Lecture Notes in Computer Science

Lecture Notes in Artificial Intelligence   16407

Founding Editor

Jörg Siekmann

Series Editors

Randy Goebel, *University of Alberta, Edmonton, Canada*
Wolfgang Wahlster, *DFKI, Berlin, Germany*
Zhi-Hua Zhou, *Nanjing University, Nanjing, China*

The series Lecture Notes in Artificial Intelligence (LNAI) was established in 1988 as a topical subseries of LNCS devoted to artificial intelligence.

The series publishes state-of-the-art research results at a high level. As with the LNCS mother series, the mission of the series is to serve the international R & D community by providing an invaluable service, mainly focused on the publication of conference and workshop proceedings and postproceedings.

Sebastian Rodriguez · Lu Feng · Jörg P. Müller
Editors

Engineering Multi-Agent Systems

13th International Workshop, EMAS 2025
Detroit, MI, USA, May 19–20, 2025
Revised Selected Papers

Springer

Editors
Sebastian Rodriguez ⓘ
RMIT University
Melbourne, VIC, Australia

Lu Feng ⓘ
University of Virginia
Charlottesville, VA, USA

Jörg P. Müller ⓘ
TU Clausthal
Clausthal-Zellerfeld, Germany

ISSN 0302-9743   ISSN 1611-3349 (electronic)
Lecture Notes in Artificial Intelligence
ISBN 978-3-032-18010-0   ISBN 978-3-032-18011-7 (eBook)
https://doi.org/10.1007/978-3-032-18011-7

LNCS Sublibrary: SL7 – Artificial Intelligence

Preface

A key unifying theme underlying Artificial Intelligence is the idea of intelligent software agents able to reason, act, interact, and learn. This metaphor has stimulated much research in AI and particularly in Autonomous Agents and Multi-Agent Systems, giving rise to research in agent-oriented software engineering, programming multi-agent systems, and declarative agent languages and technologies.

History

The International Workshop on Engineering Multi-Agent Systems (EMAS) was formed in 2013 as a merger of three long-running workshops: Agent-Oriented Software Engineering (AOSE), Programming Multi-Agent Systems (ProMAS), and Declarative Agent Languages and Technologies (DALT). This merger established EMAS as a reference venue for work that is broadly concerned with the engineering of agents and multi-agent systems.

Since its inception, EMAS has been co-located with the International Conference on Autonomous Agents and Multi-Agent Systems (AAMAS). EMAS 2013 took place in St. Paul (with post-proceedings published as Springer LNCS/LNAI volume 8245), EMAS 2014 in Paris (LNCS/LNAI 8758, and a special issue in the International Journal of Agent-Oriented Software Engineering, IJAOSE Vol. 5 No. 2/3, 2016), EMAS 2015 in Istanbul (LNCS/LNAI 9318, and a special issue in IJAOSE Vol. 6 No. 2, 2018), EMAS 2016 in Singapore (LNCS/LNAI 10093, and a special issue in IJAOSE Vol. 6 No. 3/4, 2018), EMAS 2017 in São Paulo (LNCS/LNAI 10738), EMAS 2018 in Stockholm (LNAI 11375, and a report in Software Engineering Notes), EMAS 2019 in Montreal (LNAI 12058), EMAS 2020 in Auckland (LNAI 12589), EMAS 2021 in London (LNAI 13190), EMAS 2022 in Auckland (a special issue is to appear in AMAI), EMAS 2023 in London (LNAI 14378), and EMAS 2024 in Auckland (LNCS/LNAI 15152).

From 2020 to 2022, because of the COVID-19 pandemic, AAMAS and its co-located workshops (including EMAS) were organised as online events in a fully virtual format. Since EMAS 2023 (including EMAS 2025), the workshops were held in person.

Topics

Despite the substantial body of knowledge and expertise developed in the design and development of Multi-Agent Systems (MAS), the systematic development of large-scale and open MAS still poses many challenges.

Even though various languages, models, techniques and methodologies have been proposed in the literature, researchers and developers are still faced with fundamental questions concerning MAS engineering, such as:

- How to specify, design, implement, verify, test and validate large-scale and open MAS?
- How to seamlessly integrate data-driven and machine learning techniques into design/programming languages and tool chains for agent-based systems?
- How to effectively and transparently leverage policy-based learning techniques such as reinforcement learning for the analysis, design and implementation of MAS?
- How to engineer agents and MAS that are secure, correct and protect the privacy concerns of users?
- How to ensure and control the global behaviour of decentralised, large-scale and open MAS?
- How to express the requirements for MAS and how to translate these requirements into agent goals?
- What features characterize which (multi-)agent architectures and languages are most suitable for MAS in different domains?
- How to scale to the complexity of real-world application domains?
- What are the implications of MAS engineering in the context of continuous development and deployment?
- How to seamlessly integrate MAS engineering with mainstream software engineering models, languages, frameworks and tools?
- Which processes and methodologies can integrate the above and provide a disciplined approach to the engineering of MAS?
- How can MAS be applied in specific application areas, such as Cyber-Physical Systems and Internet-of-Things?

EMAS 2025

For the 2025 edition, we especially invited contributions to a Special Theme on ML- and data-driven approaches for engineering intelligent agents and multi-agent systems.

EMAS 2025 was held in person as a 2-day workshop.[1] We received a total of 19 submissions, each of which was reviewed (single-blind) by three reviewers. In total, 15 papers were accepted for presentation at the workshop (12 regular papers, 2 short papers, and 1 student paper). After the workshop, authors of all accepted papers were invited to submit a revised and extended version of their paper to the post-proceedings. After a second round of reviews, 13 papers were selected for the post-proceedings.

EMAS 2025 provided a forum for researchers and practitioners in the domains of agent-oriented software engineering, programming multi-agent systems, declarative agent languages and technologies, artificial intelligence and machine learning to present and discuss their research and emerging results in engineering MAS. The overall purpose of the workshop was to facilitate the cross-fertilisation of ideas and experiences in the various fields to:

---

[1] The complete workshop programme and all slides used in the presentations are available online at: https://emas.in.tu-clausthal.de/2025/programme (Accessed 9 October 2025).

- Enhance our knowledge of the theory and practice of engineering intelligent agents and multi-agent systems, and advance the state of the art;
- Demonstrate how MAS methodologies, architectures, languages and tools can be used in the engineering of deployed large-scale and open MAS;
- Define new directions for engineering MAS by drawing on results and recommendations from related research areas;
- Encourage PhD and Masters students to become involved in and contribute to the area.

The best paper award went to the authors Amit K. Chopra and Munindar P. Singh for their paper "Fluid: Social Norms-Based Multiagent Systems on the Web".

This year featured a set of special events to foster discussions of new software technologies and their use for engineering multiagent systems: an invited talk by Eric Matson (Purdue University), a joint panel with the Coordination, Organizations, Institutions, Norms, Ethics for Governance of Multi-Agent Systems (COINE) workshop, and an Open Floor Workshop.

We look forward to the next edition of the EMAS workshop.

October 2025

Sebastian Rodriguez
Lu Feng
Jörg P. Müller

Organization

Program Committee Chairs

Sebastian Rodriguez	RMIT University, Australia
Lu Feng	University of Virginia, USA
Jörg P. Müller	TU Clausthal, Germany

Program Committee

Matteo Baldoni	University of Turin, Italy
Cristina Baroglio	University of Turin, Italy
Kayla Boggess	University of Virginia, USA
Rafael Bordini	Pontifical Catholic University of Rio Grande do Sul, Brazil
Maiquel de Brito	Universidade Federal de Santa Catarina, Brazil
Rafael C. Cardoso	University of Aberdeen, UK
Amit K. Chopra	University of Lancaster, UK
Andrei Ciortea	Universität St. Gallen, Switzerland
Rem W. Collier	University College Dublin, Ireland
Stefania Costantini	University of Aquila, Italy
Louise A. Dennis	University of Manchester, University of Manchester, UK
Babak Esfandiari	Carleton University, UK
Angelo Ferrando	University of Modena-Reggio Emilia, Italy
Stéphane Galland	Université de technologie de Belfort-Montbéliard, France
Zahia Guessoum	Université de Reims Champagne-Ardenne, France
Jorge J. Gómez-Sanz	Universidad Complutense de Madrid, Spain
James Harland	Royal Melbourne Institute of Technology, Australia
Vincent Hilaire	Université de technologie de Belfort-Montbéliard, France
Yves Lesperance	York University, Canada
Brian Logan	Universiteit Utrecht, The Netherlands
Viviana Mascardi	University of Genoa, Italy
Eric Matson	Purdue University, USA
Simon Mayer	University of St.Gallen, Switzerland

Roberto Micalizio	University of Turin, Italy
Luis Gustavo Nardin	École nationale supérieure des mines de Saint-Étienne, France
Alessandro Ricci	University of Bologna, Italy
Sören Schleibaum	Technische Universität Clausthal, Germany
Valeria Seidita	University of Palermo, Italy
Danai Vachtsevanou	University of St.Gallen, Switzerland
Gerhard Weiss	Maastricht University, The Netherlands
Rym Wenkstern	University of Texas at Dallas, USA
Michael Winikoff	Victoria University of Wellington, New Zealand
Yi Yang	KU Leuven, Belgium
Vahid Yazdanpanah	University of Southampton, UK
Neil Yorke-Smith	Delft University of Technology, The Netherlands
Pian Yu	University College London, UK

Steering Committee

Matteo Baldoni	Università degli Studi di Torino, Italy
Rafael Bordini	PUCRS, Brazil
Amit Chopra	Lancaster University, UK
Andrei Ciortea	University of St. Gallen, Switzerland
Mehdi Dastani	Utrecht University, The Netherlands
Jürgen Dix	Technische Universität Clausthal, Germany
Amal El Fallah Seghrouchni	Sorbonne Université, France
Brian Logan	Universiteit Utrecht (The Netherlands), and University of Aberdeen, UK
Jörg P. Müller	Technische Universität Clausthal, Germany
Alessandro Ricci	Università di Bologna, Italy
John Thangarajah	RMIT University, Australia
Michael Winikoff	Victoria University of Wellington, New Zealand
Rym Zalila-Wenkstern	University of Texas at Dallas, USA

Special Events

Invited Talk by Eric Matson, Purdue University (USA): Multiagent systems in the defense of civilian airspace against emerging UAV/UAS threats.

In 2015, a small class 1 drone flew on to the protected grounds of the White House in Washington, D.C., USA, one of the most protected spaces in the world. The ability to detect, track or remediate this threat, at that time, was basically non-existent. The capability did not exist as it was only starting to be recognized as a emerging threat. Ten years later the use of semi-autonomous to autonomous UAVs to carry out offensive threats has not only become commonplace, but a worldwide emerging industry, primarily developed by many bad actors. Given the new threat, more intense focus is being placed not on the threat, but more so on how to define, prevent, deter and mitigate these threats, over both military and civilian spaces. Agent-based systems have been employed since 2015 to detect, track, categorize, mitigate and forensically analyze autonomous UAV/UAS attacks. The ability of MAS to integrate sensors, communicate quickly and come to decisions aids the human decision-making process to successfully deter an attack that may only last a few seconds. This is why the use of MAS in the defensive function has been effective since 2015, when it was used in the first-ever documented autonomous drone-to-drone kill and has become a more effective toolset in the present day. This presentation will show the development of this MAS system.

Panel on Special Theme on ML- and Data-Driven Approaches

This year, two AAMAS workshops (EMAS and COINE) featured a special focus on the intersection of machine learning and agent-based systems. To explore this issue, we organized a panel discussion with experts from both the ML and agent communities to examine key challenges and opportunities in bridging these fields.

Panelists

- Louise Dennis (University of Manchester)
- Marc Lanctot (Google DeepMind)
- Eric Matson (Purdue University)

Moderators: Jaime Simão Sichman (COINE) and Sebastian Rodriguez (EMAS)

Open Floor Workshop: Engineering Agents in the Era of Data and LLMs: Bridging Architectures and Learning

The aim of this hands-on session was to collaboratively develop a research roadmap for the EMAS community. Participants identified key challenges and opportunities in engineering multiagent systems—particularly in contexts that integrate learning and reasoning—and propose concrete solution pathways. To anchor the discussion, we used a search and rescue scenario. The outcomes of this workshops are summarized in a joint publication with the participants in these proceedings.

Contents

A Multi-agent Collaborative Reasoning Framework for Generating
Physics Puzzles 1
Binze Li, Soham Hans, and Volkan Ustun

Adaptive Modular Agent Architecture for Hybrid Two-Level Reasoning 19
Dmitry Gnatyshak, Sergio Álvarez-Napagao, Julian Padget,
and Ulises Cortés

An Agentic System with Reinforcement-Learned Subsystem
Improvements for Parsing Form-Like Documents 27
Ayesha Amjad, Saurav Sthapit, and Tahir Qasim Syed

FALAA: Framework for the Abstraction of Language Agent Architectures 45
Nicolas Brandstetter, Felipe Bravo-Marquez, and Federico Olmedo

Fluid: Social Norms–Based Multiagent Systems on the Web 62
Amit K. Chopra and Munindar P. Singh

Holonic Active Distillation for Scalable Multi-agent Learning
in Multi-sensor Systems 80
Dani Manjah, Tim Bary, Benoit Macq, and Stéphane Galland

LTL Semantics for Tumato: A Declarative Approach to Autonomous
Agent Planning 100
Jan Vermaelen and Tom Holvoet

MEDiTATe: a First Step of a Journey from BDI to Neuroscience, and Back 117
Angelo Ferrando, Andrea Gatti, and Viviana Mascardi

Octo-Planner: On-Device Language Model for Planner-Action Agents 141
Wei Chen, Zhiyuan Li, Zhen Guo, and Yikang Shen

Oops, I Heard That! Situated Communication with Locality-Aware KQML 157
Angelo Ferrando, Andrea Gatti, and Viviana Mascardi

Teamwork in Adversarial Video Games 177
Barbara Dunin-Kęplicz and Rafał Tyl

Towards Engineering LLM-Enhanced Multi-agent Systems: A Critical
Examination of Roles 200
    Tansu Zafer Asici, Önder Gürcan, and Geylani Kardas

Towards Explainable BDI Agents for End Users 221
    Marcel Mauri and Mirjam Minor

Engineering the Next Generation of Multi-agent Systems: A Community
Roadmap from EMAS 2025 238
    *Sebastian Rodriguez, Akhila Bairy, Matteo Baldoni, Patrick Benjamin,
    Constantin Blessing, Nicolas Brandstetter, Amit K. Chopra,
    Thomas Clemen, Louise A. Dennis, Ahmad Esmaeili, Lu Feng,
    Angelo Ferrando, Zahra Ghorrati, Victor Guillet, Önder Gürcan,
    Soham Hans, James Herber, Viviana Mascardi, Marcel Mauri,
    Jörg P. Müller, John Thangarajah, Rafał Tyl, and Yi Yang*

Author Index 259

A Multi-agent Collaborative Reasoning Framework for Generating Physics Puzzles

Binze Li[1](✉), Soham Hans[2], and Volkan Ustun[2]

[1] University of California, Los Angeles, Los Angeles, USA
binzeli@ucla.edu
[2] USC Institute for Creative Technologies, Los Angeles, USA
sohamhan@usc.edu, ustun@ict.usc.edu

Abstract. Achieving expert-level performance through simulation-based training relies heavily on complex and adaptable scenarios, but creating these scenarios manually is often laborious and resource-intensive. Large Language Models (LLMs) offer a promising avenue to automate and enhance scenario generation. However, their reliance on purely sequential text generation in standard prompting settings can hinder consistent understanding in complex systems. We present a multi-agent reasoning framework to leverage LLMs for puzzle generation within the 2D Physics Puzzle Environment CREATE (Chain REAction Tool Environment) to overcome these limitations. This testbed is used as a simplified analogy for scenario generation to allow the development of fundamental LLM capabilities needed to collaboratively design and solve intricate challenges, with a long-term goal of application in domains such as military training. Our framework employs a multi-agent ReAct architecture, integrating reasoning and action feedback loops to dynamically interact with CREATE. By assigning distinct roles, such as solver and designer, to individual agents, our framework preserves the complex reasoning pathways required for solving and generating puzzles—enabling complex reasoning that was too difficult to achieve with basic prompting or single-agent approaches. This work represents a step towards more robust LLM-driven scenario generation by demonstrating the ability of a multi-agent system built on our framework, while interacting with CREATE simulations, to collaboratively perform multi-step reasoning and adapt to environmental constraints. While not yet achieving real-world scenario generation, our findings demonstrate the potential of LLMs to generate solvable puzzles aligned with user prompts. However, we also highlight and address persistent challenges with their reasoning about precise spatial relationships and understanding complex, multi-step chain reactions, which are crucial for generating more advanced scenarios. We conclude by discussing the future role of multi-agent LLM frameworks in creating realistic and adaptable training scenarios for various applications, building upon the foundational capabilities developed in this work. Examples and our full code are available at: https://github.com/binzeli/Puzzle_Generation.

B. Li and S. Hans—Contributed equally to this paper.

S. Rodriguez et al. (Eds.): EMAS 2025, LNAI 16407, pp. 1–18, 2026.
https://doi.org/10.1007/978-3-032-18011-7_1

Keywords: multi-agent systems · procedural content generation · multi-modal LLM · multi-agent LLM · multi-step reasoning

1   Introduction

In highly specialized domains, such as military training, achieving expertise through deliberate practice presents unique challenges, mainly due to the complexity and effort required to create realistic training scenarios. Creating training units is costly and requires specialized expertise, significantly limiting the number and diversity of experiential training, both live and virtual. Consequently, the available scenarios fall far short of the practice hours needed for expert-level performance [5]. Adapting these scenarios to different conditions, such as varied terrain, weather, or new objectives for opposing forces, further exacerbates these challenges.

Mastering complex tasks, such as scenario generation, demands more than raw computational power—it requires structured reasoning, adaptability, and the ability to synthesize multiple perspectives into a coherent whole. Traditional AI-driven approaches, while powerful, often struggle to balance global planning with local decision-making, long-horizon reasoning with real-time adaptability. Single-agent frameworks, constrained by their monolithic structure, lack the fluidity needed for intricate problem-solving. In contrast, intelligence in the natural world emerges from collaboration, specialization, and iterative refinement—principles that inspire our multi-agent reasoning framework. By distributing cognitive effort across specialized agents, our approach mirrors the way human teams tackle complex challenges, dynamically orchestrating expertise to generate, evaluate, and refine solutions in high-dimensional problem spaces.

Although prior research explored scenario generation for military training, the AI and ML tools available even five years ago had significant limitations and could not generate sufficiently complex or adaptable scenarios. Some systems relied on a small set of parameter sliders optimized with reinforcement learning [12], while others employed cognitive task analysis models combined with novelty search to generate new scenarios [6,7]. Although these earlier methods contributed to scenario generation, they were constrained in adapting to new contexts and producing the level of realism needed for advanced training. In contrast, today's Large Language Models (LLMs) can potentially demonstrate significant advancements in generating complex and adaptive scenarios, for instance, by leveraging vast amounts of data, including historical military operations, current geopolitical contexts, and doctrinal publications. These models may excel at creating contextually nuanced scenarios that can dynamically adapt to changes in constraints. The military is actively exploring the potential of LLMs for these purposes [3] and has recognized their value in generating more dynamic and realistic training scenarios [4].

To address the inherent complexity of scenario generation, we work towards a novel multi-agent reasoning framework that leverages the strengths of LLMs in collaborative problem-solving. Our framework integrates LLMs into a multi-agent architecture to dynamically generate and evaluate training scenarios within simulation-based environments. Unlike single-agent or basic LLM frameworks, the multi-agent approach enables distributed reasoning and specialization, addressing challenges related to maintaining coherence and context in complex systems. To build up and test the fundamental capabilities of this multi-agent framework for scenario generation, we utilized the Chain REAction Tool Environment (CREATE) [1] as a testbed. CREATE allows us to explore parallels between physics puzzles and military scenarios. For example, much like training scenarios, the physics-based movements of the balls, influenced by tool placement, demand spatial understanding, multi-step reasoning, and comprehension of interactions between different elements. Learning to effectively use a specific physics tool can also be set as a training objective. Additionally, CREATE provides an executable simulation environment to observe and analyze the outcomes of our designs. Lastly, the generation of physics puzzles is not straightforward, giving significant challenges for LLMs as they require an understanding of spatial relations, are objective-driven, and use multi-step reasoning similar to the challenges prevalent in training scenario designs.

By employing a central ReAct agent to coordinate specialized agents, such as the Solver for tool placement and the Designer for spatial planning, our approach dynamically integrates reasoning and action feedback loops. This architecture enables adaptive decision-making and more robust problem-solving capabilities than traditional methods. This paper presents our development of a novel multi-agent LLM framework that leverages the CREATE physics puzzle environment to generate and solve complex puzzles. We evaluated its performance on various navigation-based puzzles with varying difficulty, comparing it against no-agent and single-agent frameworks. Our findings aim to inform and enhance our scenario design pipeline's procedural content generation capabilities, with a long-term goal of advancing LLM-driven training scenario generation.

2   Background

As background, we briefly introduce the physics puzzle environment designed originally for reinforcement learning and discuss LLM-based approaches and inspirations that motivated our approach for a puzzle-generation pipeline.

2.1   CREATE Environment

The Chain REAction Tool Environment (CREATE) [1] is a benchmark for multi-step, physics-based puzzle reinforcement learning that includes various tools and tasks. The goal is to strategically choose and place tools, such as ramps, cannons, etc., to guide a red ball to a green goal with the help of another blue ball across different environmental setups.

In this work, we evaluate the performance of large language models (LLMs) in generating puzzles within the CREATE environment. This environment provides a standardized and flexible platform for simulating physics-based puzzles, allowing us to integrate our multi-agent LLM system into puzzle generation.

The CREATE environment allows us to run detailed simulations to observe how the placed tools interact with the balls at each step. The physics engine within the environment accurately simulates various physical interactions, including gravity, collisions, and momentum, providing a realistic assessment of the tool placements and their effects. The simulation continues iteratively, step by step, until one of the following conditions is met: (1) the red ball reaches the goal, (2) the balls move out of the frame for several consecutive steps, or (3) the balls cease to move for several steps.

2.2   LLMs for Reasoning

Generating puzzles in the CREATE environment involves a complex, multi-step reasoning process. When humans approach such challenges, they rarely conceive the entire puzzle at once. Instead, they analyze the requirements step by step, iteratively adding elements while considering their impact on the solver's experience. Similarly, supplying an LLM with a structured, multi-step reasoning process can enhance its ability to generate a complete puzzle.

Chain of Thought (CoT) [14] prompting has emerged as a valuable technique for enabling LLMs to tackle complex problems through incremental reasoning. This method encourages the model to logically build upon each step, improving its reasoning and leading to well-structured solutions, such as solvable puzzles.

However, this approach has its challenges. When given unlimited time for reasoning, LLMs may diverge from reality, creating unsolvable puzzles or introducing non-existent elements. The ReAct [13] framework, which stands for Reasoning and Action, offers a compelling solution to this issue. By prompting the LLM to take an action after each reasoning step, this approach enables the model to receive feedback from real-world observations. This feedback loop keeps the model grounded, allowing it to identify and correct errors based on action outcomes. The ReAct framework thus supports a more robust puzzle-generation process, reducing the risks of hallucinations in LLM outputs.

2.3   Related Work

Studies that have used LLMs as game-playing agents, while not a direct match, have used approaches similar to the strategies discussed in our paper. Voyager [18] describes how LLMs can play games like Minecraft by leveraging capabilities in planning and reasoning. Other notable works, such as those involving RDR2 [16], and Doom [17], utilize multimodal LLMs that unify the representation of text and images, allowing agents to perceive game states through visual inputs while seamlessly aligning this perception with text-based logical reasoning. In addition, studies like GATO [19] and SteveEye [20] rely on supervised learning with multimodal instruction sets. The Octopus [21] project showcases multimodal LLMs learning directly from environmental feedback via reinforcement learning. While our work also utilizes multimodal LLMs, we focus on enhancing reasoning mechanisms rather than just perceiving game states. By integrating visual gameplay representations, we enable LLMs to self-correct by understanding their mistakes.

Furthermore, recent works highlight the potential of LLMs in multi-agent scenarios. For example, CICERO [24] demonstrates strategic reasoning and negotiation in Diplomacy, while Du et.al [25] introduces structured debates between agents to refine factuality and reasoning. These works highlight the utility of multi-agent systems where LLMs interact dynamically to achieve a shared objective. Inspired by these advancements, we explore how multi-agent setups enhance reasoning and performance in game-based contexts.

LLMs have also been utilized in game design to varying extents. For instance, MarioGPT [22] and Todd et al.'s work [23] on generating Sokoban levels exemplify how large language models can be applied in procedural content generation. These approaches typically involve fine-tuning GPT models to generate sequences directly representing game states. In contrast, our work uses LLMs not for direct game state generation but as a tool for reasoning and logical thinking behind the design process.

Since we are testing an application using LLMs to generate training scenarios, to our knowledge, it is a domain with few comparable methods. Previous methods employed procedural techniques or evolutionary models but lacked the needed flexibility and generality [26]. While some research explored LLMs for generating word puzzles [27], they primarily focus on text-based scenarios and do not address visual or 2D environments. This highlights the novelty of our approach in combining LLMs with visual and spatial reasoning tasks to design training scenarios dynamically.

3   Experiment Design

In this section, we outline the task structure for the 2D physics puzzle environment, which consists of two primary components: **puzzle solution** and **puzzle generation**. The LLM's puzzle-solving capability is essential for generating new, solvable puzzles, allowing the LLM to create challenges that are both logical and coherent. To evaluate this capability, we defined a separate task specifically for solving puzzles. Meanwhile, the puzzle generation task is our main task, where the user verbally provides the requirements for LLMs to generate puzzles.

The primary objective of the puzzle is for the blue ball to interact with various tools to push the red ball toward the goal. We simplified the overall design and management by limiting the toolset to three essential, diverse tools, ensuring each serves a unique function and together they can solve most puzzle levels effectively:

1. **Ramp**: Simulates inclined surfaces that enable balls to roll or slide. The ramp can be set at either a 30° angle (rolling to the right) or a 150° angle (rolling to the left).
2. **Cannon**: Shoots the ball in a specified direction. It can be angled at 75° (shooting to the left) or 105° (shooting to the right).

3. **Fixed Hexagon**: Deflects the ball to a different angle.

CREATE environment offers multiple puzzle types, but for our focus, we have chosen the **navigation challenge** as a key type for both the puzzle-solving and puzzle-generation tasks. In this challenge, the blue ball must traverse complex environments using available tools, which require multi-step planning, spatial reasoning, and tool interaction. Unlike simpler, one-step puzzles (such as moving an object from point A to point B), the navigation challenge demands that the LLMs account for constraints, anticipate tool effects, and strategize efficiently to reach the goal. Our broader objective is to develop a general framework capable of tackling challenges across an entire puzzle type rather than focusing on solving individual puzzle instances.

3.1 Puzzle Solution Task

The puzzle solution task challenges the LLMs to solve 2D physics-based puzzles by strategically placing tools to enable the blue ball to push the red ball to the goal. We have divided these puzzles into five categories of our own design—ordered by increasing difficulty—as shown in Fig. 1.

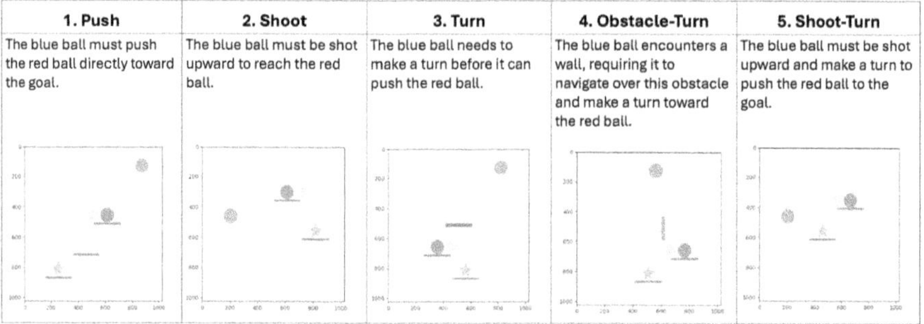

Fig. 1. Five Puzzle Categories.

The last three puzzle categories—*Turn, Obstacle-Turn, and Shoot-Turn*—require more advanced reasoning, as they involve multi-step planning and the use of multiple tools. These complex scenarios are designed to assess the LLM's ability to solve dynamic problems and execute intricate strategies.

To assist the LLMs in making better decisions, we added a sub-goal, a green circle that was not part of the original CREATE environment design. This sub-goal can help the LLMs track their progress by determining whether the ball has reached the sub-goal, enabling more informed planning and strategic adjustments throughout the puzzle.

3.2   Puzzle Generation Task

The puzzle generation task involves automatically creating solvable puzzles by placing objects such as the red ball, blue ball, goal, sub-goal, and other essential elements based on the user prompt. We adopt two complementary tasks—Layout-Specified and Tool-Specified—to examine different aspects of the LLM's puzzle generation capabilities. User prompts are shown in Table 1.

Table 1. Prompts for two puzzle generation tasks: Layout-Specified, which focuses on positioning puzzle objects according to prompt requirement, and Tool-Specified, which involves using specific tools to solve the puzzle.

Layout-Specified	Tool-Specified
Push: The blue ball on the right must push the red ball down to the goal on the left.	(1) Use a *fixed hexagon* to help the blue ball reach the red ball and push it to the goal.
Shoot: The blue ball on the left goes up to reach a red ball, then pushes it to fall onto the goal on the right.	(2) Use a *cannon* to help the blue ball reach the red ball and push it to the goal.
Turn: The blue ball on the right lands on a separate platform and pushes the red ball on the left to the goal on the right.	(3) Use a *ramp* to help the blue ball reach the red ball and push it to the goal.
Obstacle: The blue ball on the right navigates over a wall to the red ball, then pushes it to the goal on the left.	

In the **Layout-Specified** task, the user specifies the type of layout from four available categories: *Push, Shoot, Turn, Obstacle*. This task allows us to test the LLM's ability to work within predefined puzzle structures, ensuring that it correctly places tools and elements based on the chosen layout. We have tested with these four general layout types, but the framework is designed to accommodate additional layouts in the future.

In the **Tool-Specified** task, which aligns more closely with our goal of training players in tool usage, the user specifies a particular tool to be used in the prompt, and the model needs to generate a puzzle that requires that tool to solve it. The available tools include the *Ramp, Cannon*, and *Fixed Hexagon*. The motivation for this task is to evaluate how well the LLMs can design puzzles that highlight the functionality of specific tools, helping us assess whether the LLM can reason about the tool's purpose and integrate it into generating puzzles.

4   Multi-agent Puzzle Framework

In this framework, we employ a multi-agent system where multiple LLM agents collaborate to handle both puzzle generation and solution tasks. At its core is the

ReAct agent, designed using the ReAct prompting technique, which generates reasoning thoughts and executes actions by invoking predefined functions. When needed, the ReAct agent calls on specialized LLM agents to plan the placement of tools or objects.

4.1 Prompting Technique

Providing steps is a critical aspect of our prompting technique, as it offers a structured framework to guide the model through the complex task of puzzle solution and creation. By breaking the process into clear, sequential steps (e.g., Step 1: Call the designer agent, Step 2: Place objects, etc.), we ensure the model stays focused and methodical. However, these steps are not meant to restrict the model's reasoning capabilities. Instead, they act as a foundation that the model can build upon, allowing it to dynamically adapt and decide the next action based on its observations and the evolving state of the puzzle. For example, if the predefined steps suggest placing a tool and observing the outcome, but the outcome isn't successful (e.g., the blue ball doesn't reach the red ball), the model can reason that it needs to take further action—like adjusting the position of the red ball or consulting the solver agent again—even if those actions aren't explicitly listed in the original steps. In other words, the model isn't just mechanically following a script; it's using the steps as a starting point and then applying its own reasoning to solve problems creatively and effectively.

We also provide an example output format, such as "Thought: [reasoning] Action: [tool or task] Observation: [result]," which structures the model's responses and ensures transparency in its decision-making. Overall, our prompting technique provides clear guidelines to keep the model on track while empowering it to think critically and adapt as needed.

4.2 Collaborative Puzzle Agents for Solving Puzzles

The goal of the puzzle solution phase is to develop an effective strategy for solving existing 2D physics puzzles. Such a strategy involves a ReAct agent and a new LLM helper agent, the Solver, working together to determine the best tool placements to guide the blue ball in pushing the red ball to the goal. The framework is shown in Fig. 2.

The ReAct Agent serves as the primary executor in the puzzle solution process. It operates through a predefined set of actions, including "place ramp," "visualize simulation," "place fixed hexagon," "place cannon," and "call solver." These actions are functions explicitly provided to the ReAct agent at the beginning of its operation. It begins by running a simulation within the OpenAI Gym environment to observe the movement of the balls on the given puzzle layout. It then invokes the Solver agent through a function call, passing along relevant simulation data such as trajectory information and a sequence of images. The Solver suggests initial tool placements which are returned by this function. Based on the Solver's guidance, the ReAct agent reasons to place new tools, run simulations, and call the Solver to propose the next tool again. This iterative

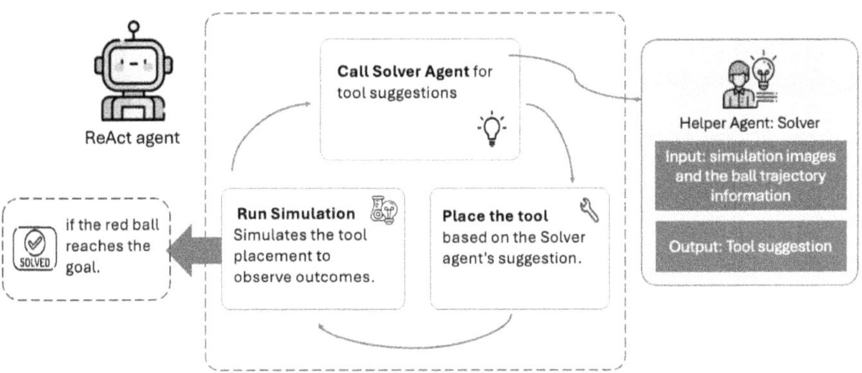

Fig. 2. Workflow for solving a 2D physics puzzle using the ReAct agent with a helper agent (Solver). The ReAct agent initially calls the Solver agent, which suggests tool placements given simulation images and ball trajectory data. The ReAct agent then places the suggested tool and runs the simulations. This loop continues until the red ball reaches the goal. (Color figure online)

approach allows the ReAct agent to refine its strategy until the puzzle is solved or no further adjustments are viable.

The **Solver Agent** is embedded as a callable function within the ReAct agent's framework. It operates as a specialized LLM tasked with analyzing the current puzzle state and recommending optimal tool placements. The Solver agent processes the input it receives from the ReAct agent to evaluate whether objectives, such as the blue ball reaching the red ball or the red ball reaching the goal, have been achieved. It then proposes specific tool placements and their relative positions, such as "place a ramp to the left of the red ball."

4.3   Collaborative Puzzle Agents for Generating Puzzles

The puzzle generation task aims to create new 2D physics puzzles that are both solvable and aligned with user prompts. This process involves a more complex multi-agent system configuration, utilizing a ReAct agent with two independent, specialized LLM helper agents: the Designer agent and the Solver agent. The workflow is shown in Fig. 3.

The ReAct Agent functions as the primary coordinator in this process, executing a sequence of defined actions through modular function calls. The generation process begins with the ReAct agent invoking the Designer agent via a "call designer" function to propose an initial object layout. The Designer agent provides precise coordinates for key objects such as the blue ball, red ball, goal, and structural elements (e.g., floors or walls) based on the user prompt. These are returned by the function to the ReAct agent who then places these objects within the environment.

After establishing the initial object layout, the ReAct agent initiates a simulation within the OpenAI Gym environment to observe interactions and trajectories. It then invokes the Solver agent to recommend tool placements that ensure the puzzle remains solvable. The ReAct agent places these tools and runs another simulation to test the effectiveness of the setup.

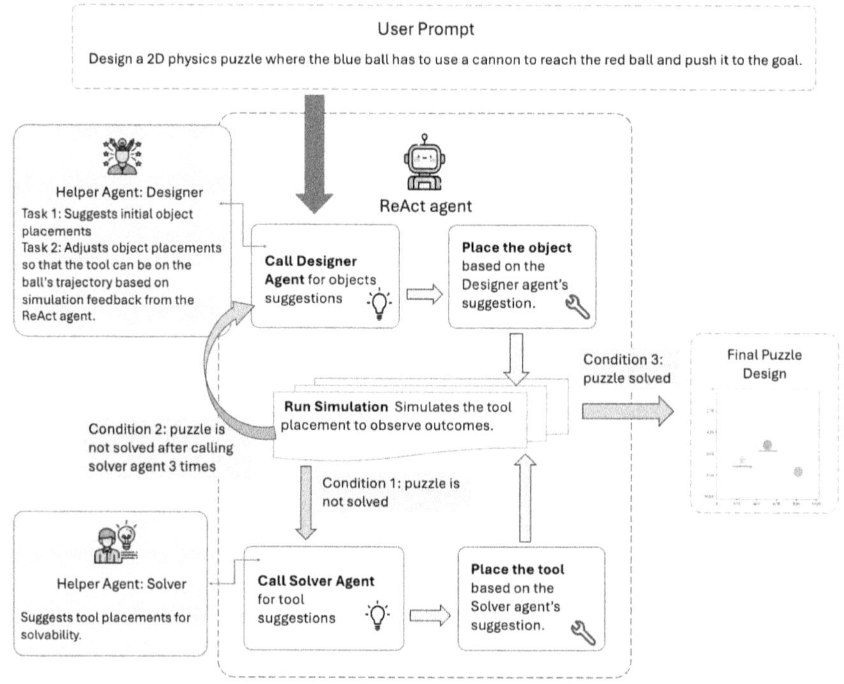

Fig. 3. Workflow for generating a 2D physics puzzle using the ReAct agent with helper agents (Designer and Solver).

If the desired outcome—such as the blue ball reaching the red ball or the red ball reaching the goal—is not achieved after three Solver calls, the ReAct agent opts to call the Designer agent to adjust the positions of existing objects. This approach is taken because adjusting the positions of objects is typically more straightforward and reliable, given the limited toolset and the challenge of precisely calibrating tool angles or lengths with the LLMs. The ReAct agent continues this cycle of adjustments and simulations until the puzzle meets the requirement for solvability.

The Designer Agent is responsible for the spatial planning and placement of objects within the puzzle environment. It performs two key tasks: proposing the initial design of objects or adjusting their positions based on simulation feedback. Initially, it sets the coordinates for the blue ball, red ball, goal, and other objects like the floor or wall according to the user's prompt. After the initial step, it proposes the adjustment of the object's position to be on the ball's trajectory to ensure that the ball's path will result in effective collisions with tools. This is done based on a series of simulation images and detailed trajectory data sent by the ReAct agent as input during the function call.

The Solver Agent in the puzzle generation task is the same agent as the Solver agent used in the puzzle solution task. It continues to provide strategic guidance on tool selection and placement to ensure the puzzle is solvable.

5   Results

In both tasks, we evaluated three approaches on both puzzle solution and generation tasks, all utilizing GPT-4o as the core LLM, with implementations conducted with LlamaIndex package [2] in Python:

1. **Basic Agent**: A single agent proposes the relative positions of the tools or object, which will be placed by us manually.
2. **Single ReAct Agent**: A single agent reasons and acts to place tools and objects using the ReAct prompting technique.
3. **Collaborative Puzzle Agents**: A single agent reasons and acts using the ReAct prompting technique with assistance from specialized helper agents (Framework described in Sect. 4).

For all approaches, we adapted in-context learning by providing the LLM with an example puzzle and its solution to ensure it understood the problem before attempting the task. The prompts were identical in both *Single ReAct Agent* and *Collaborative Puzzle Agents* approaches, as we consolidated all prompts from the Designer and Solver agents into a single prompt for the *Single ReAct Agent*. Such an approach allowed the *Single ReAct Agent* without helpers to follow the same steps and use the same prompts as the *Collaborative Puzzle Agents*. With that being said, although *Single ReAct Agent* lacks the specialized helper agents, this agent would also handle the tasks typically performed by the helper agents that are available to *Collaborative Puzzle Agents*.

During testing across all puzzle categories, we kept the context information unchanged, modifying only the input puzzle layout for the puzzle solution task and the user prompt for the puzzle generation task for each case.

5.1   Puzzle Solution Task Results

For the puzzle solution task, Fig. 4 shows the performance comparison of the three approaches across five puzzle categories: *Push, Shoot, Turn, Obstacle-Turn, and Shoot-Turn*. Each approach was tested five times in each category, and the number of successful attempts out of five was measured. This task is considered failed if the blue ball has not reached the red ball after placing three tools.

The *Basic Agent* struggled significantly, managing to solve only one puzzle in the *Turn* category while failing to solve any puzzles in the other four categories. The *Single ReAct Agent* performed much better in comparison, achieving perfect

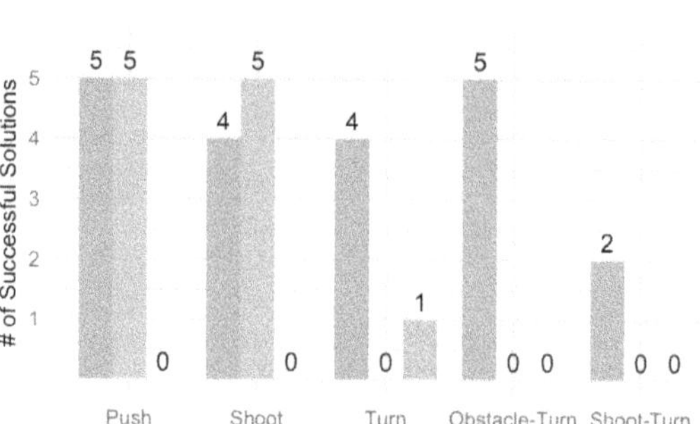

Fig. 4. Comparison of the number of successful puzzle solutions across five attempts for each of three approaches.

scores in both the Push and Shoot categories. However, it was unable to solve any puzzles in the *Turn, Obstacle-Turn*, and *Shoot-Turn* categories, suggesting that more complex puzzles require additional support. The *Collaborative Puzzle Agents* showed the most robust performance.

5.2   Puzzle Generation Task Results

We tested how those three approaches work in the puzzle generation task. The results are presented with two metrics: 1) the number of solvable puzzles generated and 2) how many of those solvable puzzles matched the user prompt requirements (evaluated manually). Failure to design a solvable puzzle is detected under two conditions (1) the red ball's position is not adjusted when the red ball has not reached the goal after placing three tools, or (2) after adjusting the ball's location, the blue ball still fails to hit the red ball, or the red ball does not reach the goal. Each agent was also tested five times in each puzzle category.

The *Basic Agent* struggled to generate solvable puzzles across all categories on Table 2. The *Single ReAct Agent* showed moderate success, managing to generate solvable puzzles in select categories, but still encountered challenges in generating puzzles that aligned with the requirement in the user prompt. The *Collaborative Puzzle Agents* demonstrated stronger performance by producing more solvable puzzles and achieved higher alignment with the user's specifications. It generated solvable puzzles in most categories, but not in the *Turn* category which requires LLM to understand how to make a turn. Additionally, it occasionally faced challenges in fully aligning with user prompts.

Figure 5 shows example puzzles and solutions from the three approaches. In the *Obstacle* category of the *Layout-Specified* type, a wall is required to serve as an obstacle that the blue ball must navigate over. The *Basic Agent* placed the wall too close to the blue ball, leaving no space to go over it and making the puzzle unsolvable. The *Single ReAct Agent* left sufficient space between the blue

Table 2. Comparison of the number of solvable puzzles generated by LLM agents and their alignment with user prompts across five attempts. The first number indicates the number of puzzles successfully solved. The second number in parentheses represents how many of those solvable puzzles align with the specified user prompt.

Layout-Specified Tasks				
Agent Type	**Push**	**Shoot**	**Obstacle**	**Turn**
Basic Agent	0 (0)	0 (0)	0 (0)	0 (0)
Single ReAct Agent	2 (2)	0 (0)	0 (0)	0 (0)
Collaborative Puzzle Agents	**5 (5)**	**5 (2)**	**3 (1)**	**1 (1)**

Tool-Specified Tasks			
Agent Type	**Fixed Hexagon**	**Cannon**	**Ramp**
Basic Agent	0 (0)	0 (0)	0 (0)
Single ReAct Agent	1 (0)	2 (0)	0 (0)
Collaborative Puzzle Agents	**4 (0)**	**3 (2)**	**4 (1)**

ball and the wall to place a tool; however, it positioned the ramp in the wrong direction. Therefore it failed to solve the puzzle despite a plausible setup. In contrast, the *Collaborative Puzzle Agents* with a designer successfully generated a solvable puzzle. The Solver helped propose a solution where the blue ball slides down a ramp, navigates over a wall and pushes the red ball to the goal. The puzzle also aligns with the prompt, as all the required objects are included and correctly positioned within the puzzle. A complete sample response generated by GPT-4o on one puzzle generation task is provided in our GitHub page.

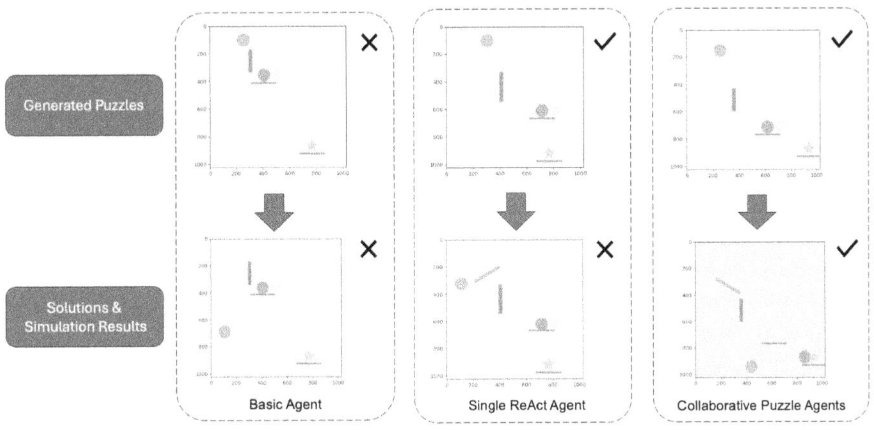

Fig. 5. Examples of generated puzzles and proposed solutions by three agents for the "Obstacle" case in the Layout-specific type.

6 Discussion

In our initial experiments using the *Basic Agent*, we encountered two key challenges: spatial relationship confusion and incorrect tool selection. One frequent issue was misinterpreting the left-right relationship between objects. For example, when the red ball was positioned to the left of the blue ball, *Basic Agent* often incorrectly suggested moving the blue ball to the right instead of to the left. Additionally, the agent struggled to select the correct tools to solve puzzles. This struggle indicated a fundamental limitation in the *Basic Agent*'s ability to process directional and spatial information.

To address the issues, we developed the *Single ReAct Agent* to leverage the LLM's reasoning abilities. Initially, we provided only visual inputs, but this led to errors such as saying the ball slides down the ramp to the left, even though the ball did not even touch the ramp. We then decided to introduce textual descriptions to accompany the visual information provided to the model. After each simulation, detailed trajectory data and positional information—such as whether the blue ball was moving to the right or positioned to the right of the red ball—were included to enhance the model's understanding. This feedback mechanism enabled the *Basic Agent* to refine its decision-making in real-time, reducing spatial confusion and allowing it to handle complex scenarios more effectively and accurately.

While the *Single ReAct Agent* showed improvements in simpler puzzle categories, its struggles with only visual data highlighted that LLMs like GPT-4o still have difficulty accurately interpreting visual details. The agent performed well in puzzles requiring basic reasoning and a single tool but struggled with more complex puzzles involving multiple tools and advanced reasoning, even with guiding questions. It also occasionally failed to follow all instructions, such as not adjusting the red ball's position after repeated failed attempts. Although ReAct prompting and additional textual information improved spatial reasoning in some cases, they were insufficient for consistently generating solvable puzzles or fully aligning with user prompts in complex scenarios.

We then transitioned to a multi-agent approach, introducing two specialized agents: the Designer and the Solver. This setup improved performance by dividing tasks between agents, allowing for more focused reasoning. The Designer agent focused on object placement, while the Solver agent concentrated on ensuring tool placement aligned with solving the puzzle. This collaborative and distributed reasoning system significantly reduced the frequency of left-right confusion and improved the model's ability to interpret directional cues derived from both textual and visual information more accurately.

However, the *Collaborative Puzzle Agents* did not always generate puzzles that matched the user prompt. For instance, in Fig. 6, the agent created a puzzle in the *Shoot* category where the blue ball will fall but it should be shot upward to reach the red ball. In another instance in the *Obstacle* category, the agent placed a wall below the red ball, which served no purpose as it did not obstruct the blue ball's path to the red ball.

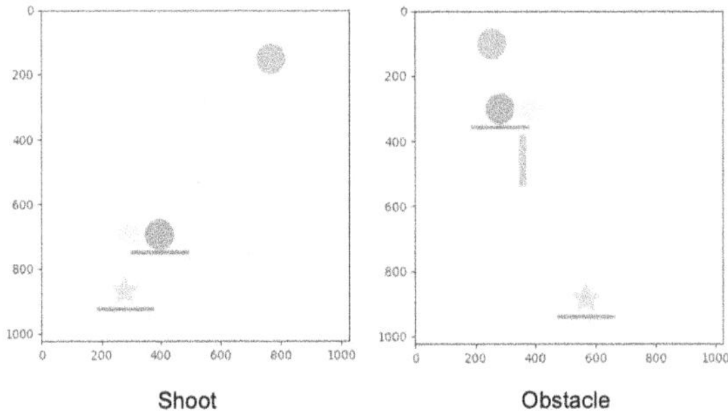

Fig. 6. Example puzzles that do not align with user prompts in the "Shoot" and "Obstacle" categories.

These examples show that LLMs may not fully understand the user prompt and instead focus primarily on adjusting the objects' positions to ensure a solution. Such issues can lead to a puzzle that technically works but doesn't match the intent or details specified by the user. The fact that LLMs did not always generate puzzle solutions shows that they also lack an inherent understanding of physical principles. This makes it challenging for them to predict how a ball's trajectory will change after interacting with tools or obstacles in the puzzle. Another reason could be that LLMs are trained on textual data and lack exposure to physical systems or spatial reasoning tasks. Generating physics-based puzzles requires balancing multiple constraints (e.g., solvability, logical object placement, adherence to user intent), which is inherently challenging for models not specifically designed for such tasks.

Furthermore, during our experiments, we observed that GPT-4o struggled to provide precise coordinates for tool placement. We tested its ability to select an exact location within the ball's trajectory to ensure proper interaction. Although GPT-4o demonstrated strong logical reasoning and could describe plausible strategies, it lacked the precision required to translate high-level reasoning into actionable, spatially accurate outputs. This limitation could arise from the inherent architecture of LLMs, which primarily rely on sequence-based token prediction and lack an explicit internal representation of spatial geometry or continuous coordinate systems. For instance, in the Turn case, it correctly suggested placing a fixed hexagon for the blue ball to bounce off and make a turn toward the red ball but failed to calculate a precise position where the hexagon would function as intended. This imprecision highlighted the gap between text-based reasoning and the model's ability to process spatially grounded tasks. This limitation led us to adjust our approach, asking the LLM agents to provide only relative locations, such as placing the tool to the left or right of an object. We wrote code to help position the tool based on that information within the functions LLM agents would call as its actions.

A fundamental improvement in the future will be fine-tuning the LLMs to enhance their ability to recognize left and right orientations when analyzing visual inputs. This adjustment aims to resolve the persistent issue of directional confusion, allowing the model to rely more on its vision rather than requiring detailed trajectory information. Another important improvement is expanding the multi-agent framework by adding a new evaluator agent dedicated to checking whether the generated puzzles align with user prompts. This agent would serve as a quality control mechanism, ensuring that puzzles more consistently meet the user's specified requirements. Finally, we plan to test newer LLM models, such as GPT-o1, to assess whether they offer improved reasoning capabilities on these complex reasoning and spatial tasks.

7   Conclusion

This paper explored the potential of Large Language Models (LLMs) in generating complex and adaptable levels within a physics-based puzzle environment. Utilizing the CREATE platform, we developed a multi-agent ReAct framework that distributes responsibilities for complex tasks across specialized models. This engineering approach enhances dynamic interaction and reasoning, addressing key challenges such as spatial understanding and multi-step problem-solving critical for advanced training scenarios. However, despite this improvement, challenges remain in ensuring that generated puzzles consistently meet user specifications. The inability of LLMs to accurately interpret visual data and spatial cues underscores the need for further research and development in this domain.

Moving forward, fine-tuning LLMs to improve their spatial reasoning capabilities, integrating evaluative agents for quality control, and exploring newer model architectures will be essential steps in enhancing the effectiveness of LLM-driven scenario generation. Ultimately, our work contributes to the growing field of AI-driven engineering solutions, particularly in specialized domains like military training. The continued exploration of multi-agent frameworks holds significant potential for advancing procedural content generation and addressing the dynamic needs of modern training.

Acknowledgments. The authors acknowledge the use of Large Language Models for assistance with proofreading and grammar checking. All content was reviewed, edited, and approved by the human authors, who take full responsibility for the final manuscript. Research was sponsored by the Army Research Office and was accomplished under Cooperative Agreement Number W911NF-14-D-0005. The views and conclusions contained in this document are those of the authors and should not be interpreted as representing the official policies, either expressed or implied, of the Army Research Office or the U.S. Government. The U.S. Government is authorized to reproduce and distribute reprints for Government purposes notwithstanding any copyright notation.

References

1. Jain, A., Szot, A., Lim, J.: Generalization to New Actions in Reinforcement Learning. In: Daumé III, H., Singh, A. (eds.) In: Proceedings of the 37th International Conference on Machine Learning, PMLR, vol. 119, pp. 4661–4672 (2020). https://proceedings.mlr.press/v119/jain20b.html
2. Liu, J.: LlamaIndex. Zenodo (2022). https://doi.org/10.5281/zenodo.1234
3. Caballero, W.N., Jenkins, P.R.: On large language models in national security applications. arXiv preprint *arXiv:2407.03453* (2024)
4. Hill, J.: Hadean builds large language model for British Army virtual training space. https://www.army-technology.com/news/hadean-builds-large-language-model-for-british-army-virtual-training-space/. Accessed 15 June 2024
5. Goldberg, B., et al.: Forging competency and proficiency through the synthetic training environment with an experiential learning for readiness strategy. In: Interservice/Industry Training, Simulation, and Education Conference (I/ITSEC), Orlando, FL (2021)
6. Dargue, B., Folsom-Kovarik, J.T., Sanders, J.: Evolving Training Scenarios with Measurable Variance in Learning Effects. In: Sottilare, R.A., Schwarz, J. (eds.) HCII 2019. LNCS, vol. 11597, pp. 40–51. Springer, Cham (2019). https://doi.org/10.1007/978-3-030-22341-0_4
7. Folsom-Kovarik, J.T., Rowe, J., Brawner, K., Lester, J.: Toward Automated Scenario Generation with GIFT. Des. Recommendations Intell. Tutor. Sys. **7**, 109–118 (2019)
8. Ericsson, K.A., Krampe, R.T., Tesch-Römer, C.: The role of deliberate practice in the acquisition of expert performance. Psychol. Rev. **100**(3), 363 (1993). American Psychological Association
9. Ericsson, K.A.: The danger of delegating education to journalists: Why the APS Observer needs peer review when summarizing new scientific developments. Unpublished manuscript, http://www.psy.fsu.edu/faculty/ericsson/ericsson.hp.html (2012)
10. Santiago III, J.M., Parayno, R.L., Deja, J.A., Samson, B.P.V.: Rolling the dice: Imagining generative AI as a Dungeons & Dragons storytelling companion. arXiv preprint arXiv:2304.01860 (2023). https://arxiv.org/abs/2304.01860
11. Zhu, A., Martin, L., Head, A., Callison-Burch, C.: CALYPSO: LLMs as Dungeon Master's Assistants. In: Proceedings of the AAAI Conference on Artificial Intelligence and Interactive Digital Entertainment, vol. 19(1), pp. 380–390 (2023)
12. Rowe, J., Smith, A., Pokorny, B., Mott, B., Lester, J.: Toward automated scenario generation with deep reinforcement learning in GIFT. In: Proceedings of the Sixth Annual GIFT User Symposium, pp. 65–74 (2018)
13. Yao, S., et al.: ReAct: Synergizing Reasoning and Acting in Language Models. arXiv preprint arXiv:2210.03629 (2022). https://api.semanticscholar.org/CorpusID:252762395
14. Wei, J., et al.: Chain-of-thought prompting elicits reasoning in large language models. Adv. Neural. Inf. Process. Syst. **35**, 24824–24837 (2022)
15. Brockman, G., et al.: OpenAI Gym. CoRR abs/1606.01540 (2016). http://arxiv.org/abs/1606.01540
16. Tan, W., et al.: Towards general computer control: A multimodal agent for Red Dead Redemption II as a case study. arXiv preprint arXiv:2403.03186 (2024)
17. de Wynter, A.: Will GPT-4 Run DOOM? arXiv preprint arXiv:2403.05468 (2024)

18. Wang, G., et alA.: Voyager: An open-ended embodied agent with large language models. arXiv preprint arXiv:2305.16291 (2023)
19. Reed, S., et al.: A generalist agent. arXiv preprint arXiv:2205.06175 (2022)
20. Zheng, S., Feng, Y., Lu, Z., et al.: Steve-eye: Equipping LLM-based embodied agents with visual perception in open worlds. In: The Twelfth International Conference on Learning Representations (2023)
21. Yang, J., et al.: Octopus: Embodied Vision-language Programmer from Environmental Feedback. arXiv preprint arXiv:2310.08588 (2023)
22. Sudhakaran, S., González-Duque, M., Freiberger, M., Glanois, C., Najarro, E., Risi, S.: Mariogpt: Open-ended text2level generation through large language models. Adv. Neural Inf. Process. Sys. **36** (2024)
23. Todd, G., Earle, S., Nasir, M.U., Green, M.C., Togelius, J.: Level generation through large language models. In: Proceedings of the 18th International Conference on the Foundations of Digital Games, pp. 1–8 (2023)
24. Bakhtin, A., et al.: Human-level play in the game of Diplomacy by combining language models with strategic reasoning. Science **378**(6623), 1067–1074 (2022)
25. Du, Y., Li, S., Torralba, A., Tenenbaum, J.B., Mordatch, I.: Improving factuality and reasoning in language models through multiagent debate. arXiv preprint arXiv:2305.14325 (2023)
26. Togelius, J., Yannakakis, G.N., Stanley, K.O., Browne, C.: Search-based procedural content generation: a taxonomy and survey. IEEE Trans. Comput. Intell. AI Games **3**(3), 172–186 (2011)
27. Merino, T., Earle, S., Sudhakaran, R., Sudhakaran, S., Togelius, J.: Making New Connections: LLMs as Puzzle Generators for The New York Times' Connections Word Game. In: Proceedings of the 20th AAAI Conference on Artificial Intelligence and Interactive Digital Entertainment, pp. 87–96 (2024)

Adaptive Modular Agent Architecture for Hybrid Two-Level Reasoning

Dmitry Gnatyshak[1,2]($\boxtimes$) , Sergio Álvarez-Napagao[1] , Julian Padget[3] ,
and Ulises Cortés[1]

[1] Universitat Politècnica de Catalunya, Barcelona, Spain
dmitry.gnatyshak@keysight.com
[2] Keysight Technologies, Barcelona, Spain
[3] University of Bath, Bath, UK

Abstract. Despite the significant advances in subsymbolic artificial intelligence over the last decade, including novel Large Language Model (LLM) based methods, this technology comes with high, even prohibitive, development and application costs. Recent research suggests that instead of blindly increasing the model sizes and deploying larger numbers of better accelerators, there are benefits from a focus on the model structures and methods employed instead. An approach that has gained in popularity lately that addresses this is neurosymbolic reasoning. By focusing on various ways of combining subsymbolic, mostly neural network-based, computations with classical symbolic reasoning, it promises to alleviate the computation demands of pure deep learning approaches by guiding the learning process with symbolic knowledge. In this paper, we introduce the Modular Hybrid Agent Architecture (MHAgentA), a cognitive agent architecture, along with a Python framework that implements it. This architecture is designed to facilitate the prototyping and deployment of neurosymbolic agents that follow Kahneman's System 1, System 2 model. We provide a breakdown of a high-level view of the architecture and outline the technical details of its implementation.

1 Introduction

The concept of an *agent* as an autonomous software program capable of pursuing goals on behalf of its owner is far from new. Envisioned in the era of symbolic artificial intelligence [32], agents have been extensively explored, with a number of classifications and even standards developed [27] formalising their potential capacities, structures, models, etc. Many *cognitive architectures* were developed, such as Soar [18], formalising potential building blocks of an intelligent agent and their internal structures facilitating the pursuit of goals. It was soon discovered, however, that the high computational complexity together with the issues in translating noisy and imprecise real-world sensor data into symbolic formats, were prohibitive for its application in complex domains [38,39]. For instance, sufficiently sophisticated planning problems in non-deterministic environments proven to be EXPTIME-complete [20,29].

Subsymbolic approaches have now become dominant in AI, trading off inherent explainability for generalisation capacity and, eventually, computational efficiency. As they evolved, the concept of agents was rediscovered, and new agent-based approaches

S. Rodriguez et al. (Eds.): EMAS 2025, LNAI 16407, pp. 19–26, 2026.
https://doi.org/10.1007/978-3-032-18011-7_2

were established. For instance, with advancements in the field of (deep) reinforcement learning (RL, DRL), many complex problems were tackled with computational agents, with particular focus on various games of high complexity [22,24,33,34,36].

Furthermore, the recent advances with large language models (LLM) show that they can be sufficient to approximate intelligent agents [26] and even imitate symbolic reasoners [25]. However, the price for these advancements is not negligible with the inherent opacity of deep models and gargantuan time, financial, and environmental costs of training complex neural architectures [7].

Neurosymbolic approaches [17], striving to combine the explainability of symbolic methods with the generalisation of neural networks, hugely vary in combination ratios of these components [8]. With the neurosymbolic approach followed in this paper, we aim to address the high computational demands of both subsymbolic and symbolic approaches when applied to complex use cases by utilising adaptive learning during the agent runtime, as well as value-based reasoning.

To facilitate efficient experimentation while pursuing these research goals, we determined the need for a computationally lightweight, highly customisable modular architecture (and corresponding agent development framework) that can be adapted and modified quickly in accordance with evolving research objectives. This work resulted in MHAgentA — Modular Hybrid Agent Architecture — a modern cognitive architecture and a Python framework designed to facilitate prototyping of neurosymbolic agents.

The rest of the paper is organised as follows. In Sect. 2, we briefly explore related research. Section 3 follows with the details on the MHAgentA. Finally, in Sect. 4, we conclude with a discussion of the scope of the work, its goals, and next steps.

2   Related Work

A significant number of cognitive architectures have been proposed over the last 40 years, many inspired by the works of Allen Newell [23] and Marvin Minsky [21]. These works outlined an intelligent agent as a system of various components defining its capacities and behaviour, such as knowledge, language, perception, decision-making, etc.

One of the most famous cognitive architectures, Soar [18], is a classical example of a symbolic agent architecture. Other notable cognitive architectures include ACT-R [5] and LIDA [6], grounded in cognitive neuroscience and modelling their reasoning processes after human cognition, and a large set of architectures inspired by the belief-desire-intention reasoning model [28], such as PRS [14], JACK [10], dMARS [12], JADEX [9], and others. However, most of them were developed a long time ago, meaning that they lack easy inherent support for more recent optimisation and deployment techniques, as well as leaning more towards symbolic agents while posing technical challenges for extensive incorporation of modern deep learning-based subsystems.

On the subsymbolic side, there is a lot of research on DRL methods [19,22,30,31]. Given enough computational and time resources (prohibitive amounts in complex real-world scenarios), they can find near-optimal solutions for many agent-based environments. Nevertheless, these costs, and the inherent opacity of DRL agents' behavioural policies, hinder their adoption in many areas.

The explainable reinforcement learning field aims to address the latter issue, but it faces its own set of problems, such as a lack of standardisation and high ambiguity in the definition of what is a (good) explanation with a promising research direction lying in extracting symbolic explanations from subsymbolic behavioural policies [13].

Large language models also seem to benefit from following the classical cognitive reasoning approaches. For instance, it was shown that a classical intelligent agent structure with its components imitated by LLMs could simulate high-level behaviour [26]. Moreover, it was shown that forcing LLM architectures to undergo internal "reasoning" cycles could vastly improve the output quality [11,25].

Finally, there exist many works on neurosymbolic methods, with various types of approaches identified in this field, from using symbols to the benefit of the otherwise purely subsymbolic systems (and vice versa) to attempts to create true hybrid solutions [4,8,37]. The last is generally regarded as the most promising way forward [17] and is the approach we follow with MHAgentA.

3   MHAgentA: Modular Hybrid Agent Architecture

3.1   Requirements

As stated above, MHAgentA is a modular and customisable cognitive architecture inspired by Kahneman's System 1 – System 2 model of human mind [15,16]. The separation into two systems implies, to a first approximation, a two-part architecture capturing a coarse division between fast and slow thinking. We also argue that the learning subsystem and the intrinsic value model are crucial for efficient *adaptive* agents capable of dynamically distributing the decision workload between the two systems.

The framework's main requirements were computational efficiency and ease of agent development and deployment. We aimed to achieve the former with multiprocessing (especially in context of high-performance computing) and the latter by using a popular programming language with a low entry threshold (Python) and with containerisation.

3.2   Cognitive Architecture

Like many other cognitive architectures, MHAgentA takes inspiration from the perception of the human mind, a complex system running many parallel processes. As stated above, we view it as two interacting systems: the faster, resource-efficient and reactive System 1, and the slower, more sophisticated, *conscious* System 2, which can generally take over control from System 1 as needed. Moreover, the separation of responsibilities between these two is not fixed: Kahneman states that while System 2 initially handles novel situations, it gradually relinquishes control to System 1 as the situation becomes more familiar. This ability to learn to adapt the workload separation between these two systems is the key feature we set as the main learn-term goal for this ongoing work.

MHAgentA's modularity and customisability allow for the creation of agents with varying capabilities implemented by a number of symbolic and subsymbolic techniques depending on the use case. Essentially, each of the provisioned module types is optional and represents a set of potential capabilities. However, for this section we will assume that the full set of module types defined below is used. The complete diagram of MHA-gentA's module types and their interactions appears in Fig. 1.

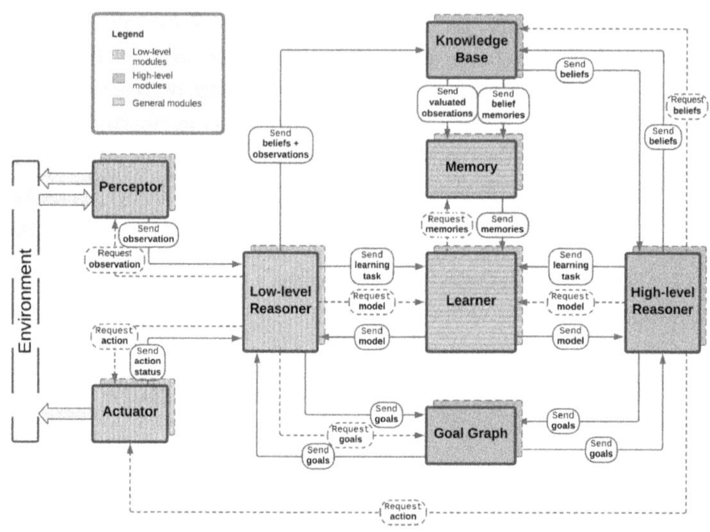

Fig. 1. MHAgentA modules and their interaction channels.

Each of these modules represents a *separate semi-autonomous process* running in parallel with other module processes and interacting with them to facilitate information processing and decision-making. Depending on the strictness of the agent and multi-agent system definitions and specifics of module implementations, a MHAgentA agent can be considered a multi-agent system itself.

The architecture does not specify the exact details of each module's implementation; instead, it focuses on the communication scheme (i.e., information flow) between them. This way, each module can be as complex or simple as needed. Moreover, it is possible to define several modules of the same type but with different purposes and capabilities.

The following paragraphs describe the architecture's modules in more detail.

Perceptors: essentially, sensors, gathering data from the environment and forwarding it to low-level reasoners for processing and belief extraction. This process can be automatic and continuous or triggered by requests from low-level reasoners. In case of several observation types or modalities, it might also be more efficient to have a set of specialised perceptors instead of a single general purpose one.

Actuators: agents' means to act upon the environment. Actions can either be performed autonomously and continuously or in response to requests from reasoners. Although actuators have the capacity to provide basic feedback on the action execution (e.g., status of its execution from the internal agent perspective), the full consequences of the performed action should be observed by perceptors.

Low-level reasoners: analogues of System 1, they are conceptualised as fast subsymbolic reactive decision-makers. Each has easy access to raw observations via its connection to perceptors and actions via actuators. It receives its current goals from the goal graph modules and works towards achieving or maintaining them. A low-level reasoner's additional responsibility crucial to the neurosymbolic reasoning capacity is processing the raw observations into sets of beliefs.

Knowledge bases: represent collections of the agent's inherent and acquired knowledge of the world. They can include the use-case-specific ontology, rules, current sets of beliefs, etc. We argue for the importance of including a value model of the agent, even as simple as a three-level partial order lattice of beliefs (e.g., like-neutral-dislike). This allows the agent to automatically assign numeric values to observations, functioning as rewards for reinforcement learning policies trained during the agent's execution.

High-level reasoners: analogues of System 2, with the role of classical, sophisticated symbolic planners making strategic decisions while leaving the minute details of the plans' execution to their low-level counterparts. However, they do have a certain level of control over an agent's actions via goals and access to actuators. The intended symbolic implementation of high-level reasoners makes the strategic level of agents' decision-making more transparent, contributing to ensuring a level of explainability and trust.

Goal graphs: used to store plans, both active and inactive, and to facilitate the exchange of their execution status between the low and high-level reasoners. They are essentially storage buffers with capacity to process existing plans and to track partial stages of their execution without taking computational resources away from reasoners.

Memory: another independent storage module type managing the information that keeps track of past information. By default, this information is used primarily for learning, e.g., for a subsymbolic RL policy or a symbolic rule-based system.

Learners: general-purpose modules responsible for learning new behaviours based on the agents' experience at the runtime. Both high and low-level reasoners can communicate with them, allowing the agent to learn both subsymbolic and symbolic behaviours. The knowledge and the memory modules play a critical role here by projecting agent values onto beliefs and observations and then storing them for learning.

3.3 Implementation Details

In addition to the cognitive architecture design, MHAgentA also comes with a direct implementation as a Python package, `mhagenta`, available through the PyPI repository[1]. It facilitates the implementation, deployment, log collection, and general runtime management of agent execution (via Orchestrator objects). Each agent is structured as a multi-process system of modules (one process per module) wrapped inside a virtual Docker container [1]. The internal module interaction is facilitated by the RabbitMQ message-broker software [3] with a simple messaging server instantiated inside each container. Individual module execution uses `subprocess` and `asyncio` Python modules, as well as a custom priority queue for scheduling the execution of internal tasks, such as incoming message processing and ticks of the user-defined internal loop. Basic module coordination (e.g., synchronous start and finish) is done via a root controller sending high-priority commands through a dedicated broadcast channel and monitoring the execution status of the modules. Beyond that, there is no internal

---

[1] https://pypi.org/project/mhagenta/.

mechanism for synchronising execution in terms of time steps; it is up to the user to ensure that each function is properly sliced to avoid execution bottlenecks at the individual module level. The module states are saved after the agent stops, with an option to resume the execution from them. Orchestrators also allows deployment of simple containerised environments. Finally, several special variants of the modules are provided (e.g., external-facing RabbitMQ-based Perceptor and Actuator), with more pending release.

4 Discussion

This paper introduces the MHAgentA cognitive architecture and an agent framework developed as part of a PhD project. The final goal of the project is to test the capabilities of the neurosymbolic adaptive learning approach for creating efficient and effective agents for complex environments.

MHAgentA is designed as a tool for rapid prototyping and iterating over possible solutions for this problem. Its Python implementation, using containerisation and multi-processing, proved to be sufficiently efficient when tested with various reinforcement learning environments of the gymnasium library [2], and is expected to scale efficiently with an increase in environment complexity. Its modularity allows for easy reutilization of the modules in different agents: for example, different agents with DRL capabilities can use the same learner module implementing the DDPG algorithm [19], along with the memory module that represents the experience replay buffer. We plan to provide implementations of common modules along with the Python package in the future. Furthermore, containerisation and the use of RabbitMQ are expected to facilitate efficient MHAgentA agents deployment on HPC clusters, with tests to support this claim scheduled. It is important to note that while the problem of formalising complex problems still affects the design of MHAgentA agents, it is possible to easily utilise existing representations, symbolic or subsymbolic, as-is as part of the design.

The current main goal is to finish the implementation and testing of a Python MHAgentA agent under the following requirements (as discussed above):

- DRL-based low-level reasoner and a symbolic planner high-level reasoner.
- Knowledge base combining the ontological representation of the environment in question with a value system over potential beliefs.
- Hieerarchical goal graphs made of primitive and compound actions.
- Learner module capable of updating its policies to shift the responsibility border between the low and high-level reasoner higher on the goal graph.

We selected NeuralMMO [35] as the experiment environment and will extensively test the agent's capabilities to solve the list of tasks provided with NeuralMMO.

Further technical optimisations, especially regarding third-party tools like Docker and RabbitMQ, are planned as future work, along with an extensive exploration of MHAgentA agents in multi-agent settings. Among the additional planned features is competence-based internal messaging and potential run-time module instantiation for error handling and load balancing based on module execution monitoring. Finally, the analysis of how various agent architectures can be represented with MHAgentA is an ongoing work that is expected to be presented in future publications.

Disclosure of Interests. The authors have no competing interests to declare that are relevant to the content of this article.

References

1. Docker: Accelerated container application development. https://www.docker.com/. Accessed 19 Feb 2025
2. Gymnasium documentation. https://gymnasium.farama.org/. Accessed 19 Feb 2025
3. RabbitMQ: One broker to queue them all | RabbitMQ. https://www.rabbitmq.com/. Accessed 19 Feb 2025
4. Acharya, K., Raza, W., Dourado, C., Velasquez, A., Song, H.H.: Neurosymbolic reinforcement learning and planning: a survey. IEEE Trans. Artif. Intell. **5**, 1939–1953 (2024). https://doi.org/10.1109/TAI.2023.3311428
5. Anderson, J.R.: Rules of the Mind. Psychology Press, Hove (1993)
6. Baars, B.J., Franklin, S.: Consciousness is computational: the LIDA model of global workspace theory. Int. J. Mach. Conscious. **1**, 23–32 (2009). https://doi.org/10.1142/S1793843009000050, https://philpapers.org/rec/BERCIC
7. Bender, E.M., Gebru, T., McMillan-Major, A., Shmitchell, S.: On the dangers of stochastic parrots: can language models be too big? In: FAccT 2021 - Proceedings of the 2021 ACM Conference on Fairness, Accountability, and Transparency, pp. 610–623 (2021). https://doi.org/10.1145/3442188.3445922
8. Bhuyan, B.P., Ramdane-Cherif, A., Tomar, R., Singh, T.P.: Neuro-symbolic artificial intelligence: a survey. Neural Comput. Appl. **36**, 12809–12844 (7 2024). https://doi.org/10.1007/S00521-024-09960-Z/TABLES/12, https://link-springer-com.recursos.biblioteca.upc.edu/article/10.1007/s00521-024-09960-z
9. Braubach, L., Pokahr, A., Lamersdorf, W.: Jadex: a short overview. In: Main Conference Net. ObjectDays, pp. 195–207. AgentExpo (2004)
10. Busetta, P., Ronnquist, R., Hodgson, A., Lucas, A.: Jack intelligent agents - components for intelligent agents in Java. AgentLink News Lett. **2**, 2–5 (1999)
11. DeepSeek-AI, Guo, D., et al.: DeepSeek-R1: incentivizing reasoning capability in LLMs via reinforcement learning (2025). https://arxiv.org/abs/2501.12948v1
12. D'Inverno, M., Luck, M., Georgeff, M., Kinny, D., Wooldridge, M.: The dMARS architecture: a specification of the distributed multi-agent reasoning system. Auton. Agents Multi-Agent Syst. **9**, 5–53 (2004). https://doi.org/10.1023/B:AGNT.0000019688.11109.19/METRICS, https://link.springer.com/article/10.1023/B:AGNT.0000019688.11109.19
13. Gimenez-Abalos, V., Alvarez-Napagao, S., Tormos, A., Cortés, U., Vázquez-Salceda, J.: Intention-aware policy graphs: answering what, how, and why in opaque agents (2024). https://doi.org/10.5281/zenodo.13862643, http://arxiv.org/abs/2409.19038
14. Ingrand, F.F., Georgeff, M.P., Rao, A.S.: An architecture for real-time reasoning and system control. IEEE Expert: Intell. Syst. Appl. **7**, 34–44 (1992). https://doi.org/10.1109/64.180407
15. Kahneman, D.: Maps of bounded rationality: psychology for behavioral economics. Am. Econ. Rev. **93**, 1449–1475 (2003). https://doi.org/10.1257/000282803322655392
16. Kahneman, D.: Thinking. Fast and Slow. Farrar, Straus and Giroux (2011)
17. Kautz, H.: The third AI summer: AAAI Robert S. Engelmore memorial lecture. AI Mag. **43**, 105–125 (2022). https://doi.org/10.1002/aaai.12036, https://ojs.aaai.org/aimagazine/index.php/aimagazine/article/view/19122

18. Laird, J.E.: The Soar Cognitive Architecture. The MIT Press, Cambridge (2019)
19. Lillicrap, T.P., et al.: Continuous control with deep reinforcement learning. In: 4th International Conference on Learning Representations, ICLR 2016 - Conference Track Proceedings (2015). https://arxiv.org/abs/1509.02971v6
20. Littman, M.L.: Probabilistic propositional planning: representations and complexity. In: AAAI/IAAI, pp. 748–754 (1997)
21. Minsky, M.: Society of Mind. Simon and Schuster, New York (1988)
22. Mnih, V., et al.: Human-level control through deep reinforcement learning. Nature **518**(7540), 529–533 (2015). https://doi.org/10.1038/nature14236
23. Newell, A.: Unified Theories of Cognition. Harvard University Press, Cambridge (1994)
24. Berner, C., et al.: OpenAI, Dota 2 with large scale deep reinforcement learning (2019). https://arxiv.org/abs/1912.06680v1
25. Hurst, A., et al.: OpenAI, GPT-4o system card (2024). https://arxiv.org/abs/2410.21276v1
26. Park, J.S., O'Brien, J., Cai, C.J., Morris, M.R., Liang, P., Bernstein, M.S.: Generative agents: interactive simulacra of human behavior. In: UIST 2023 - Proceedings of the 36th Annual ACM Symposium on User Interface Software and Technology (2023). https://doi.org/10.1145/3586183.3606763/SUPPL_FILE/3606763.ZIP, https://dl.acm.org/doi/10.1145/3586183.3606763
27. Poslad, S.: Specifying protocols for multi-agent systems interaction. ACM Trans. Auton. Adapt. Syst. (TAAS) **2** (2007). https://doi.org/10.1145/1293731.1293735
28. Rao, A., Georgeff, M.: BDI agents: from theory to practice. In: Proceedings of the First International Conference on Multi-Agent Systems (ICMAS-95), pp. 312–319 (1995)
29. Rintanen, J.: Complexity of planning with partial observability. In: ICAPS, vol. 4, pp. 345–354 (2004)
30. Schrittwieser, J., et al.: Mastering Atari, go, chess and shogi by planning with a learned model. Nature **588**(7839), 604–609 (2020). https://doi.org/10.1038/s41586-020-03051-4
31. Schulman, J., Wolski, F., Dhariwal, P., Radford, A., Openai, O.K.: Proximal policy optimization algorithms (2017). https://arxiv.org/abs/1707.06347v2
32. Shoham, Y.: AGENT0: a simple agent language and its interpreter. In: Proceedings of the Ninth National Conference on Artificial Intelligence - Volume 2, pp. 704–709. AAAI Press (1991)
33. Silver, D., et al.: A general reinforcement learning algorithm that masters chess, shogi, and go through self-play. Science **362**, 1140–1144 (2018). https://www.science.org/doi/10.1126/science.aar6404
34. Silver, D., et al.: Mastering the game of go without human knowledge. Nature **550**, 354–359 (2017). https://doi.org/10.1038/ature24270
35. Suarez, J., Du, Y., Isola, P., Mordatch, I.: Neural MMO: a massively multiagent game environment for training and evaluating intelligent agents. arXiv preprint: arXiv:1903.00784 (2019)
36. Vinyals, O., et al.: Grandmaster level in StarCraft ii using multi-agent reinforcement learning. Nature **575**(7782), 350–354 (2019). https://doi.org/10.1038/s41586-019-1724-z
37. Wang, W., Yang, Y., Wu, F.: Towards data-and knowledge-driven AI: a survey on neuro-symbolic computing. IEEE Trans. Pattern Anal. Mach. Intell. (2024). https://doi.org/10.1109/TPAMI.2024.3483273
38. Weiss, G.: Multiagent systems: a modern approach to distributed artificial intelligence (1999)
39. Wooldridge, M.: An Introduction to Multiagent Systems. John Wiley & Sons, Hoboken (2009)

An Agentic System
with Reinforcement-Learned Subsystem
Improvements for Parsing Form-Like
Documents

Ayesha Amjad[1] , Saurav Sthapit[2] , and Tahir Qasim Syed[1]([✉])

[1] Institute of Business Administration Karachi, Karachi, Pakistan
amjad@khi.iba.edu.pk, tahirqsyed@gmail.com
[2] Coventry University, Coventry, UK
ae0066@coventry.ac.uk

Abstract. Extracting alphanumeric data from form-like documents such as invoices, purchase orders, bills, and financial documents is often performed via vision (OCR) and learning algorithms or monolithic pipelines with limited potential for systemic improvements. We propose an agentic AI system that leverages Large Language Model (LLM) agents and a reinforcement learning (RL) driver agent to automate consistent, self-improving extraction under LLM inference uncertainty. Our work highlights the limitations of monolithic LLM-based extraction and introduces a modular, multi-agent framework with task-specific prompts and an RL policy of rewards and penalties to guide a meta-prompting agent to learn from past errors and improve prompt-based actor agents. This self-corrective adaptive system handles diverse documents, file formats, layouts, and LLMs, aiming to automate accurate information extraction without the need for human intervention. Results as reported on two benchmark datasets of SOIRE, and CORD, are promising for the agentic AI framework.

Keywords: agentic · multi-agent · foundation models · reinforcement learning · form-like documents

1 Introduction

A significant volume of form-like documents [14] is generated every day by several industry verticals[1], which includes invoices, purchase orders, receipts, bank statements, bills, and more. These documents require information extraction [23] to serve downstream tasks and applications in structured formats, such as efficient archiving, fast indexing, and document analytics. However, both traditional and contemporary approaches to extracting structured information from

---

[1] Industry verticals include retail, finance, healthcare, insurance, manufacturing, and businesses in general.

© The Author(s), under exclusive license to Springer Nature Switzerland AG 2026
S. Rodriguez et al. (Eds.): EMAS 2025, LNAI 16407, pp. 27–44, 2026.
https://doi.org/10.1007/978-3-032-18011-7_3

these documents are limited in their capability to efficiently deal with varying layouts, formats, and complexity [14].

Contemporary usage of deep learning algorithms such as convolutional neural networks (CNN) [1,8] and graph neural networks (GNN) [7,29], was especially influential for detecting tabular structure by leveraging its graphical properties. Methods proposing recurrent neural networks (RNN) [27], and transformer architecture for key information extraction [13,14,28,31] suggested spatial relationship, and semantic entity recognition as primary contributing factors. However, these models require large training data and boast complex architectures. Additionally, CNNs and GNNs focus primarily on the layout analysis to perform extraction, ignoring semantics and contextual awareness. Overall these models assume a list of predefined entities, hence, struggle with unseen documents and entities.

Recent studies have discovered remarkable propensity of human-like reasoning [20], planning [12], judgment, and rationality [33] in LLMs, leading to the possibility of building applications with autonomous decision-making and execution called agents [32]. To solve the complex problem of automated data extraction effectively, a system of multiple LLM agents working in a collaborative environment while learning from past experiences is presented in this study. The evaluation within the framework is done through self-feedback systems [22] as well as metrics to compute matches and similarity between raw data and its extracted counterpart. Self-learning and optimization of each LLM agent is driven through Gymnasium [30], a reinforcement learning framework, where action space is in a natural language setting.

1.1 Understanding Form-Like Documents

In form-like documents, critical information resides as key-value pairs and line items. A Key-value pair is a pair of linked data items, where a key is the unique identifier to look up the value [14], and is largely drawn from a small vocabulary of field-specific variants [23]. Line items are a list of repeated instances of items typically detailing transactional information [19] that may or may not have graphical borders.

Variations in these data artifacts are found across different document types. For example, a key phrase "Invoice#" can also be written as "Invoice Number" or "Invoice No." and its value can consist of either all digits or an alpha-numeric sequence. Moreover, a key phrase and corresponding value can be positioned relative to each other, e.g., a value can be found in the same line as the key phrase with an in-between separator such as a colon (:), or directly underneath. Certain key fields such as "Date" are found in all form-like documents, but most of the other fields are unique to the document type.

Traditionally, detecting line items on a text file has been a complex problem due to variations in its layout and the inability of models to "classify" a structure as tabular based on its content alone [19]. Computer vision algorithms using Hough transform [1] have been successful in detecting graphical borders, but challenges persist for tables without borders.

2   Related Work

Convolutional neural networks such as Fast R-CNN with Region Proposal Networks [8], and encoder-decoder architectures like Chargrid [19] were effective for table and line items detection but struggled with ambiguous or boundary-less table layouts. [1] proposed YOLOv5 for table detection and predefined keyword searches for key-value extraction. Graph-based approaches enhanced performance by encoding spatial and semantic relationships; for instance, GNN-enriched node embeddings differentiate between tables, headers, and plain text in [7]. RNN-based systems such as CloudScan [24] aided key-value extraction for invoices but were limited by their sequential processing and difficulty in generalizing to unseen layouts. Advances in representation learning [23] and contrastive learning, particularly in FormNetV2 [21], improved adaptability by encoding neighboring context and pretraining on form structure, although they still assumed predefined entities.

Transformer-based and LLM-driven methods highlights the efficacy for layout- and language-agnostic information extraction. Layout-aware transformers such as XYLayoutLM [11], spatial transformers like BROS [13], and semantic-rich models like TILT [28] and LiLT [31] significantly outperformed earlier deep learning models. LiLT, in particular, enabled multilingual document parsing. GenIE [18] autoregressively generates structured triplets (subject, relation, object), while KPVFormer [14] used a Q&A-based encoder-decoder architecture to extract key-value pairs. LLM-based frameworks offer a paradigm shift—methods such as trigger-based zero-shot extraction [3], instruction-tuned LLaMA via LoRA [17], and multimodal fine-tuned GenIK [2] demonstrate state-of-the-art flexibility, usability, and robustness, especially in low-resource or OCR-imperfect settings.

Existing models are trained on monolingual documents, except LiLT [31], finetuned for specific document categories like invoices, or assume a predefined list of entities. This limits their effectiveness with unseen documents and dynamic layouts. Their complex architectures and sensitivity to hyperparameters also hinder widespread adoption. Furthermore, standardized evaluation metrics to report the extraction accuracy and system confidence is essential for all probabilistic models in automated environments.

3   Methodology

The implemented framework (Fig. 1) introduces a novel agentic approach to automated document data extraction by combining reinforcement learning with LLMs. As detailed in Sect. 4, this framework is evaluated against a baseline using both proprietary data and public benchmarks, including CORD [25] and ICDAR-SOIRE [15]. GPT-4o-mini [16] serves as the default LLM, and LLaMA 3.3-70B [6] is an alternative for processing sensitive or confidential documents. The token limit adheres to each model's maximum capacity to handle lengthy inputs, and all responses are constrained to a strict JSON format for structured output.

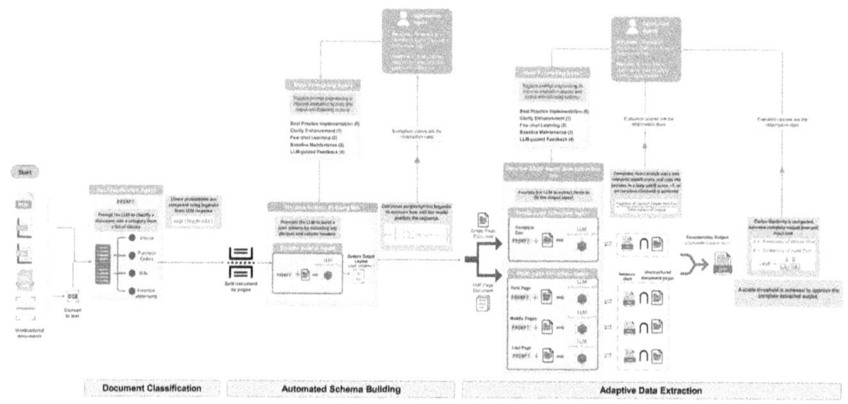

Fig. 1. Architecture of the agentic form-like document data extraction framework comprising seven agents (blue), two Gymnasium environments (dark pink), and five evaluation metrics (cyan). Agents include a document classifier, schema builder, data extractor, two Gymnasium agents, a meta-prompting agent, and an evaluator. Evaluation metrics guide iterative optimization of the environments. (Color figure online)

3.1 Document Text Reader

A document reader class reads text off of form-like documents in various formats (PDF, TXT, DOC, PNG, JPG, JPEG, TIFF, BMP), while preserving the layout of the original document. For scanned PDFs and images, it uses state-of-the-art paddle OCR [4], ensuring accurate conversion into machine-readable text along with a built-in confidence score. Text-based formats (PDF, TXT, DOC) bypass OCR for downstream processing.

To preserve the original layout of documents post-OCR, we first compute the center position of each text block using $x_{\text{center}} = \frac{\min(x_1,x_2,x_3,x_4)+\max(x_1,x_2,x_3,x_4)}{2}$. Layout preservation is then guided by a vertical threshold $\Delta y_{\text{threshold}} = h_{\text{page}} \cdot 0.015$, which helps identify line breaks and group related text blocks. To maintain appropriate spacing between elements, we calculate discrete block spacing as $\max\left(1, \left\lfloor \frac{x_{\text{current}}-x_{\text{last}}}{w_{\text{page}}\cdot 0.01} \right\rfloor\right)$. These heuristics enable the reconstruction of structured layouts while accommodating document variability.

3.2 Evaluation Metrics

Extraction accuracy is evaluated using two non-parametric scores - exact match and cosine similarity. JSON output is corroborated against its ground-truth for exact matches, calculated as a simple ratio of intersection to union. It serves as a proxy for accuracy, helping validate extracted values and identifying hallucination in an LLM-generated output.

$$\text{Exact Match} = \frac{\text{number\_of\_exact\_matches}}{\text{total\_fields}}$$

Cosine similarity score is computed between the generated JSON (A) and ground-truth JSON (B). It is robust against partial matches, and tolerant to schema variability.

$$\text{Cosine Similarity} = \cos(\theta) = \frac{\mathbf{A} \cdot \mathbf{B}}{|\mathbf{A}||\mathbf{B}|} = \frac{\sum_{i=1}^{n} A_i B_i}{\sqrt{\sum_{i=1}^{n} A_i^2} \sqrt{\sum_{i=1}^{n} B_i^2}}$$

The agentic process generates JSON schema dynamically for each document, leading to deviation in field and header names from its ground-truth and resulting in zero exact-match scores. To address this, a semantic match metric—using LLM-based evaluation but same scoring formula as exact match—is introduced.

Semantic match includes two variants: a basic version with binary field-level comparison and simple score aggregation, and an enhanced version with row alignment and cell accuracy:

$$\text{Overall Score} = f(\text{confidence\_score}, \text{table\_analysis}, \text{field\_analysis})$$

$$\text{Table Score} = \frac{\text{row\_alignment} + \text{header\_match} + \text{cell\_accuracy}}{3}$$

Classical machine learning metrics of *F1*, *precision*, and *recall* are used particularly for a comparative analysis on benchmark datasets against current state-of-the-art methods.

3.3 Baseline Data Extraction Framework

The process begins by reading text off of a form-like document, and appending it with a static "system" prompt. A real-time API call is made to the LLM, similar to a sequence-to-sequence task of Q&A [14], with upto 3 retries triggered by a predefined evaluation thresholds. The "system" prompt provides chain-of-thought instructions to establish context-aware extraction, and "user" prompt contains the source document text. The user prompt contains metadata specifying the page number, and document type (e.g. invoice, purchase order, utility bills). This contextual information helps the LLM understand the structure and semantics of the document.

4 Agentic Data Extraction Framework

The agentic framework is designed to adapt to any document type, format, and LLM. The system employs a Gymnasium-compatible environment that models the extraction process as a Markov Decision Process (MDP) [26]. It comprises of five fundamental components: actor agents, Gymnasium environments, observed evaluation space, meta-prompting [9] action space (4.4), and RL agents (4.5). These components are essential building blocks of the self-directed and self-corrected multi-agent extraction pipeline shown in Fig. 1.

4.1 Document Classification Agent

Document classification initiates the analysis of the document's first page using an LLM to categorize it into predefined classes: Invoice, Purchase Order, Utility Bill, Receipt, Financial Document (e.g., bank statements, balance sheets, investment reports), Salary Slip, or Unknown (fallback).

The classification confidence is approximated through a probabilistic approach, where the LLM's logarithmic probabilities are transformed into linear probability by taking an exponential of logprobs as shown below:

$$P_{\text{linear}} = e^{\text{logprob}} \cdot 100\%$$

Documents either failing to meet minimum P_{linear} thresholds or a known category are flagged as 'unknown' for a manual review, thereby maintaining system reliability and accuracy.

4.2 Automated Schema Building

The schema building stage implements an iterative interaction between five components of agentic framework. The custom Gymnasium environment supports an episodic learning framework for schema actor prompt with the following components:

State Representation: Two-dimensional continuous space S_s, representing perplexity score $p \in [0, \infty)$, and schema complexity $c \in [0, 1]$. Perplexity scores are computed by exponentiating the negative of the average of the logprobs. It captures the uncertainty of the generated schema, with no upper bound, its lower values indicate higher schema quality.

$$\text{p} = \exp\left(-\frac{1}{n}\sum_{i=1}^{n} logprobs\right)$$

Schema complexity is a computed score between 0 and 1. It measures the structural complexity, where scores closer to 0 indicate simpler, more maintainable schema.

$$c = \alpha N + \beta D + \gamma B + \delta R$$

where, N is the nesting depth, D is data type diversity. B is the branching factor, and R is the reference complexity. The weights are constrained such that:

$$\alpha + \beta + \gamma + \delta = 1$$

where: $\alpha = 0.4$, $\beta = 0.2$, $\gamma = 0.2$, $\delta = 0.2$.

Reward Function: Reward is computed linearly. The reward function $R_i(s_t, a_t)$ for state s_t and action a_t at time horizon t uses perplexity score p_t and complexity score c_t. Total reward is a simple aggregation of individual step rewards r_i.

$$R_i(s_t, a_t) = (p_{\text{best}} - p_t) + (c_{\text{best}} - c_t)$$

Action Space: The action space A consists of a discrete set of five prompt engineering strategies, $A = \{0, 1, 2, 3, 4\}$, each optimizing the prompts as per instructions (see 4.4).

Termination Criteria: The schema building process continues until either maximum steps are reached, or no improvements are observed in consecutive iterations.

$$\text{terminated} = \begin{cases} 1 & \text{if steps} \geq \text{max\_steps} \\ 1 & \text{if non\_improvement\_count} \geq 2 \\ 0 & \text{otherwise} \end{cases}$$

The dual optimization approaches (perplexity and complexity) provide complementary perspectives on schema quality, maintaining consistent improvement trajectories, and ensuring robustness while maintaining adaptability.

4.3   Iterative Data Extraction Environment

The multi-agent framework adopts an iterative approach, enabling interactions between the data extractor agent, extraction environment, meta-prompting action space, and an RL policy for optimizing actor prompts. It dynamically refines extraction strategies based on self-feedback.

Multi-page extraction is supported via a worker pool (Sect. 4.7), where pages are handled in parallel and results are concatenated into the final output JSON.

As part of the experiment, the framework implements three distinct environment variants with episodic learning:

1. DataExtractionEnvBase: Basic implementation with simple multiplicative reward mechanisms and fixed thresholds-based termination conditions.
2. DataExtractionEnvIterative: Enhanced version using performance plateaus $P(t)$ to implement adaptive termination $T(s, t)$, and improvement-based with bonus reward system $R(s_t, a_t, s_t')$.
3. DataExtractionEnvStepCount: Step-limited version with explicit exploration or exploitation trade-offs with time-penalization.

Following architecture discusses the second environment *DataExtractionEnvIterative* as the best performing framework for agentic data extraction.

State Representation: The state space S is defined as a continuous 3-dimensional vector. S is tracked over time horizon T, with best performing metrics and corresponding best prompt and output. For any time step $t \in T$:

$$t^* = \arg\max_{t \in T}(s^t_{exact} + s^t_{semantic} + s^t_{similarity})$$

$$\mathcal{B} = \left\{ \max_{t \in T} s^t_{exact}, \max_{t \in T} s^t_{semantic}, \max_{t \in T} s^t_{similarity}, \omega^{t^*}, \pi^{t^*} \right\}$$

where, s^t are the scores at time t, and (ω, π) represent the output-prompt pair.

Reward Function: A step function for a combined score $\sigma_t = s_{exact} + s_{semantic} + s_{similarity}$, and an improvement bonus coefficient $\beta = 0.1$

$$R(s_t, a_t, s'_t) = \begin{cases} \beta + \sigma_t - \sigma_{t-1} & \text{if } \sigma_t > \mathcal{B} \\ \sigma_t - \sigma_{t-1} & \text{otherwise} \end{cases}$$

Termination Criteria: The iterative environment implements adaptive termination $[T(s,t)$ based on performance plateaus $P(t)$ achievement and non-improvement tracking:

$$P(t) = \begin{cases} 1 & \text{if } \sigma_t \leq \sigma_{t-1} \text{ for } k \text{ consecutive steps} \\ 0 & \text{otherwise} \end{cases}$$

where, $k = 2$ (configurable non-improvement threshold)

$$T(s,t) = \begin{cases} 1 & \text{if } P(t) = 1 \\ 1 & \text{if steps} \geq \text{max\_steps} \\ 1 & \text{if threshold\_conditions\_met}(s) \\ 0 & \text{otherwise} \end{cases}$$

4.4   Meta-prompting Agent

The meta-prompting agent represents a systematic approach to dynamic prompt engineering, whereby, using driver prompts to refine and optimize actor prompts. These meta-prompting strategies makes up the discrete action space $A \in \{0, 1, 2, 3, 4\}$:

$$A = A(s, p, t, o, g) = \begin{cases} Bt(p) & \text{if } a = 0 \\ C(p) & \text{if } a = 1 \\ F(p, t_k) & \text{if } a = 2 \\ N(p) & \text{if } a = 3 \\ R(p, F(p, o, g)) & \text{if } a = 4 \end{cases}$$

1. Best Practice Strategy $(Bt(p))$: Optimize prompts by letting LLM decide and establish best prompt engineering practices.
2. Clarity Enhancement Strategy $(C(p))$: Applies process decomposition, ambiguity elimination, tone optimization, structural enhancement, and goal clarification.
3. Few-Shot Learning Strategy $(F(p, t_k))$: Implements example-based learning through carefully curated demonstrations for each task type t_k. A maximum of 3 examples are included to prevent context overflow.
4. Feedback-Refine Optimization Strategy $(R(p, F(p, o, g)))$: Takes inspiration from LLM-as-a-judge [10] policy, where an LLM evaluates and critics for complex tasks. It is a 2-stage process, where first a comprehensive feedback is provided by observing actor prompt p, generated output o and corresponding ground truth g. Followed by refinements in actor prompt to minimize differences between generated and target output.

5. Preservation Strategy (No Change) $N(p)$: Used as a control experiment that maintains original actor prompt.

4.5 Reinforcement Learning Agent

The Gymnasium agent implements a language model-guided policy $\pi(a|s)$ that observes the current state vector, current total rewards, and a boolean value for task completion, analyzes it through an LLM and maps to a meta-prompting action. This creates a closed-loop optimization system where prompt improvements are guided by both immediate feedback and long-term performance metrics.

$$\pi(a|s) : S \rightarrow P(A)$$

where, $P(A)$ is a probability distribution over action space A.

The system maintains state tracking to maximize the expected cumulative reward R for all iterative environments with minimum terminal step T:

$$argmax(\mathrm{E}[\sum_{t=0}^{T} \gamma^t R])$$

$$T = \min(T_{\max}, \inf\{t : n_t \geq N\})$$

where, $T_{\max}$ is the maximum allowed steps, n_t is the number of consecutive non-improvements, and N is the non-improvement threshold.

Exploration rate decay $\epsilon(t)$ of Gymnasium RL policy states:

$$\epsilon(t) = \epsilon_0 \cdot e^{-\delta t}$$

where, $\epsilon_0 = 1.0$ (initial exploration rate), and $\delta = 0.2$ (decay rate)

4.6 Learned Prompt Optimization

Learned Prompt Optimization (LPO) extends the capability of a simple RL agent by leveraging contextual bandit learner to iteratively explore and exploit effective meta-prompting strategies. It comprises of three core components:

1. Vector Embedding: Converts textual inputs into dense vector representations using OpenAI ada-002 embedding model.
2. Selection Scorer: Evaluates prompt strategies based on context and historical performance.
3. Policy Learner: Updates strategy selection weights using Vowpal Wabbit [5] contextual bandit implementation.

For each iteration t, the probability of selecting action $a_i \in A$ is:

$$P(a_i|C_t) = \frac{\exp(\theta_i^T \phi(C_t))}{\sum_{j=1}^{n} \exp(\theta_j^T \phi(C_t))}$$

where $\phi(C_t)$ is the context embedding and θ_i are learned parameters. After observing cumulative reward R, parameters are updated as follows, where η is the learning rate.

$$\theta_i \leftarrow \theta_i + \eta R \nabla_{\theta_i} \log P(a_i | C_t)$$

4.7 System Optimization Components

The agentic data extraction framework encounters operational challenges with multi-page documents. A single page requires time t with multiple LLM calls for optimized output, hence, processing n pages scales linearly to nt, leading to significant computational overhead. Additionally, concatenating text from all n pages into a single LLM call, while seems feasible, dampens output accuracy.

To overcome these challenges and build a robust document processing system with minimal redundant operations, parallel processing and caching mechanisms are implemented. Furthermore, our sequential framework, where the output from each step influences subsequent steps, requires comprehensive logging and error handling for debugging and monitoring to maintain system reliability.

5 Results

Results are reported for 32665 form-like documents, including 20295 proprietary documents and 11000 benchmark files, out of which approximately 93% requires an OCR processing. The largest volume of document type is invoice with 17492 files, followed by 12987 receipts. Most documents comprises of 2–3 pages (Average Number of Pages $= \frac{\text{Total Number of Pages}}{\text{Number of Files}} = 2.7$).

5.1 Baseline Framework Results

Table 1 reports the baseline results of the LLM-generated output on 32665 files, via one-shot prompting, on two metrics - exact match, and cosine similarity. All reported scores are best of 3 pooled responses averaged over # of files for each document type. Two factors have been observed to influence the evaluation performance, 1) Number of pages, 2) Scan quality.

Table 2 extends the analysis by reporting on classical machine learning metrics of $F1$, *precision*, and *recall* for benchmark datasets.

Financial documents, typically spanning 7 or more pages and available in high-quality formats, yield low extraction scores (30% exact matches, 59% similarity). In contrast, single-page images of receipts at 100 dpi (standard threshold $= 300$ dpi)—achieve higher scores (78% exact, 81% similarity). Similarly, single-page utility bills with even lower quality (89 dpi) still outperform financial documents, but falls behind receipts, in extraction accuracy (See Fig. 2).

Two patterns are observed in the extracted JSON of multi-page documents; partial extraction across all pages (often missing line items from middle pages), and complete omission of entire pages (more common). Multiple reruns revealed

Table 1. Results from the one-shot single-execution prompt

Document Type	Formats	# of Files	Exact Match	Similarity
Invoices	Images	10,000	0.43	0.61
Invoices (Australian)	Digital PDF	2202	0.58	0.74
Invoices (Australian)	Scanned PDF	5290	0.33	0.38
Purchase Orders	Digital PDF	19	0.78	0.76
Purchase Orders	Scanned PDF	138	0.43	0.55
Receipts	Images	987	0.78	0.81
Financial documents	Mixed/HTML	2,832	0.30	0.59
Utility Bills	Images	100	0.31	0.75
Salary Slips	Images	97	0.84	0.86
CORD	Images	10,000	0.71	0.90
ICDAR-SROIE	Images	1,000	0.67	0.75

Table 2. Results from baseline framework on two benchmark datasets

Document Type	F1 Score	Precision	Recall
CORD	0.886	0.902	0.871
ICDAR-SROIE	0.808	0.780	0.838

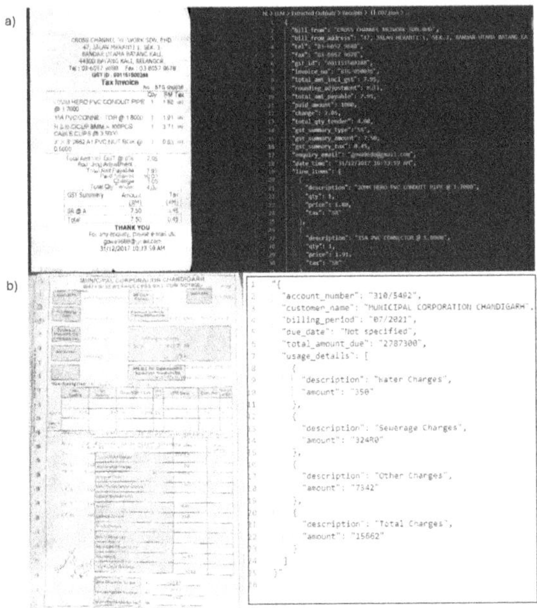

Fig. 2. a) Extracted JSON of a receipt (96 dpi) scored 90% on exact matches, 100% on semantic matches, and 96% on cosine similarity. b) Extracted JSON of a utility bill (66 dpi) scored lower: 30% exact matches, 65% semantic matches, 71% similarity.

inconsistent outputs, suggesting nondeterministic behavior from the LLM. The nondeterministic behavior worsens with poor quality scans, which sometimes returned a blank JSON or incorrect (See Fig. 3) and hallucinated response.

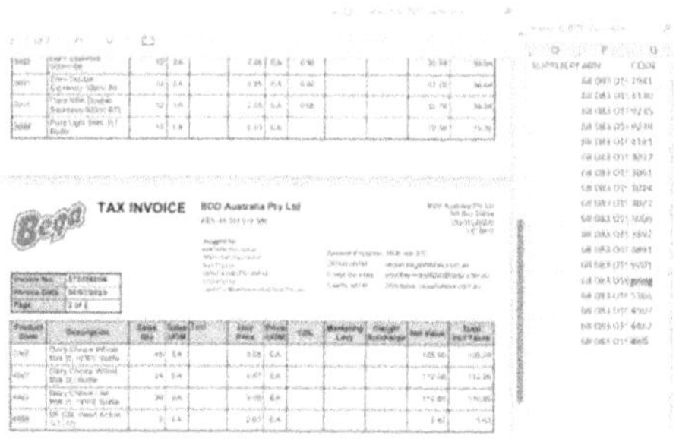

Fig. 3. Incorrect data extracted for a 2-page scanned document. "3093" is extracted as "goog" and "4155" is extracted as "4is5".

Limitations of static prompts without explicit output schema are evident in cases with atypical key phrases or headers. Cases discussed in Fig. 4 highlights the importance of including output schema in the extraction prompts. Extraction accuracy is influenced not just by page count and scan quality, but also by document formatting. Multi-line headers and dark-shaded key phrases often reduce accuracy, mainly due to issues in text conversion rather than LLM behavior. Processing documents as images generally yields more reliable results than pre-converting them to text.

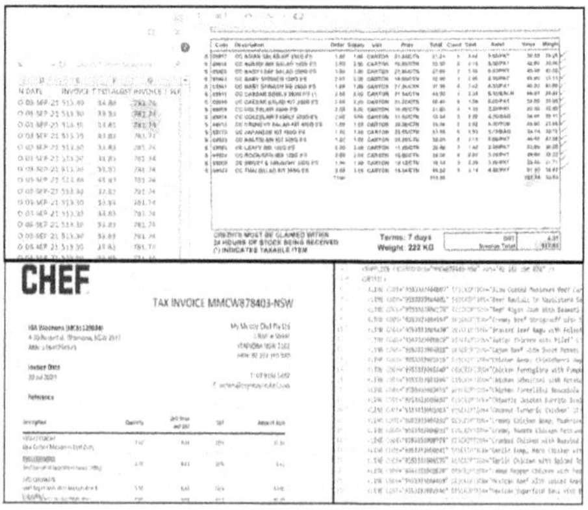

Fig. 4. Top: 'Invoice Total' is misidentified as 'total' due to semantic closeness. Bottom: explicitly specifying 'CODE' as a column header enables correct extraction, even though there is no 'CODE' column header in the document table.

The baseline monolithic prompt-based system exhibit nondeterministic behavior, producing inconsistent outputs with multi-page documents, tables with missing headers, poor quality scans, ambiguous field names, and atypical document formatting. Context window limitations further exacerbate the issue, restricting processing to shorter documents. There is also a higher likelihood of hallucination resulting from information density of multi-page documents.

5.2   Agentic Framework Results

Table 3 reports the results of agentic data extraction framework on three evaluation metrics. The exact match scores are computed after a manual verification of each output JSON against its groundtruth, therefore, depicting the most accurate picture of the output performance. Semantic match is used to balance out a score of zero on the exact match during runtime iterative processing.

Table 3. Results from the self-directed and self-corrected multi-agent system - *gpt-4o-mini*

Document Type	Formats	# of Files	Exact Match	Semantic Match	Similarity
Invoices (mixed)	Images	10,000	0.863	0.901	0.941
Invoices (Australian)	Searchable PDF	2202	0.985	0.944	0.908
Invoices (Australian)	Scanned PDF	5290	0.913	0.900	0.939
Purchase Orders	Searchable PDF	19	0.994	1.00	0.980
Purchase Orders	Scanned PDF	138	0.953	0.899	0.952
Receipts	Images	987	0.834	0.910	0.866
Financial documents	Images	2832	0.962	0.998	0.927
Utility Bills	Images	100	0.425	0.663	0.817
Salary Slips	Images	97	1.00	0.998	0.959
CORD	Images	10,000	0.866	0.812	0.921
ICDAR-SROIE	Images	1,000	0.753	0.911	0.890

A clear improvement is observed in extraction completeness from every page of financial documents. For instance, if a bank statement page lists 15 transactions, all are accurately captured in the JSON, regardless of its page index or document length. This boosts the exact match scores from 30% to 96.2% and similarity scores from 59% to 92.7%, primarily due to multi-page handling where each page is processed independently.

Searchable PDFs or high resolution single-page images achieve near-perfect extraction completeness and accuracy. Purchase Orders show a semantic score of 1.00, exact match of 0.994, and cosine similarity of 0.98. Similarly, each salary slip achieves a 100% exact match and ranks only second to Purchase Orders on other metrics.

The agentic process remains robust against large file sizes and complex structure. When a document contain multiple tables, the algorithm extracts each as a distinct child collection in the JSON output without overly complicating the schema. As shown in Fig. 5, even with duplicate tables, the schema builder agent filters out redundancies to retain only unique instances for extraction.

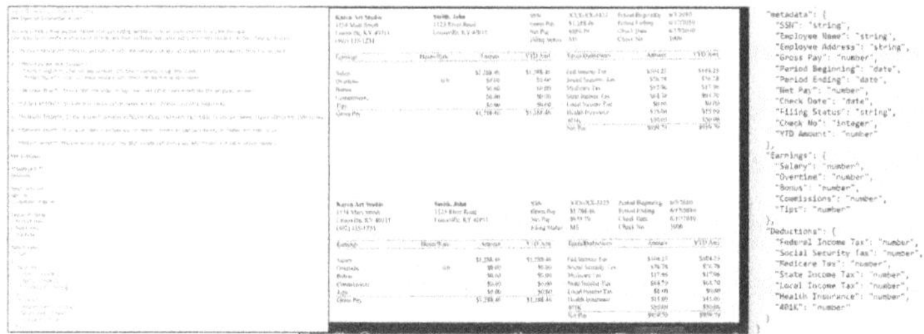

Fig. 5. This salary slip shows four tables, but only two are unique, as earnings and tax deductions each appear twice. Schema builder prompt (left) retains only unique tables.

Low-quality scans ($\leq$ 100 dpi) remain challenging due to the framework's reliance on OCR, as evident by the poor performance of utility bills scoring lowest across all metrics. A potential solution is to bypass OCR and use multimodal LLMs for direct image-based data extraction.

The agentic process dynamically generates and optimizes the schema at runtime, enabling it to extract nearly all relevant fields—often beyond the scope of benchmark groundtruth. In Fig. 6, the extracted JSON of a receipt includes all expected fields except one (address) and also captures additional fields not present in the groundtruth. To accommodate schema variations between the groundtruth and extracted output, a flexible evaluation using fuzzy matching is employed for *F1*, *precision*, and *recall* (Table 4). Values are considered a match if their similarity is $\geq$ 80%, allowing minor formatting differences to be ignored.

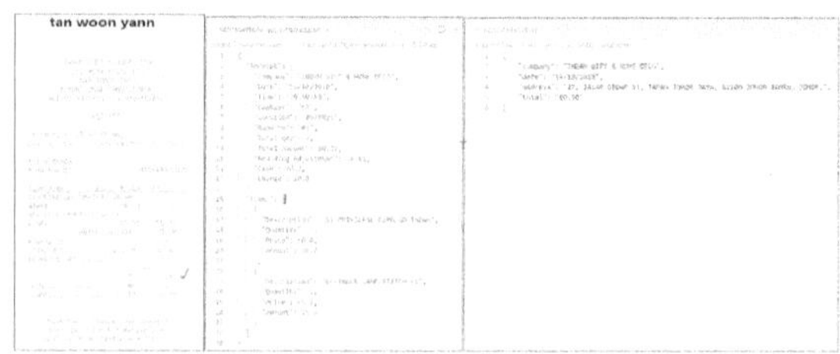

Fig. 6. ICDAR-SROIE data collection (left), agentic extracted JSON (center), groundtruth (right).

Table 4. Agentic results on benchmark shows a minimum 0.05 point boost on classical ML metrics

Document Type	F1 Score	Precision	Recall
CORD	0.965	0.966	0.964
ICDAR-SROIE	0.939	0.958	0.921

Integrating document classification and schema building stages creates a fully automated agentic extraction pipeline. Table 5 reports on classification confidence (linear probability) and schema evaluation scores—averaged per document type. These metrics are as critical in evaluating the agentic workflow.

Table 5. Evaluation report on document classification and schema generation stages

Document Type	Confidence	Accuracy	Best Complexity
Invoices	98.327%	0.84	0.547
Purchase Orders	98.196%	1.00	0.620
Receipts	87.482%	0.910	0.288
Financial documents	98.292%	0.928	0.434
Utility Bills	98.5%	0.903	0.727
Salary Slips	1.00%	1.00	0.488

Salary slips are classified with 100% confidence, while some financial documents and utility bills are misidentified as 'unknown'. This is likely due to classification relying only on the first page, which may be a cover page in financial documents, and the low-resolution images typical of utility bills. Invoices exhibit lower classification accuracy due to false positives, as many receipts are incorrectly predicted as invoices.Schema complexity is lowest for receipts due to its simple structure, and highest for utility bills. The schema building component improves the extraction but introduces variability, as each schema is tailored per document. Documents with similar layouts but different content may produce different metadata, which is acceptable for extraction but problematic for downstream ETL processes that require uniform structures.

As illustrated in Fig. 7, comparing baseline vs agentic frameworks, where latter shows improvements across all document types with financial documents and Australian invoices reporting massive ≥ 0.5 point increase in exact match scores. Same is the case for all other evaluation metrics, concluding that the agentic process has shown remarkable potential to the form-like data extraction problem in an automated environment.

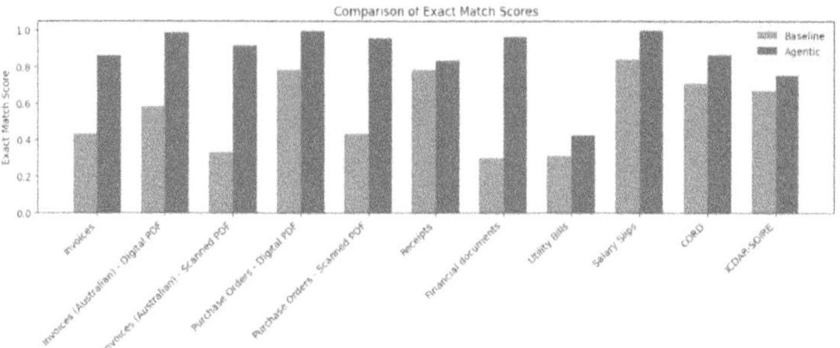

Fig. 7. Baseline vs Agentic - comparison on exact matches.

6   Conclusion

Single prompt driven applications, leveraging LLMs, have shown promising results in simple data extraction tasks. These applications are effortless, fast, and produces quality output for single-page documents. However, it faces inherent limitations in handling complex, multi-page form-like documents. Common challenges include limited context window, hallucination due to information density, and predefined prompts faltering on varying documents. This constrains the reliability and scalability of monolithic preset-prompt frameworks.

The challenges are mitigated by Agentic systems. Modular, multi-agent architectures distribute tasks and improve robustness. Systems deal inaccuracies by leveraging specialized agents for classification, splitting, schema generation and adaptive extraction. These improvements makes the process ideal for mid-size documents of good resolution. Moreover, their ability to provide confidence metrics and iterative feedback ensures higher accuracy and scalability, making them an essential evolution for form-like document data extraction.

6.1   Limitations

In addition to OCR reliance, we have observed that meta-prompting is sensitive to the wordings of the initial prompt. Processing speed is another challenge as agentic takes a minimum of 1 min to extract data, while the baseline takes less than 10 s on average. The system caters to only a handful of document categories, and there is no automated way of handling documents classified as 'unknown'. Future studies may explore multimodality of LLMs for image data extraction, in addition to adding more learnable parameters for RL policy.

6.2   Ethical Statements

The usage of cloud-based LLMs to process documents containing critical information has been under ethical scrutiny since the release of OpenAI gpt-3.5. The risks include data privacy, potential security breaches, unauthorized access, and compliance with regulatory frameworks like GDPR and HIPAA.

All data used in this study is handled in accordance with the best practices of encryption and access control. The research utilizes OpenAI's enterprise API, which is designed to ensure a secure and compliant processing. Moreover, evaluation scores are reported on benchmark datasets to compare the performance of the system with existing state-of-the-art methodologies, to avoid making confidential proprietary data public.

References

1. Arslan, H., Arslan, H.: End to end invoice processing application based on key fields extraction. IEEE Access (2022). https://doi.org/10.1109/access.2022.3192828
2. Cao, P., Wang, Y., Zhang, Q., Meng, Z.: GenKIE: robust generative multimodal document key information extraction. In: Conference on Empirical Methods in Natural Language Processing (2023). https://doi.org/10.48550/arxiv.2310.16131
3. Cao, R., Rongyu, C., Cao, R., Luo, P., Luo, P., Luo, P.: Extracting zero-shot structured information from form-like documents: pretraining with keys and triggers. In: AAAI Conference on Artificial Intelligence (2021). https://doi.org/10.1609/aaai.v35i14.17494
4. contributors, P.: PaddleOCR: awesome multilingual OCR toolkits based on PaddlePaddle. https://github.com/PaddlePaddle/PaddleOCR. Accessed 8 Dec 2024
5. Contributors, V.: Vowpal Wabbit reinforcement learning (2024). Accessed 20 Apr 2025
6. Dubey, A., et al.: The Llama 3 herd of models. arXiv preprint: arXiv:2407.21783 (2024)
7. Gemelli, A., Vivoli, E., Marinai, S.: Graph neural networks and representation embedding for table extraction in PDF documents. In: International Conference on Pattern Recognition (2022). https://doi.org/10.1109/icpr56361.2022.9956590
8. Gilani, A., et al.: Table detection using deep learning. In: IEEE International Conference on Document Analysis and Recognition (2017). https://doi.org/10.1109/icdar.2017.131
9. Goodman, N.: Meta-prompt: a simple self-improving ai design (2023). https://noahgoodman.substack.com/p/meta-prompt-a-simple-self-improving
10. Gu, J., et al.: A survey on LLM-as-a-judge. ArXiv abs/2411.15594 (2024). https://api.semanticscholar.org/CorpusID:274234014
11. Gu, Z., et al.: XYLayoutLM: towards layout-aware multimodal networks for visually-rich document understanding. Comput. Vis. Pattern Recognit. (2022). https://doi.org/10.1109/cvpr52688.2022.00454
12. Guo, T., et al.: Large language model based multi-agents: a survey of progress and challenges (2024). https://arxiv.org/abs/2402.01680
13. Hong, T., Kim, D., Ji, M., Hwang, W., Nam, D., Park, S.: BROS: a pre-trained language model focusing on text and layout for better key information extraction from documents. In: AAAI Conference on Artificial Intelligence (2021). https://doi.org/10.1609/aaai.v36i10.21322
14. Hu, K., Wu, Z., Zhong, Z., Lin, W., Sun, L., Huo, Q.: A question-answering approach to key value pair extraction from form-like document images. In: AAAI Conference on Artificial Intelligence (2023). https://doi.org/10.48550/arxiv.2304.07957
15. Huang, Z., et al.: ICDAR2019 competition on scanned receipt OCR and information extraction. In: IEEE International Conference on Document Analysis and Recognition (2019). https://doi.org/10.1109/icdar.2019.00244

16. Hurst, A., et al.: GPT-4o system card. arXiv preprint: arXiv:2410.21276 (2024)
17. Jiao, Y., et al.: Instruct and extract: instruction tuning for on-demand information extraction. In: Conference on Empirical Methods in Natural Language Processing (2023). https://doi.org/10.48550/arxiv.2310.16040
18. Josifoski, M., et al.: GenIE: generative information extraction. In: North American Chapter of the Association for Computational Linguistics (2022). https://doi.org/10.18653/v1/2022.naacl-main.342
19. Katti, A.R., et al.: Chargrid: towards understanding 2D documents. In: Conference on Empirical Methods in Natural Language Processing (2018). https://doi.org/10.18653/v1/d18-1476
20. Kojima, T., Gu, S.S., Reid, M., Matsuo, Y., Iwasawa, Y.: Large language models are zero-shot reasoners. In: Advances in Neural Information Processing Systems, vol. 35, pp. 22199–22213 (2022)
21. Lee, C.Y., et al.: FormNetV2: multimodal graph contrastive learning for form document information extraction. In: Annual Meeting of the Association for Computational Linguistics (2023). https://doi.org/10.48550/arxiv.2305.02549
22. Madaan, A., et al.: Self-refine: iterative refinement with self-feedback (2023). https://arxiv.org/abs/2303.17651
23. Majumder, B.P., et al.: Representation learning for information extraction from form-like documents. In: Annual Meeting of the Association for Computational Linguistics (2020). https://doi.org/10.18653/v1/2020.acl-main.580
24. Palm, R.B., Winther, O., Laws, F.: CloudScan - a configuration-free invoice analysis system using recurrent neural networks (2017). http://arxiv.org/abs/1708.07403 [cs]
25. Park, S.H., et al.: CORD: a consolidated receipt dataset for Post-OCR parsing. null (2019). https://doi.org/null
26. Puterman, M.L.: Markov Decision Processes: Discrete Stochastic Dynamic Programming, 1st edn. John Wiley & Sons Inc, USA (1994)
27. Palm, R.B., Winther, O., Laws, F.: CloudScan - a configuration-free invoice analysis system using recurrent neural networks. In: IEEE International Conference on Document Analysis and Recognition (2017). https://doi.org/10.1109/icdar.2017.74
28. Powalski, R., Borchmann, L., Jurkiewicz, D., Dwojak, T., Pietruszka, M., Palka, G.: Going full-tilt boogie on document understanding with text-image-layout transformer. eprint 2102.09550 (2021)
29. Riba, P., et al.: Table detection in invoice documents by graph neural networks. In: IEEE International Conference on Document Analysis and Recognition (2019). https://doi.org/10.1109/icdar.2019.00028
30. Towers, M., et al.: Gymnasium: a standard interface for reinforcement learning environments. arXiv preprint: arXiv:2407.17032 (2024)
31. Wang, J., Jin, L., Ding, K.: LiLT: a simple yet effective language-independent layout transformer for structured document understanding. Ann. Meet. Assoc. Comput. Linguist. (2022). https://doi.org/10.18653/v1/2022.acl-long.534
32. Woodridge, M., Jennings, N.: Intelligent agents: theory and practice the knowledge engineering review. Knowl. Eng. Rev. (1995)
33. Xu, L., et al.: MAgIC: investigation of large language model powered multi-agent in cognition, adaptability, rationality and collaboration (2024). https://arxiv.org/abs/2311.08562

FALAA: Framework for the Abstraction of Language Agent Architectures

Nicolas Brandstetter[1,2,3,4]([✉]), Felipe Bravo-Marquez[1,3,4][iD],
and Federico Olmedo[1,3][iD]

[1] Department of Computer Science (DCC), University of Chile, Santiago, Chile
{fbravo,folmedo}@dcc.uchile.cl
[2] Department of Electrical Engineering (DIE), University of Chile, Santiago, Chile
[3] Millennium Institute for Foundational Research on Data (IMFD), Macul, Chile
[4] National Center for Artificial Intelligence (CENIA), Santiago, Chile
nicolasbrandstetter@ug.uchile.cl

Abstract. The rapid development of LLM-based language agents has led to a proliferation of architectures described using ad hoc and inconsistent methods, making it difficult to compare, reproduce, extend or even understand them. To address this, we introduce FALAA: a framework that standardizes the description of language agent architectures through a structured set of components—Planner, Executor, Evaluator, Reflector, Memory, and Environment—and a dual-level methodology combining UML diagrams and OCL specifications.

FALAA offers both conceptual clarity and formal precision, enabling unambiguous definitions of agent behaviors and responsibilities. We illustrate its effectiveness through case studies of two representative agents: Reflexion and Retroformer. The formalization reveals critical ambiguities in both architectures, such as vague component definitions and under-specified memory handling. These results show how FALAA enhances clarity, supports architecture comparison, and uncovers design limitations, making it a promising tool for the development and analysis of future language agents.

Keywords: Language Agents · Agent Architecture · Formal Specification

1 Introduction

Language agents are a class of autonomous intelligent systems built on large language models (LLMs). They are defined by their ability to perceive, act, reason, learn, and remember, and have emerged as promising solutions for complex, multi-step tasks [1,3,8]. Recent advances in LLMs, such as GPT-4 [6] and LLaMA [11], have significantly expanded the capabilities of these agents, making them viable alternatives to traditional fine-tuned models [2]. By leveraging mechanisms like in-context learning and instruction tuning, they are able to generalize across diverse tasks without requiring parameter updates, demonstrating robust and adaptable behavior.

© The Author(s), under exclusive license to Springer Nature Switzerland AG 2026
S. Rodriguez et al. (Eds.): EMAS 2025, LNAI 16407, pp. 45–61, 2026.
https://doi.org/10.1007/978-3-032-18011-7_4

This growing potential has sparked intense research activity, with new agent architectures being proposed at an accelerating pace. However, the field's rapid expansion has not been accompanied by a corresponding standardization in how agents are designed or described [2]. In practice, most architectures are defined in an ad hoc manner, using a mix of natural language, code snippets, diagrams, and informal conventions [9,12,16]. This situation makes it difficult to reason clearly about how an agent works, compare different designs, or reuse existing components.

A central problem lies in the lack of a shared structure and vocabulary for representing language agent architectures. Descriptions based on natural language often introduce ambiguity, particularly in areas such as memory handling, control flow, or the role of reflective and evaluative components [5,17]. These ambiguities become especially problematic when selecting or comparing agents for specific tasks, as each architecture introduces its own set of assumptions and limitations. Without a common framework, researchers must interpret and reimplement agents from scratch, increasing development time and reducing consistency across systems [2].

Thus, the core issue lies in the absence of a standardized structure and shared terminology for describing language agent architectures. This gap restricts comprehension, complicates development and scalability, and hinders effective comparison and reuse of agent designs.

Several recent works have proposed partial solutions to this issue by formalizing specific aspects of agent behavior or defining taxonomies of functional components [1,2,10,13]. While valuable, these approaches typically leave unresolved the structural ambiguities and terminological inconsistencies that hinder understanding and interoperability. What is needed is a general framework that offers both a clear conceptual model and a precise formal description of language agent architectures, enabling unambiguous communication and rigorous analysis.

To address this need, we propose a framework for describing language agents that combines conceptual abstraction with formal specification. The framework introduces a standardized structure based on six essential components—Planner, Executor, Evaluator, Reflector, Memory, and Environment—each aligned with key capabilities expected in a language agent. It supports a two-level methodology: a visual-conceptual level based on UML diagrams, and a formal level using the Object Constraint Language (OCL) to specify behaviors and constraints beyond UML's expressive capacity in a precise manner. This approach (illustrated in Fig. 1) aims to reduce reliance on natural language, minimize ambiguity, and promote comparability and reuse across different agent designs.

We apply this framework to two representative agents, Reflexion [9] and Retroformer [16], and show how it reveals hidden ambiguities in their original formulations. Through these case studies, we demonstrate the framework's capacity to clarify agent structure, support systematic comparisons, and guide future development of language agent architectures.

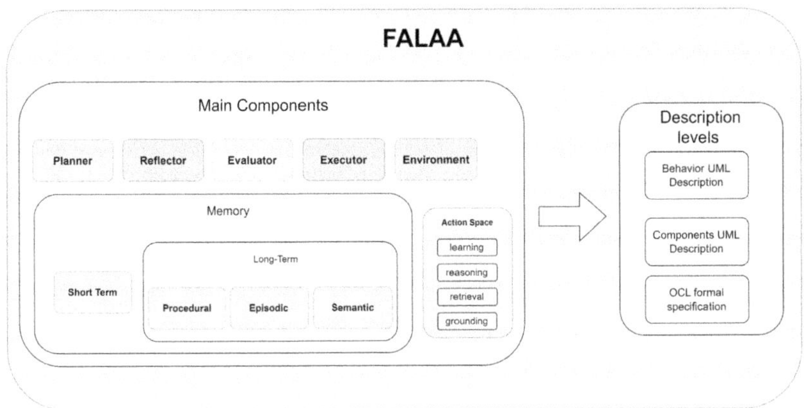

Fig. 1. Glimpse of the essential components and levels of the methodology proposed by FALAA.

The rest of the paper is organized as follows. Section 2 reviews related work on language agent frameworks and architectural formalisms. Section 3 presents our proposed framework and its methodological foundations. Section 4 applies the framework to Reflexion [9] and Retroformer [16] agents, highlighting key differences and design gaps. Finally, Sect. 5 discusses implications and future directions.

2   Related Work

This section reviews existing efforts to formalize and standardize the design of language agents. As the number and complexity of agent architectures continue to grow, several frameworks have been proposed to describe their internal structure and behavior. These approaches differ in their goals, modeling languages, and levels of abstraction. For clarity, we group them into two main categories: (1) component-based frameworks, which organize agents around functional modules inspired by cognitive or task-driven principles, and (2) formally specified frameworks, which use logical formalisms to define agent behavior with mathematical precision.

2.1   Component-Based Frameworks

Given the proliferation of new language agent architectures, many studies have proposed frameworks that decompose agents into functional components based on roles such as planning, memory, or action execution. These component-based approaches aim to provide a high-level understanding of how agents operate, often drawing inspiration from cognitive models or modular software design.

For example, [1] identifies essential capabilities such as planning, memory, execution, tool usage, and interaction with various environments. Similarly, [13] introduces a modular model with distinct roles, including profile, memory, planning, and action modules.

Some frameworks adopt cognitive architecture principles, incorporating elements inspired by human reasoning. The CoALA framework [10] organizes agents along three axes: a memory system (with short-term and long-term memory), an action space (internal and external), and a planning and execution decision process. Likewise, [15] proposes a structure with three functional areas: the Brain (housing the LLM and controlling reasoning, memory, and actions), the Perception module (translating sensory input into LLM-readable form), and the Action module (responsible for output, including tool use and physical interaction).

These frameworks contribute significantly to defining a standard structure for language agents by identifying core functionalities and modular divisions. However, despite these advances, previous frameworks do not fully address the ambiguities that arise when describing agent architectures. Their focus remains on functional decomposition rather than on providing an unambiguous, intuitive, and visual representation that facilitates the comparison and evaluation of different agents. In contrast, FALAA aims to fill this gap by offering not only a standardized structure and terminology, but a formal, visual, and standardized way to describe and analyze language agent architectures.

2.2   Formally Specified Frameworks

To address ambiguity in the behavior of language agents, some works have introduced formal specifications that define agent behavior using logical or declarative languages. These approaches prioritize rigor and verifiability, often at the expense of structural clarity.

A representative example is the framework introduced by [2], which uses Linear Temporal Logic (LTL) and S-expressions to formally specify high-level agent behavior. Their architecture includes a text generator, decoding monitor, and correction module. The agent progresses through states by generating outputs that are validated against LTL specifications. If the output fails to satisfy a goal condition, the correction module adjusts the output and reinserts it into the generation loop.

While this proposal contributes to reducing ambiguity through formal specification, its generality limits its ability to represent key architectural features of certain agents. For instance, it does not explicitly model long-term memory components such as those in Reflexion [9], which are essential for storing internal reflections and enabling self-improvement over time.

In contrast, our approach integrates the advantages of formal specification with an explicit structural model. By combining UML-based visual abstractions with formal constraints written in OCL, we offer a more comprehensive framework for describing both the behavior and architecture of language agents in a unified and unambiguous way.

3 FALAA: Framework for the Abstraction of Language Agents Architectures

This section introduces the core components of the FALAA framework, which provides a standardized structure for describing the architecture of language agents. We begin by presenting a classification of the agent's internal and external action spaces, forming the basis for a unified representation of LLM-based agents. We then detail the FALAA methodology for modeling both the architecture and behavior of such agents, structured around two complementary description levels: a conceptual-visual layer using UML Class and Sequence diagrams, and a formal specification layer based on the Object Constraint Language (OCL).

3.1 Essential Components of a Language Agent

FALAA defines a set of essential components inspired by the work of [1], which characterizes language agents as entities composed of *planning, memory, reflection, execution, tool usage,* and *interaction environments*. Building on this characterization, the proposed framework encapsulates the structure of LLM-based agents into six core components: Planner, Executor, Evaluator, Environment, Reflector, and Memory. Both the action space and the agent's memory are internally classified following the structure proposed in [10], which distinguishes four memory types—short-term, episodic, semantic, and procedural—as well as four action categories: *grounding, reasoning, retrieval,* and *learning*. While the framework allows for the inclusion of additional components when necessary to model specific behaviors, these should not override the core responsibilities assigned to the essential components.

The selection of these components is grounded in both common patterns observed across existing language agent architectures and the broader definition of LLM-based agents as autonomous entities that interact with and act upon an environment, make decisions, learn, reason, and maintain memory [4, 8, 14].

Action Space. It is defined as the set of actions a language agent can execute both externally in an environment and internally within the agent itself. Inspired by [10], we classify actions into the following categories:

- *Grounding (GRN)*: External actions to interact with the environment.
- *Reasoning (RSN)*: Internal actions to reason and generate new information from short-term memory.
- *Retrieval (RET)*: Internal actions to retrieve relevant information from long-term memories into short-term memory.
- *Learning (LRN)*: Internal actions to learn from past experiences, updating long-term memories.

Memory. Stores and provides access to information relevant to the agent. Referencing the proposal by [10], it is divided into:

- Short-term memory: Stores immediate-use information (current state, problem, proposed action). In implementations, this abstraction is sometimes represented as local variables in the code.
- Episodic memory: Records past experiences (actions, completed/failed tasks).
- Semantic memory: Contains knowledge and reflections for decision-making (summaries, learnings).
- Procedural memory: It abstracts the information used to execute actions or guide the agent's behavior. It stores two types of information: implicit and explicit. The implicit information stored in procedural memory refers to data such as that stored in the parameters of a large language model, which are not explicitly presented. Explicit information ranges from instructions for a given LLM, the external action space allowed by the environment, or even new skills acquired by the agent over time. A difference from the definition by [10] is that codes and functions that produce actions (described in the action space) are not considered part of procedural memory in this work; instead, these methods themselves are considered part of the agent's internal action space.

Both semantic, episodic and procedural memory must contain methods that allow for as many retrieval actions as necessary to provide their stored information.

Planner. Uses an LLM to reason about a problem and generate an action plan. It employs prompting techniques —such as *Chain of Thought* or ReAct— and reads instructions from long-term and short-term memories to contextualize its LLM, proposing *grounding* actions that are stored in the trajectory from short-term memory. It must contain at least a method that executes a *reasoning action* aimed at generating the action that will be returned.

Executor. Executes the *grounding* actions suggested by the Planner, interacting with the environment and receiving observations from it, storing them in the trajectory in the short-term memory, all by its own *grounding action* method.

Environment. An external component that allows the execution of actions and the reception of observations or rewards. It can be as simple as a QA environment or as complex as the one designed by [12] based on MINEFLYER, focused on interaction with Minecraft.

Reflector. Performs *reasoning* actions after the execution of the action proposed by the Planner, generating feedback about what happened. Using its instantiated LLM, it produces reflections or critiques that can be stored as knowledge or used to improve future actions proposed by the Planner. Occasionally, the Reflector is also used as an evaluator of the executed action, providing, in addition to feedback, a signal indicating the quality of the action executed by the Executor.

Evaluator. Behavior related to evaluating actions and behaviors performed by the agent, or validating outputs generated by other components, can be encapsulated in an Evaluator component. This component is responsible for evaluating and providing a signal indicating the quality of the generated action or behavior by its *reasoning action* methods.

3.2   Description Methodology

The description methodology given by FALAA, which proposes a structured way to describe and specify an LLM-based agent's architecture, is composed by two complementary levels:

(1) Conceptual Description Level. The main objective at this level is to offer a high-level understanding of the agent's architecture without ambiguity or excessive detail, clarifying relationships and behaviors in a visual-structured way. The conceptual description level should provide a concise, visual overview of the system in the standard structure proposed.

At this level, we defined the principal components and their interactions using UML Class and Sequence diagrams. By examining both diagrams, designers can quickly grasp the agent's architecture, its primary interactions, and the way in which its data and operations are logically grouped. On the other hand, following the standard structure proposed by FALAA, designers will be able to compare sections of their agents with other agents described in the literature, facilitating the understanding and comparison of behaviors and architectures of LLM-based agents.

Here is a general guideline for applying this level:

- *Identify core components:* Determine the essential building blocks of the agent (e.g. Planner, Reflector, Executor, Evaluator, various memories, and any external environment). Each essential component (proposed by FALAA) should mantain the original name, to ensure a convention is followed. Each component should be assigned a specific responsibility. Additional components can be defined if necessary to fulfill specific behaviors, but they should not replace the responsibilities of the essential components.

- *Class Diagram Abstraction:* Represent each component as a class, identifying attributes and methods that show the component's functionalities. Indicate relationships such as *composition, aggregation,* and *associations* to clarify how components depend on one another or store references to one another. This diagram also indicates the nature of each method (e.g., *reasoning, grounding, retrieval, learning*), making explicit what type of action or process is being performed. It is not necessary to assign an action type to each method, but it is encouraged to do so at least for the main functionalities.

– *Sequence Diagram Abstraction:* Model the behavior among components. Show how the agent initializes, receives tasks, proposes actions, interacts with the environment, evaluates potential results, updates memory structures and every behavior that is crucial for the agent's operation. Emphasize repeated processes (e.g., work cycles or loops) and decision points (e.g. whether a reflection it has to be generated). This helps reveal how the system behaves step by step and how information flows among components. It is encouraged to use the various sequence interaction fragments given by UML, such as *loop*, *alt*, *opt*, *par* to represent the agent's behavior more clearly and precisely. It is also encouraged to use the *ref* fragment to avoid extensive and repetitive sequence diagrams.

(2) Formal Specification Level. While UML diagrams capture the main structure and dynamics, some behaviors require a precise and unambiguous definition. The formal specification level complements the conceptual one by providing a rigorous means of describing and verifying behaviors that diagrams alone cannot capture. Designers choose which behaviors to formalize based on the system's complexity and the potential for misunderstandings. Commonly, behaviors that are pivotal to the agent's operation—such as memory handling or task verification—are prime candidates for OCL specifications. For such scenarios, this methodology incorporates the use of OCL constraints to formalize critical invariants, preconditions, and postconditions.[1] This level in FALAA is a complement and should not be seen as a alternative to the conceptual description level.

Below is a guideline for this level:

– *Identify critical behaviors:* Determine which aspects of the agent's logic could lead to ambiguity, could not be described in UML diagrams or are crucial for correctness (e.g., ensuring a specific sequence of actions and observations, conditions that define when an answer is considered complete, or methods that reset internal states).
– *Define invariants:* State the conditions that must always remain true for the system (e.g., the order in which actions and observations must alternate within a trajectory).
– *Express preconditions and postconditions:* For each significant operation, specify the required inputs or states (preconditions) and the resulting modifications (postconditions). This clarifies the exact responsibilities of a method and prevents unintended side effects, something important because, not always the functionalities assigned to a component are obvious, and can be interpreted erroneously.
– *Maintain consistency with UML:* OCL integrates naturally with the UML model. Each constraint refers to elements from the Class Diagram (attributes,

---

[1] Each OCL constraint could be named. Naming invariants or pre/postconditions is not mandatory in OCL, but it is considered good practice to facilitate the understanding of the specification.

methods, relationships), so its necessary to ensure that the constraints are consistent with the elements shown in the UML diagrams.

In summary, by combining the conceptual description level (UML diagrams) with the formal specification level (OCL), this methodology provides a comprehensive guide to accurately describe and implement LLM-based agents. The designer ultimately decides how extensively to specify each behavior, ensuring that critical aspects are addressed without overcomplicating the model.

4   Analysis of Language Agents Using FALAA

In this section, we analyze two architectures of agents based on large language models: Reflexion and Retroformer. These agents were selected due to their relevance in the field of language agents, as well as the similarities and differences they exhibit. Both Reflexion and Retroformer are designed to tackle reasoning and decision-making tasks, and have been evaluated in the same set of environments. Notably, Retroformer builds upon the Reflexion architecture, inheriting several components and behaviors. This makes them particularly well-suited for comparison under a unified descriptive framework.

The objective is to demonstrate how the standard proposed by FALAA can be used to describe each of these architectures clearly and uniformly, identifying ambiguous points, gaps, or inconsistencies in the original documentation.

Throughout the following sections, the key aspects of each agent will be reviewed, both in terms of structure and behavior (execution cycle, action and reflection generation, reward evaluations, among others). It will be illustrated how descriptions in natural language often lead to different or incomplete interpretations, and how formalization under FALAA helps to clarify and unify these aspects.

Finally, we provide a brief comparative analysis of the two agents, highlighting their similarities and differences both conceptually and operationally.[2] This approach aims to demonstrate the versatility of FALAA and its potential to facilitate the understanding and design of architectures for agents based on language models.

4.1   Reflexion

Reflexion [9] is an agent designed to enhance LLM-based systems through linguistic feedback after task failures. Upon failure, the trajectory of actions and observations generated during task solving is summarized into textual reflections that guide future attempts. Its structure defines three main components:

---

[2] It is worth noting that, to avoid overloading the paper, the full specification of Retroformer architecture under FALAA—including detailed diagrams and formal constraints—is presented for those interested in https://dccuchile.github.io/FALAA/.

an *Actor*, responsible for action generation; an *Evaluator*, which assesses trajectories by assigning rewards or ratings; and a *Self-reflection* module, which generates corrective feedback. Additionally, short-term memory (referred to as *trajectory*) and long-term memory (*Mem*) are defined to store recent experiences and accumulated reflections, respectively.

A key element of Reflexion is the *Self-reflection* module. Originally described mainly in natural language, this component relies on a dedicated LLM instance that, when the *actor* module failed in solve the current task, is prompted and generates new reflections. The prompt includes the current task, the agent's trajectory, previous reflections, instructions, examples, and a reward signal produced by the Evaluator. New reflections are stored in long-term memory, with a constraint that limits the total number to three, addressing the context window limitations of LLMs.

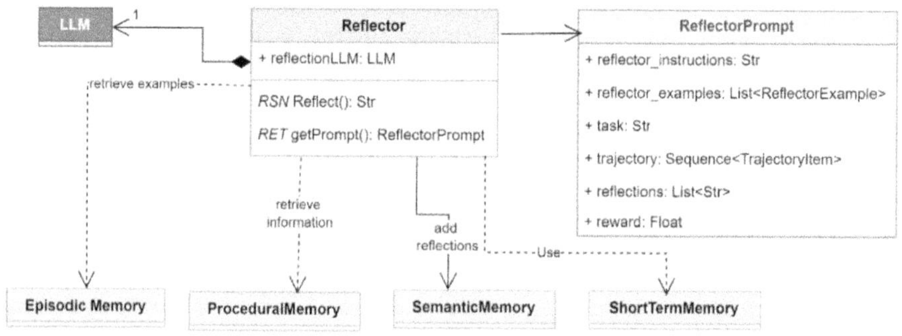

Fig. 2. UML class diagram of the reflector component of the Reflexion agent.

Under FALAA, the *self-reflection* module is formally modeled which is associated to the Reflector component, as shown in the UML class diagram in Fig. 2. The class Reflector includes an LLM instance and is associated with the ReflectorPrompt, which encapsulates the structure of the input prompt listed above. The reflection process is captured by the *Reflect()* method, whose execution is detailed in the sequence diagram of Fig. 3. The method's behavior is formally specified in OCL: the precondition 2 formally enforces that a new reflection can only be added if fewer than three are currently stored, while the invariant 1 ensures that the memory never exceeds this limit.

context SemanticMemory **inv** MaxThreeReflections :

$$\text{self.reflections} \rightarrow \text{size}() \leq 3 \tag{1}$$

context SemanticMemory :: addReflection(newReflection : Reflection): OclVoid
pre :

$$\text{self.reflections} \rightarrow \text{size}() < 3 \tag{2}$$

Ambiguities

Reflexion is described by the authors using both natural language, diagrams, and pseudocode which provide a high-level overview of their proposal. However, due to the lack of a standardized structure, ambiguities arise in its definition, which are addressed by describing Reflexion using FALAA as shown below with two examples.

1. **Scope of the *Actor* Component.** A key challenge lies in interpreting the concept of an *Actor*. According to [9], the *Actor* uses an LLM to produce text and actions, interacts with an environment, and forms a trajectory over multiple steps in a work cycle. Since it generates actions, reasons about them, and accesses a memory (though that memory belongs to the broader Reflexion agent rather than the *Actor* itself), it is not fully accurate to label this component as a standalone "agentâĂİ", because, under the language-agent structure established by FALAA, an agent must include its own memory.

   By describing Reflexion within FALAA, the Actor component is defined as an additional composite component which encompasses both the Planner and Executor components, managing the entire process of attempting to solve a given task.

   Using the above, when Reflexion mentions that other agents can be used as the Actor [9], it implies that certain elements—such as the prompting technique used by the Planner or the evaluation method implemented by the Evaluator—can be replaced with their respective counterparts from other agents.

   This perspective helps clarify the confusion noted in [2], which treated Reflexion as an extension of ReAct—another agent architecture which Reflection's authors uses as the actor in their experiments.

2. **Semantic Memory and Learning Limitations.** A notable insight gained from applying FALAA is rely to Reflexion retains only the last three reflections in its long-term memory (see Fig. 3). Although [9] briefly mentions this limitation, formalizing the agent's behavior highlights how this storage constraint—described in the FALAA's formal specification level, specification 1 and 2—prevents more extensive accumulation of knowledge. In other words, Reflexion cannot effectively learn from older tasks once it exceeds three stored reflections. This underscores a potential enhancement for future LLM-based agents aiming to incorporate deeper, more persistent learning.

4.2   Retroformer

Retroformer [16] extends the Reflexion architecture by incorporating reinforcement learning techniques to enhance the quality of its reflections. Its main contribution lies in the use of *RLHF* [7] to train an auxiliary neural network, responsible for evaluating the quality of the reflections generated by the agent's retrospective model. After training, this reward model is used to guide the reflection process: during each iteration, multiple candidate reflections are generated using a *best-of-n sampling* strategy, and the reward model selects the best reflection, aiming to maximize the agent's overall performance.

Retroformer was originally described by [16] through three main components: the *Actor*, the *Retrospective Model*, and the *Memory*, which includes a *replay buffer* for storing training data. Under the FALAA standard, these elements are mapped more precisely: the *Actor* integrates both the Planner and the Executor, as in the case of Reflexion; the *Retrospective Model* is associated with the Reflector, responsible for generating reflections; and the *Memory* is divided into FALAA's short-term and long-term memories with the *replay buffer* specifically categorized under episodic memory.

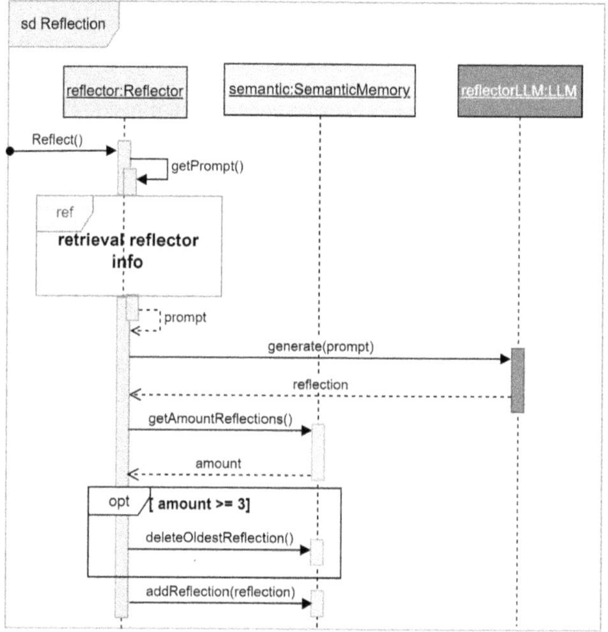

Fig. 3. UML sequence diagram of the reflection process of the Reflexion agent.

Ambiguities

Despite this more structured mapping, Retroformer exhibits greater architectural complexity than Reflexion, incorporating new components and processes. However, the absence of a standard descriptive framework led to an *ad hoc* presentation that mixes mathematical formalism with natural language explanations. As a result, ambiguities arise in key concepts—such as the reflection generation process—allowing for multiple interpretations of the original proposal.

The essential innovative aspect of Retroformer lies in its reflection process, which is based on generating multiple reflections when the agent fails a task and then selecting the best one using a pre-trained reward model. Although [16] provides more detail in describing the training of the reward and retrospective models, it does not comprehensively specify how the reflection process unfolds during the agent's normal execution.

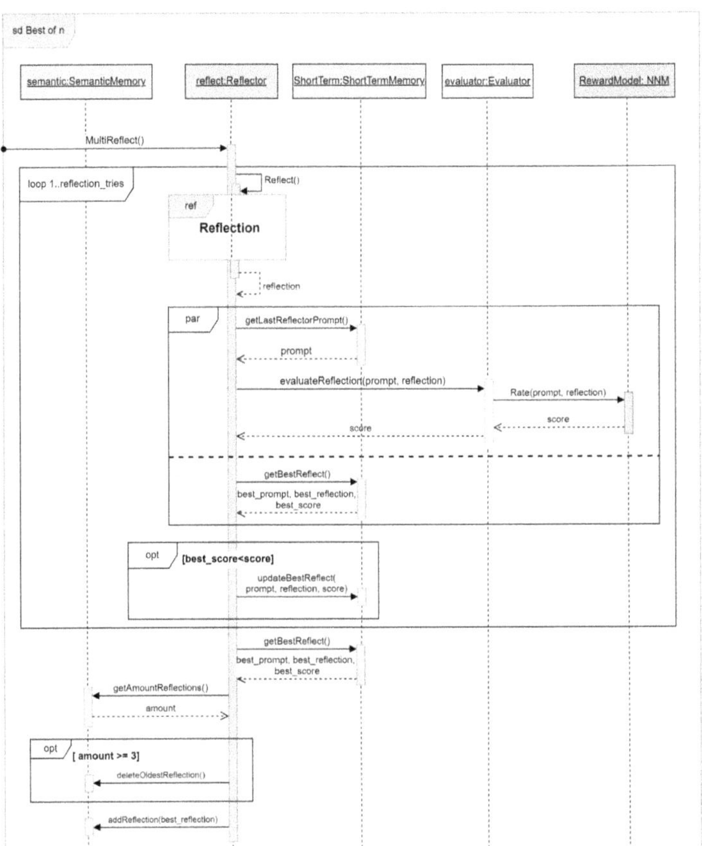

Fig. 4. UML sequence diagram of the best reflection selection process for the **Reflector** component of a **Retroformer** agent.

In the description of **Retroformer** using FALAA, this mechanism is explicitly defined (as seen in Fig. 4), reducing the likelihood of misinterpretations and facilitating an understanding of how reflections are generated and selected during a typical work cycle. In the FALAA description, it can be observed that, after detecting a failed task, the **Reflector** iterates a number of times defined by the developer, generating a reflection in each iteration (process similar to Reflexion's, presented in Fig. 3), which the **Evaluator** evaluates using the reward model.

The score obtained is compared with the score of the best prior reflection, and if it is higher, the candidate reflection and its score overwrite the current best reflection in the short-term memory. This process repeats until the specified iterations are exhausted, after which the best resulting reflection is stored in the semantic memory, following the same logic of a maximum of three reflections as proposed by Reflexion. In summary, describing Retroformer under FALAA clarifies its reflection process—based on the *best-of-n sampler* using a formal description mechanism instead of natural language.

4.3   Comparison

To better illustrate the differences and similarities between Reflexion and Retroformer, this section compares key aspects of their architectures, focusing specifically on their reflection generation processes and reward assignment strategies.

Reflection Process. Both Reflexion and Retroformer generate reflections only after failing to solve the assigned task. However, the mechanisms underlying the reflection process differ significantly. Reflexion generates a single reflection by constructing a prompt and using its LLM to produce feedback (see Fig. 3). Retroformer, on the other hand, extends this process by introducing the *best-of-n-sampler* method (see Fig. 4). Retroformer: multiple candidate reflections are generated through a similar prompting mechanism, and a trained reward model is then used to select the best reflection for subsequent use. This enhancement shows how Retroformer builds upon Reflexion by introducing a more complex reflection cycle that involves additional components and a selection phase.

Reward Assignment. In Reflexion, rewards are assigned by the Evaluator based on the overall outcome of the agent's final trajectory. In contrast, Retroformer assigns rewards incrementally after each action-observation pair generated by the agent. This difference highlights that Retroformer implements a more fine-grained evaluation strategy, assessing the agent's performance at each step rather than only at the end of the task, as in Reflexion.

5   Conclusion

In this paper, we addressed the lack of a standardized structure and a methodology for describing the architectures of LLM-based agents. Although numerous works have introduced new agent designs and paradigms, these often focus primarily on high-level concepts without exhaustively detailing essential components or behaviors, thus causing ambiguities and making comprehensive understanding, implementation, and comparison difficult. Such challenges lead to agents that do not necessarily meet every aspect required for an unambiguous definition, as seen in Reflexion or Retroformer, where certain roles and memory structures remain insufficiently specified.

We proposed FALAA (*Framework for the Abstraction of Language Agent Architectures*) to mitigate these limitations by offering a general structure belong with a dual-level specification approach. At its core, FALAA defines a minimal set of key components (Planner, Executor, Evaluator, Reflector, Memory, and Environment) and a concise action taxonomy, ensuring that every relevant aspect of LLM-based agents can be modeled consistently. On a conceptual level, UML class and sequence diagrams clarify the principal relationships and interactions among these components, while the formal specification level employs OCL to eliminate ambiguities around behaviors, invariants, preconditions, and postconditions.

From the application of this framework, several *insights* were noted:

- *Unnecessary ambiguities revealed and resolved:* By describing agents such as Reflexion and Retroformer under FALAA, it became clear how ambiguities in natural language descriptions (e.g., mixed terminologies, composition of memories or step by step reflection process) can be systematically resolved. This clarity ensures that future agent designs are easier to interpret, compare, and extend.
- *Identification of overlooked design aspects:* The formal specification process highlighted design questions not originally addressed in the literature, such as how many and which past reflections to preserve (Reflexion imposes a limit of three).
- *Natural integration across diverse agent paradigms:* FALAA does not forcibly restructure existing architectures but instead maps their essential components into a shared nomenclature (e.g. the integration of Actor component on Reflexion and Retroformer architectures). This shows that many of the behaviors in LLM-based agents are fundamentally similar, allowing for more coherent cross-agent comparisons.

Additionally, using FALAA *facilitates* the development and documentation process of LLM-based agents. By providing a clear set of responsibilities for each component and specifying how they interact, authors are steered toward more precise and transparent explanations of their systems. This enables researchers to systematically analyze which part of an agent's performance could be improved or replaced, as well as to compare existing architectures on a like-for-like basis, thus imposing a more consistent convention in the terminology of this emerging domain.

After analyzing some agents under FALAA, we have identified various opportunities for *future work*:

- **Multi-Agent Systems (MAS):** Extending this framework to scenarios where multiple LLM-based agents interact could yield significant benefits, particularly in tasks requiring collaboration or negotiation. Future work could include defining additional FALAA components and interaction protocols specific to MAS.
- **Improved Reflection Mechanisms:** Both Reflexion and Retroformer highlight reflection processes but do not reuse older reflections in subsequent task attempts. Enhancing the storage and retrieval of such knowledge in Semantic

memory (or other new memory abstractions) could allow agents to leverage insights gained from past tasks more effectively.

Overall, the proposal of FALAA aims to streamline the design, specification, and understanding of language-agent architectures by introducing a clear structure and methodology. The framework not only provide a higher degree of clarity and consistency but also leaves room for further innovation in agent design. We anticipate that FALAA, by fostering uniformity and comparability across heterogeneous research efforts, could help shape the next generation of LLM-based agents, promoting both incremental improvements and further innovation in this rapidly evolving field.

Acknowledgments. This work was supported by Millennium Institute for Foundational Research on Data (IMFD), ANID Millennium Science Initiative Program Code ICN17_002 and the National Center for Artificial Intelligence CENIA FB210017, Basal ANID.

References

1. Cheng, Y., et al.: Exploring large language model based intelligent agents: definitions, methods, and prospects (2024). https://arxiv.org/abs/2401.03428
2. Crouse, M., et al.: Formally specifying the high-level behavior of LLM-based agents (2024). https://arxiv.org/abs/2310.08535
3. Franklin, S., Graesser, A.: Is it an agent, or just a program?: A taxonomy for autonomous agents. In: Müller, J.P., Wooldridge, M.J., Jennings, N.R. (eds.) Intelligent Agents III Agent Theories, Architectures, and Languages, pp. 21–35. Springer, Berlin Heidelberg (1997)
4. Liu, Z., et al.: BOLAA: benchmarking and orchestrating LLM-augmented autonomous agents (2023). https://arxiv.org/abs/2308.05960
5. Object Management Group: Object constraint language (OCL). version 2.4. Specification formal/2014-02-03, Object Management Group (2014). https://www.omg.org/spec/OCL/2.4/PDF
6. OpenAI: GPT-4 (2023). https://openai.com/research/gpt-4. Accessed 23 Aug 2024
7. Ouyang, L., et al.: Training language models to follow instructions with human feedback (2022). https://arxiv.org/abs/2203.02155
8. Russell, S., Norvig, P.: Artificial Intelligence: A Modern Approach, 3rd edn. Prentice Hall, Hoboken (2010)
9. Shinn, N., Cassano, F., Gopinath, A., Narasimhan, K., Yao, S.: Reflexion: language agents with verbal reinforcement learning. In: Oh, A., Neumann, T., Globerson, A., Saenko, K., Hardt, M., Levine, S. (eds.) Advances in Neural Information Processing Systems, vol. 36, pp. 8634–8652. Curran Associates, Inc. (2023). https://proceedings.neurips.cc/paper_files/paper/2023/file/1b44b878bb782e6954cd888628510e90-Paper-Conference.pdf
10. Sumers, T.R., Yao, S., Narasimhan, K., Griffiths, T.L.: Cognitive architectures for language agents (2024). https://arxiv.org/abs/2309.02427
11. Touvron, H., et al.: LLaMA: open and efficient foundation language models (2023). https://arxiv.org/abs/2302.13971

12. Wang, G., et al.: Voyager: an open-ended embodied agent with large language models (2023)
13. Wang, L., et al.: A survey on large language model based autonomous agents. Front. Comput. Sci. **18**(6) (2024). https://doi.org/10.1007/s11704-024-40231-1
14. Weng, L.: LLM-powered autonomous agents (2023). https://lilianweng.github.io/posts/2023-06-23-agent/. lilianweng.github.io
15. Xi, Z., et al.: The rise and potential of large language model based agents: a survey (2023). https://arxiv.org/abs/2309.07864
16. Yao, W., et al.: RetroFormer: retrospective large language agents with policy gradient optimization (2024)
17. Zhang, Z., et al.: Igniting language intelligence: the hitchhiker's guide from chain-of-thought reasoning to language agents (2023)

Fluid: Social Norms–Based Multiagent Systems on the Web

Amit K. Chopra[1(✉)] and Munindar P. Singh[2]

[1] Lancaster University, Lancaster, UK
`amit.chopra@lancaster.ac.uk`
[2] North Carolina State University, Raleigh, USA
`mpsingh@ncsu.edu`

Abstract. A *social machine* is a Web application that enables users to interact flexibly and creatively to carry out social processes. Currently, social machines are realized via procedural technologies such as Web services. These approaches do not capture the social semantics at the heart of a social machine. Capturing the semantics of social processes would be crucial to enhancing user autonomy, accountability, interoperability, and decentralization.

We present Fluid, a decentralized multiagent architecture in which the semantics of a Web application is represented foremost as a social protocol that captures the applicable norms. Unlike data decentralization architectures such as Solid, Fluid decentralizes not just the data, but also the application logic. Our contributions are the following. One, we demonstrate how Fluid promotes user autonomy and introduces accountability as a counterbalance to autonomy. Two, we demonstrate how interesting sociotechnical patterns, e.g., relating to information governance may be captured in Fluid. Three, we demonstrate how Fluid applications may be realized using data decentralization technologies such as Solid.

1 Introduction

Berners-Lee [3] articulates a vision of *social machines* as open societies in which humans *engage creatively* with each other in social processes, leaving administrative tasks to computers. He envisions the Web (HTTP and supporting technologies and architectures) as a platform for such machines. Berners-Lee's vision has come true in some measure: many Web applications facilitate interactions among their users. We restrict attention to such Web applications, corresponding to social machines, which cover the domains of social media, e-commerce, healthcare, and e-government, among others.

Currently, a social machine is realized as a central Web service that mediates interactions between users. A crucial limitation of such an architecture is that it leaves the social and technical elements of a social machine disconnected. Specifically, a Web service provides the lowest common denominator functionality such as messaging or photo sharing (e.g., on Facebook and Twitter); however,

S. Rodriguez et al. (Eds.): EMAS 2025, LNAI 16407, pp. 62–79, 2026.
https://doi.org/10.1007/978-3-032-18011-7_5

social relationships between the users are epiphenomenal to the service: left to whatever the users make of their interaction.

User autonomy is essential to creativity and therefore crucial to Berners-Lee's vision of a social machine. However, current approaches interfere with autonomy. Instead of representing the semantics of the social process that a social machine supports and letting users interact autonomously in light of the semantics, the Web service (provider) *regiments* the social process, leaving little room for autonomous interaction between users—in effect, reflecting a procedural idealization of work—to adopt Suchman's criticism of traditional workflows [30].

Not surprisingly, the absence of a semantics of social processes hinders interoperability: users become tied to particular implementations and their APIs. Just as metadata and semantics are invaluable for linking data and services [7], so too are they essential for supporting social processes. The desired semantics should capture *social expectations* and *accountability* [15].

The foregoing motivates our research question: *How can we model and enact social machines in a semantics-driven manner that combines social and data semantics?* To answer this question, we take *Interaction-Oriented Software Engineering* (IOSE) [6] as our point of departure. What makes IOSE distinctive is that it advocates specifying a social machine in terms of a *social protocol* between users. A social protocol is framed as a set of social expectations between *roles*. Each user adopts a role in a protocol and deploys its agent as an implementation of that role. In IOSE, there is no central Web service; instead, we obtain loosely coupled agents that interoperate via a social protocol.

Our main contribution is *Fluid*, an architecture that instantiates IOSE using Web technologies. First, we specify a social machine, not as a Web service, but declaratively as a social protocol. To this end, we adopt Custard [5], a language that describes a social protocol in terms of *norms* (elaborated below) and provides a semantics that maps norms to a user's datastore. We demonstrate important norm patterns having to do with data access and privacy. We show a mapping from Custard specifications to RDF datastores by which the state of each norm (e.g., whether it is fulfilled or violated) is computed from facts in a datastore. Second, we show how to realize a user's agent as a Solid application [19,27] to take advantage of Solid's data decentralization techniques. Users engage in a social machine by enacting its social protocol with the aid of their agents. Third, we demonstrate the flexibility Fluid accords users by letting each user deploy any agent that can participate in the relevant protocol. Thus, unlike data decentralization infrastructures, Fluid decentralizes not only data but also the application logic.

Section 2 motivates our approach by comparing prevalent architectures. Section 3 describes the language and concepts underlying Fluid. Section 4 describes the key elements and an implementation of Fluid on top of Solid, and demonstrates Fluid's flexibility in supporting multiple agent implementations. Section 5 summarizes our contributions, discusses relevant literature, and lists future directions.

2   Technical Motivation

We now motivate our choice of IOSE as a foundation for Fluid. We use examples from an imaginary photosharing social machine *PhotoShare*. We consider two requirements: (1) a user may authorize another user to view a photo stream and (2) a sharing user may prohibit the viewing from forwarding photos to others.

2.1   Centralized Logic and Data

A social machine is traditionally *logically centralized* on a Web service. This service is the locus of the social machine's definitive application logic and state, which its persists in a datastore. A significant ramification of this architecture, which Fig. 1 illustrates, is that the service mediates interactions among users. The users have little control over the data the service stores—the entity that provides the service can and usually does exploit the data. Such challenges of information governance [1] and privacy [18,23] have spurred work on decentralized data architectures, such as Solid.

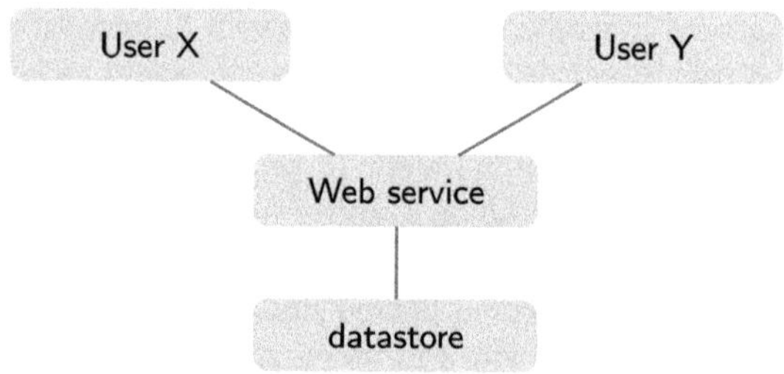

Fig. 1. A social machine implemented as a Web service.

In general, implementing an application as a Web service limits a user's autonomy to the choices made by the service provider in implementing the social machine requirements. To see this, let's assume PhotoShare is implemented as a Web service by some organization. Let's assume a user Marcy has authorized Charlie to view her photos but prohibited him from forwarding them to others. The Web service could implement this prohibition by disabling the forwarding feature for Charlie. Now suppose that Marcy is in a rural region of Italy when an earthquake hits. In this emergency situation, Charlie may wish to forward Marcy's latest photos to a rescue and relief agency (also a user of service). However, the Web service will not allow Charlie to do this.

Imagine that Charlie goes around the service by taking a screenshot of Marcy's photo and sharing it with others. Even if we trace this action to Charlie, we have no basis for claiming this is a violation of anything. If there is some textual statement that Charlie shouldn't share Marcy's photos, such a statement cannot be reasoned about computationally since it lacks a formal semantics.

In contrast, a social protocol specifies the norms (here, Marcy's prohibition on Charlie) that directly characterize Charlie's accountability. If we trace Charlie's action to him, we would know he violated the prohibition. Considerations of whether the violation itself was justified under the circumstances are subsequent to the determination of the violation and may hinge upon the user's attitudes with respect to the social interaction. For simplicity, we exclude such matters from our present scope.

2.2 Centralized Logic, Decentralized Data

Solid address challenges arising from data centralization. As Fig. 2 shows, in Solid, each user has a personal datastore. Users may grant other users access to certain content in their datastore via a fine-grained authorization and access control mechanism, which works together with identification and authentication mechanisms. An application (e.g., Solid social network application Timeline) is implemented as a Web service that takes advantage of this decentralized data via a standardized data formats.

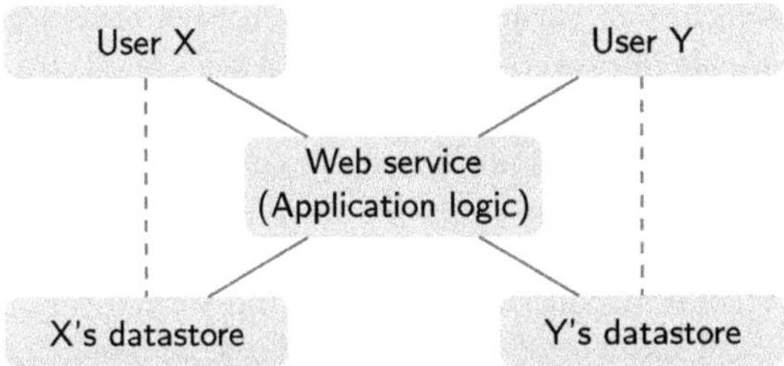

Fig. 2. A Solid application is implemented as a Web service. Users have personal datastores. The application logic comes from the Web service that executes in a user's client, and makes HTTP requests to its user's and others' datastores.

Solid tackles data decentralization, but does not address application logic decentralization. A Solid application is typically implemented as a Web service. Thus, even when the logic is physically distributed across users' browsers, it is defined by a single Web service that, in effect, mediates user interactions.

Suppose we implemented PhotoShare as a Solid Web service. Marcy and Charlie would have their own datastores. Marcy's prohibition on Charlie for forwarding would be implemented via access control attributes in Marcy's datastore and corresponding logic in the Web service. In other words, the problems of autonomy and accountability would manifest themselves in Solid applications just as for vanilla Web services, as discussed in Sect. 2.1.

Let's consider how PhotoShare might be implemented following IOSE. The authorization to view photos and the prohibition on forwarding them would both be expressed as norms. There would be no central implementation of the norms, though. Marcy could implement the authorization for Charlie by sending photos to Charlie upon request. Alternatively, she could violate the authorization by not sending Charlie photos upon request. However, if she did violate the authorization, it would be captured in both their datastores (from the absence of a message containing the requested photo). Analogously, Charlie may receive a photo from Marcy and violate the prohibition by forwarding it to the rescue agency. The violation would be inferred from the prohibition and the event in Charlie's datastore that represents communication with the rescue agency.

3   Social Protocols

We show how a social protocol, as a set of norm specifications, may be specified and realized as abstractions over RDF stores.

3.1   Norms in Custard

We adopt Custard [5] for specifying norms for two reasons. One, Custard is an expressive (supporting complex events) specification language of social protocols that covers a wide variety of norm types. Two, Custard provides a computational semantics for protocols in terms of datastores. Although Custard was developed for relational datastores, we adapt it to RDF datastores for use in Fluid.

Custard defines four types of norms: commitment, authorization, prohibition, and power. Each norm type has a specific lifecycle that determines the state of a norm based on relevant events. We explain a commitment and its lifecycle as an example. A commitment has a debtor and a creditor, representing who is committed to, and associated with two events, namely, its antecedent and consequent. For instance, a commitment in PhotoShare is that if a poster accepts a subscription request, the poster is committed to authorizing the subscriber to view her photos. In this commitment, the poster is the debtor and the subscriber is the creditor. The antecedent is the acceptance of a subscription request and the consequent is the authorization of the subscriber.

The state of a commitment is determined according to occurrence (or lack of occurrence) of its antecedent and consequent. A commitment is detached after its creation when the antecedent occurs. If the antecedent never occurs, the commitment expires. Although we conceptually say never, occurrence of the antecedent is usually associated with a deadline. A detached commitment is discharged when its consequent occurs. If the consequent never occurs (or its deadline elapses), the commitment becomes violated. Other norm types have similar lifecycle [5] which we do not present due to lack of space.

Listing 1. A relational event schema for PhotoShare.

```
SignedUp(pID) key pID
SubscRequested(sID, pID, subscID) key subscID
SubscAccepted(sID, pID, subscID) key subscID
SubscRejected(sID, pID, subscID) key subscID
```

```
ContainerURISent(sID, pID, subscID, contURI) key subscID
PhRequested(sID, pID, subscID, reqID, phID) key reqID
PhAccessed(sID, pID, subscID, reqID, phContent) key reqID
PhForwarded(sID, oID, reqID, phContent, fID) key fID
SubscCancelled(sID, pID, subscID) key subscID
```

Formally, Custard defines a social protocol as a set of norms over an *event schema*, which defines the relevant abstract event types (e.g., antecedent and consequent of a commitment). We present a relational event schema for Photo-Share in Listing 1. Each event is specified as a relation (a set of attributes) that is annotated with a key. Each event also has a timestamp to show when it has happened, which we omit from Listing 1 for brevity. For instance, a poster signs up to PhotoShare with a poster ID (pID), which is also the key for the event. A subscription request has attributes subscriber ID (sID) and poster ID (pID), to represent who makes the subscription request to whom, and also a subscription ID (subscID) as a key. Other events are specified similarly.

Two instances of an event (specification) should not have identical values for their key attributes. However, a key in one event may appear in another event as a foreign key. For instance, subscID appears in a photo request (PhRequest) as a foreign key. These foreign keys enable correlation between events. That is, a request for a photo can be correlated with a subscription. Note that a poster can send the URI of her photo container (ContainerURISent) only once for each subscription. Otherwise, different instances of ContainerURISent would share the same subscID. However, for the same subscID there can be any number of photo request events (PhRequested), since each request has its own reqID as key.

Now, we show a simple social protocol for PhotoShare in Custard. For brevity, we elide the formal syntax of Custard [5]. We start with the commitment from a poster to a subscriber to authorize the subscriber, if her request is accepted. Listing 2 shows this commitment, SubscCommr, in Custard. The first line shows the direction of the norm. That is, the poster is committed to the subscriber. The commitment is created when the poster signs up (i.e., an instance of SignedUp). The commitment becomes detached when the poster accepts a subscription request (i.e., an instance of SubscAccepted). The commitment is discharged when the poster authorizes the subscriber by creating the authorization, as we show in Listing 3. Note that the poster must authorize the subscriber within one day of accepting the request to fulfill the commitment. Otherwise, the poster violates the commitment. This deadline is defined by the expression within the brackets in the last line.

Listing 2. Commitment to authorize an approved subscriber.

```
commit SubscCommr pID to sID
  create SignedUp
  detach SubscAccepted
  discharge created SubscAuth[0, SubscAccepted + 1]
```

Listing 3 shows SubscAuth, an authorization that states the subscriber is authorized by the poster to access her photos. It is created by the poster by sending the URI of her photo container to the subscriber (i.e., the ContainerURISent event). The subscriber detaches the authorization by making a request for a photo (i.e., PhRequested), and the authorization discharges when she accesses the photo (i.e., PhAccessed). The authorization states that access should be granted to the subscriber at most in one day after her request. The authorization expires when the subscription is canceled (i.e., SubscCancelled).

Listing 3. Authorization of an approved subscriber.

```
authorize SubscAuth sID by pID
  create ContainerURISent
  detach PhRequested except SubscCancelled
  discharge PhAccessed [PhRequested , PhRequested + 1]
```

The prohibition in Listing 4 captures the expectation of posters from subscribers about not forwarding their photos to third parties. The name of the prohibition is ForwardProh. It is created when a subscriber accesses a photo by using SubscAuth. A prohibition never discharges. However, it becomes violated if the photo is forwarded by the subscriber (i.e., PhForwarded).

Listing 4. Prohibition of subscribers from forwarding photos.

```
prohibit ForwardProh sID by pID
   create discharged SubscAuth
   violate PhForwarded
```

Once the event schema and social protocol of a social machine are defined, users can start to interact according to the social protocol. As the users interact, instances of the events (e.g., subscription requests) occur, which are stored in users' datastores, who can observe them. For instance, when Charlie makes his request to subscribe to Marcy's photos, the appropriate instance of the subscription request event is stored in Charlie's and Marcy's datastores.

Each user can determine the states of the applicable norms from his or her datastore using Custard. For instance, Charlie can use the stored events to infer whether Marcy is committed to him for authorizing him to access her photos, and whether she fulfills or violates this commitment. Custard automatically generates the requisite queries for each state of a norm (e.g., a query for each commitment state, hence five in total for a commitment) to characterize the instantiation of a social protocol, as we show in Sect. 3.2.

3.2   Custard over RDF Stores

Now let us turn our attention to reasoning about norms over RDF stores. The basic idea is to store event schemas and event instances in RDF stores. The event instances explicitly represent what has happened. The stores can then be queried, in our case using SPARQL, based on each norm lifecycle event query (i.e., to determine if a norm is created, expired, detached, discharged or violated). Querying an RDF store in this manner allows us to infer the social state.

An event schema defines event types. RDF supports specifying both event types along with properties defined on them and event instances along with associated property instances.

Listing 5 declares some of PhotoShare's event types. The Custard namespace (cust) asserts Event as a class and associates a timestamp with each event. Subscription request (SubscRequested), subscription accepted (SubscAccepted) and subscription rejected (SubscRejected) are events declared in the PhotoShare (ps) namespace.

Listing 5. Event types.

```
cust : Event  rdfs : subClassOf  rdfs : Class  .
cust : timestamp  rdf : type  rdf : Property  ;
    rdfs : domain  cust : Event  ;
    rdfs : range  xsd : string  .
ps : SubscRequested  rdfs : subClassOf  cust : Event  .
ps : SubscAccepted  rdfs : subClassOf  cust : Event  .
ps : SubscRejected  rdfs : subClassOf  cust : Event  .
```

Listings 6 show specifies the attributes of event (SubscRequested). Specifically, it has properties to represent who (Subscriber) makes the request to whom (Poster). RespContURI is an rdfs:Container that the poster can use to notify the subscriber about its response. Properties of the other events are analogously specified. A 'key' property is used to refer to a relevant datum, such as a subscription identifier referring to a specific subscription instance.

Listing 6. Attributes of SubscRequested event.

```
ps : SubscID  rdf : type  rdf : Property  ;
    rdfs : domain  ps : SubscRequested  ;
    rdfs : range  xsd : string .

ps : Subscriber  rdf : type  rdf : Property  ;
    rdfs : domain  ps : SubscRequested  ;
    rdfs : range  xsd : string .

ps : Poster  rdf : type  rdf : Property  ;
    rdfs : domain  ps : SubscRequested  ;
    rdfs : range  xsd : string .
```

Listing 7 shows an event instance (ps:001) of type 'subscription requested' stored as RDF triples. Charlie makes a request to subscribe to Marcy's photo store stream at the time indicated by the timestamp.

Listing 7. An instance of SubscRequested event.

```
ps :001  a  ps : SubscRequested  ;
    ps : subscID  "Subscr1"  ;
    ps : subscriber  "Charlie"  ;
    ps : poster  "Marcy"  ;
    cust : timestamp  "1477222062829"  .
```

We now turn our attention to normative reasoning in the proposed Custard layer. Each query is generated according to Custard's semantics. However, instead of detailed semantic definitions, we demonstrate these queries via examples. The original Custard semantics is based on the relational calculus queries [5], whereas here we consider SPARQL queries. Social state inferences (e.g., that a norm is violated) are made based on SPARQL query results for event instances stored as RDF resources.

Listing 8 shows a SPARQL query for inferring whether the SubscAuth authorization, specified earlier in Listing 3, is created. All we need to check is whether the create event, ContainerURISent, has occurred and consequently we are able to infer who the authorization is by (e.g., the provider ?PID) for the benefit of whom (e.g., the subscriber ?SID) based on user variable bindings and other relevant details (e.g., the subscription identifier ?SubscID).

Listing 8. A SPARQL query generated in order to determine creation of the SubscAuth norm.

```
SELECT  ?PID  ?SID  ?SubscID  ?Time1
WHERE  {
        ?ID1  type  ContainerURISent  ;
        ?ID1  sID  ?SID  ;
        ?ID1  pID  ?PID  ;
        ?ID1  subscID  ?SubscID  ;
        ?ID1  containerID  ?ContainerID  ;
        ?ID1  timestamp  ?Time1  .
}
```

The preceding query is simple. It can be written based on the relevant event type's properties such that the ?SubscID variable is bound to the 'container URI sent' event instance's subscriber ID property subscID and so on. The only care that needs to be taken is ensuring that variables being bound to the timestamp property value (i.e., when the event occurs) of different events have unique names in case multiple events are being queried for (i.e., we do not wish to over-constrain a query to only returning simultaneously occurring events).

The SPARQL query in Listing 9 is more complicated. It tests whether the same authorization is discharged. Relying on nested clauses, it first tests whether the discharged condition has occurred, conditional on the detach having occurred previously (the first nested statement), which is conditional on the create event having occurred before the detach event (the third nested statement). By generating SPARQL queries based on norms, complex queries in application logic do not have to be handwritten, rather we can automate inferring social abstractions.

Listing 9. A SPARQL query generated in order to determine creation of the SubscAuth norm.

```
SELECT  ?SID  ?PID  ?SubscID  ?ReqID  ?PhContent  ?Time5
WHERE  {
   ?ID4  Type  PhRequested .
   ?ID4  timestamp  ?Time4 .
   ?ID4  sID  ?SID .
```

```
?ID4  pID  ?PID.
?ID4  subscID  ?SubscID
?ID4  reqID  ?ReqID
?ID4  photoID  ?PhotoID
FILTER(?Time5 >= ?Time4.  ?Time5 <= ?Time4 + 1.)
{
   SELECT  ?SID  ?PID  ?SubscID  ?ReqID  ?PhID  ?Time3
   WHERE {
      ?ID3  Type  PhRequested.
         ?ID3  timestamp  ?Time4.
         ?ID3  sID  ?SID.
         ?ID3  pID  ?PID.
         ?ID3  subscID  ?SubscID.
         ?ID3  reqID  ?ReqID.
         ?ID3  phID  ?PhID.
         MINUS { ?ID2  Type  SubscCancelled.
            ?ID2  SID  ?sID.
       ?ID2  PID  ?pID.
            ?ID2  SubscID  ?subscID.}
            FILTER(?Time2 >= ?Time1.)
            {
            SELECT  ?SID  ?PID  ?SubscID  ?Time1
            WHERE {
               ?ID1  Type  ContainerURISent.
               ?ID1  sID  ?SID.
               ?ID1  pID  ?PID.
               ?ID1  subscID  ?SubscID.
               ?ID1  containerID  ?ContainerID.
               ?ID1  timestamp  ?Time1.
      }
    }
   }
  }
 }
}
```

Such generated SPARQL queries are submitted to Solid datastores in order to infer the social state based on event instances. Algorithm 1 provides a pseudocode for submitting such queries, based on the communication methodology implemented by the Solid application dokieli [4]. The approach is quite simple: (1) create a *promise* as an asynchronous data object that initially contains no data but promises to notify the user when it is assigned data (or notify of a failure); and (2) update the promise object based on SPARQL query results for inferring whether there is a violation.

These SPARQL queries are submitted using the Solid methodology: (1) web credentials are set as being required, meaning the browser will prompt or automatically supply a certificate in order to access the Solid datastore; and (2) the SPARQL query is submitted using HTTP POST.

Algorithm 1 Sample code for posing SPARQL queries generated by Custard in order to infer the social state from Solid datastores.

```
 1: function GETVIOLATIONS(normName)
 2:     return new Promise(
 3:     function FUNCTION(resolve, reject)
 4:         httpRequest ← new httpRequest()
 5:         httpRequest.open('POST', userStoreURL)
 6:         httpRequest.withCredentials = true
 7:         ▷ Additional http request parameters should be specified.
 8:         [...]
 9:         httpRequest.onreadystatechange ←
10:         function FUNCTION(resolve, reject)
11:             [...]
12:             ▷  A function that calls the resolve and reject
                 call back functions based on the respective
                 success or failure of the http request.
13:         query ← custard.violationQuery(normName)
14:         httpRequest.send(query)
        )
```

---

4   Instantiating IOSE as Fluid

Now we present our architecture Fluid that instantiates IOSE for social machines. We first present the elements of Fluid, and then explain the implementation of agents in some detail.

4.1   Key Elements of Fluid

In Fluid, the social protocol is a refinement of a social machine's requirements. A social protocol in Fluid is specified as we explain in Sect. 3 using Custard syntax for norms and RDF serialization for the event schema. The protocol specification itself is a resource that can be accessed by all the users from a public protocol repository.

In Fluid, users of the social machine (X and Y in Fig. 3) may play one or more roles in a social machine according to their interaction with other users. For instance, in PhotoShare, Charlie plays the subscriber role when interacting with Marcy to access her pictures, and the poster role when interacting with users (including Marcy) who are subscribed to view his photos.

Users are represented by their (computational) agents. User agents are implemented on top of Solid and Custard. Solid provides the interface and middleware to access the datastores of the users. Custard provides the practical tool to reason about the social state of the social machine, which assists the agents to decide on the course of their actions and interaction with other agents. In practice, third parties would provide agent implementations that are compatible with specific roles in specific protocols.

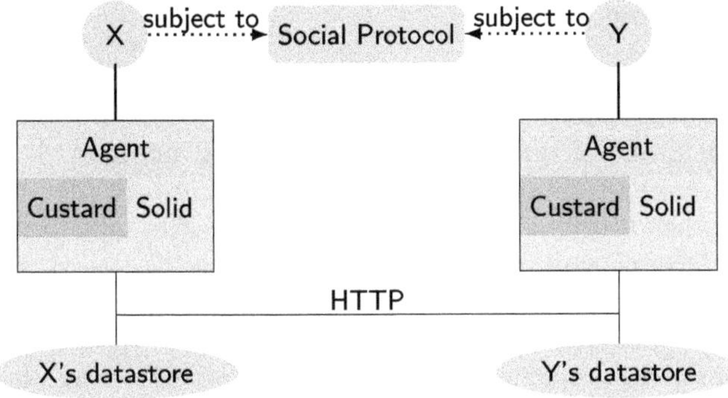

Fig. 3. Fluid decentralized social application architecture.

In Fluid, each user has a personal datastore that complies with the Solid specification [19]. The schema of a datastore is determined by the user, who owns the datastore. Fluid does not enforce any constraint on the schema of a user's datastore. In the implementation level, agents communicate with the datastores through HTTP protocol, which is encapsulated by the Solid API. Authentication and access rights on resources in datastores are also handled by Solid. Although Custard provides its own API to agents to infer the social state, in the background, Custard uses the Solid API to communicate with the user's datastore. Importantly, Custard retrieves data (through GET requests) to infer the social state, but does not modify any resources on a user's datastore.

An agent may access resources in datastores of other users if they permit. In the social level, these access rights are specified in the social protocol in terms of norms. For example, when Marcy accepts Charlie's subscription request, she authorizes him to access her photos. Solid specifies how it manages access rights on physical resources using Web Access Control.

While the social aspects of interaction are specified by the social protocol, the implementation of interaction in Fluid is by creating and updating resources in datastores that correspond to event instances. For example, in PhotoShare, each party's datastore includes a designated location—a publicly writable container as specified by the Linked Data Platform. To make his subscription request, Charlie creates a new resource in Marcy's container that corresponds to the SubscRequested event. Marcy can browse her container as she wishes. Once she observes the new resource, she can interpret the event that the resource represents to reason about the event's social meaning according to the social protocol. Then she responds to Charlie in a similar way by creating a resource that corresponds to an event (e.g., accept request) in a designated container in Charlie's datastore.

4.2   Implementing Agents

Now let us look at implementing user agents. A Fluid agent is generally crafted to meet interaction requirements for a given social protocol. Moreover, a Fluid agent, both in terms of functionality and graphical interface, is implemented according to a user's role, requirements, and preferences in the social machine. For instance, when acting as a subscriber, Charlie's agent may provide functionality, such as face recognition, to identify and tag the photos that involve him. However, Marcy may not require such functionality, and can use a simple agent that shows every photo from users whose photo streams she has subscribed to.

Furthermore, the implementations of the agents are decoupled from each other: neither depends upon the internal details of the other. Instead, interoperability is achieved by defining the semantics of interaction using a social protocol. For instance, to make his subscription request to Marcy's agent, Charlie's agent does not need to know which algorithms or data structures are used by Marcy's agent. The only necessity for interoperability is the ability to initiate the event of subscription request as it is specified by the social protocol. As a result of this decoupling, Fluid achieves both application and data decentralization.

We consider two agents Charlie uses to share and subscribe to photo streams, a flexible agent (Algorithm 2) and a rigid agent (Algorithm 3), based on different requirements. Charlie's flexible agent meets the following two requirements for automatically subverting the social protocol in extraordinary cases (i.e., emergencies) and supporting Charlie's autonomy in other cases. 1. A member of a search and rescue team may request a photo to assist in an emergency, such as to identify a person's whereabouts. In this case, Charlie wishes the photo to be forwarded automatically, even though it would violate a prohibition on forwarding. 2. Charlie would generally like to send all requested photos to a confirmed subscriber, in accordance with the authorization norm. However, he may wish to edit photos before they are sent. Hence, photos are not sent automatically, instead Charlie is prompted to send them.

The pseudocode for Charlie's flexible agent is given in Algorithm 2 (for clarity we assume norms and event schemas have corresponding types in an imperative language).

Algorithm 2 Charlie's flexible agent implementing the PhotoShare social protocol.

```
1: function ONRECEIVEPHOTOFORWARDREQUEST(request)
2:     if request.requester ∈ authorities and
           request.circumstance = emergency then
3:         ForwardPhoto(request.photo, request.requester)

4: function UPDATEDSOCIALSTATE(subscAuth, PhRequested)
5:     if SubscAuth.newstate == "detach"
           and subscAuth.complEv is PhAccessed then
6:         AccessDialog(PhRequested.photoID,
           PhRequested.subscID)
```

Charlie's rigid agent pseudocode is given in Algorithm 3 according to different user requirements. 1. Charlie does not wish photos to be automatically forwarded should doing so violate a prohibition. Accordingly, the agent should verify whether photo forwarding would violate a norm before actually forwarding the photo. 2. Charlie wishes to automatically send all requested photos that are authorized to be sent.

Algorithm 3 Charlie's rigid agent implementing the PhotoShare social protocol.

```
1: function FORWARDPHOTO(photo, request)
2:      PhForwardedEvent ←
            new forwardedEvent(photo.subscriberID,
                request.otherPartyID, request.requestID,
                photo.content)
3:      if not custard.violation(PhForwardedEvent) then
4:          ▷ Low–level photo forwarding.
5: function UPDATEDSOCIALSTATE(subscAuth, PhRequested)
6:      if SubscAuth.newstate == "detach"
            and subscAuth.complEv is PhAccessed then
7:          ProvidePhoto(PhRequested.photoID,
                PhRequested.subscID)
```

It must be emphasized that social semantics are central to the agent logic presented. An authorization dialog is not presented to the user in Algorithm 2 (Line 6) based on low-level data changes. Instead, UI elements are created and agent actions performed based on updates to the social state. Agent logic is written in terms of high–level social abstractions, aiding in understandability and providing a clear correspondence with the social protocol the agent is implemented against.

As mentioned earlier, it is impossible to regiment the involved software so that Charlie cannot forward Marcy's photos (e.g., he can take screenshots and forward them by post). Violations may therefore be undetectable to software. However, Charlie's agent can reason about potential violations in deciding its actions, as shown in Listing 3. And if Marcy's agent learns about violations, it may take actions such as unsubscribing Charlie.

5   Discussion

Table 1 identifies Fluid's distinctive features.

Fluid captures the semantics of social processes via norms that apply to users. Fluid norms are not merely documentation (as contracts in natural language are); they are first-class computational abstractions that agents can reason about. Fluid norms are not rules that are executed in a rule engine; they are elements of the social state of a social machine. Crucially, users may not comply

Table 1. Web architectures and their characteristics.

Approach	Social semantics	Decentralization
Web Service	Epiphenomenal	None
Solid	Epiphenomenal	Data
Fluid	Norms	Logic and data

with the norms that apply to them; such a conception of norms is fundamental to autonomy and creativity. As we demonstrated in Sect. 4.2, users are free to implement their agents as they please. Charlie could if he wanted deploy an agent that violates the forwarding prohibition. However, although norms can be violated, they provide an implementation-independent notion of accountability, which can be applied as a standard of correct behavior in the given social machine. For example, Charlie is accountable to Marcy for not violating her prohibition regarding her photos.

In general, balancing autonomy and accountability is crucial for ensuring that a social machine would not devolve into the extremes of chaos or tyranny. In Fluid, accountability derives fundamentally from social protocols. The above notion echoes well-known intuitions from studies in political theory [13]. This is in contrast to approaches that treat deterrence (via negative sanctions) as accountability [10,11]. Sanctioning (whether positive or negative) an accountable party is a process that is conceptually subsequent to accountability, not incorporated in its definition.

Following Hart's [14] theory of laws (broadly understood as legal norms), the violation of a norm may be disputed and may therefore require adjudication. Further, norms must also evolve to reflect changed circumstances and, in institutional settings, be recognized as the governing ones. Hart's notion of secondary rules captures the rules about rules that capture their recognition, evolution, and adjudication. Custard supports norms about norms (for example, to express sanction); however, it would be interesting to more fully examine how far it accommodates the notion of secondary rules. Metanorms, or what Hart refers to as It is also generally not possible to reference all contextual norms in the application's design.

REST [12] is an architectural style for Web applications. Ciortea *et al.* [8,9] advocate REST as a style suited to multiagent systems since agents must deal with resources in the environment. Moreover, those resources could come with interesting semantic descriptions. Extensions of Fluid to fully exploit the Web technology ecosystem would be a productive research direction.

Seneviratne [28] proposes HTTP Accountability (HTTPA) as a mechanism by providers may annotate resources with usage norms that consumers should ideally abide by but are not forced to. HTTPA supports tracking and auditing of compliance. Although the specific architectures are different, HTTPA and Fluid share similarities. It would be interesting to investigate the use of Custard in the HTTPA architecture.

Decentralized infrastructure has been a theme of growing interest in computing but much of it has focused on data, just as Solid does. This includes landmark peer-to-peer infrastructures such as Chord [29] and blockchains [31] that can be deployed to support social machines. However, these infrastructures do not address the decentralization of the social machine's application logic, as Fluid does. The logical decentralization of a social machine requires thinking in terms of a social protocol that captures the meanings of the social machine's constituent interactions. Fluid, as an instantiation of IOSE, demonstrates how social protocols may be concretely realized over the Web. Analogous instantiations can be developed over other decentralized data infrastructures. Idelberger et al. [16] report initial work on encoding blockchain applications (smart contracts) in a language that supports normative abstractions.

In security policy languages such as [21], a computer system is either obliged or prohibited from taking certain actions. These policies are programs—not social norms—that are executed by the policy engine, a distinction echoed by Polleres [24]. Fluid can be applied to specifying norms in light of which security policies are specified and thus bring sociotechnical aspects to bear. Indeed, we demonstrated how social protocols could be connected with security policies in agent implementations. Similarly, authorization framework implementations, e.g., OAuth [17], could be checked for correctness with respect to norms. Supporting sophisticated role ontologies in Fluid, as Belchior et al. [2] do for role-based access control, would be an interesting extension.

The current excitement around social machines is rooted in the potential of applying data analytics on user-generated content for solving social problems, such as earthquake prediction [26], traffic routing [22], understanding group dynamics [25], and understanding urban geographies [20]. Data analytics could benefit from Fluid's explicit representation of social norms. In particular, inference algorithms could be run on norm stores instead of lower-level data. An exciting application of such analytics would be as part of a governance feedback loop that leads to revisions of the social protocol for a social machine. In some applications, the state of a norm may be fuzzy because the underlying facts themselves are fuzzy. Approaches for fuzzy annotations for data and associated queries [32] should be valuable in extending Fluid.

Fluid supports common normative relationships such as commitment, prohibition, power, and so on. From experience though, we know that there are many more kinds of social relationships. For example, *recommends, likes, trusts* may also be seen as social relationships between users. An important direction of future work is to understand how Fluid could support idiosyncratic social relationships.

Acknowledgements. We thank Akın Günay and Thomas Christopher King for valuable discussions.

MPS thanks the US National Science Foundation (grant IIS-1908374) for partial support.

References

1. Au Yeung, C.M., Liccardi, I., Lu, K., Seneviratne, O., Berners-Lee, T.: Decentralization: the future of online social networking. In: W3C Workshop on the Future of Social Networking Position Papers, vol. 2, pp. 2–7 (2009)
2. Belchior, M., Schwabe, D., Silva Parreiras, F.: Role-based access control for model-driven web applications. In: Brambilla, M., Tokuda, T., Tolksdorf, R. (eds.) ICWE 2012. LNCS, vol. 7387, pp. 106–120. Springer, Heidelberg (2012). https://doi.org/10.1007/978-3-642-31753-8_8
3. Berners-Lee, T.: Weaving the Web: The Original Design and Ultimate Destiny of the World Wide Web. Harper Business, New York (1999)
4. Capadisli, S., Guy, A., Verborgh, R., Lange, C., Auer, S., Berners-Lee, T.: Decentralised authoring, annotations and notifications for a read-write web with dokieli. In: Proceedings of the 17th International Conference on Web Engineering, pp. 469–481. Springer, Rome (2017)
5. Chopra, A.K., Singh, M.P.: Custard: Computing norm states over information stores. In: Proceedings of the 15th International Conference on Autonomous Agents and MultiAgent Systems (AAMAS), pp. 1096–1105. IFAAMAS, Singapore (May 2016). https://doi.org/10.5555/2936924.2937085
6. Chopra, A.K., Singh, M.P.: From social machines to social protocols: Software engineering foundations for sociotechnical systems. In: Proceedings of the 25th International World Wide Web Conference, pp. 903–914. ACM, Montréal (Apr 2016) https://doi.org/10.1145/2872427.2883018
7. Christian Bizer, T.H., Berners-Lee, T.: Linked data-the story so far. Int. J. Semantic Web Inform. Syst. (IJSWIS) 5(4), 1–22 (2009)
8. Ciortea, A., Mayer, S., Gandon, F., Boissier, O., Ricci, A., Zimmermann, A.: A decade in hindsight: the missing bridge between multi-agent systems and the World Wide Web. In: Proceedings of the 18th International Conference on Autonomous Agents and Multiagent Systems (AAMAS), pp. 1659–1663. IFAAMAS (2019)
9. Ciortea, A., Mayer, S., Michahelles, F.: Repurposing manufacturing lines on the fly with multi-agent systems for the Web of Things. In: Proceedings of the 17th International Conference on Autonomous Agents and MultiAgent Systems (AAMAS), pp. 813–822. IFAAMAS, Stockholm (Jul 2018)
10. Feigenbaum, J., Hendler, J., Jaggard, A.D., Weitzner, D.J., Wright, R.N.: Accountability and deterrence in online life (extended abstract). In: Proceedings of the 3rd International Web Science Conference, pp. 7:1–7:7. ACM Press, Koblenz (Jun 2011). https://doi.org/10.1145/2527031.2527043
11. Feigenbaum, J., Jaggard, A.D., Wright, R.N.: Towards a formal model of accountability. In: Proceedings of the 14th New Security Paradigms Workshop (NSPW), pp. 45–56. ACM, Marin County, California (Sep 2011). https://doi.org/10.1145/2073276.2073282
12. Fielding, R.T.: Architectural Styles and the Design of Network-Based Software Architectures. Ph.D. thesis, University of California, Irvine (2000)
13. Grant, R.W., Keohane, R.O.: Accountability and abuses of power in world politics. Am. Political Sci. Rev. 99(1), 25–43 (2005). https://doi.org/10.1017/S0003055405051476
14. Hart, H.L.A.: The Concept of Law. Oxford University Press, Clarendon Law Series (1961)
15. Hendler, J., Berners-Lee, T.: From the semantic web to social machines: a research challenge for AI on the world wide web. Artif. Intell. 174(2), 156–161 (2010)

16. Idelberger, F., Governatori, G., Riveret, R., Sartor, G.: Evaluation of logic-based smart contracts for blockchain systems. In: Alferes, J.J.J., Bertossi, L., Governatori, G., Fodor, P., Roman, D. (eds.) RuleML 2016. LNCS, vol. 9718, pp. 167–183. Springer, Cham (2016). https://doi.org/10.1007/978-3-319-42019-6_11
17. IETF: The OAuth 2.0 authorization framework. https://tools.ietf.org/html/rfc6749 (Oct 2012)
18. Kagal, L., Finin, T., Paolucci, M., Srinivasan, N., Sycara, K., Denker, G.: Authorization and privacy for semantic web services. IEEE Intell. Syst. **19**(4), 50–56 (2004)
19. Mansour, E., et al.: A demonstration of the Solid platform for social web applications. In: Proceedings of the 25th International Conference Companion on World Wide Web (WWW), pp. 223–226. ACM, Montréal (Apr 2016). https://doi.org/10.1145/2872518.2890529
20. Nadai, M.D., Staiano, J., Larcher, R., Sebe, N., Quercia, D., Lepri, B.: The death and life of great Italian cities: a mobile phone data perspective. In: Proceedings of the 25th International Conference on World Wide Web, pp. 413–423 (2016)
21. OASIS: eXtensible Access Control Markup Language (XACML) version 3.0 specification document (Aug 2010), http://docs.oasis-open.org/xacml/3.0/xacml-3.0-core-spec-cs-01-en.pdf, OASIS Standard. Accessed 03 Feb 2022
22. Pan, B., Zheng, Y., Wilkie, D., Shahabi, C.: Crowd sensing of traffic anomalies based on human mobility and social media. In: Proceedings of the 21st ACM SIGSPATIAL International Conference on Advances in Geographic Information Systems. pp. 344–353 (2013)
23. Paradesi, S., Liccardi, I., Kagal, L., Pato, J.: A semantic framework for content-based access controls. In: International Conference on Social Computing, pp. 624–629. IEEE (2013)
24. Polleres, A.: Agreement technologies and the semantic web. In: Agreement Technologies, pp. 57–67. Springer (2013)
25. Purohit, H., Ruan, Y., Fuhry, D., Parthasarathy, S., Sheth, A.P.: On understanding the divergence of online social group discussion. In: Proceedings of the Eighth International AAAI Conference on Weblogs and Social Media (May 2014)
26. Sakaki, T., Okazaki, M., Matsuo, Y.: Earthquake shakes Twitter users: real-time event detection by social sensors. In: Proceedings of the 19th International Conference on World Wide Web, pp. 851–860. ACM (2010)
27. Sambra, A.V., Guy, A., Capadisli, S., Greco, N.: Building decentralized applications for the social Web. In: Proceedings of the 25th International Conference Companion on World Wide Web (WWW), pp. 1033–1034. ACM, Montréal (Apr 2016) https://doi.org/10.1145/2872518.2891060
28. Seneviratne, O.W.: Accountable Systems: Enabling Appropriate Use of Information on the Web. Ph.D. thesis, Massachusetts Institute of Technology (2014)
29. Stoica, I.: Chord: a scalable peer-to-peer lookup protocol for Internet applications. IEEE/ACM Trans. Network. **11**(1), 17–32 (2003)
30. Suchman, L.A.: Office procedure as practical action: models of work and system design. ACM Trans. Office Inform. Syst. **1**(4), 320–328 (1983)
31. Swan, M.: Blockchain: Blueprint for a new economy. O'Reilly (2015)
32. Zimmermann, A., Lopes, N., Polleres, A., Straccia, U.: A general framework for representing, reasoning and querying with annotated semantic web data. Web Semantics: Sci., Serv. Agents World Wide Web **11**, 72–95 (2012)

Holonic Active Distillation for Scalable Multi-agent Learning in Multi-sensor Systems

Dani Manjah[1]([⊠]) [iD], Tim Bary[1] [iD], Benoit Macq[1] [iD], and Stéphane Galland[2] [iD]

[1] Institute of Information and Communication Technologies, Electronics and Applied Mathematics (ICTEAM), UCLouvain, 1348 Louvain-la-Neuve, Belgium
`{dani.manjah,tim.bary,benoit.macq}@uclouvain.be`
[2] Université de Technologie de Belfort Montbéliard, UTBM, CIAD UR 7533, 90010 Belfort cedex, France
`stephane.galland@utbm.fr`

Abstract. The rapid expansion of sensor-based networks introduces major challenges in scalability, adaptability, and knowledge transfer, especially in open environments where new subsystems can dynamically join or leave. In this work, we propose a Holonic Active Distillation architecture within a Holonic Multi-Agent System (HMAS) to address these issues. Our approach integrates Clustered Stream-Based Active Distillation (CSBAD), a framework in which specialized student models collect local data, query pseudo-labels from teacher models, and cluster into groups of similar sensors.

Results show that the holonic organization balances local specialization with global generalization, while efficiently adapting to sensor departures and re-integrations. We also analyzed trade-offs among incremental model updates, system reorganization, and scalability limits.

Our findings highlight the advantages of holonic learning for multi-sensor systems while identifying key challenges related to model drift and long-term adaptation.

Keywords: Holonic Multi-Agent Systems · Distributed Learning · Collaborative Learning · Scalable Model Adaptation

1 Introduction

In recent years, sensor systems have evolved from isolated and manageable units to expansive and interconnected networks [42]. This transformation, while enabling broader coverage, challenges the traditional approach of deploying a single, universal Deep Neural Network (DNN) across all sensors [34]. The dynamic nature of real-world deployments, characterized by stochastic changes and the continuous addition of new sensors, introduces diverse contexts that demand ever larger training datasets and models [26]. This upscaling not only incurs significant costs, but also accumulates hidden technical debt, complicating the maintenance required to adapt to distribution shifts in sensor data [2,47].

© The Author(s), under exclusive license to Springer Nature Switzerland AG 2026
S. Rodriguez et al. (Eds.): EMAS 2025, LNAI 16407, pp. 80–99, 2026.
https://doi.org/10.1007/978-3-032-18011-7_6

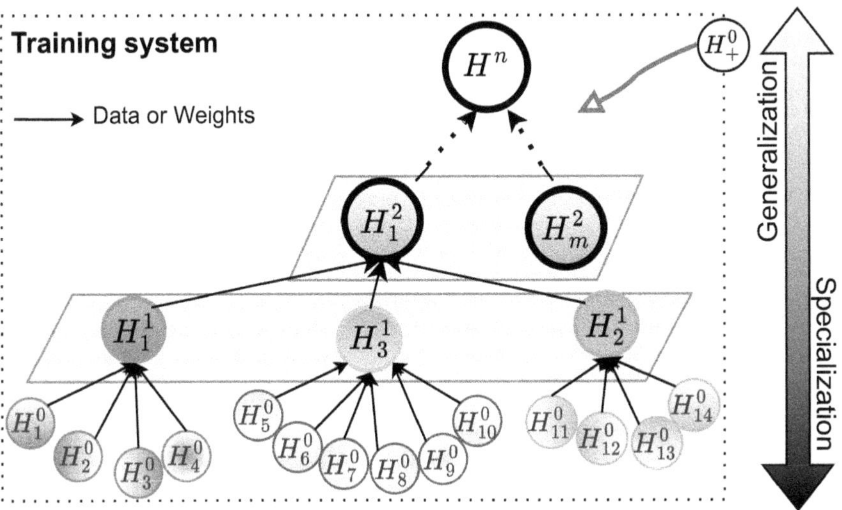

Fig. 1. A large-scale distributed training system where DNN nodes are trained on datasets built from a specificity-diversity trade-off for effective learning. Lower nodes are typically tailored to their task (*i.e.*, analytics on a sensor) and operationally more efficient. Higher nodes, trained over vaster and more diverse data, provide generalization ability. This system can scale up or down, causing challenges in integration and adaptability.

Traditional methods have relied on centralized, monolithic DNNs that struggle to scale with the increasing complexity and diversity of sensor networks. These approaches often lead to inefficiencies and increased maintenance challenges. Recent advances, such as the Holonic Learning (HoL) framework, offer a promising alternative by embracing the agent paradigm to improve scalability and flexibility [13]. HoL leverages self-nested structures of agents, known as holons, to integrate local and global perspectives, facilitating easier subsystem integration and preventing the propagation of disturbances [10,27,45]. This hierarchical learning approach improves the efficiency of data and algorithm handling, particularly for large distributed datasets [12]. A question remains related to the design of a scalable distributed learning framework that supports continuous DNN refinement with minimal refactoring, while allowing each unit to update itself online, self-organize with its peers, and transfer knowledge as the system scales.

This work builds upon the HoL framework by introducing strategies for aggregation, communication, and commitment between learning holons. The contributions are twofold:

- We augment HoL with standardized organizations and roles, allowing newcomers to integrate knowing only their role and the associated protocol, inspired by active learning and distillation of knowledge [1,34,45].
- We propose holonification mechanisms in which agents cluster horizontally and vertically based on the similarity of their sensor streams, preserving

confidentiality and balancing specificity and diversity. This recursive process improves the accuracy and resilience of the system, allowing seamless expansion or contraction without disruption [14,15].

This further advances the adaptability of multisensor holonic systems [36], materializing continuous learning in dynamic environments.

The remainder of this paper is structured as follows. Section 2.2 provides background and current related works. Section 3 presents the high-level formulation of the organizations for the Holonic Active Distillation (HAD) architecture and the relationships between super- and subholons. Section 4 introduces a distributed, multi-tiered, self-nested structure for DNNs and the self-organization mechanisms that realize the specificity–diversity trade-off. Section 5 describes the materials used in the experiment, while Sect. 6 reports the results on sensor addition and removal, comparing partial reorganizations with complete retraining and measuring knowledge-transfer speed. Finally, Sect. 7 discusses the insights, limitations, and perspectives, followed by the conclusion in Sect. 8.

2   Related Works

We set the foundational machine learning frameworks to continuously adapt to incoming data. Next, we discuss the landscape of learning in Multi-Agent System (MAS) motivated by the ability of agent-oriented design to minimize refactoring and support isolated updates. The section is then concluded by reviewing organizational methodologies for seamless integration of a new sensor, model, or more generally, a subsystem of sensors and models in MAS.

2.1   Online Test-Time Adaptation

Adapting machine learning models at test-time is crucial to preserve their performance [4,7,32]. Stream-Based Active Distillation (SBAD) [35] addresses the challenges of the **lack of labeled data at test time** by selecting, from sensor streams, samples to constitute a training set representative of the sensor's characteristics,*i.e.*, features space. To alleviate annotation costs, SBAD relies on annotation by other models within the system in a **Teacher-Student** scheme. Fine-tuning a model per device does not scale well, as it requires maintaining a separate model for each additional sensor [17,47].

Clustered SBAD [34] diminishes the number of models by grouping sensors using a similarity distance of their features and by training one model per cluster. This also improves the accuracy of models by striking a balance between tailoring models to their data streams and generalization capabilities by training on enough diverse samples [56]. CSBAD's limitation is not to retain knowledge for successive re-training of current models, nor provide knowledge transfer mechanisms to new sensors.

Inspired by human organizations, this paper proposes a design where higher layers of systems build structural knowledge **to seamlessly integrate agents and avoid the pitfalls of abrupt failures, environmental changes, or knowledge loss,** especially with new or varied data classes [18,29].

2.2   Learning in Multi-agent Systems

Adaptive MAS networks leverage online learning strategies to dynamically respond to environmental changes, highlighting the importance of distributed and collaborative learning [38].

Wolpert and Macready [52] introduce a system utilizing reinforcement learning to align agent actions with collective goals, minimizing human oversight. Agents are organized into "sub-worlds" for focused collaboration, yet the application of reinforcement learning in complex scenarios with varied sensors and methods encounters obstacles such as unclear rewards and limited exploration, which hinders the required diversity of learning [43,52,55].

Organizational learning considers agents evolving through both personal and collective learning efforts, enhancing agents' abilities in MAS through management mediated interactions and task alignment to boost system efficiency [20,49]. This model emphasizes the role of knowledge sharing in improving workflows and establishing structural knowledge, crucial for system resilience. Social science research [11] reflects on the applicability of this framework to understand the impact of staff turnover on management, analogous to agent dynamics in open MAS.

Hierarchical learning [12] uses hierarchical MAS to streamline model training in various geographical locations. By modeling challenges as a hypergraph, the system organizes agents, each with unique skills and knowledge, into a structured multitiered network. This design not only facilitates the decentralized handling of Machine Learning (ML) algorithms and data, but also significantly improves the efficiency and scalability of processing large distributed datasets.

In the context of distributed ML, Gupta and Raskar [23] pioneered Federated Learning (FL) to train neural networks in distributed datasets, prioritizing data privacy and computational efficiency. However, FL faces hurdles in communication and training reliability. Hierarchical FL addresses these by grouping users to improve FL security and efficiency through group-specific updates [54]. Personalized FL [33] methods aim to produce personalized models for different users or groups of users [21] to keep track of their individualized requirements. Hierarchy has also been instrumental in Fog Learning. Unlike FL, which is based on a star topology of device-server interactions, Fog Learning explicitly considers the network and topology structures among devices and enables intelligent device collaborations through data and parameter offloading [24].

Esmaeili et al. [13] abstract FL and CSBAD with HoL, applying holonic principles to a collaborative learning framework. In that sense, **FL and CSBAD can be seen as a first-order HoL**. HoL enhances model cooperation with specific strategies for aggregation, communication, and commitment within holons, facilitating complex yet intuitive collaboration of nodes compared to Fog Learning. In this balance between local autonomy and coordinated decision making, holonic systems are better equipped to tackle challenges such as adaptability, and scalability.

HoL does not specify how learning agents should (re)organize, nor how a system can seamlessly expand to new domains or safely unlearn obsolete ones; shortcomings that become acute in applications requiring auto-scaling and auto-tuning [13,51].

2.3 Organizational Multi-agent Systems

Agent-oriented software engineering addresses the limitations of traditional methods like UML in managing complex, distributed, expanding and self-adaptive systems [1,2,10,22,31,36,50,51]. Organizational theory from social science inspired software designers who developed methodologies for the development of MAS to break down design complexity via 1) the use of metaphors that are more accessible to software engineers and 2) a focus on high levels of abstraction to enable the integration of new agents, even when they differ significantly from existing ones [19,28,46]. In fact, MASs are best viewed as organizational structures of autonomous, proactive agents interacting to achieve shared or individual goals [28].

Many agent-oriented methodologies have been developed last decades, such as, ADELFE [3,22], ASPECS [9], Gaia [53], INGENIAS [41], PASSI [8], Prometheus [40], SODA [39], Tropos [6], MOISE [25]. Each has its own specificities: ADELFE is dedicated to adaptive system and cooperative agents design, ASPECS is dedicated to holonic multi-agent systems, Gaia focuses on static organization and roles, whereas PASSI focuses on agent social aspects thanks to ontology, SODA highlights the notion of environment. MOISE focuses on explicit organisational modelling—defining roles, groups, missions, and deontic norms—to balance agent autonomy and coordinated behaviour.

Given our choice of the holonic learning paradigm, we adopt the ASPECS methodology [9].

2.4 Conclusion

We address scalability limitations of continuous adaptation in machine learning systems by enriching the holonic learning paradigm with *organizations* and *roles*. These concepts provide an abstract interaction pattern that improves the architecture's robustness and flexibility. Furthermore, our *Teacher–Student* stream-based distillation scheme supplies pseudo-labels that calibrate online incoming *Students*, thereby enabling auto-tuning. Finally, self-organization emerges from a specificity–diversity trade-off among *Students*, while integration and deletion protocols dynamically scale sensor subsystems. Collectively, these mechanisms yield **the first HoL variant that supports self-organization and auto-scaling.**

3 Holonic Active Distillation Architecture

We seek a design that minimizes refactoring and supports isolated updates, simplifying the integration of a new sensor, model, or more generally a subsystem of sensors and models [17,47]. From the literature, we derived five main recommendations to **design scalable, multimethod learning systems:**

1. Establish standardized interaction protocols, aggregation strategies, commitment, and communication patterns within components. This facilitates the integration of new units, as they only need to understand their role and communication methods within the system, regardless of their operating mode [1, 45].
2. Render a method, a sensor, or by construction a subsystem as independent and self-contained as possible to limit the complexity between units. This aims to simplify a local update or maintenance [1, 22, 50].
3. Recursively divide a system into subsystems based on a key criterion. This prevents the propagation of disturbances [45]. Furthermore, integration of a new component requires less communication as it requires only coordination with the upper layers of the system instead of with each subsystem [10].
4. Place units at certain levels of the hierarchy and provide representations of how other levels can contribute "information" or "models". This division simplifies the complexity of programming, allowing designers to focus on each module and facilitating reuse between different systems [10].
5. Exploit *Active Distillation*, where each *Student* unit collects data on the fly from its streams to train on them. Training is performed by querying a model *Teacher* [35].

Given our choice of the organizational holonic paradigm, we adopt the ASPECS methodology [9]. The latter starts by defining an **Organization**, which denotes a subsystem in which components play a role and interact to achieve a shared goal in the context of this organization. Next, the **Roles** which are both expected behaviors to fulfill (part of) requirements, and status to the role's agent in the organization (Sect. 3.1). The subsequent activity (Sect. 3.2) is the definition of relationships between superholons (higher-level entities) and subholons (lower-level entities). As a reference later, a **holarchy** denotes the hierarchy of self-regulating holons.

3.1 Teacher-Specialized Student

Building on the Active Distillation framework and the specificity-diversity trade-off from [34], we developed an organizational model that incorporates the roles of **Specialized Student** and **Teacher**, as illustrated in Fig. 2.

The **Specialized Student** role is designed to continuously collect data on subparts of the system's deployment environment. Under the oversight of a higher-order **Teacher** entity, these *Students* learn from these data, adapting their models' weights accordingly.

3.2 Holarchy

The section begins with introducing a new notation. Then we present an example of a three-tiered holarchy structure. Each level of this holarchy is a possible

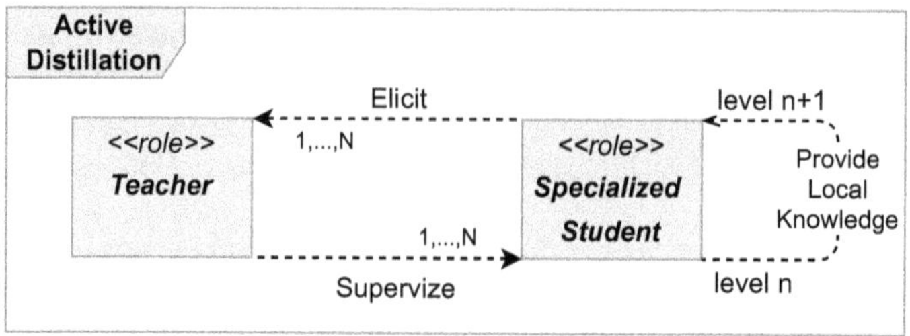

Fig. 2. Organizational model of the ***Teacher-Student***, using the ASPECS notation [9]. The ***Specialized Student*** role involves a component tasked with building expertise over a delineated sub-domain in the system, *i.e.*, a regional distribution. The ***Teacher*** role supervizes the learning processes of the *Students*.

instance of an organization defined in Sect. 3.1. To provide a more holistic perspective, we depict the Cyber-Physical Platform (CPP) data processing organization (see our previous work [36]) alongside the TSS but CPP is not the main focus of this paper[1].

Notations. A holarchy $\mathcal{H}_O^L$ includes up to L vertical layers instantiating an organization O. A holon i in layer l, where l ranges from 0 to L, is denoted by $\hbar_i^l$ and comprises:

- X_i^l: Set of operating data streams of a holon $\hbar_i^l$.
- $\mathcal{T}_i^l$: Training set of a holon $\hbar_i^l$.
- $\mathcal{V}_i^l$: Validation set of a holon $\hbar_i^l$.
- $\theta^{\hbar_i^l}$: Processing model of a holon $\hbar_i^l$.
- SUB_i^l: Inner members corresponding to layer $l-1$ of a holon $\hbar_i^l$.
- SUP_i^l: Superior holon of a holon $\hbar_i^l$.

Multi-scale Hierarchical Architecture. The system architecture, shown in Fig. 3, includes two holarchies: $\mathcal{H}_{CPP}^3$ that processes data on three levels and $\mathcal{H}_{TSS}^2$ managing knowledge on two levels.

- **At level 0:** agents are the primary functional layer. They employ models designed for specific data streams. Proximity to other agents, geographically or related to the task, allows them to merge outputs and reduce errors. For example, $\hbar_1^0$ and $\hbar_2^0$ form Group G1 to fuse their outputs to feed the data request of a higher-order holon $\hbar_1^1$.

---

[1] As a more detailed context, ***CPP*** is designed to respond to external requests with perceptions and to manage its finite resources to ensure fair access across multiple surveillance operations. The ***Resource Provider*** role ensures a fair distribution of the resources among all parties. The ***Observer*** role has the ability to produce perceptions thanks to the data acquired by the ***Sensor*** role. The data acquisition could be based on another CPP.

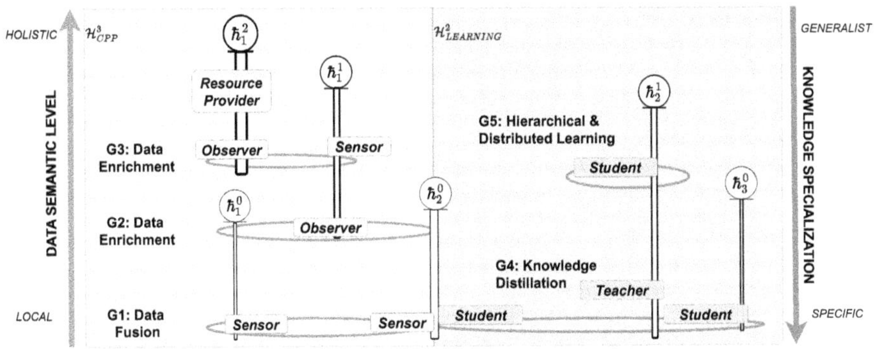

Fig. 3. Holonic architecture inspired by the "cheese board" notation [9,16]. Each level represents a different hierarchical position, defining both the semantic level of data and the degree of knowledge specialization. On the left, the $\mathcal{H}^3_{CPP}$ instantiates the *CPP* organization, and on the right, the $\mathcal{H}^2_{TS}$ is responsible for active learning. Agents may assume multiple roles and participate in multiple holarchies simultaneously.

However, agents monitoring the same area may employ different models if their functions require learning different features. Consequently, $\hbar^0_2$ and $\hbar^0_3$, as *Specialized Students*, form Group G4 to learn a shared model under the supervision of a *Teacher* holon via Group G5.

- **At levels 1 and 2:** higher levels above the agents integrate and synthesize data from specific areas of the system (*e.g.*, data streams that share attributes). The holons in the role *Observer*, such as $\hbar^1_1$ and $\hbar^2_1$, elevate the collected data to a new semantic level.
  Holon $\hbar^1_2$, a higher order *Specialized Student*, aggregates validation sets from $\hbar^0_2$ and $\hbar^0_3$ (*i.e.*, $\mathcal{T}^1_2 = \mathcal{V}^0_2 \cup \mathcal{V}^0_3$), to create a broader and generalized model.

Generally, each semantic level consolidates knowledge across **broader areas of the system, fostering a holistic view, such as city-scale tracking.** Meanwhile, intermediate layers consisting of *Specialized Students* synthesize knowledge from lower levels, to **deepen collective task understanding** and **increase holons' universality**.

4   Holonic Learning Framework

This section presents mechanisms to create a multilevel learning framework. Next, it introduces a mechanism to incorporate new nodes by coordinating with the top layers and assigning each new node to the group whose DNN model is most accurate in its data stream.

4.1 Holonification

In the holonic terminology, *holonification* is the process of grouping agents into a holarchy, resembling complex clustering based on criteria like capabilities and resource access [14, 15].

In this Section, we propose a multi-tiered learning structure (illustrated in Fig. 1), comprising a portfolio of models that range from sensor-specific to universal, deployable across the entire network. Specifically, upper-layer models are trained on larger datasets for broader coverage, while lower-layer models use smaller, more similar datasets for increased specificity. Having intermediate models at various levels of granularity not only ensures adaptability, **but also supports robust knowledge organization.** For example, city-wide vehicle detection may require multiple models specializing in certain domain representations [34]. However, these domain-specific models **benefit from interactions with peer models or a more fundamental model** that develops a fundamental understanding of object detection tasks [56]. Our agent-based modeling offers this flexibility to develop these vertical and horizontal interactions.

Formally, each holon in a layer $l > 0$ is allocated a budget $B^l = B_0 \cdot 10^l$, where B_0 represents the number of images used for model fine-tuning. This budget limits the training of each layer to at most 10^l from the preceding levels, ensuring that the size of the data set of any holon $\hbar_i^l$ does not exceed B^l, *i.e.*, $|\mathcal{T}_i^l| \leq B^l$.

To merge holons, we adopt the premise from Manjah et al. [34] that models with similar performance have learned from comparable data.

The remainder of this section describes the holonification process.

STEP 1 – Cross-Performance Vector. Assuming holons can transfer their model weights to each other within the same layer. Each holon $\hbar_i^l$ computes a performance vector P_i by evaluating the effectiveness of models from other holons and itself in the same layer on its own validation data $\mathcal{V}_i^l$, according to Eq. 1.

$$P_i^l := \left[f\left(\theta_1^l, \mathcal{V}_i^l\right) ; \cdots ; f\left(\theta_{N^l}^l, \mathcal{V}_i^l\right) \right]^T \tag{1}$$

where θ_j denotes the model parameters of the j-th holon $\hbar_j^l$, $j \in 1, \cdots, N^l$ and $f(\theta, \mathcal{V})$ the score of a model performance θ against a validation set $\mathcal{V}$.

STEP 2 – Pair-Wise Distance Computation. To quantify the differences between models trained in different domains, holons broadcast their cross-perfor-mance vectors P_i^l defined in Eq. 1 and compute a pairwise distance between their performance in the datasets and the performance of the other holons. Generally, for a holon $\hbar_i^l$, the distance to a holon $\hbar_j^l$ is given by Eq. 2.

$$D_i(\hbar_j^l) = \sqrt{\sum_{k=1}^{N^l} (P_{ik}^l - P_{jk}^l)^2} \tag{2}$$

STEP 3 – Agglomerative Merging using Single Linkage. The merging of the holons is an iterative process. The set of holons $\{\hbar_1^l, \cdots, \hbar_{N^l}^l\}$ creates a higher-order holarchy $\mathcal{H}^{l+1}$ to which they belong.

At each iteration, the set of holons $\hbar^l$ transmits their smallest linkage distance. This is defined as the minimal distance between the inner members of the holons. Formally, for two holons $\hbar_A^l$ and $\hbar_B^l$, the single link distance $L(\hbar_A^l, \hbar_B^l)$ is given by Eq. 3.

$$L(\hbar_A^l, \hbar_B^l) = \min\{D_{ij} : \hbar_i^{l-1} \in \mathsf{SUB}(\hbar_A^l),\ \hbar_j^{l-1} \in \mathsf{SUB}(\hbar_B^l)\} \tag{3}$$

After all linkages are evaluated, the pair with the smallest distance merges, involving a combination of their datasets. After merging, the set of holons has decreased, $\{\hbar_1^l, \cdots, \hbar_{N^l-1}^l\}$, and the linkage distances are updated for all agents.

The process ends if there remains only one holon or if the previous merge leads to a holon with a dataset size that exceeds B^{l+1}. In the second scenario, the process goes back to STEP 1 for the set $\{\hbar_1^{l+1}, \cdots, \hbar_{N^{l+1}}^l\}$.

STEP 4 – Model Training. The final steps consist in training the cluster models on the aggregated data sets.

4.2   Domain Integration Process

A new holon $\hbar_+$ joins a holarchy $\mathcal{H}^L$ of L levels. Its integration starts at the highest hierarchical level, L, and progresses downward to the level 1. At each level, $\hbar_+$ is associated with the holon $\hbar_*^1$ that shows the highest performance in the new set of unit validations, $\mathcal{V}_+$, subject to meeting budget constraints, *i.e.*, $|\mathcal{T}_*^l \cup \mathcal{T}_+| \leq B^l$. Once integrated, $\hbar_+$'s dataset merges with that of the selected holon, $\hbar_*^l$, necessitating a retraining of the aggregated dataset. If no appropriate holons are available at a required level, the system can initiate reholonification, integrating $\hbar_+$ with the set $\{\hbar_1^l, \cdots, \hbar_{N^l}^l\}$. A pseudocode is provided in Algorithm 1.

Remark 1. **The cost of holonification** is compared to integration on-the-fly on the basis of the amount of communication between the holons. It is built on a single linkage-Hierarchical Clustering, with a **complexity of** $\mathcal{O}\left(N^2\right)$ [48].

On the other hand, the **on-the-fly mechanism has a** $\mathcal{O}(N + L)$ **complexity.** This corresponds to the worst-case scenario in which the new agent is compared to all holons from the upper layer L to layer 0. This mechanism thus offers a cost-effective integration in comparison with a reholonification.

4.3   Research Questions

From the setup and challenges described above, we formulate the following research questions:

1. Given a new data stream, how can we determine the most suitable existing model for fine-tuning?

Algorithm 1 Integration of a New Holon into a Holarchy

Require: $\mathcal{H}^L$: L-level learning holarchy
Require: $\hbar_+$: A holon
  1: **for** $l = L$ downto 1 **do**
         $\triangleright$ **Identify sub-holons whose training sets do not exceed budget constraints**
  2:     FreeHolons $\leftarrow \hbar^l : |\mathcal{T}^l \cup \mathcal{T}_+| \leq B^l$
  3:     **if** FreeHolons $= \emptyset$ **then**
  4:        Reholonification with the set $\{\hbar_1^l, \cdots, \hbar_{N^l}^l\} \cup \hbar_+$.
  5:        **break**
  6:     **end if**
         $\triangleright$ **Select the optimal sub-holon for integration**
  7:     FreeModels $\leftarrow$ FreeHolons's models
  8:     $\theta_*^l \leftarrow \arg\max_{\theta^l \in \text{FreeModels}} f\left(\theta^l, \mathcal{V}_+\right)$
  9:     Update model parameters θ_*^l using $\mathcal{T}_*^l \cup \mathcal{T}_+$.
         $\triangleright$ **Integrate $\hbar_+$ into holon of θ_*^l**
10:     SUB$(\hbar_*^l) \leftarrow$ SUB$(\hbar_*^l) \cup \hbar_+$
11: **end for**

---

2. Assume an effective integration of new sensors based on similarity with a group of sensors from the system:
   (a) What are the consequences on model accuracy upon the integration of a new agent?
   (b) How does the accuracy of the model scale when incrementally integrating N_+ new agents versus performing a full system reorganization?
3. What are the long-term accuracy trade-offs between retaining versus discarding data from removed sensors?

5 Materials and Methods

The datasets, the training procedure, and the evaluation protocol are presented in this Section.

5.1 Datasets

We used two city-focused video datasets for a total of 16 cameras.

WALT [44] features footage from nine static cameras over 1–4 weeks. Sampling rates vary (5,000–40,000 frames/week), with temporal bursts and diverse weather conditions (snow, rain, day/night).

AI-City [37] features seven annotated videos, each approximately five minutes at 10 FPS. Camera angles and sensor types vary (vertical, dome, PTZ), ensuring coverage of multiple representation contexts.

5.2 Model Training

We follow SBAD [34] sampling 256 images per camera. A large YOLOv8x6 Teacher (261.1 GFLOPs) pseudolabels these samples. Each Student model is a YOLOv8n (8.7 GFLOPs), initialized with COCO weights [30], then fine-tuned at a learning rate of 0.01 (unless otherwise indicated).

5.3 Evaluation of mAP50-95

We report the *"mAP50-95"* as the **mean A**verage **P**recision across various intersection over union thresholds, spanning from **0.50 to 0.95** in increments of 0.05 . We evaluated the holon's performance on its associated datasets.

6 Results

We begin by evaluating our holonification approach under different budgets and then proceed with incremental integration, departure handling, and knowledge-transfer experiments.

6.1 Holonification Baseline Performance

We conducted a holonification, as proposed in Sect. 4.1, on a dataset comprising sixteen cameras. We set a multilayer budget framework $B^l = 256 \cdot 10^l$, implying that layer 0 holons do not exceed 256 training samples, and successive layers cannot exceed 10^l sub-holons for a holon $\hbar^l$.

Table 1. Holonification with varying budgets. Shown are the final groupings and average mAP50-95 for the 16-camera dataset.

Layer	B^l	mAP50-95	Holonic Structure
2	25600	0.65	$\mathcal{H}^2 : \{\hbar_0^1, \hbar_1^1, \hbar_2^1\}$
1	2560	0.66	$\mathcal{H}_0^1 : \{\hbar_0^0, \hbar_1^0, \hbar_2^0, \hbar_8^0\}$ $\mathcal{H}_1^1 : \{\hbar_3^0, \hbar_4^0, \hbar_5^0, \hbar_6^0, \hbar_7^0\}$ $\mathcal{H}_2^1 : \{\hbar_9^0, \hbar_{10}^0, \hbar_{11}^0, \hbar_{12}^0, \hbar_{13}^0, \hbar_{14}^0, \hbar_{15}^0\}$
0	256	0.67	$\mathcal{H}^1 : \{\hbar_0^0, \ldots, \hbar_{15}^0\}$
YOLOv8n^{COCO}	N.A	0.498	N.A

Table 1 confirms that the models require specificity to achieve maximum performance.

6.2   Transfer, Integration and Departure

Model Transfer Upon Increment The transferability of holons across new, although similar, domains is investigated. Table 2 details the performance results for models trained in an all-but-one combination of domains as well as across all domains.

Table 2. mAP50-95 scores for models trained under an all-but-one camera to assess the transferability of those models on the remaining camera. A baseline is also provided where the model is trained across all cameras. Each model is trained for 10000 iterations.

Cluster	$f(\theta, \mathcal{V}_i)$			
	$\mathcal{V}_0^0$	$\mathcal{V}_1^0$	$\mathcal{V}_2^0$	$\mathcal{V}_3^0$
$\theta^{\mathcal{H}_1^1} \setminus \{\hbar_0^0\}$	0.38	0.65	0.65	0.47
$\theta^{\mathcal{H}_1^1} \setminus \{\hbar_1^0\}$	0.46	0.57	0.66	0.46
$\theta^{\mathcal{H}_1^1} \setminus \{\hbar_2^0\}$	0.49	0.66	0.65	0.48
$\theta^{\mathcal{H}_1^1} \setminus \{\hbar_8^0\}$	0.47	0.64	0.66	0.42
$\theta^{\mathcal{H}_1^1}$	0.46	0.65	0.66	0.47

The results indicate that models struggle to transfer, even across similar camera domains, reinforcing the need to integrate the newcomer in a cluster, and the local retraining the cluster.

Incremental Integration We evaluated the impact of integrating N_+ new units into a holonified system, structured with budget limits of $B^l = 256 \cdot 10^l$. Using our integration mechanism described in Algorithm 1, we evaluated two scenarios: integrating one ($N_+ = 1$) and three ($N_+ = 3$) additional agents.

In 16 agent configurations, the incremental integration maintained an average mAP50-95 of 0.66 ± 0.003 ($N_+ = 1$) and 0.66 ± 0.006 ($N_+ = 3$), showing no degradation compared to the baseline in Table 1.

Agent Departure. When a sensor $\hbar_i^0$ leaves, its data $\mathcal{T}_i$ may be retained or discarded. We successively simulate the exit of each agent and track the accuracy of the global model on (i) remaining and (ii) left sensors. As Fig. 4 shows, removing a sensor's data yields small gains for the remaining sensors, but severely reduces performance if that sensor later re-enters the system. Note that, upon the departure of an agent, their data set $\mathcal{T}_i^0$ is removed from the collective data set $\mathcal{T}^2$, and the model is re-trained for 10,000 iterations at a learning rate of 0.005.

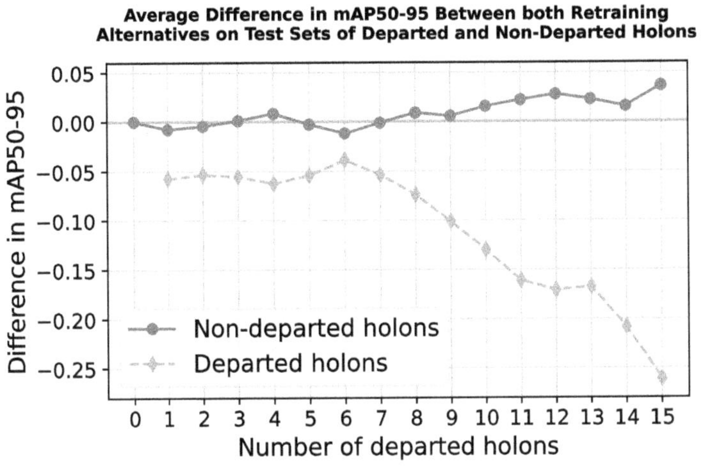

Fig. 4. Difference in $\hbar^2$ model performance between retaining and discarding each departed sensor's data. Blue: remaining sensors; yellow: departed sensors. Results show marginal gains for remaining sensors but a marked degradation on departed sensors.

6.3 Inter-holonic Knowledge Transfer

We test how effectively a holon trained on existing cameras can accelerate training and improve the peak accuracy of a newcomer domain. Specifically, we conducted 16 trials, each excluding one camera from the data set to simulate a "newcomer". The following pre-trained models serve as initial weights:

- θ^2: Global holon (trained on 15 cameras),
- θ_*^1: Group-specific holon,
- YOLOv8n^{COCO}: General-purpose off-the-shelf model.

Fig. 5 shows that θ^2 or θ_*^1 consistently outperform the generic COCO baseline when fine-tuning the newcomer camera. Training spanned 5 epochs with a learning rate of 0.005.

7 Discussion

7.1 Insights

Our experiments confirm that a certain level of domain specificity improves accuracy (Sect. 6.1), though it also increases the number of models to maintain. Budget constraints help contain this growth but can reduce performance gains from specialized holons. Meanwhile, leveraging broader universal models accelerates learning for new domains (Sect. 6.3).

In the context of open systems (Sect. 6.2), our sanity check shows that a straightforward model transfer performs under, even when the model comes from similar domains. The observed performance gap motivated the development of

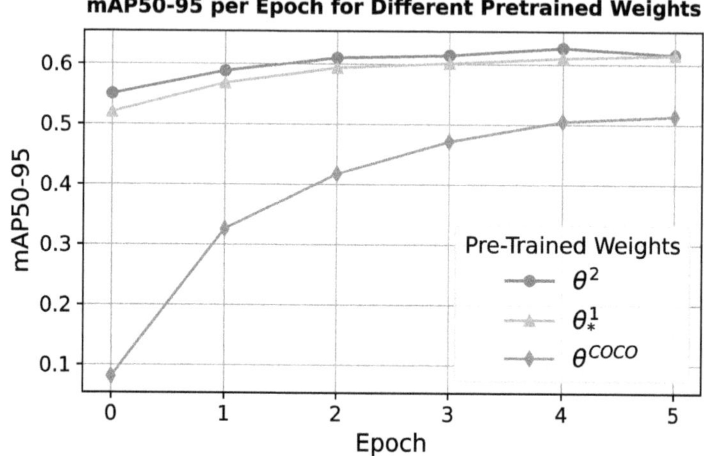

Fig. 5. mAP50-95 per epoch for a new model starting from universal model θ^2, group-specific θ^1_*, and general-purpose θ^{COCO}. The superiority of θ^2 highlights the efficiency of selecting a pretrained model closer to the source.

integration mechanisms, which proved effective, but the experiments do not provide conclusive evidence regarding the maximum number of agents that can be integrated without a performance decline. Finally, agent departure highlights a trade-off between short-term gains and relearning costs if the environment reappears. In other words, discarding data should be considered in terms of agents' turnover rate.

7.2   Limitations

Machine Learning Lifecycle. Machine learning based models are also subject to feedback loops, where data and interactions with the external world influence their behavior in unintentional ways [47]. The subsequent design of machine learning systems should account for the fact that their behavior evolves with environmental data and user interactions. This includes providing control mechanisms to avoid the accumulation of errors due to the self-supervised nature of the system.

Stress-Tests. We need to further stress test the system; that is, starting with a system of size N, stress tests can evaluate how many new components (N_+) can be integrated without compromising the quality of service.

7.3   Perspectives

Modern systems integrate heterogeneous approaches (*e.g.*, physics-based modeling vs. deep learning) and diverse sensing modalities (*e.g.*, cameras, radar), producing richer analytics [5,36]. Our architecture abstracts the holonic paradigm sufficiently to accommodate such heterogeneity. However, specialized coordination modules could further optimize collaborative performance among different modalities.

8 Conclusions

We present an organizational holonic learning design coupled with active learning to address the challenges of scaling learning in multisensor networks. Our self-organization mechanism, grounded in the specificity-diversity trade-off, allows for the establishment of various granularity levels and handles sensor addition and removal while maintaining strong predictive performance. Experimental results highlight the benefits of vertical and horizontal knowledge transfer, although more stress testing is needed to refine the upper limits on system growth. We also note that self-supervised processes risk model drift without robust monitoring, which may cause issues in autoscaling and autotuning. Future work aims to design colearning mechanisms for heterogeneous methods.

Acknowledgments. This work was partially funded by PIT ATMP - Convention 8881. T. Bary is funded by the MedReSyst project, supported by FEDER and the Walloon Region.

Disclosure of Interests. The authors have no competing interests to declare that are relevant to the content of this article.

References

1. Abbas, H.A.: Organization of multi-agent systems: an overview. Int. J. Intell. Inform. Syst. **4**(3), 46 (2015). https://doi.org/10.11648/j.ijiis.20150403.11
2. Beal, J., Viroli, M., Pianini, D., Damiani, F.: Self-adaptation to device distribution changes. In: 2016 IEEE 10th International Conference on Self-Adaptive and Self-Organizing Systems (SASO), pp. 60–69 (2016). https://doi.org/10.1109/SASO.2016.12
3. Bernon, C., Gleizes, M.-P., Peyruqueou, S., Picard, G.: ADELFE: a methodology for adaptive multi-agent systems engineering. In: Petta, P., Tolksdorf, R., Zambonelli, F. (eds.) ESAW 2002. LNCS (LNAI), vol. 2577, pp. 156–169. Springer, Heidelberg (2003). https://doi.org/10.1007/3-540-39173-8_12
4. Brion, E., Léger, J., Javaid, U., Lee, J., Vleeschouwer, C.D., Macq, B.: Using planning CTs to enhance CNN-based bladder segmentation on cone beam CT. In: Fei, B., Linte, C.A. (eds.) Medical Imaging 2019: Image-Guided Procedures, Robotic Interventions, and Modeling, vol. 10951, p. 109511M, International Society for Optics and Photonics, SPIE (2019). https://doi.org/10.1117/12.2512791
5. Campagner, A., Ciucci, D., Cabitza, F.: Aggregation models in ensemble learning: A large-scale comparison. Inform. Fusion **90**, 241–252 (2023). ISSN 1566-2535. https://doi.org/10.1016/j.inffus.2022.09.015
6. Castro, J., Kolp, M., Mylopoulos, J.: Towards requirements-driven information systems engineering: the tropos project. Inform. Syst. **27**(6), 365–389 (2002), ISSN 0306-4379. https://doi.org/10.1016/S0306-4379(02)00012-1

7. Cioppa, A., Deliege, A., Istasse, M., De Vleeschouwer, C., Van Droogenbroeck, M.: Arthus: adaptive real-time human segmentation in sports through online distillation. In: Proceedings of the IEEE/CVF Conference on Computer Vision and Pattern Recognition (CVPR) Workshops (June 2019)
8. Cossentino, M., Gaglio, S., Sabatucci, L., Seidita, V.: The passi and agile passi mas meta-models compared with a unifying proposal. In: Multi-Agent Systems and Applications IV, pp. 183–192, Springer Berlin Heidelberg, Berlin, Heidelberg (2005). ISBN 978-3-540-31731-9
9. Cossentino, M., Gaud, N., Hilaire, V., Galland, S., Koukam, A.: Aspecs: an agent-oriented software process for engineering complex systems. Auton. Agent. Multi-Agent Syst. **20**(2), 260–304 (2010). https://doi.org/10.1007/s10458-009-9099-4
10. Diaconescu, A., Frey, S., Müller-Schloer, C., Pitt, J., Tomforde, S.: Goal-oriented holonics for complex system (self-)integration: Concepts and case studies. In: 2016 IEEE 10th International Conference on Self-Adaptive and Self-Organizing Systems (SASO), pp. 100–109 (2016). https://doi.org/10.1109/SASO.2016.16
11. Dong, J., Liu, R., Qiu, Y., Crossan, M.: Should knowledge be distorted? managers' knowledge distortion strategies and organizational learning in different environments. The Leadership Quarterly **32**(3), 101477 (2021) ISSN 1048-9843
12. Esmaeili, A., Gallagher, J.C., Springer, J.A., Matson, E.T.: Hamlet: a hierarchical agent-based machine learning platform. ACM Trans. Auton. Adapt. Syst. **16**(3–4) (Jul 2022), ISSN 1556-4665
13. Esmaeili, A., Ghorrati, Z., Matson, E.T.: Holonic learning: a flexible agent-based distributed machine learning framework. In: Proceedings of the 23rd International Conference on Autonomous Agents and Multiagent Systems, pp. 525–533, AAMAS '24, International Foundation for Autonomous Agents and Multiagent Systems, Richland, SC (2024), ISBN 9798400704864
14. Esmaeili, A., Mozayani, N., Jahed-Motlagh, M.R., Matson, E.T.: Towards topological analysis of networked holonic multi-agent systems. In: Advances in Practical Applications of Survivable Agents and Multi-Agent Systems: The PAAMS Collection, pp. 42–54, Springer International Publishing, Cham (2019), ISBN 978-3-030-24209-1
15. Esmaeili, A., Mozayani, N., Motlagh, M.R.J., Matson, E.T.: The impact of diversity on performance of holonic multi-agent systems. Eng. Appl. Artif. Intell. **55**, 186–201 (2016), ISSN 0952-1976
16. Feraud, M., Galland, S.: First comparison of sarl to other agent-programming languages and frameworks. Proc. Comput. Sci. **109**, 1080 – 1085 (2017), ISSN 1877-0509. https://doi.org/10.1016/j.procs.2017.05.389
17. Fowler, M.: Refactoring: improving the design of existing code. Addison-Wesley Professional (2018)
18. French, R.M.: Catastrophic forgetting in connectionist networks. Trends Cogn. Sci. **3**(4), 128–135 (1999), ISSN 1364-6613, https://doi.org/10.1016/S1364-6613(99)01294-2
19. Garcia, E., Argente, E., Giret, A., Botti, V.: Issues for organizational multiagent systems development. In: Sixth International Workshop From Agent Theory to Agent Implementation (AT2AI-6), pp. 59–65, Citeseer (2008)
20. Gherardi, S.: Learning: organizational. In: International Encyclopedia of the Social & Behavioral Sciences (Second Edition), pp. 695–698, Elsevier, Oxford, second edition edn. (2015), ISBN 978-0-08-097087-5
21. Ghosh, A., Chung, J., Yin, D., Ramchandran, K.: An efficient framework for clustered federated learning. In: Advances in Neural Information Processing Systems, vol. 33, pp. 19586–19597, Curran Associates, Inc. (2020)

22. Gleizes, M.P.: Self-adaptive complex systems. In: Multi-Agent Systems, pp. 114–128, Springer, Berlin, Heidelberg (2012), ISBN 978-3-642-34799-3

23. Gupta, O., Raskar, R.: Distributed learning of deep neural network over multiple agents. J. Netw. Comput. Appl. **116**, 1–8 (2018), ISSN 1084-8045, https://doi.org/10.1016/j.jnca.2018.05.003

24. Hosseinalipour, S., Brinton, C.G., Aggarwal, V., Dai, H., Chiang, M.: From federated to fog learning: distributed machine learning over heterogeneous wireless networks. IEEE Commun. Mag. **58**(12), 41–47 (2020)

25. Hübner, J.F., Boissier, O., Kitio, R., Ricci, A.: Instrumenting multi-agent organisations with organisational artifacts and agents: "giving the organisational power back to the agents.âĂİ Auton. Agent. Multi-Agent Syst. **20**(3), 369–400 (2010)

26. Jocher, G., Chaurasia, A., Qiu, J.: Ultralytics YOLO (2023). https://github.com/ultralytics/ultralytics

27. Koestler, A.: The Ghost in the Machine. Hutchinson, London, UK (1967)

28. Kolp, M., Giorgini, P., Mylopoulos, J.: Multi-agent architectures as organizational structures. Auton. Agent. Multi-Agent Syst. **13**, 3–25 (2006)

29. Le, J., Lei, X., Mu, N., Zhang, H., Zeng, K., Liao, X.: Federated continuous learning with broad network architecture. IEEE Trans. Cybern. **51**(8), 3874–3888 (2021), ISSN 2168-2275, https://doi.org/10.1109/TCYB.2021.3090260

30. Lin, T., Maire, M., et al.: Microsoft COCO: common objects in context. CoRR **abs/1405.0312** (2014)

31. Lippi, M., Mariani, S., Martinelli, M., Zambonelli, F.: Individual and collective self-development: Concepts and challenges. In: 2022 17th Conference on Computer Science and Intelligence Systems (FedCSIS), pp. 15–21 (2022)

32. Léger, J., Brion, E., Desbordes, P., De Vleeschouwer, C., Lee, J.A., Macq, B.: Cross-domain data augmentation for deep-learning-based male pelvic organ segmentation in cone beam ct. Appl. Sci. **10**(3) (2020), ISSN 2076-3417, https://doi.org/10.3390/app10031154

33. Ma, Z., Xu, Y., Xu, H., Liu, J., Xue, Y.: Like attracts like: Personalized federated learning in decentralized edge computing. IEEE Trans. Mobile Comput. **23**(2), 1080–1096 (2024), ISSN 1558-0660

34. Manjah, D., Cacciarelli, D., De Vleeschouwer, C., Macq, B.: Camera clustering for scalable stream-based active distillation. Expert Syst. Appl. **290**, 128408 (2025), ISSN 0957-4174, https://doi.org/10.1016/j.eswa.2025.128408

35. Manjah, D., et al.: Stream-based active distillation for scalable model deployment. In: Proceedings of the IEEE/CVF Conference on Computer Vision and Pattern Recognition (CVPR) Workshops, pp. 4998–5006 (2023)

36. Manjah, D., Galland, S., Vleeschouwer, C.D., Macq, B.: Autonomous methods in multisensor architecture for smart surveillance. In: Proceedings of the 16th International Conference on Agents and Artificial Intelligence, vol. 3, pp. 824–832 (2024), ISBN 978-989-758-680-4, ISSN 2184-433X

37. Naphade, M., et al.: The 5th ai city challenge. In: The IEEE Conference on Computer Vision and Pattern Recognition (CVPR) Workshops (2021)

38. Nezamoddini, N., Gholami, A.: A survey of adaptive multi-agent networks and their applications in smart cities. Smart Cities **5**(1), 318–347 (2022), ISSN 2624-6511

39. Omicini, A.: Soda: societies and infrastructures in the analysis and design of agent-based systems. In: Agent-Oriented Software Engineering, pp. 185–193, Springer Berlin Heidelberg (2001), ISBN 978-3-540-44564-7
40. Padgham, L., Winikoff, M.: Prometheus: a methodology for developing intelligent agents. In: Agent-Oriented Software Engineering III, pp. 174–185, Springer Berlin Heidelberg, Berlin, Heidelberg (2003), ISBN 978-3-540-36540-2
41. Pavón, J., Gómez-Sanz, J.: Agent oriented software engineering with ingenias. In: Multi-Agent Systems and Applications III, pp. 394–403, Springer, Berlin, Heidelberg (2003), ISBN 978-3-540-45023-8
42. Perera, C., Zaslavsky, A., Christen, P., Georgakopoulos, D.: Sensing as a service model for smart cities supported by Internet of Things. Trans. Emerg. Telecommun. Technol. **25**(1), 81–93 (2014). ISSN 2161-3915
43. Porter, B., Rodrigues Filho, R.: Distributed emergent software: assembling, perceiving and learning systems at scale. In: 2019 IEEE 13th International Conference on Self-Adaptive and Self-Organizing Systems (SASO), pp. 127–136 (2019)
44. Reddy, N.D., Tamburo, R., Narasimhan, S.G.: Walt: Watch and learn 2D a modal representation from time-lapse imagery. In: Proceedings of the IEEE/CVF Conference on Computer Vision and Pattern Recognition (CVPR), pp. 9356–9366 (2022)
45. Rodriguez, S., Hilaire, V., Gaud, N., Galland, S., Koukam, A.: Holonic Multi-Agent Systems. Natural Comput. Series **37**, 251–279 (2011). https://doi.org/10.1007/978-3-642-17348-6_11
46. Schatten, M., Grd, P., Konecki, M., Kudelić, R.: Towards a formal conceptualization of organizational design techniques for large scale multi agent systems. Procedia Technology **15**, 576–585 (2014), ISSN 2212-0173, https://doi.org/10.1016/j.protcy.2014.09.018, 2nd International Conference on System-Integrated Intelligence: Challenges for Product and Production Engineering
47. Sculley, D., et al.: Hidden technical debt in machine learning systems. In: Advances in Neural Information Processing Systems, vol. 28, Curran Associates, Inc. (2015)
48. Sibson, R.: SLINK: an optimally efficient algorithm for the single-link cluster method. Comput. J. **16**(1), 30–34 (1973), ISSN 0010-4620
49. Terabe, M., Washio, T., Katai, O., Sawaragi, T.: A study of organizational learning in multiagents systems. In: Distributed Artificial Intelligence Meets Machine Learning Learning in Multi-Agent Environments, pp. 168–179, Springer Berlin Heidelberg, Berlin, Heidelberg (1997), ISBN 978-3-540-69050-4
50. Wautelet, Y., Schinckus, C., Kolp, M.: Agent-based software engineering, paradigm shift, or research program evolution. In: Research Anthology on Recent Trends, Tools, and Implications of Computer Programming, pp. 1642–1654, IGI Global (2021)
51. Weyns, D., et al.: Self-adaptation in industry: a survey. ACM Trans. Auton. Adapt. Syst. **18**(2) (2023), ISSN 1556-4665
52. Wolpert, D.H., Macready, W.G.: No free lunch theorems for optimization. IEEE Trans. Evol. Comput. **1**(1), 67–82 (1997), ISSN 1089778X, https://doi.org/10.1109/4235.585893
53. Wooldridge, M., Jennings, N.R., Kinny, D.: The gaia methodology for agent-oriented analysis and design. Auton. Agent. Multi-Agent Syst. **3**(3), 285–312 (2000). https://doi.org/10.1023/A:1010071910869
54. Xu, B., Xia, W., Wen, W., Liu, P., Zhao, H., Zhu, H.: Adaptive hierarchical federated learning over wireless networks. IEEE Trans. Veh. Technol. **71**(2), 2070–2083 (2021)

55. Yang, Y., et al.: Diverse auto-curriculum is critical for successful real-world multiagent learning systems. In: Proceedings of the 20th International Conference on Autonomous Agents and MultiAgent Systems, pp. 51–56, AAMAS '21, International Foundation for Autonomous Agents and Multiagent Systems, Richland, SC (2021), ISBN 9781450383073
56. Yin, D., Pananjady, A., Lam, M., Papailiopoulos, D., Ramchandran, K., Bartlett, P.: Gradient diversity: a key ingredient for scalable distributed learning. In: Proceedings of the Twenty-First International Conference on Artificial Intelligence and Statistics, Proc. Mach. Learn. Res. **84**, 1998–2007 PMLR (2018)

LTL Semantics for Tumato: A Declarative Approach to Autonomous Agent Planning

Jan Vermaelen[✉] and Tom Holvoet

DistriNet, KU Leuven, 3001 Leuven, Belgium
`{jan.vermaelen,tom.holvoet}@kuleuven.be`

Abstract. This paper explores the semantics of Tumato 2.0, a constraint-based planning framework, through the lens of Linear Temporal Logic (LTL). Tumato enables the generation of policies for autonomous agents, ensuring safe and robust goal-oriented behavior. The framework guarantees that critical safety constraints hold across all potential outcomes of non-deterministic actions, while pre-computed policies eliminate the need for runtime decision-making. By translating Tumato's language constructs into LTL, we formalize its approach to handling safety, liveness, and robustness properties. This contribution offers a foundation for reliable agent behavior under real-world uncertainties, as well as improved interpretability.

We further demonstrate the semantics of Tumato's specification language through a case study, demonstrating how LTL guides system specification and supports potential formal verification efforts. These contributions align with key challenges in engineering intelligent and multi-agent systems, focusing on safety, correctness, and robust operation within complex environments. Overall, this work emphasizes the importance of declarative approaches in delivering reliable solutions for real-world applications.

Keywords: Tumato 2.0 · Linear Temporal Logic (LTL) · Autonomous Agents

1 Introduction

Autonomous agents and multi-agent systems require rigorous planning frameworks to operate safely and effectively in complex, real-world environments. The Tumato framework, originally introduced by Hoang Tung Dinh et al. [3], is a constraint-based planning tool designed to generate safe, goal-oriented behavior policies. However, the uncertainty inherent in real-world conditions—such as unexpected obstacles and sensor and actuator inaccuracies—demands that an agent's planning framework be robust. By incorporating these non-deterministic action outcomes within its constraint-based structure, Tumato 2.0 [8] ensures that agents can reliably face these challenges, making it particularly relevant for the engineering of robust autonomous agents.

© The Author(s), under exclusive license to Springer Nature Switzerland AG 2026
S. Rodriguez et al. (Eds.): EMAS 2025, LNAI 16407, pp. 100–116, 2026.
https://doi.org/10.1007/978-3-032-18011-7_7

The approach adopted by Tumato—offline, complete policy generation—further enhances robustness by eliminating the need for real-time re-planning. In safety-critical applications, where stable and reliable behavior is required, re-planning under computational constraints can introduce risk and latency. By generating policies ahead of runtime, Tumato reduces computational demands during operation, enabling agents to execute predefined, guaranteed safe, and goal-oriented behavior. Furthermore, the planning approach generates complete policies, specifying which actions to execute in every potential state of the system. The approach is valuable for systems deployed in industries such as autonomous logistics, healthcare robotics, and field operations.

To fully value Tumato's capabilities, we analyze it through the lens of formal logic, which provides a structured, rigorous way to evaluate and reason about agent behavior. Tumato's declarative specification language enables users to specify desired outcomes and constraints without detailing the specific actions required to achieve them. A natural choice for such an analysis is Linear Temporal Logic (LTL), which facilitates reasoning about sequences of actions and states over time. LTL enables the specification of safety and liveness properties, providing a foundation for well-defined behaviors.

This paper formalizes Tumato's specification framework using LTL. We focus on the guarantees Tumato provides: safety (avoiding dangerous actions and states), robustness (handling non-determinism), and goal achievement (meeting specified objectives). While Tumato, the planning tool itself, is not formalized in this work, nor can it be fully expressed in LTL, this paper focuses on the semantics of Tumato's specification framework. The presented formalization improves the interpretability of Tumato's guarantees but does not aim to redefine or enhance the planning tool's underlying mechanisms. For a deeper exploration of Tumato's planning capabilities, we refer to [8]. By mapping Tumato's functionalities into LTL, we analyze its alignment with formal methods and assess its implications for reliable agent planning. To demonstrate its practical utility, we include a case study that represents Tumato's features as LTL expressions, in a robotic pick-and-place scenario. Tumato's declarative specification framework inherently supports multi-agent systems, as multi-agent interactions can be implemented in a state-action-based manner. This work does not delve into the modeling of multi-agent-specific features. Additionally, probabilistic approaches—which Tumato avoids by design—and detailed implementation aspects fall outside the scope of this work.

The remainder of this paper is structured as follows. Section 2 provides the background and related work, introducing LTL-based approaches as well as Tumato. Section 3 shows the relationship between Tumato specifications and LTL, offering insights into Tumato's approach. Section 4 presents the case study, followed by Sect. 5 discussing the findings. Finally, Sect. 6 concludes.

2   Background and Related Work

To ensure reliable and safe operation in autonomous systems, formal methods such as temporal logic are often essential for specifying and verifying system properties. This section introduces LTL and explores its applications and adaptations in autonomous systems, before focusing on the Tumato framework.

2.1   Linear Temporal Logic (LTL)

Temporal logic, especially LTL, has become a natural choice for specifying (and verifying) properties on safety and liveness in autonomous and multi-agent systems [1].

LTL enables reasoning about sequences of states and events over paths using propositional variables (such as *at_charger* and *object_loaded*) which can be either *true* or *false*, logical operators ($\neg$, $\vee$, $\wedge$, $\rightarrow$, $\leftrightarrow$), and temporal modal operators (X, F, G, U, R). The temporal operators allow for describing the progression of states over time:

- X *(Next)*: Specifies that a condition will hold in the next state. For example, Xp means that p is true in the state immediately following the current one.
- F *(Eventually)*: Specifies that a condition will hold at some point in the future. For example, Fq means that q will become true at least once.
- G *(Globally)*: Specifies that a condition holds in all future states. For example, Gr means that r is true in every state.
- U *(Until)*: Specifies that one condition must hold at least until another becomes true. For example, $p\,U\,q$ means that p must hold continuously up to the point where q becomes true.
- R *(Release)*: Specifies that one condition releases another. For example, $p\,R\,q$ means that q must hold until and including the point where p becomes true. If p never becomes true, q must hold indefinitely.

As mentioned before, the suitability of looking at LTL to understand Tumato arises from its ability to capture conditions critical to safety, liveness, and robustness. Common properties in robotics, for example in a (mobile) pick and place application, include:

- **Safety**:
    - $G\neg u$ (with an unsafe condition u, which should never occur),
    - e.g. $G\neg$collision (a collision should never happen),
    - e.g. G(loaded $\rightarrow$ $\neg$pickup) (a pickup should never execute if the robot is already loaded).
- **Liveness**:
    - Ft (with single task formula t) or GFg (with repeating goal formula g),
    - e.g. $G(\neg$loaded $\rightarrow$ Floaded) (if the robot is not loaded, it should be loaded in the future), and
    e.g. G(loaded $\rightarrow$ $F\neg$loaded) (if the robot is loaded, it should be unloaded in the future),
    - e.g. $G(F$loaded $\wedge$ $F\neg$loaded) (true liveness).
    From a more practical (yet more procedural) viewpoint, one could also consider G(at_delivery_station $\rightarrow$ (loaded $\rightarrow$ Xdeliver)). That is, if the robot is at the delivery station while loaded, it should deliver, next.

- **Robustness** (regarding the *failure* of actions):
  - of the form $v\, U\, w$ (with formula v the intended operation and formula w the desired effect),
  - e.g. $G(\text{pickup} \rightarrow \text{pickup}\, U\, \text{loaded})$ (pickup should be executed until successfully loaded).

Looking at related work in this context, LTL-based approaches have focused on managing conflicting objectives and handling constraints imposed by the environment, as in the work by Tumova et al. [6,7], where methods are developed to minimize specification violations. This line of work emphasizes practical adaptability by finding the *least-violating* control strategy. In contrast, Tumato ensures absolute safety without compromise, opting instead to only generate behavior that succeeds in maintaining and restoring safety. If safety can not be guaranteed, it refrains from generating behavior.

Handling both high-level abstraction and continuous low-level observation and execution remains a universal challenge in autonomous control [4]. This challenge has been observed using Tumato as well, and is addressed by using *monitoring modules* that translate low-level observations into high-level states [8], although the details are beyond this paper's scope.

Various approaches include probabilistic aspects in agent planning, potentially combined with LTL. An example is a method to generate a control strategy that maximizes the probability of accomplishing a task given as an LTL formula [2]. Tumato, however, avoids probabilistic dependencies to mitigate the complexities of obtaining and maintaining reliable probabilities in dynamic environments. Instead, it assumes (biased) foreseeable, non-deterministic action outcomes, enabling robust planning while maintaining a declarative approach to safety.

LTL frameworks are often capable of real-time plan (re)calculation, for dynamic tasks or changing environments [11]. Tumato, however, generates complete, sound policies offline, enabling it to preemptively address safety constraints and remove the need for runtime recalculations. This pre-planned robustness ensures that no additional runtime intervention is needed beyond executing the existing policy.

LTL has been effectively applied to task assignment and planning in multi-robot systems, leveraging techniques like *lazy collision checking* to simplify the planning problem [5]. Although multi-agent applications are beyond this paper's immediate focus, Tumato's planning structure inherently supports multi-robot scenarios. It enables flexible, high-level task allocation and, when needed, communication among agents. Since planning is handled offline, the required computational power is readily available.

Other advancements have led to the development of HyperLTL [10], which extends LTL to express planning objectives like optimality, robustness, and privacy across multiple paths. Tumato's approach to non-determinism shares a related concept by ensuring safety across multiple possible outcomes for each action, illustrating a comparable need for handling relationships among multiple possible execution paths.

Overall, a range of LTL adaptations has been investigated before. In this work, we align Tumato with such efforts, seeking to provide a comprehensive understanding of the semantics within its specification framework.

2.2 Tumato

As introduced earlier, the Tumato 2.0 framework is a constraint-based planning tool designed to generate policies for autonomous systems, emphasizing safety, robustness, and goal-oriented behavior [8]. Tumato enables users to specify system behavior in a declarative manner, which is then automatically translated into sets of constraints. These constraints allow for the generation of a sound and complete policy that ensures safe and robust operation, even in realistic, non-deterministic environments. A Tumato-generated policy is a state-based behavior mapping, in which each state is associated with a set of actions to be executed. A recent empirical evaluation has demonstrated Tumato's effectiveness when compared to other, more ad-hoc approaches [9].

Tumato is not directly applicable to arbitrary problems in a fully observable non-deterministic (FOND) planning context, nor does it employ PDDL syntax. Instead, Tumato is a hands-on practical behavior planning tool that generates robust, constraint-based policies for autonomous agents. The focus of this work is on the formalization of its specification framework, rather than on Tumato itself.

Tumato's Specification Language. Tumato employs a high-level declarative specification language for modeling autonomous systems. This language allows users to express system behavior in terms of states, actions, safety constraints, and goals. Below, we outline the core constructs of the Tumato language, along with examples to clarify their use.

States. System states are defined using state variables, specifying all possible configurations of the system and its environment:

```
state <StateVarName> can be <StateValue> [, <StateValue> ...]
```

Here, *StateVarName* represents the name of the state property, and *StateValues* define its discrete possible values. For example:

```
state location can be pickup, dropoff, corridor
```

This definition specifies that the robot's location can be one of three discrete values: `pickup`, `dropoff`, or `corridor`.

Actions. Actions define the operations the system can perform and are specified as follows:

```
action <ActionName>
[duration: <Cost>]
[controlled resources: <ActionResource> [, <ActionResource> ...]]
preconditions: [none | <Predicate> [, <Predicate> ...]]
nominal effects: [none | <Predicate> [, <Predicate> ...]]
[alternative effects: [none | <Predicate> [, <Predicate> ...]]];
```

The key components of an action are:

- **<ActionName>:** The name of the action being defined.
- **Preconditions:** Conditions (written as predicates) that must hold before the action can be executed.
- **Nominal Effects:** Expected outcomes of the action under normal circumstances.
- **Alternative Effects:** (Zero or more) less desirable and less likely but possible deviations from the nominal effects.

Additionally, **controlled resources** can be specified, preventing two actions from executing simultaneously if they require the same resource. The optional **duration** parameter is used exclusively for prioritizing safety restoration actions: when safety must be restored, actions with shorter durations are prioritized. If safety is not violated, the duration parameter is ignored.

For example, a `pickup` action might be defined as:

```
action pickup
preconditions: location is pickup
nominal effects: object_status is loaded
alternative effects: object_status is free
```

This action requires the robot to be at the pickup location (`preconditions`) and results in the object being loaded (`nominal effects`) or failing to load (`alternative effects`).

Safety Rules. Safety rules in Tumato ensure that the system maintains or restores safety. Rules are defined using the following syntax:

```
rule: <Predicate>
```

Tumato supports two types of rules:

- **Reaction Rules:** These enforce immediate actions or prohibit actions under specific conditions. They are expressed in the following form:

  ```
  rule: IF <condition> THEN [NOT] executing <action>
  ```

  This rule specifies reactive behavior triggered by the given condition.
- **State Rules:** These define conditions that must hold across all state-action outcomes. They are expressed in the following form:

```
rule: IF <condition> THEN <other condition>
```

State rules specify safety constraints that must hold in the next state, after the effects of the action have taken place.

Goals. Goals specify the desired states or conditions the system must achieve. Tumato supports both unconditional and conditional goals:

```
goal: <goal condition> // unconditional
when <condition> then goal: <goal condition> // conditional
```

In the second case, the goal is pursued only while the condition holds.

Maximum Plan Length. The maximum plan length is specified using:

```
max_plan_length: <value>
```

This parameter sets an upper bound on the number of steps considered during offline planning. By limiting the plan length, Tumato ensures computational feasibility while still focusing on generating effective plans.

Core Features of Tumato. Tumato's offline policy generation process eliminates the need for real-time re-planning during execution. This precomputed approach guarantees stable and predictable behavior, which is especially important in safety-critical environments. As described, the system specifications are transformed into constraints that are solved by a constraint solver. This ensures:

- **Completeness:** Every possible state has an associated action or set of actions.
- **Soundness:** No unsafe (or resource-conflicting) actions are executed, adhering to all specified safety rules, while the goals are pursued.
- **Robustness:** The system accounts for non-deterministic outcomes by considering both nominal and alternative effects of actions.

Tumato's declarative approach simplifies system modeling by abstracting procedural details. Users can modify high-level constraints as needed, and Tumato automatically regenerates the corresponding policy. This flexibility makes Tumato suitable for evolving system requirements.

Another key strength is Tumato's handling of non-deterministic action outcomes. Actions are modeled with both nominal and alternative effects to account for possible deviations. For example, a robot tasked with moving to a location might encounter obstacles or actuator malfunctions, resulting in delays or failures. Tumato considers such foreseeable alternatives during planning, ensuring that the policy remains safe. The completeness of the policy ensures that, regardless of the outcomes of actions, the system can keep progressing toward its goals.

By combining offline policy generation, a declarative specification language, and a robust constraint-based backbone, Tumato provides a comprehensive solution for generating safe, goal-oriented policies for autonomous systems operating in uncertain environments.

Further details on Tumato's capabilities (and a case study) can be found in [8].

3   Mapping Tumato to LTL and CTL

We use LTL (and CTL) to formalize the semantics of Tumato's specification constructs. While these logics provide a way to reason about the behavior, they can not capture the decision-making process. They are suited for specifying properties over paths of states (and actions) during execution. By translating elements of a Tumato specification into LTL, we enable formal reasoning about the properties of the generated policy.

The completeness of Tumato's generated policy refers to the existence of a set of actions for every possible state—unless explicitly assumed otherwise in the specification. This completeness can be trivially verified since each state is guaranteed to have a corresponding state-action mapping generated by Tumato.

The specification of a maximum plan length in Tumato contains a parameter that guides the offline planning process, defining the execution horizon over which the planning system reasons. However, this does not constrain the infinite execution traces of the policy at runtime.

Using LTL formulas for state transitions, goals, and safety, Tumato policies can be verified to be sound, as claimed by the tool. The entries in a policy can also be represented using LTL as:

$$G(s \to a),$$

meaning that in a state s, action(s) a is (are) executed. In turn, potential state transitions resulting from actions can be expressed as

$$G((s_1 \wedge a) \to X(s_{2a1} \vee s_{2a2} \vee \ldots)),$$

where $s_{2a1}, s_{2a2}, \ldots$ represent all possible individual next states after executing action a in s_1. More details about the effects of actions can be found in Sect. 3.1.

3.1   Modeling Actions

In Tumato, actions are associated with preconditions and effects that can be mapped into LTL.

Preconditions. Preconditions specify conditions that must hold before an action can be executed. If an action a_1 has preconditions $c_1, c_2, \ldots$, they can be represented in LTL as:

$$G(a_1 \to (c_1 \wedge c_2 \wedge \ldots)).$$

This ensures that action a_1 is only taken when its preconditions are satisfied.

Resource Constraints. In Tumato, actions that use the same resources are mutually exclusive. LTL can also enforce that no two actions with overlapping resource needs execute simultaneously. For a pair of actions a_i and a_j (with $i \neq j$) that require the same resource, mutual exclusion is expressed as:

$$G(a_i \rightarrow \neg a_j), \quad \text{or equivalently} \quad G\neg(a_i \wedge a_j).$$

This guarantees that resources can be allocated without conflict.

Effects of Actions. Effects describe the outcomes of executing an action. The resulting next state depends on the effects of the action(s)—executed in a specific state.

In an idealized setting (without external interference and no intermediary states), we assume that executing an action a leads directly to its nominal effect $\text{effect}_{\text{nom}}$ in the next state. This idealized effect can be expressed in LTL as:

$$G(a \rightarrow X(\text{effect}_{\text{nom}})).$$

In realistic settings, action outcomes are often non-deterministic, meaning that an action a may lead to one of several possible effects $\text{effect}_{\text{nom}}$, $\text{effect}_{\text{alt1}}$, $\text{effect}_{\text{alt2}}$, ... To model this uncertainty, we can express that one of these effects will eventually occur if the action is executed:

$$G(a \rightarrow F(\text{effect}_{\text{nom}} \vee \text{effect}_{\text{alt1}} \vee \text{effect}_{\text{alt2}} \vee \ldots)).$$

However, this formulation assumes that the effects occur regardless of whether the action continues to be executed, which may not always be accurate.

A more realistic formulation incorporates the condition that the effects only occur as long as the action a is being executed. This relationship can be captured as:

$$G(a \rightarrow (a \ U \ (\text{effect}_{\text{nom}} \vee \text{effect}_{\text{alt1}} \vee \text{effect}_{\text{alt2}} \vee \ldots \vee \neg a))).$$

This formula states that while a is being executed, it must continue until one of its effects occurs, unless a is stopped.

Further, Tumato addresses the frame problem implicitly. While we do not represent this in LTL, it is assumed that any state variables not affected by an action's outcome remain unchanged. In Tumato, all relevant variables are updated explicitly in the effects of actions, and those not mentioned are understood to persist by default.

If multiple actions are executed simultaneously, Tumato treats each action's effects as a distinct potential outcome.[1] At runtime, the effects of one action occur first, followed by an evaluation of the new state and corresponding actions. When modeling in LTL, simultaneous actions can be modeled by a composite action with all possible effects. However, in Tumato we should keep actions separate to maintain the notion of bias toward nominal effects.

---

[1] If actions directly interfere with each other, they should be modeled with shared resources to prevent conflicts.

Indeed, Tumato introduces a bias toward nominal outcomes, which represent the expected result of actions, while alternatives model less likely deviations. This bias is not probabilistic but semantic: Tumato assumes that if an action is executed repeatedly, its nominal effect will occur. In logical terms, this reflects a fairness assumption—namely, that the system is fair with respect to nominal outcomes and does not indefinitely fail. The bias can not be expressed directly in LTL.

3.2   Modeling Goals

Liveness properties in Tumato ensure that certain desirable states or conditions will eventually be reached or maintained:

- **Basic Goals**: The simplest form of a goal in Tumato can be interpreted as GFg, meaning that a goal condition g will eventually be reached and reoccur (or be maintained) indefinitely. This is useful for specifying tasks that should continue to be achieved, unconditionally.
  Multiple goals can be conjoined using Tumato's *constraint* goal option. The conjunction of all goals g_i for $i = 1, 2, \ldots, n$ is represented as $g \leftrightarrow (g_1 \wedge g_2 \wedge \ldots \wedge g_n)$.
- **Conditional and Prioritized Goals**: Tumato enables more complex goal structures, where goals are prioritized and active only under certain conditions. These prioritized conditional goals can be represented in LTL as follows:

$$G(c_1 \rightarrow (c_1 U(g_1 \vee \neg c_1)))$$

$$G((c_2 \wedge \neg c_1) \rightarrow ((c_2 \wedge \neg c_1)U(g_2 \vee \neg c_2)))$$

$$\ldots$$

$$G((c_n \wedge \neg c_1 \wedge \neg c_2 \wedge \ldots \wedge \neg c_{n-1}) \rightarrow$$

$$((c_n \wedge \neg c_1 \wedge \neg c_2 \wedge \ldots \wedge \neg c_{n-1})U(g_n \vee \neg c_n))).$$

These formulas ensure that a goal g_i is pursued when its corresponding condition c_i holds, provided no higher-priority goals (depending on their order) are active under their respective conditions. This ensures that goals are pursued in priority order when their conditions are met.

Under the fairness assumption (with respect to nominal outcomes), Tumato's planner synthesizes strong cyclic plans. Such plans guarantee that the goals will eventually be reached from all states. The argument can be made by contradiction: assume there exists an infinite execution where the goal is never reached. Consider the closest state to the goal—according to some distance metric—that is revisited infinitely often without progressing toward the goal. The planner associates each state with an action whose nominal effect moves closer to the goal. Therefore, the only way to never reach the goal is if the nominal effects never occur, which contradicts the fairness assumption. It follows that, under fairness, the generated policy ensures goal reachability.

3.3   Handling Safety

Safety constraints in Tumato take the form of either reaction rules or state rules:

- **Reaction Rules**: These are typically expressed as $G(c \rightarrow a)$, where c is a condition under which action a should (or should not: $G(c \rightarrow \neg a)$) be executed. For example, if a robot detects an obstacle, it should execute a braking action.
- **State Rules**: State rules push the constraint to *the next state* and are used to specify conditions that must hold after state transitions. State rules can be interpreted as GXb in LTL, where b represents a safe condition. Whichever actions are executed, they should always lead to a state where a safety constraint b holds.

When including potential alternative outcomes of actions, LTL theoretically falls short, as it can not reason about different possible futures or guarantee safety across all outcomes. Branching-time logic, such as CTL, may be more suitable, as it can express properties over different possible execution paths. For example, $A(GXb)$ specifies that b must always hold for all possible next outcomes, ensuring safety across all paths. While LTL cannot fully express Tumato's bias toward nominal outcomes or its handling of safety regarding potential alternative outcomes, it does still provide a foundational framework for reasoning about Tumato's (safety) semantics.

4   Case Study: a Mobile Pick-and-Place Robot

In this case study, we examine a pick-and-place robot tasked with moving objects from a pickup location to a drop-off location. The robot operates in a well-defined environment with a corridor between the two locations, and it must adhere to specific safety and liveness requirements. This example highlights Tumato's semantics, expressed in LTL, and its approach to generating robust policies. These policies ensure safety across all potential action outcomes while achieving liveness goals.

4.1   Model in LTL

To express this system in LTL, we define atomic propositions representing actions and states:

Actions:

- *pickup*: object pickup action (precondition: at pickup location),
- *drop_off*: object unload action (precondition: at drop-off location),
- *move_to_a*: move to pickup location,
- *move_to_b*: move to drop-off location,
- *secure*: secure object if one is present on the robot,
- *release*: release (or *unsecure*) the secured object, if any.

States:

- a: robot is at the pickup location,
- b: robot is at the drop-off location,
- c: robot is in between locations, in the corridor,
- obj: an object is present on the robot,
- sec: the object on the robot is secured for transport,
- bat: the battery level is in range for normal operation.

Please note that a, b, and c are mutually exclusive. The robot will always be at one (and only one) of those locations.

These propositions enable us to formalize both liveness properties—ensuring transport goals are reached—and safety properties—ensuring objects are secured before transport.

The robot's states and actions (state transitions) can be represented in an automaton, see Fig. 1, including nominal and alternative outcomes. The transitions show the non-deterministic nature of actions, where the robot cannot predict which outcome will occur at runtime but ensures safety regardless of the result. Battery levels have been omitted in this overview for readability. Please note, the action $move\_to\_b$ (moving to the drop-off location) could be executed after $pickup$ and before $secure$ as moving has no preconditions. Since (one outcome of) this action is not safe—see later in this section—it has not been included in the figure. Similarly, moving to a workstation without (un)loading first does not progress the system and is not included—although again, possible.

For goal-oriented planning, Tumato assumes nominal outcomes of actions over the far less likely and less desirable alternative ones. When guaranteeing safety, however, also the alternative outcomes are considered. Tumato's policies ensure that actions exist for all states, enabling continuous operation without the need for runtime decision-making.

Action Preconditions. For some actions, certain preconditions must be satisfied to ensure appropriate execution. For instance, the robot must be at the pickup location before it can execute the $pickup$ action. In LTL, we can enforce this precondition by requiring that the action only occurs when the robot is indeed at the pickup location:

$$G(pickup \rightarrow a)$$

This formula states that $pickup$ implies a (the robot being at the pickup location), ensuring that the action $pickup$ can only occur when a is $true$.

Robust Operation. To ensure robust operation, the robot must handle potential failures, requiring retries of actions when necessary. For example, if the robot attempts to pick up an object, the object may occasionally fall back down. To handle such failures, one can include robustness in that the robot will persist in attempting the pickup action until it succeeds.

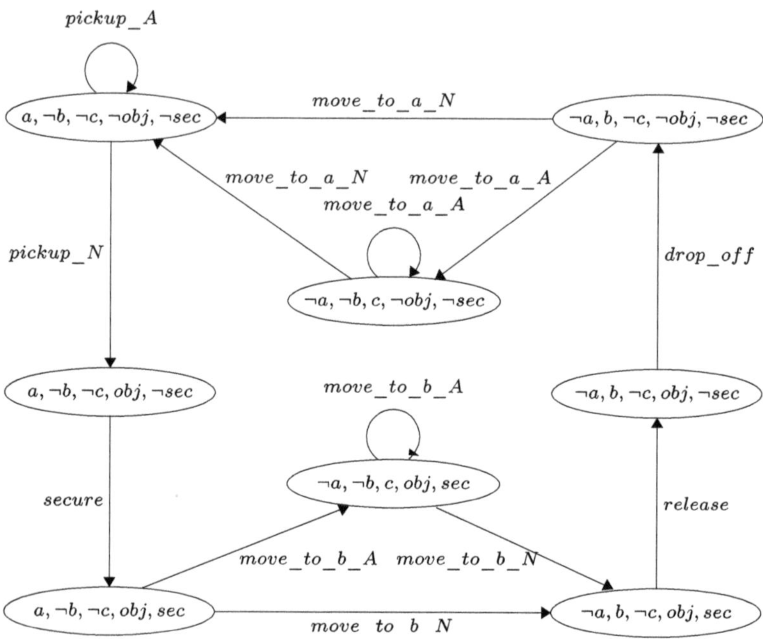

Fig. 1. An automaton showing the state transitions, visualizing both nominal and alternative effects of actions as $<action>\_N$ and $<action>\_A$ respectively

Using LTL, we define this as follows:

$$pickup\, U\, obj$$

This expression denotes that the robot will continue attempting the pickup action *pickup* until the object is successfully loaded onto the robot, indicated by *obj*.

Tumato's policy structure inherently guarantees robustness by ensuring that each state has associated actions. This ensures the system can retry failed actions or correct deviations caused by unintended action outcomes, without additional runtime decision-making.

Liveness Properties. The robot is expected to continuously fulfill its objective of picking up and delivering objects, represented in LTL by goals that must be repeatedly achieved.

General Liveness of Pickup and Delivery: $G(F pickup)$ denotes that the robot will always eventually pick up an object. Similarly, $G(F drop\_off)$ denotes that the robot will always eventually deliver an object.

Refined Liveness Properties: Using conditions to define when specific goals must be met:

- If the robot is not currently carrying an object, it should obtain an object. We use "*condition U goal*" rather than "*F goal*" to emphasize a required continuous condition:

$$G(\neg obj \rightarrow (\neg obj \, U \, obj)).$$

- If the robot has an object loaded, it should eventually unload it:

$$G(obj \rightarrow (obj \, U \, \neg obj)).$$

After also including the battery level:

$$G((\neg obj \wedge bat) \rightarrow ((\neg obj \wedge bat) \, U \, (obj \vee \neg bat))),$$

$$G((obj \wedge bat) \rightarrow ((obj \wedge bat) \, U \, (\neg obj \vee \neg bat))),$$

$$G(\neg bat \rightarrow (\neg bat \, U \, bat)).$$

These formulas ensure the robot continuously attempts to pick up and deliver objects while prioritizing battery constraints and hence charging.

Safety Properties. The safety requirements aim to prevent the robot from entering unsafe states, such as moving (in the corridor) with an unsecured object. Most practically, with a procedural mindset, we write:

$$G(obj \rightarrow ((secure \vee sec) \, U \, drop\_off))$$

where we have to assume that securing happens instantly since moving is not prohibited.

In practice, however, actions do not effectuate instantly. Furthermore, unlike in this *secure* example, action outcomes are seldom purely deterministic, making it necessary to include robustness to account for these potential failures or delays.

To more directly address this safety property, we can require the robot to explicitly (successfully) secure any object before movement is permitted. This can be captured as:

$$G((obj \wedge \neg sec) \rightarrow X(sec \, R \, \neg c)).$$

Or more generally applicable, reflecting Tumato's state rules, if an object is present but not secured, the robot is not allowed to be in the corridor:

$$G(X((obj \wedge \neg sec) \rightarrow \neg c))$$

4.2   Enabling Policy Verification

The derived LTL formulas provide the necessary elements to formally reason about state transitions, goal satisfaction, and safety constraints in Tumato's policies. In principle, model-checking techniques could be employed to verify that Tumato's policies comply with specified safety and liveness properties.

However, explicit verification is unnecessary as Tumato's constraint-solving approach inherently guarantees compliance with these properties by construction. The policy generation process ensures:

- All specified constraints are enforced, ensuring soundness.
- All reachable states have corresponding actions, ensuring completeness.
- Robustness is achieved through precomputed policies that account for non-deterministic outcomes.

Nonetheless, the formalization provided here enables verification if needed for specific cases or additional validation.

By addressing safety and liveness requirements while accounting for non-deterministic outcomes, Tumato effectively tackles key challenges in generating reliable policies for autonomous systems. These contributions also align with broader challenges in multi-agent engineering, particularly for systems deployed under real-world uncertainties.

5   Discussion

The mapping of Tumato's specifications into LTL highlights its contribution to generating sound and robust policies for autonomous systems. This formalization reveals how Tumato aligns with key safety and liveness properties while managing uncertainties, offering valuable insights for engineering intelligent agents.

Tumato's policy generation relies on constraint-solving to meet safety and goal requirements by construction. It ensures policies are sound, adhering to safety rules, and complete, covering all possible states. This inherent reliability guarantees that the generated policies align with specifications whose semantics can be appreciated through LTL, eliminating the need for (runtime) verification. The approach is particularly effective in environments where action outcomes are non-deterministic.

The offline nature of Tumato's policy generation eliminates the need for dynamic, on-the-fly planning. By pre-computing policies that address all reachable states, all contingencies are accounted for. This avoids reliance on ad-hoc re-planning, which poses challenges in real-world environments and distributed settings. As such, Tumato is particularly advantageous for applications where safety guarantees are critical, such as autonomous robotics.

The alignment of Tumato's policies with the safety and liveness properties expressed in LTL is observed. Safety properties, such as ensuring that objects are secured before transport, map directly to constraints that must always hold. Similarly, liveness properties, such as continuous pickup and delivery of objects, are represented as recurring goals within Tumato. This connection underscores Tumato's suitability for systems requiring operational guarantees.

LTL provides a solid foundation for specifying safety and liveness properties. In this work, it was used to provide the semantics of Tumato's specification constructs. However, LTL can not represent the explicit accounting for alternative effects of actions in terms of safety nor the bias toward nominal outcomes. Also, the approach of restoring safety the most preferred way, based on a *duration* is outside LTL's scope. These discrepancies are due to Tumato's origin of addressing practical needs in engineering (robotic) agents. Rather than focusing on LTL's expressiveness, Tumato employs a constraint-solving mechanism that directly integrates robustness into policy generation, ensuring safety even when actions have multiple possible outcomes. The balance between formal logic and practical needs sets Tumato apart from prior works, which often prioritize theoretical guarantees over real-world applicability.

Tumato also differs from approaches based on probabilistic models, which rely on accurate probabilistic information to guide decision-making. While these models are mathematically powerful, they are challenging to apply in uncertain environments where probabilities are difficult to estimate. By avoiding such dependencies, Tumato ensures greater reliability in dynamic and non-deterministic scenarios.

6   Conclusion

This work formalizes the semantics of Tumato's constraint-based planning framework using LTL. We investigated the specification used to generate sound, complete, and robust policies for autonomous systems by satisfying safety and liveness requirements. The obtained semantics form a structured way to interpret Tumato's specifications and understand its guarantees, particularly in non-deterministic and safety-critical settings.

Tumato's focus on nominal outcomes, while accounting for other contingencies, provides a practical solution for real-world applications. Although LTL cannot fully capture every aspect of Tumato's safety handling, it provides a valuable framework for understanding specifications and verifying policies. By combining explicit robustness with pre-computed, complete policies that eliminate runtime checks, Tumato effectively balances theoretical rigor with practical applicability, making it highly effective for engineering safe and robust autonomous (robotic) systems.

Future work should investigate Tumato's capabilities regarding dynamic goal assignment and explicit support for multi-agent collaboration, which would enhance its utility in evolving tasks and cooperative planning. Additionally, the use of machine learning techniques could be explored to assist users in adequately representing real-world systems without relying on probabilistic models. Furthermore, prioritizing safety rules could enable Tumato to weigh more critical constraints more heavily when resolving unsafe situations. Finally, exploring the possibility of temporarily allowing (transient) *less safe* states before fully restoring safety could expand Tumato's flexibility in highly constrained environments. This trade-off must be carefully examined to ensure alignment with safety-critical requirements. Such advancements would broaden Tumato's applicability and contribute to ongoing efforts to engineer intelligent agents capable of operating in complex, real-world scenarios.

Acknowledgments. This research is partially funded by the Research Fund KU Leuven.

Throughout this work, the authors used *Grammarly* and, to a lesser extent, *ChatGPT* for grammar and readability improvements. All edits were reviewed and refined by the authors, who take full responsibility for the publication's content.

Disclosure of Interests. The authors have no competing interests to declare that are relevant to the content of this article.

References

1. Baier, C., Katoen, J.P.: Principles of model checking. MIT press (2008)
2. Ding, X.C.D., Smith, S.L., Belta, C., Rus, D.: LTL control in uncertain environments with probabilistic satisfaction guarantees. IFAC Proc. Vol. **44**(1), 3515–3520 (2011)
3. Dinh, H.T., Cruz Torres, M.H., Holvoet, T.: Sound and complete reactive UAV behavior using constraint programming (2017). https://lirias.kuleuven.be/retrieve/470086
4. Fainekos, G.E., Kress-Gazit, H., Pappas, G.J.: Temporal logic motion planning for mobile robots. In: Proceedings of the 2005 IEEE International Conference on Robotics and Automation, pp. 2020–2025. IEEE (2005)
5. Luo, X., Zavlanos, M.M.: Temporal logic task allocation in heterogeneous multirobot systems. IEEE Trans. Rob. **38**(6), 3602–3621 (2022). https://doi.org/10.1109/tro.2022.3181948
6. Tumova, J., Castro, L.I.R., Karaman, S., Frazzoli, E., Rus, D.: Minimum-violation LTL planning with conflicting specifications. In: 2013 American Control Conference, pp. 200–205. IEEE (2013).https://doi.org/10.1109/acc.2013.6579837
7. Tumova, J., Karaman, S., Belta, C., Rus, D.: Least-violating planning in road networks from temporal logic specifications. In: 2016 ACM/IEEE 7th International Conference on Cyber-Physical Systems (ICCPS), pp. 1–9. IEEE (2016https://doi.org/10.1109/iccps.2016.7479106
8. Vermaelen, J., Holvoet, T.: Tumato 2.0-a constraint-based planning approach for safe and robust robot behavior. Ann. Math. Artif. Intell. 1–27 (2024https://doi.org/10.1007/s10472-024-09949-3
9. Vermaelen, J., Holvoet, T.: An empirical evaluation of a formal approach versus ad hoc implementations in robot behavior planning. Sci. Comput. Programm. **241**, 103226 (2025). https://doi.org/10.1016/j.scico.2024.103226
10. Wang, Y., Nalluri, S., Pajic, M.: Hyperproperties for robotics: planning via HyperLTL. In: 2020 IEEE International Conference on Robotics and Automation (ICRA), pp. 8462–8468. IEEE (2020https://doi.org/10.1109/icra40945.2020.9196874
11. Xu, N., Li, J., Niu, Y., Shen, L.: An LTL-based motion and action dynamic planning method for autonomous robot. IFAC-PapersOnLine **49**(5), 91–96 (2016)

MEDiTATe: a First Step of a Journey from BDI to Neuroscience, and Back

Angelo Ferrando[1], Andrea Gatti[2], and Viviana Mascardi[2]([✉])

[1] University of Modena-Reggio Emilia, Modena, Italy
angelo.ferrando@unimore.it
[2] University of Genova, Genoa, Italy
andrea.gatti@edu.unige.it, viviana.mascardi@unige.it

Abstract. The connections between neuroscience findings and Artificial Intelligence (AI) are very strong, but literature that analyzes how neuroscience inspired AI, and viceversa, mainly takes a machine learning point of view. However, intelligent software agents modeled after the Belief-Desire-Intention (BDI) architecture have many ties with neuroscience. Some are explicitly expressed, others are less evident and deserve to be better addressed and understood. In order to explore such ties and make their hidden potential exploitable, we introduce the BDI-inspired MEDiTATe conceptual framework encompassing theory of **M**ind, **E**motions, **D**eep **TA**lk, and small **T**alk.

MEDiTATe is intended as a principled means to analyze the connections between neuroscience and BDI approaches in a systematic way, and to interact with neuro-scientists by sharing a common terminological ground. The main contribution of this paper is indeed to survey the relevant scientific literature and organize the findings of this review coherently with the MEDiTATe vision.

Nonetheless, most modules of MEDiTATe have been, or may be, implemented using a well known toolkit for BDI agents, Jason. In this sense, the possibility to move MEDiTATe from the conceptual level to the practical one is backed up by existing software tools. Targeting Jason and its JaCaMo extension only is a limitation of the current MEDiTATe approach, but it is the limitation that makes a shift from theory to practice feasible.

MEDiTATe features *small talk* and *deep talk* that we conjecture to be related but distinct cognitive functions, each with its own purpose and possibly dedicated different brain areas. We expect that MEDiTATe – once fully developed in a practical Jason-based toolkit – may support the study of these functions and of their relations with other, better understood, cognitive processes, possibly inspiring experiments by neuro-scientists to validate the hypothesis.

In fact, in our long-term vision, MEDiTATe should offer to computer scientists and neuro-scientists a shared gym for experimenting models and theories of brain functioning.

Keywords: MEDiTATe, Deep Talk, Small Talk, Neuroscience, Mind, Emotions, Beliefs-Desires-Intentions, BDI, Cognitive Agents, Jason

S. Rodriguez et al. (Eds.): EMAS 2025, LNAI 16407, pp. 117–140, 2026.
https://doi.org/10.1007/978-3-032-18011-7_8

1   Introduction

Since its conception in the mid-1950, Artificial Intelligence (AI) – envisioned by John McCarthy as *the science and engineering of making intelligent machines* – was interconnect with sciences studying human intelligence from a biological, functional, medical, and psychological perspective.

Even before the term AI was born, the studies carried out by McCulloch and Pitts on artificial neural networks were directly rooted in neuroscience [77], and Reinforcement Learning is inspired by animal learning psychology, which states that responses followed by rewarding outcomes are more likely to be repeated [112].

These examples show that, often, computer science and AI rely on discoveries by psychologists and neuroscientists. Some times, however, computer science and AI anticipate discoveries made later on. One example is the idea that memory might consist of a fast access, short term component, and a slower access, long term one. The cache computer memory, implementing this idea, was first developed by Wilkes in 1965 [121], but systematic and coherent models of short term and long term human memory appeared only later, as discussed by Squire [110] and Baddeley [7].

Interestingly, in some cases AI systems show unanticipated similarities with human cognitive functions, suggesting that the exploration of how the AI system works might lead to a better understanding of how the brain works. As an example, in a very recent work co-authored by the Director of the Center of Computational Brain Science at Brown University [115], the open question of how Transformer models solve tasks that appear to require complex cognitive branching is addressed. The authors conclude that *finding connections between emergent behavior of Transformer models and human working memory serves to benefit both computational cognitive neuroscience and AI.*

Moving to one of the most disruptive technological advancements we are witnessing, Large Language Models (LLMs), being based on statistical prediction and leaving room to hallucination, they turn out to be aligned with findings in neuroscience too [48,107]: mechanisms underlying LLMs might indeed allow neuroscientists in better understanding mechanisms underlying cognition.

Exploring the connections between neuroscience and AI is hence extremely relevant for both communities, and some reviews analyze how neuroscience inspired AI, and viceversa [57,64]. Unfortunately – but not surprisingly – they mainly assume that artificial intelligence is machine learning. To make an example, Gopinath [54] states that "AI can be broken down into two subsets, machine learning and deep learning", and Onciul et al. [84] assert the same when they write that the "two fundamental pillars of AI are ML and DL". This perspective is the only one that scholars and scientists may find online.

In this review paper we complement those works via a principled discussion of the connections between neuroscience findings and intelligent software agents modeled after the Belief-Desire-Intention (BDI) architecture [94]. We limit our investigation to theory of mind, emotions and language, and we envision MEDi-

TATe (theory of **M**ind, **E**motions, **D**eep **TA**lk, and small **T**alk) that is rooted on the BDI architecture and provides a conceptual framework for our investigation.

Two innovative elements characterize this paper.

On the neuroscience side, we consider *small talk* and *deep talk* as two distinct cognitive functions, pursuing different goals. While this is based on psychological studies [6,66,80,105], we formulate the hypothesis that – in the same way as different parts of the brain are involved in fast and slow thinking [35], in short and long term memory, etc. – the brain's areas specifically devoted to small talk and deep talk are different, and this is reflected in the MEDiTATe framework.

On the Engineering Multiagent Systems side, we envision that being based in solid scientific studies from both computer science and neurosciences, MEDiTATe may represent the first step towards the development of an effective playground for experimenting not only sophisticated models of cognitive software agents and of their communication mechanisms, but also theories on the brain functioning.

The MEDiTATe vision is grounded in recent scientific literature and has a practical flavor: working prototypes of most of its components have been – or might be – implemented in Jason [15], one very popular implementation of the AgentSpeak(L) language [93] for programming BDI agents. To this aim, we reference literature in the BDI field describing such prototypes or – at least – their design. The big, open challenge – whose solution goes far beyond the purpose of this research – is how to integrate them.

The paper is organized in the following way: we provide some background information on the BDI architecture and on Jason in Sect. 2; Sects. 3 and 4 analyze the BDI $\rightarrow$ neuroscience and neuroscience $\rightarrow$ BDI influences, respectively. To deepen the discussion on deep and small talk, Sect. 5 presents ChatBDI, an implemented tool integrating LLMs, used as "communication sensors and actuators", in Jason; once integrated and extended, ChatBDI may represent a concrete step toward the MEDiTATe implementation. Finally, Sect. 6 concludes and outlines some future directions for our work.

2   Background

2.1   The BDI Architecture

Figure 1 sketches the BDI architecture, taking the Jason interpreter of the AgentSpeak(L) language, detailed below, as a reference model for the BDI functioning. Agents are equipped with beliefs, desires (goals in the picture), intentions, plans. Beliefs are symbolic representations of what the agent knows. Goals are symbolic representations of the states of the world that the agents want to achieve. Plans are not generated at runtime, but they are associated with the agent at design time (although – when a sophisticated behavior is needed – agents can exchange plans and can autonomously add new plans to their own plan library). They represent recipes that agents may adopt to try to achieve their goals. Intentions are partially instantiated plans. They are data structures used at runtime, that usually developers do not need to be aware of and to access (again, unless they want to implement sophisticated meta-behaviors).

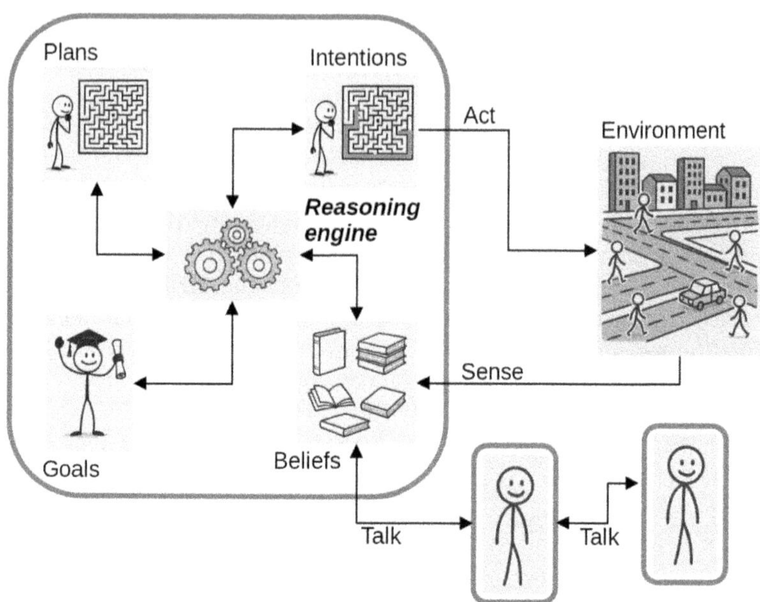

Fig. 1. BDI architecture.

Agents sense the environment via sensors: the sensed events are turned into a symbolic form, and enter the belief base of the agent possibly triggering the execution of plans. On the other way round, agents act on the environment. Actions belong to the plans' body. When a plan is selected for execution and becomes an intention, actions in its body are executed[1].

Finally, agents may communicate with each other. Assuming communication based on the Knowledge Query and Manipulation Language, KQML [46,68,117], depending on the KQML performative (the communicative act type) new beliefs, new goals, or new plans may be "planted" inside the receiver's brain. In Fig. 1 arrows labeled with *Talk* model *Tell* performatives that allow the sender agent to add a new belief in the belief base of the receiver. *Achieve* performatives generate a new goal in the receiver's goal base, while *TellHow* adds a new plan. Other KQML performatives exist, for querying the receiver's belief base.

A reasoning engine, also named BDI interpreter, is in charge for properly connecting all the BDI components. For example, when the agent acquires a

---

[1] Designing the transformation from real events in the environment to their symbolic representation, and from actions in the plan's body into real actions in the environment falls outside the purpose of the BDI architecture. Jason, as an example, represents the environment as a Java class and implements a bidirectional mechanism for sensing and acting. Also the way plans are selected and intentions progress in their execution, is more complex than how sketched above, and duly described by the AgentSpeak(L) operational semantics [117].

new goal, looking for the right plans to cope with that goal and selecting one for execution is up to the reasoning engine.

2.2   AgentSpeak(L), Jason and JaCaMo

AgentSpeak(L) [93] is an agent programming language based on a restricted first order logics with events and actions. Jason [15] is an interpreter for an extended version of AgentSpeak(L), and JaCaMo [14] integrates Jason with artifacts [96], useful for interacting with the environment.

To gently introduce Jason, we use the `auction` example available from the Jason web site[2].

The agent named `ag3` has various beliefs, among which `ally(ag2).` and plans, among which *Plan1*:

```
+auction(N)[source(S)]
    :   .my_name(I) & not winner(I) &
        ally(A) & not alliance(I,A)
    <- !alliance(A); !bid_normally(S,N).
```

Listing 1.1. *Plan1* in Jason.

`+auction(N)[source(S)]` is the *triggering event* of this plan: its syntax (+B) means that the plan can be used when a new belief (+) unifying with B (in this case with `auction(N)` with `source(S)`) enters the agents' belief base. The plan is applicable if its *plan context*, `.my_name(I) & not winner(I) & ally(A) & not alliance(I,A)`, is a logical consequence of the current belief base. In the plan's context, `&` is the logical conjunction, `.my_name(I)` is a call to an internal action (we understand this by the `.` before the function's name), `not` implements negation as failure, the other components are beliefs that the agent might have since the beginning, like `ally(ag2)`, or might have acquired at runtime via communication, perception, or internal generation of new beliefs. The *body* consists of two *achievement goals*, `!alliance(A)` and `!bid_normally(S,N)`, as suggested by the `!` before the predicate symbols. The semicolon represents sequence of actions/goals in the plan body.

In order to achieve an achievement goal *!G*, a plan with triggering event *+!G* is needed. In this example, *Plan2* below can be used to achieve `!alliance(ag2)` (we have propagated the unification A←ag2 created in the plan context of *Plan1*, to the body).

```
+!alliance(R) : true <- .send(R,tell,alliance).
```

Listing 1.2. *Plan2* in Jason.

The only action in the body of *Plan2* is `.send`. It takes the receiver R (`ag2` in the example, where we assume that free variables have been associated with ground terms via unification), the illocutionary force, or performative (`tell`), and the content (`alliance`) as its arguments , and adds the content to the receiver's beliefs, with a `+` in front of it (`+alliance`) to mean "addition".

---

3   From BDI to Neuroscience

The work by Georgeff and Rao on BDI agents was inspired by the philosophical studies on intentionality by Brentano [20], Dennet [39], Bratman [19]. To the best of our knowledge, they did not explicitly take neuroscience findings into account. Nevertheless, generation and management of Beliefs, Desires, Goals, Intentions, Plans, namely of the key components of the BDI architecture, are necessarily brain functionalities, and we now know that they are supported by specific areas in the brain.

In this section we make the connection between Beliefs, Desires, Goals, Intentions, Plans and brain functionalities explicit: for each of them we discuss what it serves for (its *function*), the ***major anatomical structures involved*** in the brain, according to recent literature and accurate brain maps[3], and one ***feasible implementation in Jason***. The Theory of Mind, Emotions, Deep and Small Talk components are presented in Sect. 4, following the same schema.

3.1   Beliefs

Although the most immediate counterpart of Beliefs is memory, memory also involves unconscious procedural information which has no "twin" in the BDI architecture. Budson and Price's [21] provide a clear introduction to human memory by classifying memory systems in explicit (associated with conscious awareness) and declarative (that can be consciously recalled), versus implicit (associated with change in behavior) and nondeclarative (unconscious). They also present four different kinds of memory: episodic, semantic, procedural, and working.

Episodic Memory

Function: Episodic memory refers to the explicit and declarative memory system used to recall personal experiences framed in our own context.

Major Anatomical Structures Involved: Prefrontal cortex, medial temporal lobes, anterior thalamic nucleus, mammillary body, fornix.

Feasible Implementation in Jason: Beliefs with `personal, long-term` annotation.

Semantic Memory

Function: Semantic memory refers to our general store of conceptual and factual knowledge not related to any specific memory. It is a declarative and explicit memory system.

---

[3] See for example https://dana.org/resources/neuroanatomy-the-basics/.

Major Anatomical Structures Involved: Temporal lobes.

Feasible Implementation in Jason: Beliefs with `factual, long-term` annotation.

Procedural Memory

Function: Procedural memory refers to the ability to learn behavioral and cognitive skills and algorithms that are used at an automatic, unconscious level. Procedural memory is nondeclarative but during acquisition may be either explicit or implicit.

Major anatomical structures involved: Basal ganglia, cerebellum, supplementary motor area.

Feasible Implementation in Jason: No explicit and direct BDI twin exists for procedural memory, as the BDI architecture does not integrate "cognitive skills used in an automatic way". However, Jason internal actions may represent a feasible way for the agent to run an algorithm "without thinking about it", so in an "unconscious", "automatic" way. Jason internal actions are implemented in Java and support is given, e.g., for binding of logical variables. This paves the way to model (simulated, but also real, in principle) actions like "driving in a known road with light traffic", a typical example of skill that becomes a "think fast" ability, albeit initially requiring to "think slow". What cannot be easily supported by Jason, w.r.t. human procedural memory, is the ability to learn such internal actions, and to move them from System 2 (deliberative, slow) to System 1 (unconscious, fast) [35]. While we are not aware of proposals dealing with this specific capability in the BDI literature, Ramirez and Fasli [74] describe a plan acquisition strategy addressing the cases of learning plans composed of one action, sequences or a repetition of actions that allow an agent to improve its behavior at run-time, and Ciatto et al. [29] generate BDI plans using LLMs, when no plan is available for achieving the current goal.

Working Memory

Function: Working memory is an explicit and declarative memory system combining the fields of attention, concentration, and short-term memory. It refers to the ability to temporarily maintain and manipulate information that one needs to keep in mind.

Major Anatomical Structures Involved: Prefrontal cortex, Broca's area, Wernicke's area (limited to phonologic working memory).

Feasible Implementation in Jason: Beliefs with `short-term` annotation instead of `long-term` one.

Desires and Goals

Function: Pleasure serves to motivate individuals to pursue rewards necessary for fitness, and rewards involve a composite of several psychological components: liking (core reactions to hedonic impact), wanting (motivation process of incentive salience), and learning (Pavlovian or instrumental associations and cognitive representations) [13]. Intuitively, goals are usually states we want but have difficulty achieving even when we know they are achievable. Discriminating between desires and goals in neurobiology is difficult, as desires may be seen as one of the two goals' dimensions, *the will*, with the other dimension being *the way* [12].

Major Anatomical Structures Involved: Prefrontal cortex [10,79,97].

Feasible Implementation in Jason: The support that Jason offers to representing goals and to managing them during the agent's reasoning cycle directly comes from the AgentSpeak(L) operational semantics, and is described in the Jason related resources.

As far as liking is concerned, besides ad-hoc beliefs that model what agents like and dislike, or annotations to beliefs, there is no directly supported counterpart in Jason. We may consider preferences associated with goals, along the lines of [25–27].

When learning comes into play, we may mention the recent proposals to integrate Reinforcement Learning (RL) in Jason [8,9,16,86,91,119]. While the idea of injecting some RL into BDI agents dates back to the beginning of the millennium [2,71–73,83,92,113], implementations in Jason became available only recently.

3.2   Intentions and Plans

Function: Intentions operate at the interface of thought and action, translating cognitive states into detailed motor coordination. Jahanshahi [62] and Brass and Haggard [18] suggests that intentions consist of a "what to do" component, a decision "when to act", and an inhibitory process (a "whether" element in Brass and Haggard model). Apparently, plans should be easier to characterize than intentions. Their behavioral and psychological intuition is clear, and their computational counterpart is even clearer: a plan is a sequence of actions, and planning is a process that considers actions and their sequential interdependence in terms of the desirability of their outcomes. However, planning *remains one of the most elusive cognitive processes at the neural level* [76].

Major Anatomical Structures Involved: Prefrontal cortex.

Feasible Implementation in Jason: Jason agents – coherently with AgentSpeak(L) – consist of a belief set and a plan set; when relevant (namely, triggered by the current event selected by the *event selection function*) and applicable (namely, characterized by a context that is a logical consequence of the current beliefs) plans are selected for execution, they become intentions. Intentions are data structures used at runtime by the Jason interpreter, and correspond to stacks of partially instantiated plans.

While structures named plans and intentions are already integrated in Jason, no dynamic, first-principles planning is supported by design. However, both old [38,109,118] and recent [78,123] proposals for extending the basic BDI model with dynamic planning exist. Some of them target Jason or its JaCaMo extension [14] as their implementation framework [23].

4   From Neuroscience to MEDiTATe

In this section, we focus on the "from neuroscience to MEDiTATe" direction by looking at brain science outcomes that do not fit the original BDI architecture, but that might be integrated into its MEDiTATe extension. The MEDiTATe components, as well as a rough sketch of the input, output, and working interpreter, are shown in Fig. 2, while the functional brain map is shown in Fig. 3. For all the MEDiTATe components we highlighted their cognitive function (top, in bold), the brain areas involved, and feasible implementations in Jason, if available.

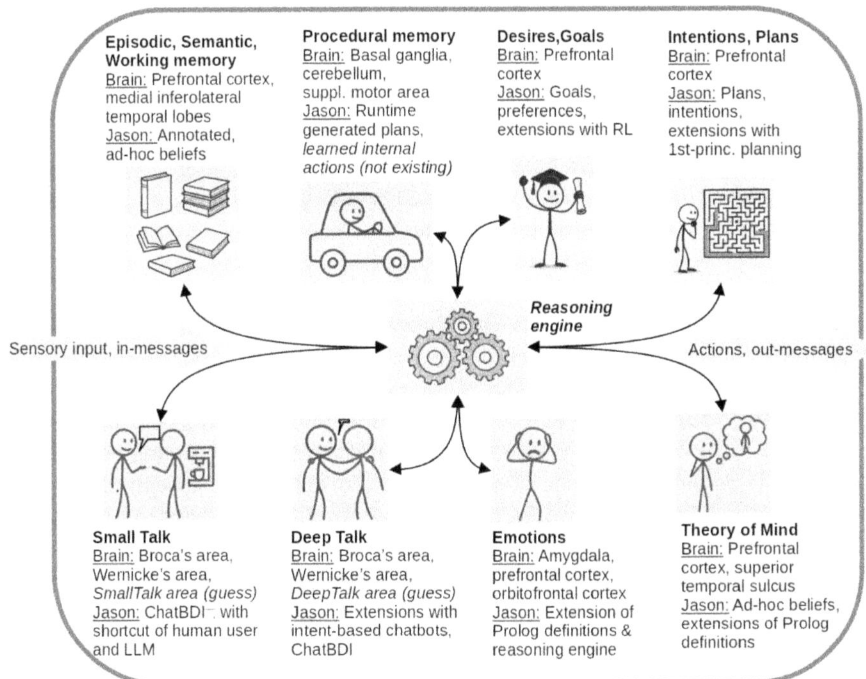

Fig. 2. MEDiTATe framework.

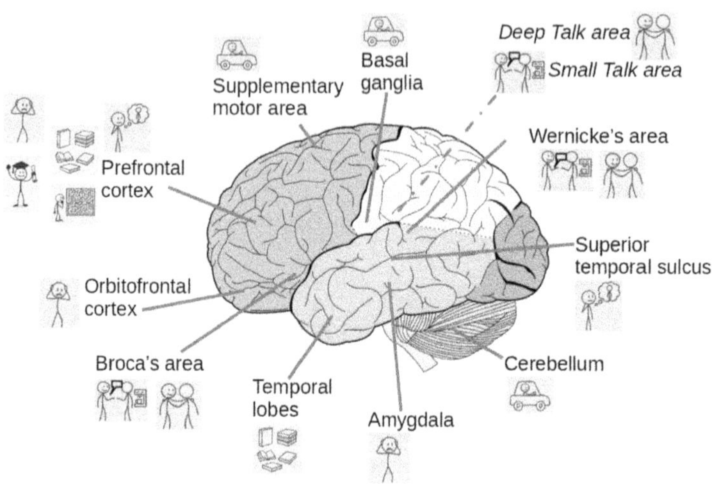

Fig. 3. Functional brain map.

Following the MEDiTATe acronym we start with Theory of **M**ind; we move then to **E**motions, and we conclude with **D**eep **TA**lk, and small **T**alk.

4.1   Theory of Mind

Function: Theory of Mind (ToM) is the ability to reason about mental states, such as beliefs, desires, and intentions, in order to explain and predict people's behavior [4], and to plan how to behave in social situations [58][4]. Neuroimaging findings suggest that there are several core regions in the brain, including parts of the prefrontal cortex and superior temporal sulcus, that contribute to ToM reasoning [24].

Major Anatomical Structures Involved: Prefrontal cortex, superior temporal sulcus.

Feasible implementation in Jason: The idea that autonomous agents and robots need a ToM to engage into social interactions with humans and among themselves is as old as the idea of agent itself [36,37], and it is still objective of active research [108]. Many works explore how intelligent agents may exhibit a ToM [98] and the BDI architecture is a very natural framework for this investigation [17,56]. Various proofs of concept have been developed in Jason or JaCaMo [22,34,81,85,104,106,124], often by annotating extensional beliefs or exploiting the Prolog intensional definition of beliefs with abduction and other ToM-related

---

[4] Whether ToM is unique to our species was, and still is, a challenging and exciting open question [67,89]. Given that artificial intelligences do not belong to our species, this debated question applies to them as well.

rules. This suggests that an implementation (or better, an approximation) of ToM in Jason is feasible.

4.2   Emotions

Function: Emotions play a myriad of roles at intrapersonal, interpersonal, and social and cultural levels [59,99]. At the intrapersonal level, they prepare us for behavior with minimal thinking [32] and associate memories with the emotions experienced at those times the facts occurred, allowing us to create "emotional connections" among disparate facts [120]. At the interpersonal level, they send non verbal signals to others and influence others and our social interactions [41]. Finally, the development and transmission of attitudes, values, beliefs, and norms related to emotions, is part of cultural transmission and operates then at the cultural level [75]. The brain areas devoted to managing emotions have been studied for more than thirty years [69,70,99], with the amygdala playing a major role in processing emotions and linking them to memories, learning, and sensing, and – due to the complexity of emotions and of their relation with cognitive processes – with many other central and peripheral areas involved.

Major Anatomical Structures Involved: Amygdala, prefrontal cortex, orbitofrontal cortex.

Feasible Implementation in Jason: Various extensions of the BDI architecture and of its underpinning formal model have been proposed over the last years, aimed at integrating emotions [5,87,90,111]. Sánchez and Cerezo's survey is a good starting point for overviewing the literature on the topic [102]. Not surprisingly, Jason is often used as a handy and flexible tool to experiment with BDI emotional agents [3,28,114].

4.3   Deep and Small Talk

In this section we put forward the most visionary and unexplored component of MEDiTATe, namely the one related with language, and we differentiate between talking deep, and talking small. We keep the distinction because it is very relevant from a computational point of view although – to the best of our knowledge – no neurological studies have been specifically performed on localization of these two functions.

According to the Cambridge Dictionary, *small talk* is a conversation about things that are not important, often between people who do not know each other well[5]. This is often used in contrasts with *deep talk,* meaning a conversation involving increasingly greater self-disclosure[6].

---

[5] https://dictionary.cambridge.org/dictionary/english/small-talk.
[6] https://www.linkedin.com/pulse/why-deep-meaningful-conversations-important-ray-williams-mpjbc/.

The language area involved in turning thoughts into words is Broca's area, while Wernicke's areas is involved in language understanding and processing. The angular gyrus processes concrete and abstract concepts and plays a role in verbal working memory during retrieval of verbal information. While not all the scientists agree on the localization of language functions [116], the Broca-Wernicke's theory still holds a dominant position in neurosciences [101].

Talk Deep

Function: While it is not always possible to engage into deep, intimate and self-disclosing talk, recent experimental studies show that people feel more connected to deep conversation partners than shallow conversation partners [66,80]. Deep talk may strengthen social connections, besides leaving lasting memories [31].

Major Anatomical Structure Involved. Not explored; we name it "TalkDeep area".

Feasible Implementation in Jason: The literature on BDI implementations of conversational agents and dialogue systems is almost rich [40,60,82,122], but just a few recent papers use Jason as implementation language. In a set of papers published between 2021 and 2023 [42–45], Engelmann et al. present Dial4JaCa. Dial4JaCa integrates JaCaMo and Dialogflow [53], an intent-based chatbot platform developed by Google. VEsNA [49,50] originally exploited Dial4JaCa to bridge a human user speaking in natural language, and a Virtual Reality (VR) environment. These works exploit a chatbot platform driven by the recognition of "intents" of the user, and keep the control of the conversation on the Jason side: "what to say, why, and when" is hence the result of a Jason-driven rational process based on the users intentions, that we associate with deep thinking. ChatBDI [51,52] provides an integration of BDI agents and LLMs that supports deep talk in its default implemented setting, where sentences by the human user are sent to agents for reasoning, and answers are sent to LLMs for being properly expressed in natural language. The work by Frering et al. [47] is similar to ChatBDI, but lacks its generality.

Talk Small

Function: Experiments from psychologists, sociologists and neuroscientists show that small talk with "weak ties" generates well-being [6,103,105].

Major Anatomical Structure Involved. Not explored; we name it "TalkSmall area".

Feasible Implementation in Jason: In the Generative AI and Large Language Models era, our vision of talking small is "talking as an LLM would talk". While this does not mean that an interaction with an LLM always looks like being shallow, or "chit-chat", LLMs are not reasoners [65], and are not even speakers because they lack goals and intentions [55,88,100]. We claim that not being intention-driven speakers prevents LLMs from talking deep. Still, they generate very fluent and believable sentences, making them suitable for talking small. Hence, a feasible Jason implementation of small talk might integrate LLM-based generation of sentences as actions that agents may perform without needing to "reason on what to say" and, most importantly, without needing to recall the contents and the context of the conversation. A restricted version of ChatBDI, let us name it ChatBDI$^-$, may serve this purpose, as discussed in Sect. 5. Besides ChatBDI, in [61], Ichida et al. exploit LLMs and reinforcement learning to bootstrap the reasoning capabilities of NatBDI agents, which is not what we need. In [95], Ricci et al. envision generative BDI architectures, namely architectures based on the BDI model integrating generative AI technologies, but no implemented integration in Jason is available.

5   MEDiTATe on a Jason-Based Framework

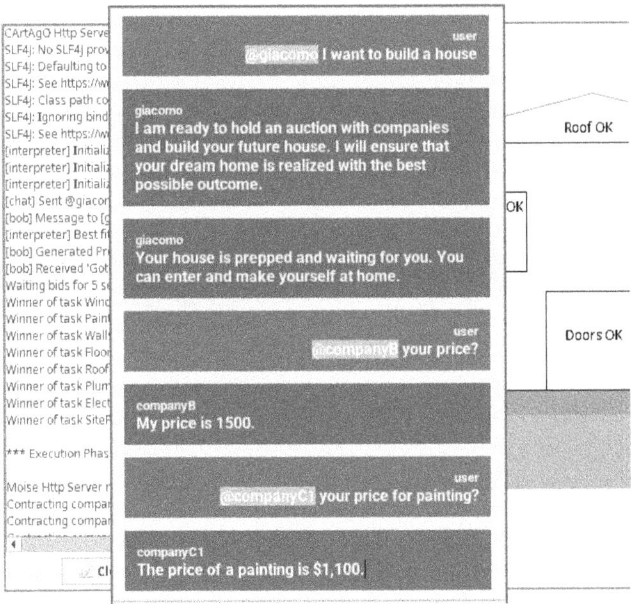

Fig. 4. Chattification of a JaCaMo MAS via ChatBDI, from [51].

One first practical step towards implementing the MEDiTATe vision is represented by ChatBDI[7] and by PlanchBDI [1], an envisioned integration between ChatBDI and Ciatto et al.'s dynamic plan generation [29].

---

[7] https://github.com/VEsNA-ToolKit/chatbdi, accessed on February 9, 2026.

ChatBDI allows the human user to enter the conversation in a Jason or JaCaMo MAS, that may also be a legacy one. In fact, ChatBDI requires no changes to the agents' source code to "chattify" them.

Through the graphical ChatBDI chat interface shown in Fig. 4, each message exchanged among agents can be visualized by the user after being converted into its natural language representation. The user, in turn, can send natural language messages either as broadcasts or to specific recipients by prefixing the agent's name with the @ symbol. These user-generated messages are then translated into KQML so that the agents can correctly interpret and process them.

More specifically, ChatBDI features:

(i)   a graphical, chat-style interface that facilitates user interaction;
(ii) a *kqml2nl* function, which translates agent-generated KQML messages into natural language for user comprehension;
(iii) an *nl2kqml* function, which converts user inputs from natural language into KQML for agent understanding; and
(iv) the ChatBDI interpreter that mediates communication between natural language and KQML representations.

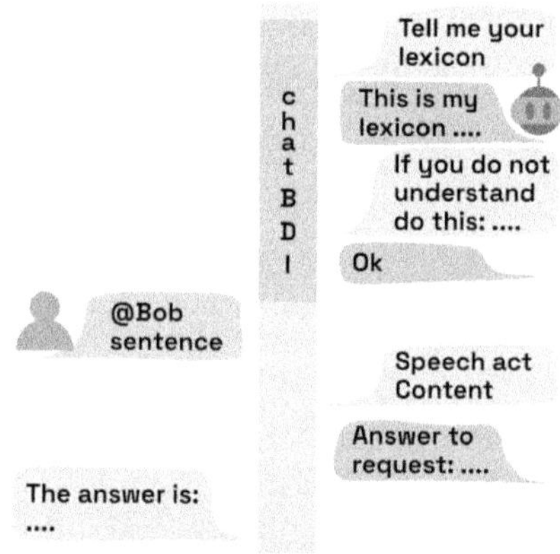

Fig. 5. Information flow in ChatBDI: messages are in natural language in the left-hand side, and in the KQML Agent Communication Language (ACL) in the right-hand side, from [52].

Humans naturally adapt their language to their interlocutors by adjusting both lexical choices and stylistic features [11,30]. Similarly, ChatBDI incorporates an adaptation mechanism, as illustrated in Fig. 5. Specifically, ChatBDI instructs the agents within the MAS on how to interact with humans and subsequently functions as an intermediary between the human and the agents, facilitating mutual understanding.

The task of *teaching* agents in the MAS exploits the *meta-programming capabilities* provided by Jason, which enable one agent to instruct another agent

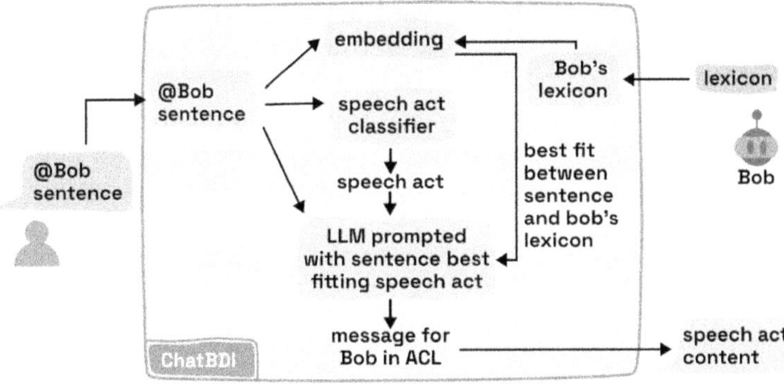

Fig. 6. Exploitation of embeddings in ChatBDI, to adapt to the agent's lexicon, from [52].

on "how to perform specific tasks". The process of identifying the lexicon element that best corresponds to a user's utterance is addressed through the use of *embeddings*, as depicted in Fig. 6. Both the lexicon-based translation from natural language to ACL and the reverse translation from ACL to natural language are performed through an *LLM*.

For the implementation of the *kqml2nl* function, we evaluated several Ollama models, as these are considerably more lightweight and sustainable than GPT. The model qwen2.5:7b[8] turned out to offer the best balance between being lightweight and having good accuracy.

The implementation of *nl2kqml* is also based on a well crafted prompt passed to qwen that was used after the embedding creation step carried out with all-minilm[9], for both speech act and content extraction.

The results of the experiments with *nl2kqml* are browsable in our Streamlit dashboard[10], showing that classifying the KQML intent (speech act) of a sentence is doable, but correctly generating its content is hard.

ChatBDI already implements the deep talk functionality, following the paradigm "think BDI, talk LLM". The reasoning stage performed in the BDI brain might be however bypassed, for a talk small conversation.

We might indeed suppress the delivery of user messages to the BDI brain, and only use the BDI infrastructure to interface users and LLMs, inside a MAS, leading to a ChatBDI⁻ implementation.

With minor extensions, however, ChatBDI could be used for a double purpose, switching between talking deep and talking small depending on the classification of the user's sentence as 'serious' or 'chit-chat'.

PlanchBDI – for "PLAN and CHat LLM, but (Still!) Think BDI" – will integrate automatic, on-demand plan generation via LLMs – as opposed to call-

---

[8] https://ollama.com/library/qwen.
[9] https://ollama.com/library/all-minilm.
[10] https://vesna-toolkit-chatbdi-testsdashboard-svwkjh.streamlit.app.

ing some first-principles planner – with ChatBDI, paving the way towards BDI agents that can invent plans for goals they do not know how to pursue, and can talk deep and small.

We are currently adding personality traits, mood and propensities to BDI agents and to plans, and we are designing and implementing automatic mechanisms to select plans and intentions driven by such emotional features.

6   Conclusions

Albeit just sketched, all the MEDiTATe modules shown in Fig. 2 are rooted on neuro-scientific or agent-oriented literature and are coherent with the most recent MAS meta-models, such as CATALINA [33]; however, the main challenge in implementing MEDiTATe is not in the implementation of its components, but *in fully understanding their connections* (on the neuro-scientific side) and *in seamlessly integrating them* (on the agent-oriented software engineering side). As the title of the paper says, this is a first step in the journey of bridging neuroscience outcomes and achievements in the BDI research field. A first – even small – step is always needed to start a journey and, to the best of our knowledge, no systematic analysis of the BDI and neuro-scientific literature had been carried out so far. While accommodating results from neuroscience into the MEDiTATe conceptual framework, we aimed at achieving two different goals: making the MEDiTATe vision more coherent, and looking for gaps in the neuro-scientific literature, where some implemented tools exist that have no counter-part in the brain. This is what happened with deep and small talk.

The most innovative element of MEDiTATe is indeed the distinction between deep and small talk. ChatBDI already supports the deep talk functionality, and extending it to support small talk seems a feasible extension, as well as adding mood and personality traits to cope with emotional notions. Ciatto et al.'s work supports a kind of procedural memory, and we are collaborating towards an integration of their work and ours: despite the many open challenges, some core functionalities are already available.

We hope that MEDiTATe may become a theoretical, methodological and practical framework where achievements from experts in different disciplines can find a natural positioning, because it may offer a more controllable, explainable, and transparent approach for testing their hypotheses than emerging in silico experimentation using deep learning-based encoding models [63].

Stickpersons in Figs. 1, 2, and 3 have been generated using GPT4-o, and a few sentences (less than 5%) were improved using ChatGPT. No other use of generative AI has been made to write this paper.

Acknowledgments. This work was partially supported by *ENGINES – ENGineering INtElligent Systems around intelligent agent technologies,* funded by the Italian MUR program PRIN 2022 under grant number 20229ZXBZM and *FAIR – Future Artificial Intelligence Research,* PNRR MUR Project PE0000013 funded by the European Union – NextGenerationEU, CUP J33C24000420007.

References

1. Aguzzi, G., Ciatto, G., Ferrando, A., Gatti, A., Mascardi, V.: LLMs as agents, LLMs at the service of agents, or agents at the service of LLMs? In: Preproceedings of the Agent Toolkits Community Session. Bucharest (2025). available at https://interactions.ics.unisg.ch/agent-toolkits-2025/papers/aguzzi-et-al.pdf
2. Airiau, S., Padgham, L., Sardiña, S., Sen, S.: Enhancing the adaptation of BDI agents using learning techniques. Int. J. Agent Technol. Syst. **1**(2), 1–18 (2009). https://doi.org/10.4018/JATS.2009040101
3. Alfonso, B., Vivancos, E., Botti, V.J.: Toward formal modeling of affective agents in a BDI architecture. ACM Trans. Internet Techn. **17**(1), 5:1–5:23 (2017)
4. Apperly, I.A.: What is "theory of mind"? concepts, cognitive processes and individual differences. Quart. J. Exper. Psychol. **65**(5), 825–839 (2012)
5. Argente, E., del Val Noguera, E., Pérez-García, D., Botti, V.J.: Normative emotional agents: a viewpoint paper. IEEE Trans. Affect. Comput. **13**(3), 1254–1273 (2022)
6. Ascigil, E., Gunaydin, G., Selcuk, E., Sandstrom, G.M., Aydin, E.: Minimal social interactions and life satisfaction: the role of greeting, thanking, and conversing. Social Psychol. Person. Sci. (2023). https://doi.org/10.1177/19485506231209793
7. Baddeley, A.: Working memory: theories, models, and controversies. Ann. Rev. Psychol. **63**, 1–29 (2012). https://doi.org/10.1146/annurev-psych-120710-100422
8. Badica, A., Badica, C., Ivanovic, M., Mitrovic, D.: An approach of temporal difference learning using agent-oriented programming. In: 20th International Conference on Control Systems and Computer Science, CSCS 2015, Bucharest, Romania, May 27-29, 2015, pp. 735–742. IEEE (2015). https://doi.org/10.1109/CSCS.2015.71
9. Badica, C., Becheru, A., Felton, S.: Integration of jason reinforcement learning agents into an interactive application. In: Jebelean, T., Negru, V., Petcu, D., Zaharie, D., Ida, T., Watt, S.M. (eds.) 19th International Symposium on Symbolic and Numeric Algorithms for Scientific Computing, SYNASC 2017, Timisoara, Romania, September 21-24, 2017, pp. 361–368. IEEE Computer Society (2017). https://doi.org/10.1109/SYNASC.2017.00065
10. Bechara, A., Damasio, A.R., Damasio, H., Anderson, S.W.: Insensitivity to future consequences following damage to human prefrontal cortex. Cognition **50**(1–3), 7–15 (1994)
11. Bell, A.: Language Style as Audience Design. In: Coupland, N., Jaworski, A. (eds.) Sociolinguistics. MLS, pp. 240–250. Macmillan Education UK, London (1997). https://doi.org/10.1007/978-1-349-25582-5_20
12. Berkman, E.T.: The neuroscience of goals and behavior change. Consult. Psychol. J.: Pract. Res. **70**(1), 28 (2018)
13. Berridge, K.C., Kringelbach, M.L.: Pleasure systems in the brain. Neuron **86**(3), 646–664 (2015). https://doi.org/10.1016/j.neuron.2015.02.018, https://pmc.ncbi.nlm.nih.gov/articles/PMC4425246/
14. Boissier, O., Bordini, R.H., Hübner, J.F., Ricci, A.: Multi-agent oriented programming: programming multi-agent systems using JaCaMo. MIT Press (2020)
15. Bordini, R.H., Hübner, J.F., Wooldridge, M.J.: Programming multi-agent systems in AgentSpeak using Jason. J. Wiley (2007)

16. Bosello, M., Ricci, A.: From programming agents to educating agents - A jason-based framework for integrating learning in the development of cognitive agents. In: Dennis, L.A., Bordini, R.H., Lespérance, Y. (eds.) Engineering Multi-Agent Systems - 7th International Workshop, EMAS 2019, Montreal, QC, Canada, May 13-14, 2019, Revised Selected Papers. Lecture Notes in Computer Science, vol. 12058, pp. 175–194. Springer (2019). https://doi.org/10.1007/978-3-030-51417-4_9

17. Bosse, T., Memon, Z.A., Treur, J.: A recursive BDI agent model for theory of mind and its applications. Appl. Artif. Intell. **25**(1), 1–44 (2011)

18. Brass, M., Haggard, P.: The what, when, whether model of intentional action. Neuroscientist **14**(4), 319–325 (2008). https://doi.org/10.1177/1073858408317417 pMID: 18660462

19. Bratman, M.: Intention, plans, and practical reason (1987)

20. Brentano, F.: Psychology From an Empirical Standpoint. Routledge (1874)

21. Budson, A.E., Price, B.H.: Memory dysfunction. N. Engl. J. Med. **352**(7), 692–699 (2005). https://doi.org/10.1056/NEJMra041071, https://www.nejm.org/doi/full/10.1056/NEJMra041071

22. Cantucci, F., Falcone, R.: A computational model for cognitive human-robot interaction: An approach based on theory of delegation. In: WOA. CEUR Workshop Proceedings, vol. 2404, pp. 127–133. CEUR-WS.org (2019)

23. Cardoso, R.C., Ferrando, A., Papacchini, F.: Automated planning and BDI agents: A case study. In: PAAMS. Lecture Notes in Computer Science, vol. 12946, pp. 52–63. Springer (2021)

24. Carrington, S.J., Bailey, A.J.: Are there theory of mind regions in the brain? a review of the neuroimaging literature. Hum. Brain Mapp. **30**(8), 2313–35 (2009). https://doi.org/10.1002/hbm.20671

25. Casali, A., Godo, L., Sierra, C.: Graded BDI models for agent architectures. In: CLIMA. Lecture Notes in Computer Science, vol. 3487, pp. 126–143. Springer (2004)

26. Casali, A., Godo, L., Sierra, C.: A graded BDI agent model to represent and reason about preferences. Artif. Intell. **175**(7–8), 1468–1478 (2011)

27. Casali, A., Godo, L., Sierra, C.: A language for the execution of graded BDI agents. Log. J. IGPL **21**(3), 332–354 (2013)

28. Chella, A., Lanza, F., Seidita, V.: Decision process in human-agent interaction: extending Jason reasoning cycle. In: EMAS@AAMAS. Lecture Notes in Computer Science, vol. 11375, pp. 320–339. Springer (2018)

29. Ciatto, G., Aguzzi, G., Battistini, R., Baiardi, M., Burattini, S., Ricci, A.: Exploiting GenAI for plan generation in BDI Agents. In: European Conference on Artificial Intelligence, ECAI 2025. Bologna (2025)

30. Clark, H.H., Murphy, G.L.: Audience design in meaning and reference. In: Le Ny, J.F., Kintsch, W. (eds.) Language and Comprehension, Advances in Psychology, vol. 9, pp. 287–299. North-Holland (1982). https://doi.org/10.1016/S0166-4115(09)60059-5

31. Cooney, G., Boothby, E.J., Lee, M.: The thought gap after conversation: Underestimating the frequency of others' thoughts about us. J. Exp. Psychol. Gen. **151**(5), 1069–1088 (2022). https://doi.org/10.1037/xge0001134

32. Cosmides, L., Tooby, J.: Evolutionary psychology and the emotions (2000)

33. Cossentino, M., Averna, G., Pilato, G., Mylopoulos, M., Mylopoulos, J.: The agent working cycle in CATALINA. In: WOA, pp. 1–6. CEUR-WS (2025)

34. Costantini, S., De Gasperis, G., Migliarini, P., Salutari, A.: Proposal of a empathic multi-agent robot design based on theory of mind. In: Proceedings of cAESAR (2020)
35. Daniel, K.: Thinking, Fast and Slow. Farrar, Straus and Giroux (2011)
36. Dautenhahn, K.: Getting to know each other - artificial social intelligence for autonomous robots. Robotics Auton. Syst. **16**(2–4), 333–356 (1995)
37. Dautenhahn, K.: Socially intelligent agents and the primate social brain - towards a science of social minds (1999). AAAI Technical Report FS-00-04
38. De Silva, L., Padgham, L.: Planning on demand in BDI systems. In: ICAPS, pp. 37–40 (2005)
39. Dennett, D.C.: The Intentional Stance. The MIT Press, Cambridge, MA (1987)
40. Dennis, L.A., Oren, N.: Explaining BDI agent behaviour through dialogue. Auton. Agents Multi Agent Syst. **36**(1), 29 (2022)
41. Elfenbein, H.A., Ambady, N.: On the universality and cultural specificity of emotion recognition: a meta-analysis. Psychol. Bull. **128**(2), 203 (2002)
42. Engelmann, D.C., Cezar, L.D., Panisson, A.R., Bordini, R.H.: A conversational agent to support hospital bed allocation. In: BRACIS (1). Lecture Notes in Computer Science, vol. 13073, pp. 3–17. Springer (2021)
43. Engelmann, D.C., et al.: Dial4jaca - A demonstration. In: PAAMS. Lecture Notes in Computer Science, vol. 12946, pp. 346–350. Springer (2021)
44. Engelmann, D.C., et al.: Dial4jaca - a communication interface between multi-agent systems and chatbots. In: PAAMS. Lecture Notes in Computer Science, vol. 12946, pp. 77–88. Springer (2021)
45. Engelmann, D.C., Panisson, A.R., Vieira, R., Hübner, J.F., Mascardi, V., Bordini, R.H.: MAIDS - A framework for the development of multi-agent intentional dialogue systems. In: AAMAS, pp. 1209–1217. ACM (2023)
46. Finin, T.W., Fritzson, R., McKay, D.P., McEntire, R.: KQML as an agent communication language. In: Proceedings of the Third International Conference on Information and Knowledge Management (CIKM'94), Gaithersburg, Maryland, USA, November 29 - December 2, 1994, pp. 456–463. ACM (1994). https://doi.org/10.1145/191246.191322
47. Frering, L., Steinbauer-Wagner, G., Holzinger, A.: Integrating belief-desire-intention agents with large language models for reliable human-robot interaction and explainable artificial intelligence. Eng. Appl. Artif. Intell. **141**, 109771 (2025)
48. Friston, K.: The free-energy principle: a unified brain theory? Nat. Rev. Neurosci. **11**(2), 127–138 (2010)
49. Gatti, A., Ferrando, A., Mascardi, V.: Integrating virtual reality, chatbots, and BDI agents: VEsNA goes fast! In: Collier, R., Mascardi, V., Ricci, A. (eds.) Agents and Multi-Agent Systems Development – Platforms, Toolkits, Technologies. Springer (2025)
50. Gatti, A., Mascardi, V.: Vesna, a framework for virtual environments via natural language agents and its application to factory automation. Robotics **12**(2), 46 (2023)
51. Gatti, A., Mascardi, V., Ferrando, A.: ChatBDI: Think BDI, Talk LLM. In: AAMAS. International Foundation for Autonomous Agents and Multiagent Systems / ACM (2025)
52. Gatti, A., Mascardi, V., Ferrando, A.: Let me talk to you! Natural language interaction between humans and BDI agents via ChatBDI. In: European Conference on Artificial Intelligence, ECAI 2025. Bologna (2025)
53. Google: Dialogflow (2017). https://cloud.google.com/dialogflow/. Accessed 23 Jan 2026 12:36:17

54. Gopinath, N.: Artificial intelligence and neuroscience: an update on fascinating relationships. Process Biochem. **125**, 113–120 (2023). https://doi.org/10.1016/j.procbio.2022.12.011, https://www.sciencedirect.com/science/article/pii/S1359511322004512

55. Gubelmann, R.: Large language models, agency, and why speech acts are beyond them (for now)-a kantian-cum-pragmatist case. Philos. Technol. **37**(1), 32 (2024)

56. Harbers, M., van den Bosch, K., Meyer, J.C.: Modeling agents with a theory of mind. In: IAT, pp. 217–224. IEEE Computer Society (2009)

57. Hassabis, D., Kumaran, D., Summerfield, C., Botvinick, M.: Neuroscience-inspired artificial intelligence. Neuron **95**(2), 245–258 (2017). https://doi.org/10.1016/j.neuron.2017.06.011, https://www.sciencedirect.com/science/article/pii/S0896627317305093

58. Ho, M.K., Saxe, R., Cushman, F.: Planning with theory of mind. trends Cogn. Sci. **26**(11), 959–971 (2022). https://doi.org/10.1016/j.tics.2022.08.003, https://www.sciencedirect.com/science/article/pii/S1364661322001851

59. Hwang, H., Matsumoto, D.: Functions of Emotions. Psychology, Noba textbook series (2018)

60. Ichida, A.Y., Meneguzzi, F.: Modeling a conversational agent using BDI framework. In: Hong, J., Lanperne, M., Park, J.W., Cerný, T., Shahriar, H. (eds.) Proceedings of the 38th ACM/SIGAPP Symposium on Applied Computing, SAC 2023, Tallinn, Estonia, March 27-31, 2023, pp. 856–863. ACM (2023). https://doi.org/10.1145/3555776.3577657

61. Ichida, A.Y., Meneguzzi, F., Cardoso, R.C.: BDI agents in natural language environments. In: AAMAS, pp. 880–888. International Foundation for Autonomous Agents and Multiagent Systems / ACM (2024)

62. Jahanshahi, M.: Willed action and its impairments. Cogn. Neuropsychol. **15**(6–8), 483–533 (1998)

63. Jain, S., Vo, V.A., Wehbe, L., Huth, A.G.: Computational language modeling and the promise of in silico experimentation. Neurobiol. Langu. **5**(1), 80–106 (04 2024). https://doi.org/10.1162/nol_a_00101

64. Jiao, L., et al.: Brain-inspired learning, perception, and cognition: a comprehensive review. IEEE Transactions on Neural Networks and Learning Systems, pp. 1–21 (2024). https://doi.org/10.1109/TNNLS.2024.3401711

65. Kambhampati, S.: Can Large Language Models reason and plan? Ann. N. Y. Acad. Sci. **1534**(1), 15–18 (2024). https://doi.org/10.1111/nyas.15125

66. Kardas, M., Kumar, A., Epley, N.: Overly shallow?: Miscalibrated expectations create a barrier to deeper conversation. J. Pers. Soc. Psychol. **122**(3), 367–398 (2022). https://doi.org/10.1037/pspa0000281, https://pubmed.ncbi.nlm.nih.gov/34591541/

67. Krupenye, C., Call, J.: Theory of mind in animals: Current and future directions. WIREs Cognit. Sci. **10**(6), e1503 (2019). https://doi.org/10.1002/wcs.1503, https://wires.onlinelibrary.wiley.com/doi/abs/10.1002/wcs.1503

68. Labrou, Y., Finin, T.W.: A semantics approach for KQML - A general purpose communication language for software agents. In: CIKM, pp. 447–455. ACM (1994)

69. Ledoux, J.E.: Cognitive-emotional interactions in the brain. Cogn. Emot. **3**(4), 267–289 (1989). https://doi.org/10.1080/02699938908412709

70. LeDoux, J.E.: The emotional brain: The mysterious underpinnings of emotional life. Simon and Schuster (1998)

71. Lee, S., Son, Y.J.: Dynamic learning in human decision behavior for evacuation scenarios under BDI framework. In: Proceedings of the 2009 INFORMS Simulation Society Research Workshop. INFORMS Simulation Society: Catonsville, MD, pp. 96–100 (2009)
72. Lokuge, P., Alahakoon, D.: Handling multiple events in hybrid BDI agents with reinforcement learning: a container application. In: Chen, C., Filipe, J., Seruca, I., Cordeiro, J. (eds.) ICEIS 2005, Proceedings of the Seventh International Conference on Enterprise Information Systems, Miami, USA, May 25-28, 2005, pp. 83–90 (2005)
73. Lokuge, P., Alahakoon, D.: Reinforcement learning in neuro BDI agents for achieving agent's intentions in vessel berthing applications. In: 19th International Conference on Advanced Information Networking and Applications (AINA 2005), 28-30 March 2005, Taipei, Taiwan, pp. 681–686. IEEE Computer Society (2005). https://doi.org/10.1109/AINA.2005.293
74. Luna-Ramírez, W.A., Fasli, M.: Plan acquisition in a BDI agent framework through intentional learning. In: Berndt, J.O., Petta, P., Unland, R. (eds.) Multiagent System Technologies - 15th German Conference, MATES 2017, Leipzig, Germany, August 23-26, 2017, Proceedings. Lecture Notes in Computer Science, vol. 10413, pp. 167–186. Springer (2017). https://doi.org/10.1007/978-3-319-64798-2_11
75. Matsumoto, D., Hwang, H.C.: Assessing cross-cultural competence: A review of available tests. J. Cross Cult. Psychol. **44**(6), 849–873 (2013)
76. Mattar, M.G., Lengyel, M.: Planning in the brain. Neuron **110**(6), 914–934 (2022). https://doi.org/10.1016/j.neuron.2021.12.018, https://www.sciencedirect.com/science/article/pii/S0896627321010357
77. McCulloch, W., Pitts, W.: A logical calculus of the ideas immanent to nervous activity. Bull. Math. Biophys. **5**(4), 115–133 (1943)
78. Meneguzzi, F., de Silva, L.: Planning in BDI agents: a survey of the integration of planning algorithms and agent reasoning. Knowl. Eng. Rev. **30**(1), 1–44 (2015)
79. Miller, E.K., Cohen, J.D.: An integrative theory of prefrontal cortex function. Annu. Rev. Neurosci. **24**(1), 167–202 (2001)
80. Molla, H., Smadi, S., Lyubomirsky, S., Li, T., de Wit, H.: Immediate and enduring effects of deep and shallow conversations on feelings of closeness in healthy adults (2022). https://doi.org/10.31234/osf.io/p62va
81. Montes, N., Luck, M., Osman, N., Rodrigues, O., Sierra, C.: Combining theory of mind and abductive reasoning in agent-oriented programming. Auton. Agents Multi Agent Syst. **37**(2), 36 (2023)
82. Mustapha, A., Ahmad, M.S., Ahmad, A.: Conversational agents as full-pledged BDI agents for ambient intelligence. In: ISAmI. Advances in Intelligent Systems and Computing, vol. 219, pp. 221–228. Springer (2013)
83. Norling, E.: Folk psychology for human modelling: Extending the BDI paradigm. In: 3rd International Joint Conference on Autonomous Agents and Multiagent Systems (AAMAS 2004), 19-23 August 2004, New York, NY, USA, pp. 202–209. IEEE Computer Society (2004). https://doi.org/10.1109/AAMAS.2004.10066, https://doi.ieeecomputersociety.org/10.1109/AAMAS.2004.10066
84. Onciul, R., et al.: Artificial intelligence and neuroscience: Transformative synergies in brain research and clinical applications. J. Clin. Med. **14**(2) (2025). https://doi.org/10.3390/jcm14020550
85. Panisson, A.R., Sarkadi, S., McBurney, P., Parsons, S., Bordini, R.H.: On the formal semantics of theory of mind in agent communication. In: AT. Lecture Notes in Computer Science, vol. 11327, pp. 18–32. Springer (2018)

86. Parmiggiani, M., Ferrando, A., Mascardi, V.: Together is better! Integrating BDI and RL agents for safe learning and effective collaboration. In: ICAART, p. 12. SCITEPRESS (2025)

87. Pereira, D., Oliveira, E., Moreira, N., Sarmento, L.: Towards an architecture for emotional BDI agents. In: 2005 portuguese conference on artificial intelligence. pp. 40–46 (2005). https://doi.org/10.1109/EPIA.2005.341262

88. Piwek, P.: Are conversational large language models speakers? In: Proceedings of the 28th Workshop on the Semantics and Pragmatics of Dialogue - Poster Abstracts (2024)

89. Premack, D., Woodruff, G.: Does the chimpanzee have a theory of mind? Behav. Brain Sci. 1(4), 515–526 (1978)

90. Puica, M.A., Florea, A.M.: Emotional belief-desire-intention agent model: previous work and proposed architecture. Int. J. Adv. Res. Artif. Intell. 2(2), 1–8 (2013)

91. Pulawski, S., Dam, H.K., Ghose, A.: Bdi-dojo: developing robust BDI agents in evolving adversarial environments. In: El-Araby, E., Kalogeraki, V., Pianini, D., Lassabe, F., Porter, B., Ghahremani, S., Nunes, I., Bakhouya, M., Tomforde, S. (eds.) IEEE International Conference on Autonomic Computing and Self-Organizing Systems, ACSOS 2021, Companion Volume, Washington, DC, USA, September 27 - Oct. 1, 2021, pp. 257–262. IEEE (2021). https://doi.org/10.1109/ACSOS-C52956.2021.00066

92. Qi, G., Bo-ying, W.: Study and application of reinforcement learning in cooperative strategy of the robot soccer based on BDI model. Int. J. Adv. Rob. Syst. 6(2), 15 (2009). https://doi.org/10.5772/6795

93. Rao, A.S.: AgentSpeak(L): BDI agents speak out in a logical computable language. In: 7th European Workshop on Modelling Autonomous Agents in a Multi-Agent World, Eindhoven, The Netherlands, January 22-25, 1996. Lecture Notes in Computer Science, vol. 1038, pp. 42–55. Springer (1996). https://doi.org/10.1007/BFb0031845

94. Rao, A.S., Georgeff, M.P.: BDI agents: from theory to practice. In: ICMAS, pp. 312–319. The MIT Press (1995)

95. Ricci, A., Mariani, S., Zambonelli, F., Burattini, S., Castelfranchi, C.: The cognitive hourglass: agent abstractions in the large models era. In: AAMAS, pp. 2706–2711. International Foundation for Autonomous Agents and Multiagent Systems / ACM (2024)

96. Ricci, A., Viroli, M., Omicini, A.: Programming MAS with artifacts. In: PROMAS. Lecture Notes in Computer Science, vol. 3862, pp. 206–221. Springer (2005)

97. Ridderinkhof, K.R., Ullsperger, M., Crone, E.A., Nieuwenhuis, S.: The role of the medial frontal cortex in cognitive control. Science 306(5695), 443–447 (2004)

98. Rocha, M., da Silva, H.H., Morales, A.S., Sarkadi, S., Panisson, A.R.: Applying theory of mind to multi-agent systems: a systematic review. In: BRACIS (1). LNCS, vol. 14195, pp. 367–381. Springer (2023)

99. Rolls, E.T.: On the brain and emotion. Behav. Brain Sci. 23(2), 219–228 (2000). https://doi.org/10.1017/S0140525X00512424

100. Rosen, Z.P., Dale, R.: LLMs don't "do things with words" but their lack of illocution can inform the study of human discourse. In: Proceedings of the 46th Annual Meeting of the Cognitive Science Society, pp. 2870–2876 (2024)

101. Rutten, G.J.: Chapter 2 - Broca-Wernicke theories: A historical perspective. In: Hillis, A.E., Fridriksson, J. (eds.) Aphasia, Handbook of Clinical Neurology, vol. 185, pp. 25–34. Elsevier (2022). https://doi.org/10.1016/B978-0-12-823384-9.00001-3, https://www.sciencedirect.com/science/article/pii/B9780128233849000013

102. Sánchez, Y., Cerezo, E.: Designing emotional BDI agents: good practices and open questions. Knowl. Eng. Rev. **34**, e26 (2019)

103. Sandstrom, G.M., Dunn, E.W.: Is efficiency overrated?: Minimal social interactions lead to belonging and positive affect. Social Psychol. Person. Sci. **5**(4), 437–442 (2014). https://doi.org/10.1177/1948550613502990

104. Sarkadi, S., Panisson, A.R., Bordini, R.H., McBurney, P., Parsons, S.: Towards an approach for modelling uncertain theory of mind in multi-agent systems. In: AT. Lecture Notes in Computer Science, vol. 11327, pp. 3–17. Springer (2018)

105. Schroeder, J., Lyons, D., Epley, N.: Hello, stranger? pleasant conversations are preceded by concerns about starting one. J. Exp. Psychol. Gen. **151**(5), 1141–1153 (2022). https://doi.org/10.1037/xge0001118

106. Seidita, V., Sabella, A.M.P., Lanza, F., Chella, A.: Agent talks about itself: an implementation using Jason. CArtAgO and speech acts. Intelligenza Artificiale **17**(1), 7–18 (2023)

107. Seth, A.: Being You: A New Science of Consciousness. Faber & Faber (2021)

108. Sgorbissa, A., Morocutti, L., D'Angelo, I., Recchiuto, C.T.: Machiavellian robots and their theory of mind. IEEE Trans. Affect. Comput. 1–18 (2024). https://doi.org/10.1109/TAFFC.2024.3494595

109. de Silva, L., Sardiña, S., Padgham, L.: First principles planning in BDI systems. In: AAMAS (2), pp. 1105–1112. IFAAMAS (2009)

110. Squire, L.R.: Memory systems of the brain: A brief history and current perspective. Neurobiol. Learn. Mem. **82**(3), 171–177 (2004). https://doi.org/10.1016/j.nlm.2004.06.005, https://www.sciencedirect.com/science/article/pii/S1074742704000735, multiple Memory Systems

111. Steunebrink, B.R., Dastani, M., Meyer, J.C.: A formal model of emotion triggers: an approach for BDI agents. Synth. **185**(Supplement-1), 83–129 (2012)

112. Sutton, R.S., Barto, A.G.: Reinforcement learning - an introduction. adaptive computation and machine learning, MIT Press (1998). https://www.worldcat.org/oclc/37293240

113. Tan, A., Ong, Y., Tapanuj, A.: A hybrid agent architecture integrating desire, intention and reinforcement learning. Expert Syst. Appl. **38**(7), 8477–8487 (2011). https://doi.org/10.1016/J.ESWA.2011.01.045

114. Taverner, J., Alfonso, B., Vivancos, E., Botti, V.J.: Integrating expectations into jason for appraisal in emotion modeling. In: IJCCI (ECTA), pp. 231–238. SciTePress (2016)

115. Traylor, A., Merullo, J., Frank, M.J., Pavlick, E.: Transformer mechanisms mimic frontostriatal gating operations when trained on human working memory tasks. CoRR **abs/2402.08211** (2024)

116. Tremblay, P., Dick, A.S.: Broca and Wernicke are dead, or moving past the classic model of language neurobiology. Brain Lang. **162**, 60–71 (2016) .https://doi.org/10.1016/j.bandl.2016.08.004, https://www.sciencedirect.com/science/article/pii/S0093934X16300475

117. Vieira, R., Moreira, Á.F., Wooldridge, M.J., Bordini, R.H.: On the formal semantics of speech-act based communication in an agent-oriented programming language. J. Artif. Intell. Res. **29**, 221–267 (2007). https://doi.org/10.1613/jair.2221, https://doi.org/10.1613/jair.2221

118. Walczak, A., Braubach, L., Pokahr, A., Lamersdorf, W.: Augmenting BDI agents with deliberative planning techniques. In: PROMAS. LNCS, vol. 4411, pp. 113–127. Springer (2006)
119. Wan, Q., Liu, W., Xu, L., Guo, J.: Extending the BDI model with q-learning in uncertain environment. In: Proceedings of the 2018 International Conference on Algorithms, Computing and Artificial Intelligence, ACAI 2018, Sanya, China, December 21-23, 2018, pp. 33:1–33:6. ACM (2018). https://doi.org/10.1145/3302425.3302432
120. Wang, Q., Ross, M.: Culture and memory. Handbook Cult. Psychol. **18**, 645–667 (2007)
121. Wilkes, M.V.: Slave memories and dynamic storage allocation. IEEE Trans. Electron. Comput. **14**(2), 270–271 (1965)
122. Wong, W., Cavedon, L., Thangarajah, J., Padgham, L.: Flexible conversation management using a BDI agent approach. In: Nakano, Y., Neff, M., Paiva, A., Walker, M. (eds.) IVA 2012. LNCS (LNAI), vol. 7502, pp. 464–470. Springer, Heidelberg (2012). https://doi.org/10.1007/978-3-642-33197-8_48
123. Xu, M., Bauters, K., McAreavey, K., Liu, W.: A formal approach to embedding first-principles planning in BDI agent systems. In: Ciucci, D., Pasi, G., Vantaggi, B. (eds.) SUM 2018. LNCS (LNAI), vol. 11142, pp. 333–347. Springer, Cham (2018). https://doi.org/10.1007/978-3-030-00461-3_23
124. Yan, E., Burattini, S., Hübner, J.F., Ricci, A.: Towards a multi-level explainability framework for engineering and understanding BDI agent systems. In: WOA. CEUR Workshop Proceedings, vol. 3579, pp. 216–231. CEUR-WS.org (2023)

Octo-Planner: On-Device Language Model for Planner-Action Agents

Wei Chen[1]([✉]) [iD], Zhiyuan Li[1] [iD], Zhen Guo[2] [iD], and Yikang Shen[3] [iD]

[1] Nexa AI and Stanford, cupertino, USA
`{alexchen,zack}@nexa.ai`
[2] MIT EECS, Cambridge, USA
`zguo0525@mit.edu`
[3] MIT-IBM Watson AI Lab, Cambridge, USA
`yikang.shen@ibm.com`
`https://www.nexa.ai, https://www.mit.edu, https://research.ibm.com`

Abstract. AI agents have become increasingly significant in various domains, enabling autonomous decision-making and problem-solving. To function effectively, these agents require a planning process that determines the best course of action and then executes the planned actions. In this paper, we present an efficient on-device Planner-Action framework that separates planning and action execution into two components: a planner agent, or Octo-planner, optimized for edge devices, and an action agent using the Octopus model for function execution. Octo-planner first responds to user queries by decomposing tasks into a sequence of sub-steps, which are then executed by the Octopus action agent. To optimize performance on resource-constrained devices, we employ model fine-tuning instead of in-context learning, reducing computational costs and energy consumption while improving response times. Our approach involves using GPT-4 to generate diverse planning queries and responses based on available functions, with subsequent validations to ensure data quality. We fine-tune the Phi-3 Mini model on this curated dataset, achieving a 97% success rate in our in-domain test environment. To address multi-domain planning challenges, we develop a multi-LoRA training method that merges weights from LoRAs trained on distinct function subsets. This approach enables flexible handling of complex, multi-domain queries while maintaining computational efficiency on resource-constrained devices. To support further research, we have open-sourced our model weights at NexaAI Hugging Face repo. For its performance on mobile devices, please refer to our YouTube video demo.

Keywords: On-Device AI · Multi-LoRA Training · Large Language Model · AI Agent

---

W. Chen, Z. Li, Z. Guo and Y. Shen—Equal contribution.

S. Rodriguez et al. (Eds.): EMAS 2025, LNAI 16407, pp. 141–156, 2026.
https://doi.org/10.1007/978-3-032-18011-7_9

1   Introduction

Artificial intelligence (AI) agents [17,31] have significantly transformed various industries by enabling autonomous decision-making and improving operational efficiencies [6,8,9,18,19,41,42,46]. These agents rely on a critical planning process that involves determining the optimal course of action, executing the planned actions, and summarizing the outcomes. Large Language Models (LLMs) such as Gemini-Pro [12] and GPT-4 [29] have shown potential in this domain. While these models face challenges in executing complex planning tasks at a level comparable to human performance [39,47], they remain effective in addressing simpler tasks, thereby facilitating practical applications (Fig. 1).

One such application is the emergence of AI assistant tools from companies like MultiOn [26], Simular AI [35], and Adept AI [1], which leverage the capabilities of LLMs to provide intelligent assistance across various domains. Additionally, consumer-oriented AI hardware products, such as Rabbit R1 [32], Humane AI Pin, and Limitless Pendant [23], integrate LLMs into user-friendly devices, making intelligent assistance more accessible and driving significant traction.

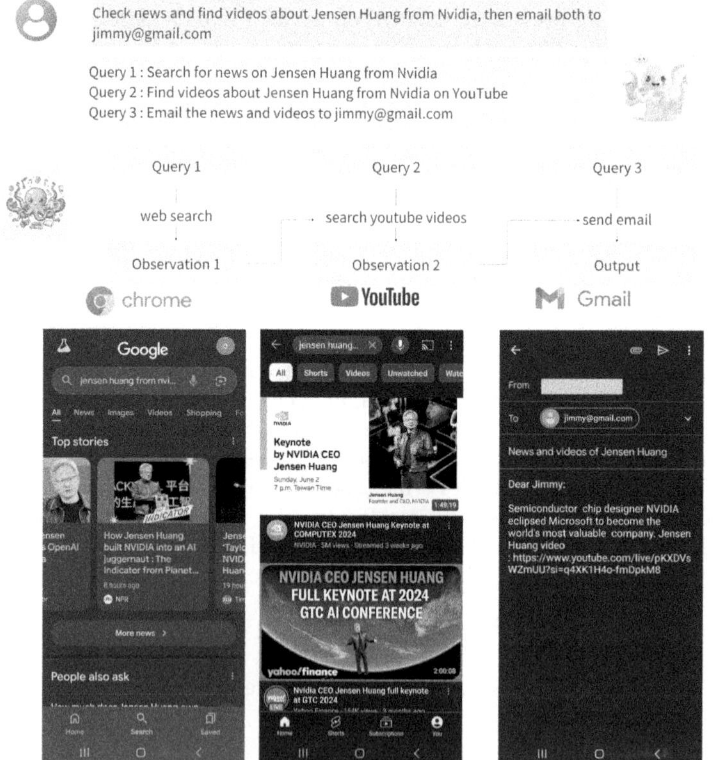

Fig. 1. Planner-Action Agent in smartphone using Octopus models.

The success of AI agents depends on the performance of the underlying LLMs. Agents using pre-trained models without fine-tuning on tasks demonstrations have relatively low success rates, ranging from 12% on desktop applications [40] to 46% on mobile applications [4], while those leveraging fine-tuned models can achieve up to 80% success rate on tasks similar to their training data [13,27]. However, using LLMs for AI agents is costly due to high computational demands and infrastructure expenses, limiting widespread adoption. The lack of on-device AI agents restricts applications requiring real-time processing, offline functionality, or enhanced privacy.

On-device AI agents offer advantages including reduced latency, offline operation, lower costs, and improved data security [3,24,33,44]. While action models like Octopus V2 achieve over 95% accuracy for function calling [7], an on-device planning model is still missing. General agent frameworks use single-model in-context learning, requiring lengthy function descriptions and planning instructions in each prompt. This approach is impractical for on-device models with limited context lengths, causing high latency and battery consumption on edge devices.

In this paper, we introduce Octo-planner, an on-device planning agent that addresses the key challenges of efficiency, adaptability, and resource constraints. Our Planner-Action framework separates planning and action execution into two components: a planner agent, or Octo-planner, optimized for edge devices, and an action agent using the Octopus model for function execution. By prioritizing fine-tuning over few-shot prompting, we reduce computational costs and minimize key-value (KV) cache requirements. Our approach uses GPT-4 to generate and validate planning data, which is then used to fine-tune Phi-3 Mini for on-device deployment. In-domain tests demonstrate that this fine-tuning improves planning success rates to 97%. To address multi-domain planning challenges, we develop a multi-LoRA training method that merges weights from LoRAs trained on distinct function subsets. This enables flexible handling of complex, multi-domain queries while maintaining computational efficiency on resource-constrained devices. By focusing on pre-defined functions for simpler tasks and leveraging fine-tuning, we aim to make AI agents more practical, accessible, and cost-effective for real-world applications.

This work aims to contribute to the ongoing efforts to make AI more accessible and practical for everyday use. By bridging the gap between AI agent potential and edge computing constraints, we seek to facilitate the adoption of intelligent, on-device assistants across various domains. Through open-sourcing our approach, we hope to inspire further innovations in on-device AI, expanding the reach of advanced planning capabilities to a broader range of applications.

2   Related Works

2.1   Planner Agent

Language models have become essential in planning agent systems. Proprietary models like OpenAI's assistant API [28] excel in generating strategies based on user queries and available functions. Recent advancements have further expanded the capabilities of language models in planning. The ReAct framework [43] integrates planning and acting for limited action spaces, while research from Alibaba Group [34] highlights the effectiveness of separate planning and action models for complex tasks. In robotics, language models are also increasingly applied to task-level planning [11,16]. Notable examples include SayCan [2], which uses LLMs to break high-level tasks into concrete sub-tasks, and Video Language Planning (VLP) [10], which enhances long-horizon planning through a text-to-video dynamics model.

2.2   Fine-Tuning to Replace Long Context

Fine-tuning language models to internalize specific prompts or context information reduces input length and improves efficiency [21,22]. This approach involves training models on carefully curated, task-specific datasets. For models with limited context windows, this technique is particularly valuable as it enables more efficient query processing without sacrificing response quality. The success of fine-tuning largely depends on the use of diverse, high-quality datasets, which ensure the model can generalize across various prompt phrasings [5,30,37,38]. When implemented effectively, fine-tuning streamlines application-specific interactions, addressing both context length limitations and computational challenges in practical deployments.

2.3   LoRA and Multi-LoRA

Low-Rank Adaptation (LoRA) efficiently adapts pre-trained language models to specific tasks [15]. Unlike fine-tuning, which updates all parameters, LoRA freezes pre-trained weights and adds trainable low-rank matrices to each layer, significantly reducing trainable parameters and computational demands. Multi-LoRA extends this concept by enabling multiple task-specific adapters to be trained, combined, or switched during inference, allowing a single base model to handle various tasks efficiently [36]. Building on these approaches, researchers have developed several related variants of the original LoRA to address different aspects of model adaptation: LoRA+ optimizes learning rates [14], VeRA uses random projections [20], AdaLoRA implements adaptive rank [45], DoRA decomposes weights [25], and Delta-LoRA updates pretrained weights [48]. These variations aim to further refine efficiency or performance in specific scenarios.

3   Method

This section presents our framework for on-device Planner-Action agents. We first describe the integration of planning and action agents for efficient problem-solving. We then detail our approach to dataset design and the training process for the planning agent, including support for extensive functions and a plug-and-play capability for additional function sets. Finally, we outline our benchmark used to evaluate agent performance.

3.1   Planner and Action Agents Framework

Our Planner-Action approach distinguishes itself from general agent frameworks by separating the planning and action execution processes into two components. This separation improves modularity and allows for specialized optimization of each component. The framework operates as follows.

Planner Phase: Given a user query q, our planning model π_{plan} decomposes the task into a sequence of sub-steps. Formally:

$$\{\tau_1, \tau_2, \ldots, \tau_n\} = \pi_{\text{plan}}(q; F) \tag{1}$$

where F is the set of available function descriptions, and τ_i is the ith execution step. π_{plan} internalizes F during instruction fine-tuning.

Action Phase: For each step in the execution sequence, we employ an action model π_{action}. At step i, given the observation of the current state O_i, the action model performs:

$$O_{i+1} = \pi_{\text{action}}(\tau_i, O_i) \tag{2}$$

where O_{i+1} and τ_{i+1} are passed to the next step for continued execution.

For the action model, we utilize the Octopus model, which is specifically designed for on-device function calling. Figure 2 illustrates the difference between our Planner-Action framework and the single-model approach for LLM agents.

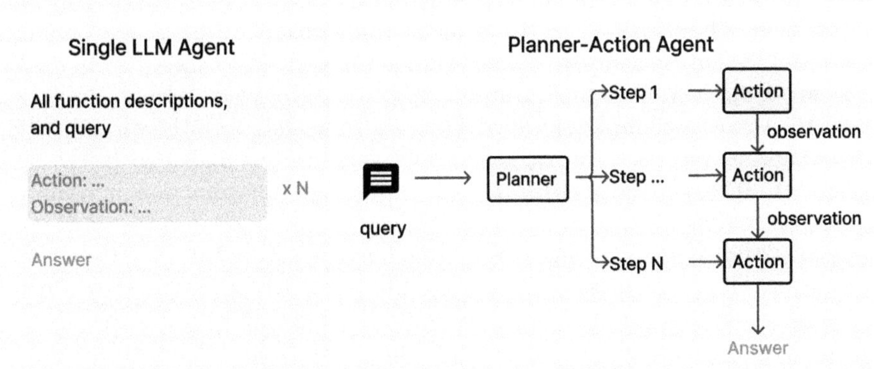

Fig. 2. Comparison of Single LLM Agent and Planner-Action Agent frameworks. (Left) Single LLM Agent: A unified model performs both task planning and action execution. (Right) Planner-Action Agent: A specialized planner model decomposes the task into subtasks, while a separate action model executes each subtask sequentially.

The modular design of our framework offers several advantages:

- **Specialization**: Separating planning and action execution allows optimization of each model for its specific role, enhancing performance in complex tasks.

- **Scalability**: Independent scaling of planning and action capabilities efficiently accommodates varying task complexities.
- **Interpretability**: Explicit separation of phases improves transparency in the decision-making process.
- **Adaptability**: Easier integration of domain-specific knowledge or constraints into either phase without system-wide changes.

3.2 Planning Dataset

Our framework uses the Octopus model as the action model, requiring training only for the planner agent. We fine-tune the planner agent with the following dataset format:

<|user|>{user's query}<|end|>

<|assistant|> {query₁}<nexa_split>{query₂}<nexa_split>...
<nexa_split>{queryₙ}.<|end|>

Special tokens like `<|user|>` and `<|assistant|>` are used for chat model pretraining but are optional otherwise. We set n as 1–5, based on our finding that most of tasks on mobile app consist of fewer than 5 steps. The dataset generation and curation process includes:

1. **Dataset collection**: Given the available functions F, we use a large language model (GPT-4) to generate diverse queries answerable by these functions. We increase the model's temperature setting to ensure query variety. Responses are then generated in the specified dataset format. Importantly, while function descriptions are used during generation, they are not included in the final dataset. Instead, the planner model internalizes this function information during training.
2. **Data validation**: We employ the same language model as a validation tool to assess the correctness of query-response pairs. Despite some errors in the initial generation process, we found that the model effectively classifies generated content as valid or invalid, allowing us to filter out incorrect outputs and maintain dataset quality.

Example data points with different number of sub-steps are shown below:

Planning Dataset example:

query: Tell me today's stock market.
response: Search for today's stock market news and latest updates<|end|>

Two-step example:

query: Find and email me Jensen Huang's news in English.
response: Find articles about Jensen Huang in English<nexa_split> Email the first article found to myself<|end|>

Three-step example:

query: Find and increase the screen brightness by 20% to better view the quarterly report document before connecting to the office printer via Bluetooth.
response: Find the quarterly report document in the system<nexa_split> Increase screen brightness by 20% to improve visibility<nexa_split> Connect to the office printer via Bluetooth to print the quarterly report<|end|>

Four-step example:

query: Find and email the project proposal document to project.manager@company.com, then look up the submission deadline and schedule it in my calendar with a reminder.
response: Locate the project proposal document<nexa_split> Send the project proposal via email to the project manager at project.manager@company.com<nexa_split> Find the project proposal submission deadline<nexa_split> Schedule a calendar event for the project proposal submission deadline with a reminder<|end|>

Five-step example:

query: I have a meeting tomorrow morning, please find my presentation then connect to the conference room projector via Bluetooth. After that, increase the screen brightness then take a screenshot of the final summary slide and email it to all participants.
response: Find the presentation for the meeting tomorrow<nexa_split> Connect to the conference room projector via Bluetooth<nexa_split> Increase screen brightness by 20%<nexa_split> Take a screenshot of the final summary slide<nexa_split> Email the screenshot to all meeting participants<|end|>

For the visualization of the dataset collection, please see Fig. 3. Example function descriptions are in Appendix 8.1.

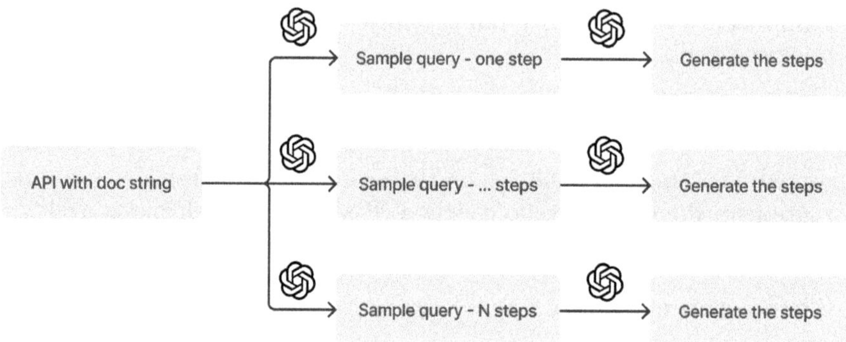

Fig. 3. Dataset Collection Process for Planner Model Training. We generate queries that require between 1–5 steps, verify correctness, and retain only high-quality samples.

3.3   Benchmark Design

Our evaluation relies on a carefully constructed test dataset. This dataset is designed to represent the complexities of real-world planning, employing a multi-stage approach that integrates automated generation, expert validation, and empirical testing.

The process begins with the automated generation of an initial dataset comprising 1,000 data points using GPT-4. These data points then undergo a rigorous quality assurance process to ensure their integrity and relevance. The quality assessment criteria are as follows:

- Each step must correspond to an existing function;
- The sequential order of steps must be correct.

To ensure the reliability of our evaluation, we incorporate an additional phase of manual verification. This phase involves selecting a subset of examples for end-to-end model execution, thereby validating the accuracy of our results and providing a comprehensive assessment of our model's performance.

For the evaluation of our proposed planning model, we employ GPT-4 as an oracle to determine the correctness of the generated plans. This choice is based on empirical observations indicating GPT-4's high proficiency in our specific use case.

4   Experimental Design

Our experimental design assesses the Octo-planner's performance for on-device AI agent planning. We aim to determine the optimal configuration for deploying efficient, accurate planning models on resource-constrained devices while maintaining adaptability to new domains and functions. Our experiments focus on four key areas:

1. Performance and efficiency trade-offs between full fine-tuning and LoRA.
2. Multi-LoRA accuracy in handling different function sets simultaneously.
3. Performance comparison across various base models and sizes.
4. The impact of dataset size on accuracy, ranging from 100 to 1000 training examples.

We conduct supervised fine-tuning on our curated dataset, using Phi-3 Mini and a few other alternatives as the base model. Training includes both full fine-tuning and LoRA techniques. For all experiments, we set the dataset size to be 800 times the number of available functions, and the multiplier was determined empirically through initial pilot studies. We perform fine-tuning on an NVIDIA A100 GPU using optimized hyperparameters for both approaches: a learning rate of 5×10^{-6}, batch size of 4, a warm-up ratio of 0.2, and 2 training epochs. For LoRA, we set the `target_modules` to be `all-linear`.

5   Results

5.1   Full Fine-Tuning Vs LoRA

Table 1 presents a detailed comparison of full fine-tuning and LoRA approaches for our planning model. Our experiments reveal significant differences in performance across these methods. Full fine-tuning achieves the highest accuracy at 98.1%, demonstrating superior performance. In contrast, LoRA performance depends on rank size. With rank 64 and alpha 256, LoRA achieves 85.1% accuracy, while reducing to rank 16 and alpha 32 drops accuracy to 72.9%. These results highlight the trade-off between model performance and computational efficiency when using LoRA. While full fine-tuning provides better accuracy, LoRA offers a more resource-efficient alternative, with performance varying based on rank configuration.

Table 1. Full Fine-Tuning vs. LoRA

Training Configuration	Benchmark Accuracy
Full model training	98.1%
LoRA (rank=64, alpha=256)	85.1%
LoRA (rank=16, alpha=32)	72.9%

5.2   Multi-loRA Training and Merging

While LoRA-based training is effective for specific function sets, real-world applications often require handling new or expanded sets of functions. To address this challenge, we propose merging multiple LoRA weights, each trained on distinct function subsets, with the same base model. This approach creates a composite model that combines knowledge from various function sets, offering a scalable solution for complex, multi-domain queries in resource-constrained environments.

To evaluate this method, we constructed a benchmark dataset by randomly selecting functions from each LoRA's domain with equal probability, combining them into workflows. Queries and plans were generated using GPT-4. For example, when testing two merged LoRAs, queries may involve Android functions, E-commerce functions, or both, with equal likelihood.

The code block below shows sample queries from our benchmark dataset and the corresponding inference results from the multi-LoRA merged model:

Android functions only:

query: Find the quarterly report for Q3 and print it for the upcoming board meeting.
response: Locate the quarterly report document for Q3<|nexa_split|>Print the located quarterly report document<|end|>

E-commerce functions only:

query: Find ergonomic office chairs and then buy the selected one using my default shipping address and credit card
response: Search for ergonomic office chairs<nexa_split>Purchase the selected ergonomic office chair using the default shipping address and credit card<|end|>

Android and E-commerce functions:

query: Find ergonomic office chair list doc and print it for my shopping
response: Search for ergonomic office chair list doc<nexa_split>Print the ergonomic office chair list doc <|end|>

Table 2 presents the performance results of our multi-LoRA merging technique. Each individual LoRA was trained with consistent hyperparameters: rank 64, lora_alpha 256, and target_modules set to "all-linear". The single-domain Android function set LoRA achieves 85.1% accuracy. When merging LoRAs from two domains (Android and E-Commerce), accuracy slightly decreases to 82.2%. Further merging yields lower accuracies: 78.9% for three domains (adding Video

Streaming), and 69.7% for four domains (adding Travel). These results reveal a pattern of gradual accuracy decline as we integrate more function sets, with a steeper drop occurring after the third domain is added.

Table 2. Multi-LoRA Benchmark

Training Configuration	Benchmark Accuracy (%)
LoRA for Android	85.1
Merged for Android, E-Commerce	82.2
Merged for Android, E-Commerce, video streaming	78.9
Merged for Android, E-Commerce, video streaming, travelling	69.7

5.3   Full Fine-Tuning with Different Base Models

We also tested multiple base models in full fine-tuning. Table 3 shows that Google Gemma 2b achieved 85.6% accuracy, Gemma 7b reached 99.7%, and Microsoft Phi-3 Mini got 98.1%. The results indicate that while smaller models can be adapted quickly, larger models generally achieve higher accuracy.

Table 3. Different Base Model Benchmark

Base Model	Benchmark Accuracy
Google Gemma 2b	85.6%
Google Gemma 7b	99.7%
Microsoft Phi-3 Mini	98.1%

5.4   Full Fine-Tuning with Different Dataset Sizes

Our default training dataset has 1,000 data points, with an even distribution across 1–5 step sequences. We investigate how dataset size affects performance, balancing the cost of synthetic data generation with accuracy. Table 4 shows the results. Accuracy grows with dataset size, suggesting that at least 1,000 data points is recommended for robust performance.

Table 4. Dataset Size Benchmark

Training Dataset Size	Benchmark Accuracy
1,000 data points	98.1%
500 data points	92.5%
250 data points	85.3%
100 data points	78.1%

6   Conclusion

We presented the Octo-planner, an on-device planning agent designed to work alongside action agents like Octopus V2. By separating planning and action execution, we improve specialization and adaptability. Our approach fine-tunes Phi-3 Mini (a 3.8B parameter LLM) to serve as a planning agent capable of running locally on edge devices, achieving a 97% success rate in-domain tests. We reduce computational demands, improve latency, and introduce a multi-LoRA approach for easily expanding model capabilities without full retraining.

This contribution addresses key deployment concerns—data privacy, latency, and offline functionality—moving toward practical, sophisticated AI agents that function entirely on-device. By open-sourcing our model weights, we hope to spur innovation in on-device AI, advancing efficient and privacy-protecting applications that serve everyday needs.

7   Limitations and Future Work

While our model is effective for specific mobile phone use cases, it lacks the iterative refinement seen in frameworks like ReAct [43], which alternate between planning steps and real-time execution based on feedback. Our upfront planning approach is efficient for straightforward tasks but may be less adaptable to changing conditions mid-execution.

Future work will explore incremental plan refinement using real-time observations to handle dynamic environments more effectively. We also intend to integrate our planning model with a broader range of action models, extending beyond mobile applications to IoT and robotics. These steps aim to address current limitations and broaden the versatility of on-device planning.

Acknowledgments. We thank the Nexa AI and MIT community for valuable feedback and support.

Disclosure of Interests. The authors have no competing interests to declare that are relevant to the content of this article.

8   Appendix

8.1   Function description examples

Note: Empty **Returns** sections are omitted for brevity.

```
def get_trending_news(query, language):
    """
    Retrieves a collection of trending news articles.

    Parameters:
    - query (str): Topic for news articles.
    - language (str): ISO 639-1 language code, default is English ('en').
```

```
    Returns:
    - list[str]: A list of strings, where each string represents one news.
    """

def get_weather_forecast(location):
    """
    Provides a weather forecast for a specified location.

    Parameters:
    - location (str): Location for the forecast (city name, ZIP code).

    Returns:
    - list[str]: A list of daily forecasts (date and weather).
    """

def send_email(recipient, title, content):
    """
    Sends an email to a specified recipient.

    Parameters:
    - recipient (str): Recipient's email address.
    - title (str): The subject line of the email.
    - content (str): The body content of the email.
    """

def search_youtube_videos(query):
    """
    Searches YouTube for videos matching a query.

    Parameters:
    - query (str): Search query.

    Returns:
    - list[str]: Each element includes the video name and URL.
    """

def find_route_google_maps(origin, destination, mode):
    """
    Computes a route using Google Maps from origin to destination.

    Parameters:
    - origin (str): Starting location.
    - destination (str): Target location.
    - mode (enum): 'driving', 'walking', 'bicycling', or 'transit'.

    Returns:
    - list[str]: Route details, including directions and distances.
    """

def send_text_message(contact_name, message):
    """
    Sends a text message to a specified contact.

    Parameters:
    - contact_name (str): The name of the recipient contact.
    - message (str): The content of the message.
    """

def create_contact(name, phone_number):
    """
    Creates a new contact in the device's address book.
```

```
    Parameters:
    - name (str): Full name of the contact.
    - phone_number (str): Phone number (preferably in E.164 format).
    """

def set_timer_alarm(time, label):
    """
    Sets a timer or alarm for a specified time.

    Parameters:
    - time (str): Alarm time in "HH:MM" (24-hour format).
    - label (str): Custom label (default is "alarm").
    """

def create_calendar_event(title, start_time, end_time):
    """
    Schedules a new event in the calendar.

    Parameters:
    - title (str): Event title.
    - start_time (str): ISO 8601 format (YYYY-MM-DD-HH-MM).
    - end_time (str): ISO 8601 format; must be after start_time.
    """

def set_volume(level, volume_type):
    """
    Sets the volume level for a specified type ('ring', 'media', 'alarm').

    Parameters:
    - level (int): 0 (mute) to 10 (max).
    - volume_type (enum): One of 'ring', 'media', 'alarm'.
    """
```

References

1. Adept Team: Adept ai. https://www.adept.ai (2024)
2. Ahn, M., Chen, D., et al.: Do as i can, not as i say: Grounding language in robotic affordances. arXiv preprint (2022)
3. Alwarafy, A., Barnawi, A., et al.: A survey on iot-based edge computing for streaming data analytics. IEEE Access **8** (2020)
4. Bishop, W., Song, Y., Chen, R.: Latent planning in LLM-based mobile agents. under review (2024)
5. Cao, J., Giannini, S., Guo, D., et al.: Instruction-tuning data generation for domain-specific tasks. arXiv preprint (2023)
6. Chen, W., Li, Z.: Octopus v4: Graph of language models. arXiv preprint (2024)
7. Chen, W., Li, Z., Guo, Z., Shen, Y.: Octopus v2: On-device function calling with 95% accuracy. under review (2024)
8. Chen, W., Li, Z., Ma, M.: Octopus: On-device language model for function calling of software apis. arXiv preprint (2024)
9. Deng, B., Xiao, W., Lin, X., et al.: Mind2web: toward a generalist agent for the web. arXiv preprint (2023)
10. Du, Y., Zhang, S., Kemp, C., et al.: VLP: video language planning for long-horizon tasks. arXiv preprint (2023)

11. Firoozi, T., Lan, R., Magnus, G., et al.: Foundation models in robotics: a survey. arXiv preprint (2023)
12. Gemini Team: Gemini: Next-generation large language model from google. under review (2024)
13. Gur, I., Friedman, E., Heilbron, F.C., et al.: Real-world agent tasks: a fine-tuned LLM approach. under review (2024)
14. Hayou, S., Gurram, A., Ingold, R.: Lora+: Learning rate aware lora for efficient adaptation. under review (2024)
15. Hu, E.J., Shen, Y., et al.: Lora: Low-rank adaptation of large language models. arXiv preprint (2021)
16. Hu, Z., Zhu, Y., Farn, C., et al.: General-purpose robotics via large language models. arXiv preprint (2023)
17. Jennings, N.R., Wooldridge, M.: Applications of intelligent agents. In: Agent Technology, pp. 3–28. Springer (1998)
18. Kim, B., Gao, J., He, J., et al.: Language models are multilingual chain-of-thought reasoners. arXiv preprint (2023)
19. Koh, S., Wang, Y., Xu, A., et al.: Visualwebarena: a benchmark for vision-based web manipulation. under review (2024)
20. Kopiczko, P., Foltyn, R., et al.: Vera: very efficient random adaptation. under review (2024)
21. Lester, B., Al-Rfou, R., Constant, N.: The power of scale for parameter-efficient prompt tuning. arXiv preprint (2021)
22. Li, X.L., Liang, P.: Prefix-tuning: Optimizing continuous prompts for generation. In: Proceedings of ACL 2021 (2021)
23. Limitless Lab: Limitless pendant. https://www.limitlessai.com (2024)
24. Lin, X., Gan, Y., Xu, A., et al.: AWQ: activation-aware weight quantization for LLMs. under review (2024)
25. Liu, K., Hayes, T., Barnett, M.: Dora: Decomposed rank adaptation for parameter-efficient tuning. under review (2024)
26. MultiOn Team: Multion: An ai assistant for multi-step tasks. https://www.multion.ai (2024)
27. Nakano, R., Hilton, J., Balaji, S., et al.: Webgpt: Browser-assisted question-answering with human feedback. arXiv preprint (2022)
28. OpenAI: Openai assistant api overview. https://platform.openai.com/docs/guides/gpt (2023)
29. OpenAI: Gpt-4 technical report. https://openai.com/research/gpt-4 (2024)
30. Paul, M., Kolesnikov, A., Reinhard, E., et al.: Deep training data curation. arXiv preprint (2023)
31. Poole, D.L., Mackworth, A.K.: Artificial Intelligence: Foundations of Computational Agents. Cambridge University Press (2010)
32. Rabbit Team: Rabbit r1: On-device ai phone. https://www.rabbitphone.com (2024)
33. Ranaweera, P., Ramasamy, S., Jayarathna, S.: A survey on security in edge computing. IEEE Access **9** (2021)
34. Shen, Y., Chen, W., Zhuang, T., et al.: Small LLM, big skills: a multi-agent approach for complex tasks. under review (2024)
35. Simular AI Team: Simular: Ai in everyday workflows. https://simular.ai (2024)
36. Wang, R., Zhu, Y., Zhang, R.: Multi-lora: Fine-tuning large language models across domains. arXiv preprint (2023)
37. Wang, Y., Zhang, T., Kong, Y., et al.: On the importance of diverse synthetic data for instruction tuning. under review (2024)

38. Xia, T., Wei, Y., Huang, H., et al.: Less is more: Efficient sample generation for large instruction tuning. under review (2024)
39. Xie, Q., Zhu, W., Li, D., et al.: Evaluating LLM-based agent for real-world travel itinerary planning. under review (2024)
40. Xie, Z., Gao, X., Yuan, Y., et al.: Osworld: evaluating LLM-based agent for OS-level tasks. under review (2024)
41. Xu, J., Li, Z., Chen, W., et al.: On-device language models: a comprehensive review. arXiv preprint (2024)
42. Yan, S., Wang, W., Fang, Y., et al.: Exploring GPT-4v as a multi-modal agent for vision-based tasks. arXiv preprint (2023)
43. Yao, S., Yu, P.S., Wang, S.: React: Synergizing reasoning and acting in language models. arXiv preprint (2023)
44. Yu, H., Wang, M., Chen, J., et al.: A survey on security issues of on-device ai. IEEE Communications Surveys & Tutorials (2017)
45. Zhang, X., Jiang, Y., et al.: Adalora: Fine-tuning large language models with adaptive rank. arXiv preprint (2023)
46. Zheng, W., Song, W., Liu, X., et al.: Gpt-4v in the loop: multimodal chain-of-thought reasoning for web navigation tasks. under review (2024)
47. Zheng, X., Chen, Y., Wu, S., et al.: The limit of LLM's planning ability for real-world tasks. arXiv preprint (2024)
48. Zi, W., Wei, J., Lin, Z., et al.: Delta-lora: Revisiting the tradeoff between model adaptation and stability. arXiv preprint (2023)

Oops, I Heard That! Situated Communication with Locality-Aware KQML

Angelo Ferrando[1]([✉])[iD], Andrea Gatti[2][iD], and Viviana Mascardi[2][iD]

[1] University of Modena-Reggio Emilia, Modena, Italy
`angelo.ferrando@unimore.it`
[2] University of Genova, Genoa, Italy
`andrea.gatti@edu.unige.it`, `viviana.mascardi@unige.it`

Abstract. In traditional BDI (Belief-Desire-Intention) Multiagent Systems (MAS), agent communication languages such as KQML (Knowledge Query and Manipulation Language) facilitate structured message exchange and are supported by widespread BDI implementations like Jason. However, KQML lacks mechanisms to account for the situatedness of agents within dynamic environments. This paper proposes an extension to KQML, KQML-S, that incorporates the notion of locality, enabling message semantics to adapt based on the agents' shared context. Specifically, we introduce a framework where agents within the same logical communication space, or "logical room", perceive indirect updates from interactions occurring within their locality. We present the theoretical foundations of KQML-S and its implementation within VEsNA (Virtual Environments via Natural language Agents), a framework extending Jason with chatbots for natural language interaction, and a Virtual Reality environment implemented in Godot.

KQML-S bridges two foundational features of agents: social ability and situatedness.

VEsNA agents, being natively situated in Virtual Reality and inheriting KQML communication from Jason, fully exploit the potential of KQML-S and showcase its usefulness in those scenarios where agents are logically or physically embodied in a discrete, "room-based" environment.

Keywords: Belief-Desire-Intention · KQML · Situated Communication · Virtual Communication Spaces · VEsNA

1 Introduction

To achieve goals they cannot satisfy individually, agents must coordinate. This coordination typically relies on one of three mechanisms: (i) *point-to-point* private communication; (ii) *direct interaction* via coordination artifacts; and (iii) *indirect interaction* through the environment.

Examples of the first mechanism include the Knowledge Query and Manipulation Language (KQML), developed within the "Knowledge Sharing Effort"

S. Rodriguez et al. (Eds.): EMAS 2025, LNAI 16407, pp. 157–176, 2026.
https://doi.org/10.1007/978-3-032-18011-7_10

project [22], and FIPA-ACL [15], standardized by the Foundation for Intelligent Physical Agents (FIPA). Frameworks like Jason [6] and Jade [2] adopt, respectively, KQML and FIPA-ACL. Jadescript [3] uses a subset of FIPA-ACL performatives, while Jadex [33] uses point-to-point communication but remains agnostic with respect to the language.

Coordination artifacts provide shared interaction media, giving agents access to local resources, enabling discovery of other agents, and supporting cooperative behaviors [35]. TuCSoN [32] is a well-known example, using tuple centers to support mediated coordination. In the Agents and Artifacts (A&A) meta-model [31,37], agents are proactive entities that pursue goals, while artifacts are reactive components providing shared services. This model is implemented in frameworks like CArtAgO [36] and integrated into JaCaMo [4].

Situated agents also interact indirectly with their environment, sensing and modifying it to influence others. Swarm intelligence, for example, emerges from simple agents coordinating via local interactions and environmental cues [5]. Frameworks such as NetLogo [42], Mason [29], and Repast [30] rely on the environment as the primary shared medium, with stigmergy [24,40] as the central coordination mechanism.

Point-to-point communication is typically private and lacks locality, which is instead a native feature of environment-based and artifact-mediated coordination. Locality may be physical (e.g., an agent near a pheromone trail) or logical (e.g., participation in an online chat group). However, even point-to-point messaging in Multiagent Systems (MAS) is not always private in practice. In shared physical or virtual spaces, messages may be overheard, spread unintentionally, or interpreted based on context. Traditional models like KQML and FIPA-ACL support direct dialogue but overlook these emergent dynamics, which are central to coordination. By treating overhearing and context-sensitive responsiveness as first-class features, we enable more realistic and adaptive agent interaction.

KQML transport model is assumed to employ unidirectional communication links, to be reliable and order-preserving (messages are received in the order they were sent) [27]. These assumptions do not depend on the KQML language itself but on its implementation, and do not capture relevant aspects of real agent communication—see for example [11,12] for a discussion of order-preserving communication and its consequences on protocol enactability. Also, interactions shaped by spatial or social proximity are not captured by these assumptions. Besides these limitations, KQML has also been criticized for its lack of formal semantics and the perceived arbitrariness of its performatives [38], but it is nevertheless the foundation for communication in widely adopted agent-oriented frameworks like Jason and JaCaMo, and by far a well known format for message exchange among agents: at the time of writing, the citations of [13,14,27] on Google Scholar sum up to more than 4700. Our choice to extend KQML is thus pragmatic: instead of proposing a new model, we enrich existing infrastructure with locality-aware semantics, enabling context-sensitive agent interaction without sacrificing compatibility.

Our work does not discard message routing or private messaging—in fact, KQML-S is a conservative extension of KQML and hence supports them, as long as the underlying KQML implementation does. Instead, we generalize KQML's semantics to better accommodate contexts where communication is inherently observable to co-located agents. By elevating locality to a first-class concept—rather than hiding it inside assumptions on the transport model—and distinguishing between public and private communication modes, KQML-S enables both deliberate and incidental communication in shared environments. This promotes more expressive, flexible interaction in open MAS, where transparency, coordination, and social influence are essential.

To achieve our goal we enrich communication in the AgentSpeak(L) agent-oriented programming language [34], for which Jason provides an extended interpreter [41], by incorporating locality—modeled as logical rooms populated by potentially overlapping agent subsets—into the environment configuration and by distinguishing between private and public message modes. Logical rooms are not MASs themselves: they are more similar to organizations within MASs, where agents may enter and leave, and may reside in more than one logical room at the same time. However, logical rooms may have a digital—or even physical—twin, that automatically drives how communication inside a room works. For example, if the room is physical, we may expect that agents physically located inside the room may overhear messages exchanged there, but those outside the room cannot. In our work, we also model agents' attitudes toward overheard information, influencing whether and how they respond to it. Our formal setting is AgentSpeak(L)'s speech act semantics, using KQML as the base communication language and Jason as the implementation platform. We focus on the KQML `Achieve` and `Tell` performatives. The resulting extension, KQML-S, is integrated into VEsNA [17,19–21], a framework that connects Jason agents to Virtual Reality environments developed in Godot [23], and enables natural language interaction. Because agents in VEsNA are spatially situated in Virtual Reality (VR), the adoption of KQML-S, with logical rooms corresponding to physical rooms in VR, is both natural and effective.

2 Motivation

Let us consider five scenarios taken from daily life of academic computer scientists.

Scenario 1. Alice enters the open space of her lab and says to her colleague Bob *"Hi Bob, I'm late... I forgot to make two further copies for today's exam, may you kindly print them?"*. Alice believes that Bob—who is an early bird—is already at his desk, not visible from Alice's desk, and that the point to point `Achieve` message just sent was properly received. She starts collecting all the stuff she needs for running the exam, counting on the two further copies appearing soon, but Bob is enjoying a coffee in another room and does not hear. Alice has to print the copies herself, the toner is low, the paper is missing, and the exam starts late...

Scenario 2. At the other extreme, a message is (unexpectedly) heard by too many agents. Alice enters the lab very early in the morning, when Bob is

- usually - the only one already there, and she says *"Hi Bob, we won that big project on BDI agents with Carol... We have plenty of money, but do not tell the PhD students..."*. Today Frank, George, and Hilary, three PhD students, have a deadline and are already in the lab, although not visible from the door. The point to point `Tell` message was meant from Alice to Bob but the space where it was sent was not a private one. What Alice says when she is in her lab, cannot be heard elsewhere, as locality poses constraints on which agents may receive messages that were not directed to them. However, Frank and George—that believe everything they hear—have already recorded that there is more money for them. Hilary is instead skeptical, and just ignores it.

Scenario 3. Let us suppose that Alice and Bob are in the same WhatsApp group with Carol: a safer way for Alice to share the good news of the funded project would be to send a WhatsApp message there. Even if Alice and Bob are in the same physical room, other "logical rooms" exist: they can be in more rooms at the same time, with different persons. Although incautious communications may lead to eavesdropping, it may also happen that unexpected hearing is beneficial. Let us consider a fourth scenario.

Scenario 4. Alice asks Bob to look for the funded projects' rules, but Bob is sipping his second coffee somewhere else. However, Dave is at his desk. He hears the request and, being altruistic, says *"I can do it"* to Alice. Although Alice asked Bob for the favor, she happily accepts Dave's help.

A last, different situation is the following.

Scenario 5. Alice enters the lab and says *"Hi, may anyone print one copy of the EMAS 2025 call for papers? It's online..."*. We distinguish this message, having a generic "anyone in the lab, although I do not know who is in" recipient, from a broadcast message intentionally sent to a specific set of receivers, or to *all* the agents in the MAS. In fact, in this case, the request might be heard by Irene, a new PhD student that Alice does not even know, who is in the lab and volunteers to make the print. Bob is at the coffee machine in another room and, again, sneaks out of work. Messages sent to anyone in a logical room raise the problem of coordination among those persons that might achieve the goal, resulting into dozens copies of the paper printed. It will be up to Alice to decide to whom assigning the task.

These examples show that even KQML-like, speech-act-based communication—typically point-to-point and independent of coordination artifacts or environmental mediation—can be affected by situatedness. In Virtual Reality environments structured as rooms or regions, communication must account for spatial context. Shared environments introduce phenomena like overhearing, which traditional models such as KQML overlook. KQML-S treats overhearing as a meaningful event that shapes reasoning, allowing agents to make context-sensitive decisions that go beyond standard point-to-point messaging.

3 Preliminaries

In this section, mainly based on the paper by Vieira et al. [41], we introduce the foundational concepts necessary to understand the paper.

AgentSpeak(L). AgentSpeak(L) is a logic programming language that provides an abstract framework for programming BDI agents [34].
The beliefs of an agent determine what an agent currently knows about itself, the other agents in the system, and the environment. They are defined as atomic formulae, as follows:

$$b ::= P(t_1, \ldots, t_n) \quad (n \geq 0)$$

where P denotes a predicate symbol, and $t_1, \ldots, t_n$ are standard terms of first-order logic. A belief base is a sequence of beliefs:

$$beliefs ::= b_1 \ldots b_n \quad (n \geq 0)$$

The beliefs defined by the programmer at design time make up for the initial belief base. The rest of the beliefs are then added dynamically during the agent's lifetime.

An achievement goal in AgentSpeak(L) is specified as:

$$g ::= \ !at$$

where at is an atomic proposition.
Finally, an action in AgentSpeak(L) is defined as:

$$a ::= A(t_1, \ldots, t_n) \quad (n \geq 0)$$

Action are written using the same notation as predicates, except that an action symbol A is used instead of a predicate symbol.

Plans are used to define the course of action for the agent to fulfill its goals. A plan has three main components: a triggering event te, denoting the event triggering the execution of the plan, a context $ctxt$, denoting the conditions that must hold to consider the plan applicable, and a body h consisting of a sequence of steps to be executed. A plan in AgentSpeak(L) is defined as:

$$p ::= te : ctxt \leftarrow h$$

The triggering event is defined as follows:

$$te ::= +b \mid -b \mid +g \mid -g$$

meaning the addition (resp. deletion) of a belief b, and the addition (resp. deletion) of a goal g. A plan is relevant for a triggering event if the event can be unified with the plan's head.

For a plan to be considered applicable a condition $ctxt$ must hold as a logical consequence of the agent's belief.

The body of a plan is composed of actions (a), belief updates ($+b$, $-b$), and achievement goals (g). We omit test goals for brevity. The sequence of formulae denoting the body of a plan is:

$$h ::= a \mid g \mid +b \mid -b \mid h; h'$$

An agent program contains a plain library with a set of plans:

$$plans ::= p_1 \ldots p_n \quad (n \geq 1)$$

Finally, we define an agent through its beliefs and plans:

$$agent ::= beliefs\ plans$$

KQML. One of the earliest formal definitions of KQML semantics was provided by Labrou and Finin [26], building on the foundational work of Cohen and Perrault on action-theoretic semantics for natural language speech acts [8]. Their key insight was that if utterances are considered actions, then formal action-reasoning frameworks, such as STRIPS-style pre- and post-conditions, can be applied to model their effects. Specifically, Cohen and Perrault used this approach to define the semantics of the "inform" and "request" speech acts, framing them in terms of the beliefs, desires, and abilities of conversation participants.

$$
\begin{array}{ll}
\text{Pre-condition}(S)\text{:} & \text{bel}(S, X) \wedge \text{know}(S, \text{want}(R, \text{know}(R, \text{bel}(S, X)))) \\
\text{Pre-condition}(R)\text{:} & \text{intend}(R, \text{know}(R, \text{bel}(S, X))) \\
\text{Post-condition}(S)\text{:} & \text{know}(S, \text{know}(R, \text{bel}(S, X))) \\
\text{Post-condition}(R)\text{:} & \text{know}(R, \text{bel}(S, X)) \\
\text{Action Completion:} & \text{know}(R, \text{bel}(S, X))
\end{array}
$$

Fig. 1. Semantics for `Tell` (Labrou & Finin, 1994).

Figure 1 illustrates the semantics of the KQML performative `Tell(S, R, X)` (where S informs R that it believes X to be true), following [26].

With `Achieve`, R is asked to want to try to make the content X true of the system. With respect to `Tell`, the `Achieve` performative makes sense when the receiver R has a representation of the real world in its belief base and the result of the attempt to "make the content true" is some action in the real world [27].

3.1   Speech Act Communication in AgentSpeak(L)

KQML messages in AgentSpeak(L) follow the format $\langle mid, id, ilf, cnt \rangle$, where mid uniquely identifies the message, id specifies the recipient when sending or the sender when receiving, ilf denotes the illocutionary force (namely, the performative), and cnt contains the message content.

Messages are exchanged asynchronously and stored in a mailbox, with one message processed at the start of each reasoning cycle. The transition system manages three key sets: M_{In}, which holds received but unprocessed messages; M_{Out}, containing messages awaiting transmission; the set of suspended intentions awaiting responses to previously sent information requests is also needed in the general case, but not in this paper.

Messages of type "ask" (AskIf, AskAll, AskHow) suspend intentions and we do not deal with them in this paper. The rule *ExecActSnd-noAsk* below provides the semantics of sending a message different from an ask one. To keep the presentation simple, we discuss only those elements in the configuration of an agent, that are affected by the .send action.

$$(\textit{ExecActSnd-noAsk})\ \frac{\text{next action to be executed by } ag \text{ is } .send(id, ilf, cnt) \quad ilf \notin AskSet}{\langle ag, C, M, T, ExecInt\rangle \rightarrow \langle ag, C', M', T, ClrInt\rangle}$$

$$\textit{where} \quad AskSet = \{AskIf, AskAll, AskHow\}$$
$$M'_{Out} = M_{Out} \cup \{\langle mid, id, ilf, cnt\rangle\}$$
$$\text{with } mid \text{ a new message identifier;}$$
$$.send(id, ilf, cnt) \text{ is removed from the intention it belonged to}$$

The semantics of sending involve adding a well-formed message to the agent's mail outbox, as defined by the *ExecActSnd* rule. For non-suspended intentions, the cycle proceeds with *ClrInt*, ensuring that the updated intention—now without the sending action—undergoes the necessary clearing.

On the receiver side, receiving a message with Tell performative and Bs content, where Bs is a set of beliefs, has the following semantics:

$$(\textit{Tell})\ \frac{\begin{array}{c} S_M(M_{In}) = \langle mid, id, Tell, Bs\rangle \\ (mid, i) \notin M_{SI} \quad \text{for any intention } i \end{array}}{\langle ag, C, M, T, ProcMsg\rangle \rightarrow \langle ag', C', M', T, SelEv\rangle}$$

$$\textit{where} \quad M'_{In} = M_{In} \setminus \{\langle mid, id, Tell, Bs\rangle\}$$
$$\text{for each } b \in Bs$$
$$ag'_{bs} = ag_{bs} + b$$
$$C'_E = C_E \cup \{\langle +b[id], T\rangle\}$$

A Tell message can be received either as a reply or as an **inform** action. When received as an **inform**, the AgentSpeak(L) agent incorporates the message content into its belief base, tagging the sender as the source of that information. This reflects the "action completion" condition outlined by [26], where the receiver acknowledges the sender's perspective on the belief.

The rule for receiving a message with Achieve performative and at content, where at is an atom, is

$$(\textit{Achieve})\ \frac{\begin{array}{c} S_M(M_{In}) = \langle mid, id, Achieve, at\rangle \\ (mid, i) \notin M_{SI} \quad [\text{for any intention } i] \end{array}}{\langle ag, C, M, T, ProcMsg\rangle \rightarrow \langle ag, C, M', T, SelEv\rangle}$$

$$where \quad M'_{In} = M_{In} \setminus \{\langle mid, id, Achieve, at\rangle\}$$
$$C'_E = C_E \cup \{\langle +!at, T\rangle\}$$

In an appropriate social context (e.g., when the sender holds authority), receiving an `Achieve` message prompts the agent to execute a plan triggered by `+!at`, attempting to fulfill the goal specified in the message. This adds an external event to the event set, linked to an empty intention (T). With `Achieve` messages, new intention stacks can be created directly from incoming goals, and these plans may themselves include further achievement goals, pushing additional plans onto the stack. The rule *MsgExchg* provides a semantics to KQML communication at the MAS level:

$$(\text{MsgExchg}) \frac{\langle mid, id_j, ilf, cnt\rangle \in M_{id_iOut}}{\{AG_{id_1}, ..., AG_{id_i}, AG_{id_j}, ..., AG_{id_n}, env\} \rightarrow \{AG_{id_1}, ..., AG'_{id_i}, AG'_{id_j}, ..., AG_{id_n}, env\}}$$

$$where \quad M'_{id_iOut} = M_{id_iOut} \setminus \{\langle mid, id_j, ilf, cnt\rangle\}$$
$$M'_{id_jIn} = M_{id_jIn} \cup \{\langle mid, id_i, ilf, cnt\rangle\}$$

It means that if agent id_i sends a message to agent id_j in a MAS where there are id_1, ..., id_n agents, the only two agents affected by the communication are id_i, whose mailbox is updated by removing $\langle mid, id_j, ilf, cnt\rangle$ and id_j whose mailbox is updated by adding it. The environment env is not affected by the communication.

From a technical point of view, Jason provides a `.send( Receiver, Performative, Cnt, Answer, Timeout )` action where `Receiver` can be either the name of another agent or a list of names, `Performative` is one of the known KQML illocutionary forces, or performatives (`tell`, `askOne`, `achieve`, ...), `Cnt` is the content, `Answer` is an optional parameter used with `ask` messages to unify the answer from `Receiver` and `Timeout` is an optional parameter that sets a timeout in case the agent is waiting for an answer. When `.send` is called, the message is sent.

4   Formalization of KQML-S

In this section, we present the design of KQML-S. We begin by illustrating how the standard KQML semantics must be adapted to account for the situatedness of agents. Following this, we show how KQML-S can be integrated into the operational semantics of AgentSpeak(L). Both modifications are implemented modularly, preserving the existing syntax and semantics of KQML and AgentSpeak(L). New performatives and their corresponding semantics are introduced, ensuring full backward compatibility.

4.1 How to Make KQML Situated

We now focus on extending KQML to incorporate the situatedness of agents within a MAS by introducing the concept of a *room*, which serves as a logical representation of agent locality.

We identify the set of logical rooms with *Rooms*. *Rooms* may evolve over time, as does the set $Ags = \{AG_{id_1}, ..., AG_{id_i}, AG_{id_j}, ..., AG_{id_n}\}$ of agents in the MAS, and the enviroment *env*. For example, logical rooms might include the `coffee machine room`, the `MAS lab`, and a `WhatsApp chat`. It is important to note that a logical room does not need to correspond to a physical space in the real world; for instance, the `WhatsApp chat` represents a logical communication group rather than a physical location.

Given a set of rooms, we define a function $loc : Ags \rightarrow \mathcal{P}(Rooms)$ mapping each agent to a set of logical rooms the agent currently occupies.

The first data structure that must be extended is the one modeling the MAS: in KQML-S, we add a *loc* element to the tuple, that becomes

$$\{AG_{id_1}, ..., AG_{id_i}, AG_{id_j}, ..., AG_{id_n}, env, loc\}$$

All the agents in the MAS are, by default, in the *mas* logical room and they cannot exit it, unless they leave the MAS. If one agent is in more than one room, it will receive all the messages—either private and directed to it, or public—that are sent by agents in that room. Agent locations, as given by the *loc* function, may evolve over time due to agent movement or actions, and new logical rooms may also be introduced dynamically.

The second data structure that we must change is the one for messages, that is extended with a *mode*. In the simplest setting that we address in this paper, *mode* is a couple whose first element is one room identifier (*mas* for the logical room where all the agents are located, by default), and the second element is either *public* or *private*. Independently from the room, agents may communicate privately, for example using private chats on social media, or whispering in a crowded room, or in *public* mode, meaning that communication is meant to be received by one agent, but both the sender and the receiver (should...) know that all the other agents in the room will hear what they say.

A KQML-S message looks like $\langle mid, id_j, ilf, cnt, (room, how) \rangle$. The id_j receiver can assume the *all* value. This should not be confused with a broadcast message. In broadcast, we expect that the list of receivers is known to the sender: we do not cope with broadcast explicitly, as it can be resorted to as many individual point-to-point private messages as the intended recipients. The *all* receiver identifier, instead, stands for "all agents in *room*, whoever they are". For simplicity and coherence with our intended use, *all* is allowed only in *public* mode.

The standard KQML semantics is a special case of the KQML-S one obtained by setting $loc = \{(AG_{id_1}, \{mas\}), ..., (AG_{id_i}, \{mas\}), ..., (AG_{id_n}, \{mas\})\}$ and $mode = (mas, private)$. Apart from the addition of *loc* and *mode*, only a few rules of the KQML semantics are affected by the KQML-S extension.

4.2 Extension of Global Rules

In KQML-S the behavior of the MAS remains the same as in KQML, if communication is *private*. However, if it is *public*, all the agents in the same room as the speaker are affected. Interestingly, the receiver of the message might not be affected, if it is not in the same room as the speaker. And interestingly, in the default setting, the speaker will still believe that the intended receiver got the message, and will make plans accordingly.

The KQML-S extension of *MsgExchg* is

$$\text{(MsgExchg-S one)} \frac{\langle mid, id_j, ilf, cnt, (room, public)\rangle \in M_{id_i Out}}{\{AG_{id_1}, ..., AG_{id_i}, AG_{id_j}, ..., AG_{id_n}, env, loc\} \rightarrow \{AG'_{id_1}, ..., AG'_{id_i}, AG'_{id_j}, ..., AG'_{id_n}, env, loc\}}$$

$$where \quad 1. \quad M'_{id_i Out} = M_{id_i Out} \setminus \{\langle mid, id_j, ilf, cnt, (room, public)\rangle\}$$

$$2. \quad M'_{id_j In} = M_{id_j In} \cup \{\langle mid, id_i, ilf, cnt, (room, public)\rangle\}$$
$$\text{if } room \in loc(id_j);$$

$$3. \quad M'_{id_k In} = M_{id_k In} \cup \{\langle mid, id_i, Notify, sent(id_j, ilf, cnt), (room, public)\rangle\}$$
$$\text{for all agents } id_k \neq id_j \text{ such that } room \in loc(id_k);$$

$$4. \quad M'_{id_k In} = M_{id_k In}$$
$$\text{for all agents } id_k \text{ (possibly including } id_j\text{) s.t. } room \notin loc(id_k).$$

The semantics is as follows: if agent id_i sends a message to id_j in *public* mode (analogous to speaking loudly in a room), all agents present in the same room will become aware that the message was sent. The intended recipient, id_j, if present in the room, will receive and process the message directly, triggering the standard message-handling mechanism (Condition 2: $M_{id_j In} \cup \{\langle mid, id_i, ilf, cnt, (room, public)\rangle\}$). All other agents in the room will update their knowledge to reflect that id_i sent a message to id_j (Condition 3: $M'_{id_k In} = M_{id_k In} \cup \{\langle mid, id_i, Notify, sent(id_j, ilf, cnt), (room, public)\rangle\}$). Agents not present in the room (including id_j if located elsewhere) remain unaffected (Condition 4). Public messages may be perceived by multiple agents, but remain intentionally directed at a specific recipient. The receiver field encodes this intent, enabling overhearers to infer the message was not meant for them and decide whether to act. This supports socially aware reasoning, unlike broadcast or artifact-based communication, where intent is implicit or absent.

The `Notify` performative is new in KQML-S, and its effect on the agent's semantics is described in Sect. 4.3.

In KQML-S, messages sent in public mode retain their recipient field. This field defines the sender's communicative intent, which is used both by the designated receiver and by overhearing agents to interpret the social context of the message. For example, an overhearing agent may infer that the message was not intended for them, and adjust their behavior accordingly (e.g., ignoring it, intervening altruistically, or reacting with skepticism). Thus, the recipient field is essential for interpreting the semantics of overheard messages.

A different situation is when Alice says *"May anyone print this paper?"*, without directing the information to anyone. This implicitly means that it is directed to all the colleagues in the lab, and can be modelled by setting *all* as the intended receiver:

$$(\text{MsgExchg-S all}) \quad \frac{\langle mid, all, ilf, cnt, (room, public) \rangle \in M_{id_i Out}}{\{AG_{id_1}, ..., AG_{id_i}, AG_{id_j}, ..., AG_{id_n}, env, loc\} \rightarrow \{AG'_{id_1}, ..., AG'_{id_i}, AG'_{id_j}, ..., AG'_{id_n}, env, loc\}}$$

$$where \quad \begin{aligned} &1. \quad M'_{id_i Out} = M_{id_i Out} \setminus \{\langle mid, all, ilf, cnt, (room, public) \rangle\} \\ &2. \quad M'_{id_k In} = M_{id_k In} \cup \{\langle mid, id_i, ilf, cnt, (room, public) \rangle\} \\ &\qquad \text{for all agents } id_k \text{ such that } room \in loc(id_k). \end{aligned}$$

Differently from *MsgExchg-S one*, *MsgExchg-S all* changes the message queues of all the agents in the room in the same way, as if all of them were the intended receivers. While KQML-S supports public message exposure in shared contexts (e.g., rooms), it maintains point-to-point communication at the intentional level: each message specifies a receiver as the intended addressee. This differs from environment-based communication, where messages are undirected and lack explicit intent. In our model, overhearing arises naturally from co-location, not by design. The receiver field remains semantically meaningful, allowing overhearing agents to determine whether to respond, based on their attitude.

4.3   Extension of Local Rules

In the previous section, we examined how the operational semantics of AgentSpeak(L) must be adapted to account for the situatedness of agents involved in the communication. This led to the introduction of a new performative, Notify, used to create messages that inform agents within the same logical room where the communication occurs.

In this section, we detail how AgentSpeak(L)'s semantics is extended to handle this addition. Specifically, we introduce two new rules to manage messages with the Notify performative. In our framework, notifications relate to either a Tell or an Achieve messages, sent to one agent sharing the same logical room, as outlined in the extended global rules. Although additional rules could be defined to cover other interpretations of Notify, this work focuses on these two primary and common cases to maintain clarity and conciseness.

The first rule, *NotifyTell*, handles the notification of a Tell message. This rule governs the reception of the notification and updates the agent's belief base based on its current *mood*. The mood set defines characteristics that influence an agent's behavior when receiving `Tell` or `Achieve` messages. An agent may be `Credulous` and/or `Altruistic`. We assume a closed world assumption in interpreting the agent's mood: if an agent is not `Credulous`, it is skeptical. If it is not `Altruistic`, it is selfish. There is no need to be explicit on being skeptical or selfish: they are just a consequence of not being `Credulous` or `Altruistic`. If the agent is in an `Credulous` mood, it fully trusts the information overheard in its logical room and updates its belief base as if it were the direct recipient of the original `Tell` message.

$$(\text{NotifyTell}) \frac{S_M(M_{In}) = \langle mid, id, Notify, sent(\_, Tell, Bs), mode\rangle \quad (mid, i) \notin M_{SI} \quad \text{for any intention } i}{\langle ag, C, M, T, ProcMsg, mood\rangle \rightarrow \langle ag', C', M', T, SelEv, mood\rangle}$$

$$\begin{aligned} where \quad & M'_{In} = M_{In} \setminus \{\langle mid, id, Notify, sent(\_, Tell, Bs), mode\rangle\} \\ & \text{if } Credulous \in mood \text{ then} \\ & \quad \text{for each } b \in Bs \\ & \quad ag'_{bs} = ag_{bs} + b \\ & \quad C'_E = C_E \cup \{\langle +b[id], T\rangle\} \end{aligned}$$

The second rule, *NotifyAchieve*, handles the notification of an `Achieve` message. The agent's response to this notification depends on its current *mood*. If the agent is in an `Altruistic` mood, it checks whether it possesses any relevant plans—applicable given its current beliefs—that can achieve the goal overheard in the logical room. In this scenario, the receiving agent recognizes that the sender requires assistance in achieving a goal and acknowledges its own ability to help. However, it would be inappropriate for the agent to autonomously pursue the goal without coordinating with the sender. To address this, the *NotifyAchieve* rule specifies that if the notified agent can assist (*i.e.*, it has an applicable plan), it sends a message to the sender, offering to achieve the goal on their behalf. What follows is domain-dependent and must be programmed by the developer: it is up to the sender agent to autonomously decide whether to accept the offer, delegate the goal, or continue pursuing other strategies.

Similar to the previous rule, if the agent is not in an `Altruistic` mood, it simply discards the message and takes no action.

$$(\text{NotifyAchieve}) \frac{S_M(M_{In}) = \langle mid, id, Notify, sent(\_, Achieve, at), mode\rangle \quad (mid, i) \notin M_{SI} \quad [\text{for any intention } i]}{\langle ag, C, M, T, ProcMsg, mood\rangle \rightarrow \langle ag, C, M', T, SelEv, mood\rangle}$$

$$\begin{aligned} where \quad & M'_{In} = M_{In} \setminus \{\langle mid, id, Notify, sent(\_, Achieve, at), mode\rangle\} \\ & \text{if } Altruistic \in mood \text{ then} \\ & \quad \text{if } AppPlans(ag_{bs}, RelPlans(ag_{ps}, at)) \neq \emptyset \\ & \quad M'_{Out} = M_{Out} \cup \{\langle mid', id, Tell, can\_achieve(at), mode\rangle\} \end{aligned}$$

5   Implementation

Here, we present the instantiation of KQML-S inside the VEsNA framework. The code is available to the community from the KQML-S repository [18].

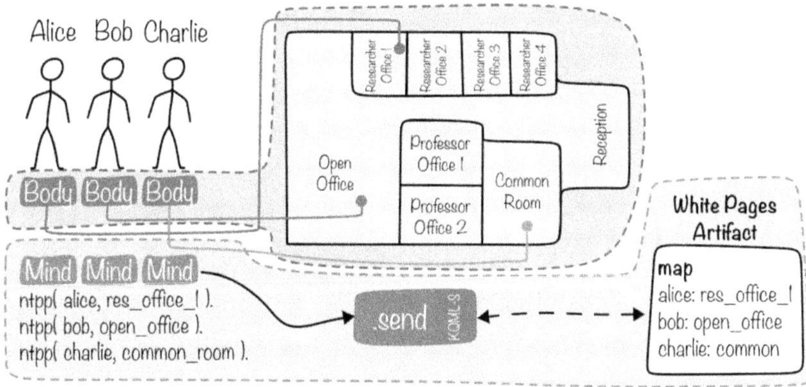

Fig. 2. VEsNA KQML-S design. Each agent has a body and a mind, it is physically located inside a region, and models (and stores) this information using Region Connection Calculus [9]. Whenever the agent moves, it updates the White Pages artifact. When an agent **a** calls the `.send` action in Jason, the action accesses the White Pages to check which other agents are in the same region as **a**.

VEsNA [17,21] extends Jason by enabling peer-to-peer connections between an agent and its body and uses some features of JaCaMo [4] when artifacts are needed. Jason, implemented in Java, provides the foundation for this extension. In Jason a class `Agent` manages the agent's lifecycle and reasoning process, interpreting the AgentSpeak(L) source, and agents have a predefined set of internal actions implemented through the `DefaultInternalAction` class. VEsNA extends the default Jason implementation in three ways:

1. the `Agent` class is extended into `VesnaAgent`, which creates a WebSocket client for bidirectional communication with the body;
2. a new `DefaultInternalAction walk` is introduced, enabling agents to perform walking actions;
3. a set of high-level plans is provided to facilitate agent implementation.

VEsNA agents reason logically on space using the Region Connection Calculus (RCC) [16]. In RCC, the relation `ntpp(X, Y)` describes that X *is strictly contained in* Y. This property is crucial for the implementation, as it naturally expresses an agent **a**'s situatedness within a region **r** as `ntpp(a, r)`. In the current KQML-S in VEsNA implementation, we only consider situatedness in regions: logical rooms like `WhatsApp` are not yet supported. Figure 2 shows the architecture we implemented.

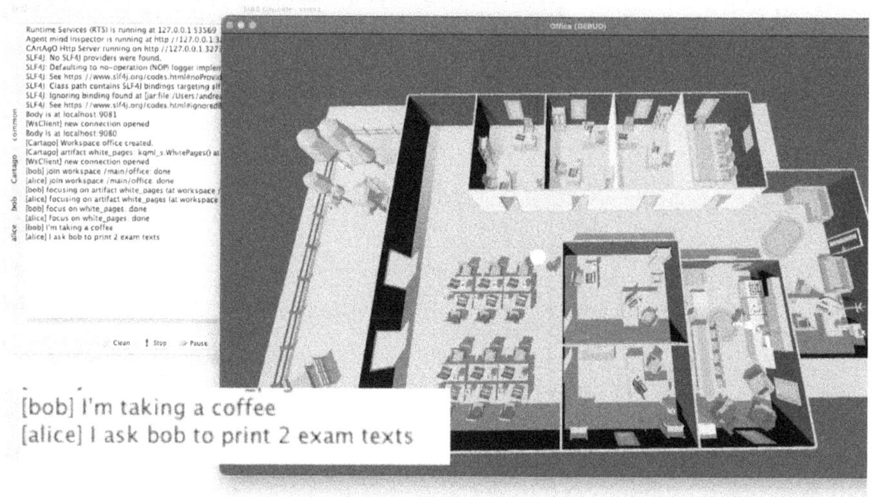

Fig. 3. Scenario 1. Alice (red agent) asks Bob (white agent) to print two copies of the exam. The request is heard by nobody.

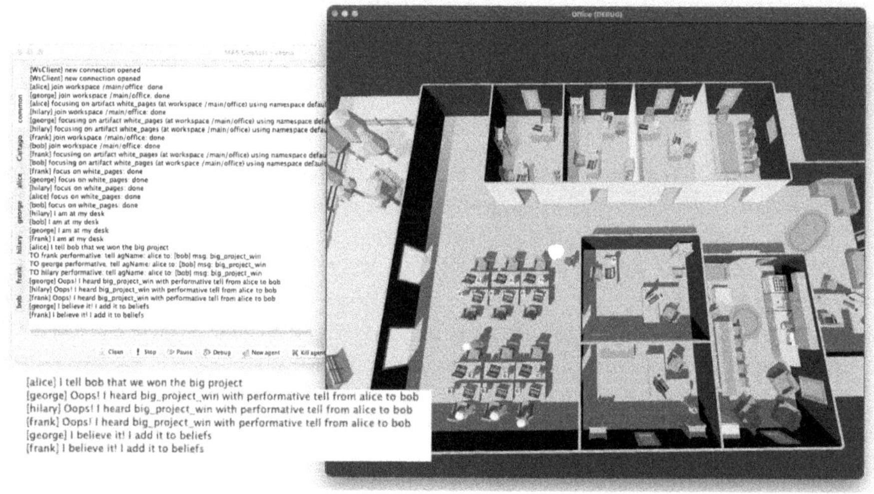

Fig. 4. Scenario 2. Alice (red agent) tells Bob (one of the white agents) they won a big project. The message is heard also by Frank, George and Hilary who are in the room. As shown in the MAS Console, Frank and George are credulous and they add the content to their belief base while Hilary does nothing.

To implement the KQML-S extension a new `DefaultInternalAction` `.send` has been developed starting from the `.send` standard one: the KQML-S `.send` action provides this API

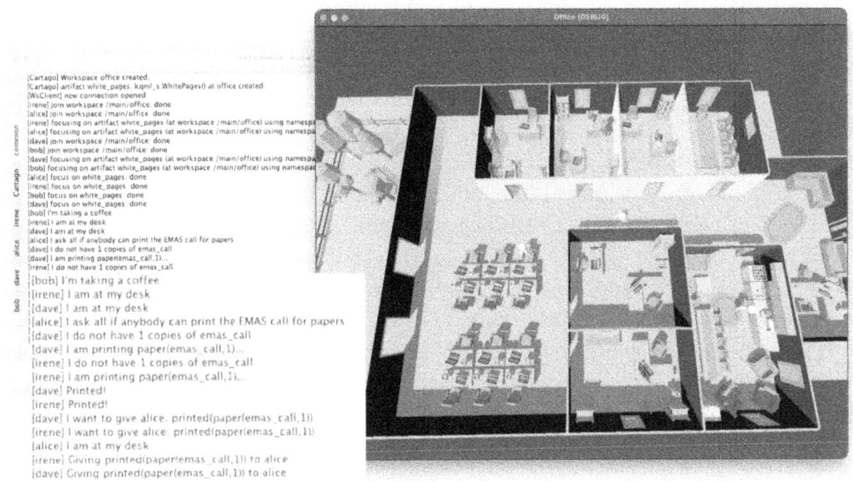

Fig. 5. Scenario 5. Alice (red agent) requests **all** agents inside the office room to print EMAS call for papers. The message is received from Bob and Irene, and both print it.

```
.send( Mode, Receiver, Performative, Cnt, Answer, Timeout )
```

where **Mode** can be set to either **private** or **public** to change the privacy level of the message and the other parameters are the same as the default one. The message is sent only if the sender and **Receiver** are in the same region. Since in this current implementation we only support region-based situatedness, the **Mode** actual parameter, that in our formalization is a couple (**Room, How**), only needs to state the **How** (**private** or **public**), as the **Room** is computed automatically as "the RCC region in the Virtual Environment where the sender is" by taking advantage of the *White Pages* artifact. If **Mode** is **public** all the agents in the region that are neither **Receiver** nor in **Receiver** list will find the **notify(Performative, Receiver, Cnt)[source(Sender)]** belief among their mental notes. In addition, an agent can perform a **.send** with **all** as **Receiver**. Here, the message is sent to all the agents present in the region.

Agents update their location via the *White Pages* artifact when moving between regions. The **.send** action delivers messages only to agents currently in the same room. This preserves individual perspectives, allowing agents to hold outdated beliefs or remain unaware of others unless explicitly informed.

The implementation covers four of the five scenarios in Sect. 2; Scenario 3 is excluded due to reliance on unsupported logical rooms. Scenario 4 is implemented but omitted here for space. Agents act within a virtual office built in Godot. The screenshots show a single execution frame, while the MAS Console logs all events and real-time interactions.

Scenario 1. Alice moves to the open area of the office, where Bob is usually present, to request that he prints two copies of the exam. Alice performs `.send(public, bob, achieve, print(paper(exam, 2)))`; and Bob has indeed a plan to print but, as shown in Fig. 3, he is enjoying a coffee in the common room.

Scenario 2. Alice returns to the open office where Bob is and announces that they won a big project, speaking loudly without realizing that Frank, George, and Hilary are also present, as shown in Fig. 4.

Scenario 5. Alice enters the office and asks if anyone can print a copy of the EMAS 2025 call for papers. In the office there are Bob and Irene, that she does not know. Alice sends the request using `send` with `all` as the receiver, ensuring that everyone in the room directly receives the `achieve` message. Since, in this simplified setting, no coordination mechanism is in place, both Bob and Irene print the document and provide a copy to Alice, as illustrated in Fig. 5.

6   Related and Future Work

KQML-S extends KQML with locality and public/private communication, enabling agents to interact within shared logical spaces and model effects like overhearing. This enriches coordination and awareness in MAS. Our interest, shaped by work on VEsNA, reflects the growing need for locality-aware communication as distributed systems increasingly rely on spatial or logical co-location.

KQML-S treats overhearing as a first-class communication feature, capturing key aspects of situated interaction in virtual and physical environments. Rather than avoiding unintended perception, it leverages it as a channel for partial information, implicit coordination, and timely intervention—without requiring subscriptions or explicit sharing. This supports more natural, context-aware agent behavior in spatially structured settings.

Previous approaches have touched on related aspects. CG-KQML+ [7] extends KQML with conceptual graphs and enhanced performatives, but lacks the focus on spatial context. Coo-BDI [1] enables plan sharing among trusted peers, emphasizing structural cooperation rather than dynamic, context-driven communication. Moise+ [25] models role-based social behavior, while KQML-S focuses on how locality and presence influence message propagation. Liu et al. [28] offer a domain-specific KQML adaptation for control systems, whereas KQML-S remains general-purpose. Dell'Anna et al. [10] address norm revision, which aligns with our interest in context-sensitive message interpretation.

Unlike these works, KQML-S introduces a communication layer grounded in environment-aware semantics and agent attitudes (e.g., altruistic, skeptical), supporting nuanced responses based on message content and context.

Looking ahead, several directions could extend KQML-S. Adding KQML performatives like `Ask` or `TellHow` would support richer agent dialogues and a wider range of communication behaviors. We also plan to explore the effects of *nested* or *connected logical rooms* on message propagation, moving beyond isolated spaces. Incorporating *social structures*—such as norms, roles, and hierarchies—would allow agents to adapt communication based on trust, authority, or group membership. Finally, linking situated communication to *information protocols* like BSPL [39] could broaden the applicability of our model.

Another important future direction is the integration of *coordination* and *conflict resolution protocols* to enhance the robustness of KQML-S. This would be especially useful in scenarios where multiple agents respond to a single overheard message, potentially leading to conflicts (e.g., multiple agents pursuing the same goal). Large-scale experiments will also be essential to assess how KQML-S scales in more complex MAS environments, testing its performance and scalability as the number of agents and logical spaces increases.

Beyond virtual environments, extending KQML-S to interact with physical systems and IoT devices could enable applications in smart homes, autonomous vehicles, and robotic swarms, where agents must respond to both digital and physical cues. Integrating privacy-preserving mechanisms—such as encryption or access control—would also enhance security, allowing agents to reason about both visibility and confidentiality in communication. Together, these directions aim to evolve KQML-S into a comprehensive framework for situated communication in dynamic, socially rich MAS environments.

Acknowledgements. This work was partially supported by ENGINES âĂŞ ENGineering INtElligent Systems around intelligent agent technologies, funded by the Italian MUR program PRIN 2022 under grant number 20229ZXBZM and by FAIR âĂŞ Future Artificial Intelligence Research, PNRR MUR Project PE0000013 funded by the European Union âĂŞ NextGenerationEU, CUP J33C24000420007.

References

1. Ancona, D., Mascardi, V.: Coo-BDI: Extending the BDI model with cooperativity. In: Leite, J.A., Omicini, A., Sterling, L., Torroni, P. (eds.) Declarative Agent Languages and Technologies, First International Workshop, DALT 2003, Melbourne, Australia, July 15, 2003, Revised Selected and Invited Papers. Lecture Notes in Computer Science, vol. 2990, pp. 109–134. Springer (2003). https://doi.org/10.1007/978-3-540-25932-9_7
2. Bellifemine, F.L., Caire, G., Greenwood, D.: Developing Multi-Agent Systems with JADE. John Wiley & Sons (2007)
3. Bergenti, F., Caire, G., Monica, S., Poggi, A.: The first twenty years of agentbased software development with JADE. Auton. Agents Multi Agent Syst. **34**(2), 36 (2020)
4. Boissier, O., Bordini, R., Hubner, J., Ricci, A.: Multi-Agent Oriented Programming: Programming Miuted-Agent Systems Using JaCaMo. Intelligent Robotics and Autonomous Agents series, MIT Press, United States (2020). https://books.google.com.br/books?id=GM_tDwAAQBAJ
5. Bonabeau, E., Dorigo, M., Theraulaz, G.: Swarm Intelligence - From Natural to Artificial Systems. Santa Fe Institute Studies in the Sciences of Complexity, Oxford University Press (1999)

6. Bordini, R., Hübner, J., Wooldridge, M.: Programming Multi-Agent Systems in AgentSpeak Using Jason, vol. 8. John Wiley & Sons, Ltd, United Kingdom (10 2007). https://doi.org/10.1002/9780470061848
7. Bouzouba, K., Moulin, B., Kabbaj, A.: CG-KQML+: an agent communication language and its use in a multi-agent system. In: Proceedings of the 9th International Conference on Conceptual Structures, pp. 1–14 (2001)
8. Cohen, P.R., Perrault, C.R.: Elements of a plan-based theory of speech acts. Cogn. Sci. 3(3), 177–212 (1979). https://doi.org/10.1016/S0364-0213(79)80006-3, https://www.sciencedirect.com/science/article/pii/S0364021379800063
9. Cohn, A.G., Bennett, B., Gooday, J., Gotts, N.M.: Qualitative spatial representation and reasoning with the region connection calculus. GeoInformatica **1**(3), 275–316 (1997). https://doi.org/10.1023/A:1009712514511
10. Dell'Anna, D., Dastani, M., Dalpiaz, F.: Runtime revision of sanctions in normative multi-agent systems. Auton. Agent. Multi-Agent Syst. **34**(2), 1–54 (2020). https://doi.org/10.1007/s10458-020-09465-8
11. Ferrando, A., Winikoff, M., Cranefield, S., Dignum, F., Mascardi, V.: On enactability of agent interaction protocols: Towards a unified approach. In: EMAS@AAMAS. Lecture Notes in Computer Science, vol. 12058, pp. 43–64. Springer (2019)
12. Ferrando, A., Winikoff, M., Cranefield, S., Dignum, F., Mascardi, V.: On enactability of agent interaction protocols: towards a unified approach. In: AAMAS, pp. 1955–1957. International Foundation for Autonomous Agents and Multiagent Systems (2019)
13. Finin, T., Fritzson, R., McKay, D., McEntire, R.: KQML as an agent communication language. In: Proceedings of the Third International Conference on Information and Knowledge Management, pp. 456–463. CIKM '94, Association for Computing Machinery, New York, NY, USA (1994). https://doi.org/10.1145/191246.191322
14. Finin, T., McKay, D.P., Fritzson, R., McEntire, R.: KQML - a language and protocol for knowledge and information exchange. IOS Press (September 1994), revised paper from the 13th International Distributed Artificial Intelligence Workshop, July 28-30 (1994)
15. Foundation for Intelligent Physical Agents: FIPA ACL Message Structure Specification (2002). http://www.fipa.org/specs/fipa00061/SC00061G.html. Accessed 23 Jan 2026 09:47:13
16. Gatti, A.: Reason logically, move continuously. In: Ferrando, A., Cardoso, R.C. (eds.) Agents and Robots for reliable Engineered Autonomy, pp. 115–127. Springer Nature Switzerland, Cham (2025)
17. Gatti, A., Ferrando, A., Mascardi, V.: Integrating virtual reality, chatbots, and BDI agents: VEsNA goes fast! In: Collier, R., Mascardi, V., Ricci, A. (eds.) Agents and Multi-Agent Systems Development – Platforms, Toolkits, Technologies. Springer (2025)
18. Gatti, A., Ferrando, A., Mascardi, V.: KQML-S web site (2025). https://github.com/VEsNA-ToolKit/KQML-S. Accessed 23 Jan 2026 09:47:13
19. Gatti, A., Ferrando, A., Mascardi, V.: VEsNA-Toolkit web site (2025). https://github.com/VEsNA-ToolKit. Accessed 23 Jan 2026 09:47:13
20. Gatti, A., Mascardi, V.: Towards VEsNA, a framework for managing virtual environments via natural language agents. In: AREA@IJCAI-ECAI. EPTCS, vol. 362, pp. 65–80 (2022)

21. Gatti, A., Mascardi, V.: VEsNA, a framework for virtual environments via natural language agents and its application to factory automation. Robotics **12**(2), 46 (2023)
22. Genesereth, M.R., Ketchpel, S.P.: Software agents. Commun. ACM **37**(7), 48–ff. (Jul 1994). https://doi.org/10.1145/176789.176794
23. Godot foundation: Godot web site (2025). https://godotengine.org/. Accessed on 2026/01/23 09:47:13
24. Hadeli, Valckenaers, P., Kollingbaum, M., Van Brussel, H.: Multi-agent coordination and control using stigmergy. Comput. Ind. **53**(1), 75–96 (Jan 2004). https://doi.org/10.1016/S0166-3615(03)00123-4
25. Hübner, J.F., Sichman, J.S., Boissier, O.: Developing organised multiagent systems using the MOISE+ model: programming issues at the system and agent levels. Int. J. Agent Oriented Softw. Eng. 1(3/4), 370–395 (2007). https://doi.org/10.1504/IJAOSE.2007.016266
26. Labrou, Y., Finin, T.: A semantics approach for KQML – a general purpose communication language for software agents. In: Proceedings of the Third International Conference on Information and Knowledge Management, pp. 447–455. CIKM '94, Association for Computing Machinery, New York, NY, USA (1994). https://doi.org/10.1145/191246.191320
27. Labrou, Y., Finin, T.: A proposal for a new KQML specification. Tech. rep., TR CS-97-03 from UMBC (1997)
28. Liu, Y., Zhang, X., Wu, Q.: Optimizing KQML for usage in wood drying multi-agent coordination system. In: 2011 Chinese Control and Decision Conference (CCDC), pp. 3725–3730 (2011). https://doi.org/10.1109/CCDC.2011.5968872
29. Luke, S., Balan, G.C., Sullivan, K., Panait, L.: Mason (2003). https://cs.gmu.edu/~eclab/projects/mason/, george Mason University
30. North, M.J., Collier, N.T., Vos, J.R.: Repast (2006). https://repast.github.io/, argonne National Laboratory
31. Omicini, A., Ricci, A., Viroli, M.: Artifacts in the A&A meta-model for multi-agent systems. Auton. Agents Multi Agent Syst. **17**(3), 432–456 (2008)
32. Omicini, A., Zambonelli, F.: Coordination for internet application development. Auton. Agents Multi Agent Syst. **2**(3), 251–269 (1999)
33. Pokahr, A., Braubach, L.: From a research to an industry-strength agent platform: JADEX V2. In: Wirtschaftsinformatik (1). books@ocg.at, vol. 246, pp. 769–780. Österreichische Computer Gesellschaft (2009)
34. Rao, A.S.: AgentSpeak(L): BDI agents speak out in a logical computable language. In: 7th European Workshop on Modelling Autonomous Agents in a Multi-Agent World, Eindhoven, The Netherlands, January 22-25, 1996. Lecture Notes in Computer Science, vol. 1038, pp. 42–55. Springer (1996). https://doi.org/10.1007/BFb0031845
35. Ricci, A., Omicini, A., Denti, E.: The TuCSoN coordination infrastructure for virtual enterprises. In: Proceedings Tenth IEEE International Workshop on Enabling Technologies: Infrastructure for Collaborative Enterprises. WET ICE 2001, pp. 348–353 (2001). https://doi.org/10.1109/ENABL.2001.953442
36. Ricci, A., Piunti, M., Viroli, M., Omicini, A.: Environment programming in CArtAgO. In: Multi-Agent Programming, Languages, Tools and Applications, pp. 259–288. Springer (2009)
37. Ricci, A., Viroli, M., Omicini, A.: Give agents their artifacts: the A&A approach for engineering working environments in MAS. In: AAMAS, pp. 150. IFAAMAS (2007)

38. Singh, M.P.: Agent communication languages: rethinking the principles. Computer 31(12), 40–47 (1998). https://doi.org/10.1109/2.735849
39. Singh, M.P.: Information-driven interaction-oriented programming: BSPL, the blindingly simple protocol language. In: The 10th International Conference on Autonomous Agents and Multiagent Systems - Volume 2, pp. 491–498 (2011)
40. Theraulaz, G., Bonbeau, E.: A brief history of stigmergy. Artif. Life 5(2), 97–116 (Apr 1999). https://doi.org/10.1162/106454699568700
41. Vieira, R., Moreira, Á.F., Wooldridge, M.J., Bordini, R.H.: On the formal semantics of speech-act based communication in an agent-oriented programming language. J. Artif. Intell. Res. 29, 221–267 (2007). https://doi.org/10.1613/jair.2221
42. Wilensky, U.: Netlogo (1999). http://ccl.northwestern.edu/netlogo/, center for Connected Learning and Computer-Based Modeling, Northwestern University

Teamwork in Adversarial Video Games

Barbara Dunin-Kęplicz[1] and Rafał Tyl[2,3]($\boxtimes$)

[1] Faculty of Mathematics, Informatics and Mechanics, University of Warsaw,
Warsaw, Poland
[2] Gentle Viking, Warsaw, Poland
[3] Grail, Warsaw, Poland
`rafftyl@wp.pl`

Abstract. In adversarial video games, human players and non-player characters (NPCs) compete to win certain goods or targets. To gain an advantage and create realistic behaviors, NPCs could cooperate by forming groups or coalitions. Surprisingly enough, they typically do not. Consequently, we have concentrated our efforts on providing game developers with the necessary tools to enhance virtual characters with teamwork capabilities. To start with, we address this challenge by observing that a classical Reconfiguration Algorithm, known in MAS, can serve as an umbrella for teamwork-related activities of NPCs. Reconfiguration amounts to intelligent replanning in response to changing circumstances. By analogy, our solution, inspired by the reconfiguration process, takes the control over the game and keeps it going by utilizing mechanisms that facilitate cooperation under adversarial conditions.

As a proof of concept, we have developed, implemented, and tested ARA, the Adversarial Reconfiguration Algorithm, alongside an encompassing agent-oriented framework called ARAG and a simple stealth video game called Treasure Hunt. ARAG facilitates a flexible approach to aspects of teamwork such as belief representation, communication, reconfiguration, and task allocation. As demonstrated by Treasure Hunt, NPCs coordinated by ARAG outperform those lacking cooperative capabilities, even with the adopted simplifying design choices.

Keywords: methodology of teamwork · reconfiguration algorithm · adversarial video games

1 Introduction

Teamwork matters. This paradigmatic statement is true in multiagent systems. But how about video games? Most games include non-player characters, NPCs, who engage human players by providing adequate challenges and exhibiting convincing behaviors [29]. In adversarial video games, opposing parties compete to win certain goods or targets. NPC teammates could work together to gain an advantage, but despite recent attempts to improve NPCs cooperation with basic communication and coordination [1], this is often neglected [2,29].

The multi-billion dollar gaming market, projected to grow dynamically, is overlooking mature teamwork solutions from MAS, despite enormous financial

© The Author(s), under exclusive license to Springer Nature Switzerland AG 2026
S. Rodriguez et al. (Eds.): EMAS 2025, LNAI 16407, pp. 177–199, 2026.
https://doi.org/10.1007/978-3-032-18011-7_11

potential and the technological sophistication of the products themselves. In the context of MAS, with the emphasis on autonomy, cooperation, and communication among intelligent agents, advanced models for coordination, dependency management, and conflict resolution have been developed over the years. By not using these frameworks, the gaming industry misses its full potential in modeling the teamwork of NPCs and human players. What is also surprising is that the MAS community does not allocate more effort to adapt its solutions to such a large industry. The state of the art motivated us to investigate how to automatically orchestrate NPCs' teamwork in adversarial video games with the help of MAS-related techniques.

Teamwork, typically regarded in the literature as a collective accomplishment of common goals [7,8,23,30–32], can take various forms [18]. Traditionally, the study of cooperation belongs to MAS, so we searched for a relevant methodology there, choosing TeamLog, a formal Belief-Desire-Intention (BDI) model of agents' cooperation introduced in [7]. Based on multi-modal logic, TeamLog, has been designed to model group attitudes like collective intentions and collective commitments during teamwork. Their role is highlighted in the classical model of teamwork, consisting of stages of potential recognition, team formation and plan generation, culminating in team action. Namely, a collective intention constitutes a strictly cooperative team during team formation, while a plan-based collective commitment, implementing the specifics required for a group to cooperate, is set up during planning. Ultimately, reconfiguration, as a form of intelligent replanning, is carried out throughout team actions and implemented as a Reconfiguration Algorithm [7].

For several reasons, we are hesitant to use TeamLog directly, even though it would be natural to consider it as the underlying teamwork modeling formalism. First, while situated at the core of TeamLog, complete BDI agents with groups equipped with collective attitudes are not really needed at the current stage. Second, by turning the player into an opponent, the video game generates an entirely distinct situation. Specifically, the NPCs' team must make a clear distinction between the effects of the enemy's actions and those arising from the environment's variability. Third, industry standards of game specification have to be taken into account. All in all, we do not adhere to the logic-based formalism of TeamLog, while still remaining inspired by its methodology.

Taking this into account, we developed the Adversarial Reconfiguration Algorithm (ARA) to dynamically manage team actions in response to game state changes. It draws from MAS-related Reconfiguration Algorithm and AI planning, providing an orchestration of NPC behavior in adversarial video games. The entire process is implemented as the Adversarial Reconfiguration Algorithm for Games (ARAG) framework, automatically integrating teamwork into games.

Although the burden of game design and implementation remains with the developers, ARAG organizes teamwork among otherwise uncooperative NPCs. As an input, a developer provides an implementation of an adversarial video game along with components required by ARAG. As a result, ARAG produces a realistic teamwork of NPCs, turning an uncooperative video game into a cooperative one.

The presented version of ARAG deals with one team of NPCs, competing against a human player. In future, this simplifying assumption might be relaxed.

Compared to ad hoc solutions, ARAG offers innovative game possibilities, by combining MAS methodologies with game industry experience. A typical challenge in agent-based programming is merging goal-directed reasoning with data-driven stream reflecting the environmental circumstances. Even though game environments are usually simpler than those in MAS, one must still account for unanticipated events brought on by human players. ARAG addresses this issue.

Overall, the original contributions of this paper include:

- ARA: the algorithm for managing team actions in reaction to changes,
- ARAG: the framework for orchestrating NPCs' teamwork, encompassing ARA,
- a prototype implementation for a simple stealth video game - Treasure Hunt.

The paper is structured as follows. In Sect. 2, we discuss teamwork in adversarial video games, while Sect. 3 describes ARAG's role in coordinating teamwork. Section 4 is devoted to the ARAG architecture. Section 5 presents the core of our research: ARA with the auxiliary procedures. In Sect. 6 we discuss the design choices underlying ARAG, while Sect. 7 presents a proof of concept. Section 8 discusses related work and, Sect. 9 concludes the paper.

2   Teamwork and Adversarial Video Games

Video games are complex systems, where an audiovisual apparatus is orchestrated by game engines facilitating the development of components like resource management, rendering, game loop management, physics simulation, etc. [9]. Thanks to the availability of affordable game engines [22], developers do not have to build games from scratch, but provide game-specific components solely. A perception of the game depends on the level of realism in each individual action and on the complexity of the NPCs' interactions. Moreover, cooperative teams of NPCs must battle against (human) player and be able to:

- operate in a physical environment with interactive elements (e.g. doors),
- coordinate actions with others,
- access the game world data,
- adequately react to adversarial actions of others,
- communicate beliefs or actions by graphical symbols (icons and indicators) or sounds (so called "barks").

In multi-agent environments, actions may fail due to unexpected circumstances. In adversarial video games, one needs to distinguish situations resulting from a natural variability of the environment from those caused by an enemy. This requires a proper separation of:

- observed phenomena,
- messages explicitly/implicitly dealing with adversarial acts,
- a lack of contact with some agents.

Video games typically progress according to scenarios scriptwrited by game designers. These scenarios outline the principles governing dynamic alterations to the surroundings, such as those that occur naturally (like an accident), on a regular basis (like day-night cycle mechanics), or as a result of player or NPCs activity (like opening and closing a door). Thus, a key concern is how to strike a balance between a designer's control and the autonomy of NPCs.

In our approach, the adherence to scripts is ensured by plans applicable in specific circumstances: individual plans, reflecting individual behavior and social ones, reflecting team behavior. Both types are constructed from actions to be performed by particular NPCs in a given order. Thus, ARAG utilizes a user-defined plan library as the foundation of teamwork, while still being able to enhance the game with complex and diverse teamwork functionalities.

During team action, a hostile interruption of a plan's execution necessitates an appropriate response. Although plan adaptation is prevalent in MAS, in games a team must explicitly monitor individuals for prospective attacks. Thus, replanning during reconfiguration influences both group and adversary behavior. These aspects are implemented in ARA.

3   ARAG as a Teamwork Coordinator

In video games, most of the time NPCs fight human players. The idea of ARAG is to give NPCs the opportunity to cooperate in order to increase their gains and make the task more difficult for their opponents. To achieve this, ARAG serves as a coordinator of NPCs' teamwork, while maintaining the individual roles assigned to them by the game designer.

3.1   ARAG and NPCs

ARAG takes control over NPCs in the game. Functionally, it can be thought of as a software agent whose responsibility is to manage game-specific behaviors of NPC agents. As its input, ARAG receives an implementation of an adversarial game. As usual, the game is created and implemented by the game creator. The use of ARAG adds an additional overhead, including some situation-specific preferences and game-related strategies (listed in Sect. 4.3) that need to be made available via an ARAG-imposed API. As the result, ARAG enhances the game by automatically created realistic teamwork of autonomous NPCs.

The ARAG's operations, encapsulated in ARA, lead to the creation, execution, and intelligent modification of social plans, accomplished by techniques derived from distributed AI and MAS. Consecutive phases of the entire process allow to change a plan or a team, according to the hazards of the game.

NPCs and ARAG maintain some explicit representation of beliefs, commitments and reports, but we are not concerned with their specific representations. As regards beliefs, we assume that there is an interface to the belief base providing fused beliefs of all NPCs, abstracting from specific belief fusion methods. They may vary from the simplest belief union to sophisticated fusion methods, e.g. eliminating noise or resolving potential uncertainty, inconsistencies and/or disagreements. In contrast to real-world applications, in video games NPCs typically have a direct access to the virtual environment. Thus their observations can be interpreted unambiguously so a simple sum of beliefs is often sufficient.

3.2   Plan Skeletons and Social Plans

ARAG realizes the two main aspects of teamwork – task sharing and result sharing [31]. Task sharing involves the decomposition of a comprehensive task into subtasks assigned to individual agents. These tasks form social plans that transform a loosely connected NPCs into a cooperative team. Result sharing pertains to supplying teammates with relevant information.

The social plan construction pertains to a user-provided library of plan skeletons, defined as a partially ordered set of tasks, in particular denoting tasks to be performed sequentially. A complete social plan is a defined as a partially ordered set of task-agent pairs, where each pair denotes an agent allocated to a specific task [7]. A transition from a plan skeleton to a social plan is shown in Fig. 1.

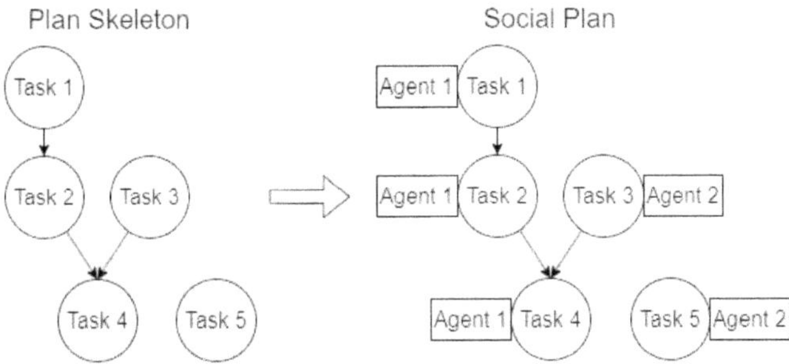

Fig. 1. Transformation of plan skeleton into a social plan.

The ARAG activity starts from team formation and task allocation, resulting in a social plan. Ultimately it leads to a team action, that is, to collective execution of this plan by a team of NPCs under ARAG's supervision. During plan execution, ARAG determines the status (*in progress*, *completed*, or *failed*) of the plan as a whole. If a task fails, ARAG reconfigures the plan, as described in the sequel. In short, ARAG is responsible for:

– choosing the plan to achieve the objective,
– identifying the most suitable NPCs,
– creating a cooperating team,
– developing a social plan,
– distributing tasks to NPCs,
– creating bilateral commitments between NPCs and itself,
– supervising a plan execution and reconfiguring it,

- changing the plan in the case of emergency/lost connection,
- dissolving the team, when needed,
- announcing failure/success/abort of the plan.

Commitments between ARAG and NPCs are created by ARAG sending a task execution request and the NPC confirming its ability to perform this task. Then NPCs carry out tasks and report to ARAG their progress and observations pertinent to the team. This way ARAG becomes the central node of the commitment network. Such a star topology centralizes some agent management aspects while reducing the need for group interactions.

An NPC is primarily responsible for carrying out agent-specific tasks. What counts to ARAG is whether the NPC is capable of performing the tasks, as indicated by its opportunities and abilities reflecting its objective possibilities and subjective skills, respectively [11,15]. That is, NPCs are heterogeneous.

4   The Architecture of ARAG

ARAG consists of multiple interacting components and databases (Fig. 2):

- *Belief Base* of beliefs about the world and NPCs;
- *Report Base* of task status reports,
- *Plan Library* of plan skeletons.

Information stored in the databases (denoted as ovals) is processed in order to create, monitor and reconfigure social plans by the following processes (denoted as rectangles):

- *Reasoner*, responsible for reasoning about beliefs,
- *Opportunity Analyzer*, producing feasible tasks, based on the current beliefs about the environment,
- *Report Analyzer*, checking the current plan's status and generating new tasks based on monitoring results,
- *Filters: Compatibility Filter, Task Override Filter*, narrowing down the stream of tasks,
- *Task Selector*, selecting the most suitable task,
- *Means-End Reasoner*, selecting applicable plans from Plan Library,
- *Adversarial Reconfiguration Algorithm* ARA, creating the details of a *social plan* and reconfiguring it, when necessary,
- *Communication Layer*, facilitating communication between ARAG and NPCs.

In contrast to Reasoner and Means-End Reasoner that are adequate to the representation of beliefs and plans, Filters, Task Selector, Report Analyzer and Opportunity Analyzer are game-specific and their content should be delivered by the user (e.g., as a set of rules).

The communication layer serves as the interface between ARAG and the team, ensuring effective information exchange. Even though MAS are known for complex interactions, in ARAG, designed for real-time video games, they should

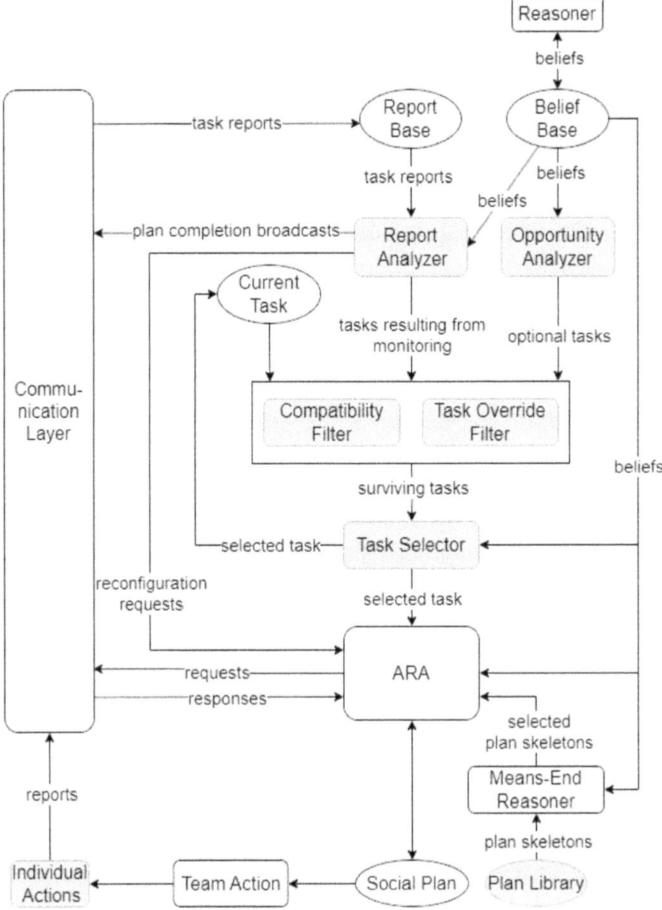

Fig. 2. ARAG architecture.

be as simple and balanced as possible. Therefore, only the most fundamental speech acts—a bilateral communication between two actors and an announcement, when the message reaches all teammates simultaneously—are considered. Facilities ensuring proper communication are a part of ARAG, while the potential presentation layer (sounds, animations etc.) should be delivered by the user.

4.1   Combining Various Streams of Options

Adversarial Reconfiguration Algorithm refers to optional tasks originating from:

- the current plan: goal-directed aspect,
- the observed/communicated environmental changes: data driven aspect,
- the monitoring process: potentially generating new options.

Given the recent circumstances, all tasks originating from the above three sources compete to become the winner - the task to be executed next. This issue is central in intelligent decision systems and may be solved in a variety of ways. Based on the experience acquired in MAS, a filtering system inspired by a well known system IRMA [4] was designed in a relatively transparent way. As filters aim to reduce computational complexity during task selection, their sensitivity is crucial: too sensitive might destabilize the ARAG's operation, while too rough might downplay potential threats [4].

4.2   The ARAG's Lifecycle

ARAG is incorporated into the game as a software framework, meaning that the user provides required data and procedures for calculating game-specific parameters (like abilities and opportunities), as outlined in Sect. 4.3. On the other hand, ARAG dictates the flow of control inside its update function called periodically from the game loop. Namely, on each update the lifecycle of ARAG starts with generating three streams of optional tasks, then sent to the Compatibility Filter to assess their consistency with the current task. Importantly, the rejected options are not simply discarded. They pass through the Task Override Filter to determine whether the current situation requires a radical change of the plan. In such cases, for example, after detecting hazardous conditions, relevant options are passed to the Task Selector. Out of surviving tasks, the Task Selector chooses the best one to pursue. A relevant social plan is formed using Adversarial Reconfiguration Algorithm, described in Sect. 5. Whenever the system is updated, the plan is modified or the task is modified in response to environmental changes.

4.3   ARAG's Setup Step by Step

The user is required to provide the following game-specific elements:

- plan skeletons for the Plan Library,
- filtering rules,
- option generation rules for the Report Analyzer,
- option generation rules for the Opportunity Analyzer,
- option selection rules for the Task Selector,
- game-specific actions of the NPCs,
- functions to compute individual opportunities and abilities.

In Fig. 2, the modules containing user-provided data are indicated in green. They are user-tailored and establish the level of detail of the team's interactions. The rules from analyzers, together with filtering and task selecting mechanisms, ensure a deliberative aspect of ARAG, leading to the choice of the next task for the team. On the other hand, user-provided plan skeletons enable scenario-driven means-end reasoning as well as event-driven reactions to both environmental changes and enemy activity.

As a core of teamwork, ARAG produces a social plan to achieve the current task by NPCs. Then it monitors the execution of the resulting team action.

Specifically, this social plan and coordinated team action constitute ARAG's output. A higher level view of inputs and outputs is shown in Fig. 3.

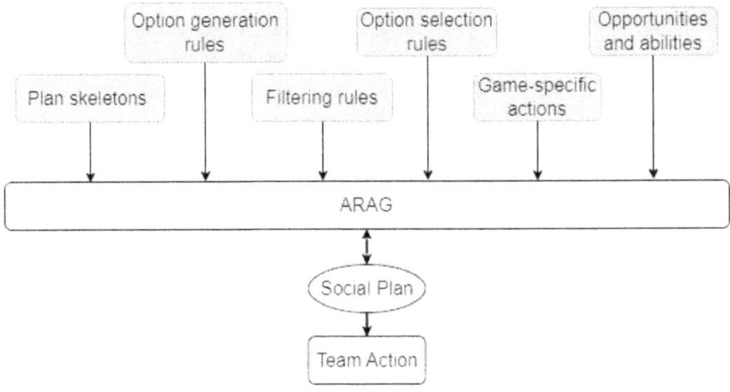

Fig. 3. ARAG inputs and outputs.

5   Adversarial Reconfiguration Algorithm

The Adversarial Reconfiguration Algorithm, ARA, provides the overall control structure of a team. It applies practical reasoning [7,31] to create social plans. The necessary plan modifications are accomplished by separating successive phases of the algorithm and controlling their complex interplay. In contrast to the classical Reconfiguration Algorithm [7], ARA consists of five phases, differing from the original ones. In each phase, the algorithm moves towards creating a team that executes a social plan, possibly returning to an earlier phase in the case of failure. These phases are implemented in pseudocode as:

1. plan selection - in Algorithm 1,
2. team formation - in Algorithm 1,
3. task allocation - Algorithm 2,
4. commitment distribution - Algorithm 3,
5. team action monitoring - Algorithm 4.

To avoid nested loops and improve readability we use 'go to' statements.

5.1   Plan Selection

Planning boils down to taking the next plan skeleton from the sequence of applicable plans, returned by the Means-End Reasoner and sorted by preferences. Each plan contains information about the optimal size of the team that will be consumed during team formation. The entire procedure fails in the absence of a plan, indicating that the task is not feasible given the current situation and the pool of potential NPCs.

Algorithm 1: ARA

Input: *task* - the current task
Input: *potentialTeammates* - the list of potential teammates
Input: *planToReconfigure* - the social plan to be reconfigured. If null, a new social plan will be created.
Data: *beliefBase* - the belief base
Output: a social plan realizing the current task

```
/* if the current plan is reconfigured, start with team formation first       */
if planToReconfigure ≠ null then
    plan ← planToReconfigure
    go to TEAM_FORMATION;
end
plans ← queue of plan skeletons from Means-End Reasoner suitable for task
PLANNING:
/* if the algorithm returned to planning after a failed reconfiguration, start over  */
if planToReconfigure ≠ null then
    plans ← queue of plan skeletons suitable for task from Means-End Reasoner
    planToReconfigure ← null
end
if plans is empty then
    return null; // fail and stop the algorithm
end
plan ← dequeue the first element of plans
teamSize ← team size from plan's metadata
/* team index is reset after getting a new plan, to be used during team formation  */
currentTeamIndex ← −1

TEAM_FORMATION:
consideredAgents ← filter potentialTeammates by ability
if size of consideredAgents < teamSize then
    go to PLANNING
end
/* produce the next team of the given size using Revolving Door algorithm        */
increment currentTeamIndex
team ← RevolvingDoor(consideredAgents, teamSize, currentTeamIndex)
/* team formation fails if there are no more teams of the given size             */
if failed then
    go to PLANNING
end

TASK_ALLOCATION:
globalContext ← construct global context based on beliefs from beliefBase
socialPlan ← Allocate(plan, team, globalContext)
if failed then
    go to TEAM_FORMATION
end

COMMITMENT_DISTRIBUTION:
DistributeCommitments(socialPlan)
if failed then
    clean up commitments
    go to TEAM_FORMATION
end
return socialPlan
```

5.2   Team Formation

Once a plan is selected, unsuitable NPCs are eliminated, based on their abilities and opportunities for specific tasks. Then, Payne's revolving door algorithm [12] allows to choose subgroups of the necessary size by selecting k-subsets that differ by only one member. These subgroups are successively passed to task allocation. If all accessible teams have been tried and failed, or if there are not enough NPCs, the algorithm returns to planning to select an alternative plan.

5.3 Task Allocation

The allocation phase assigns teammates to tasks from the plan skeleton. For each task ready for execution, the most suitable NPC is selected by computing a quality score based on opportunity and ability scores. If no NPC achieves a score above a user-specified threshold, the algorithm reverts to team formation. The procedure is repeated until all tasks are assigned, completing the social plan.

5.4 Commitment Distribution

The goal of this phase is to build commitments based on the established social plan. For every task in the plan, ARAG sends a task execution request to the appropriate NPC via the Communication Layer. The commitment is made and saved in the belief base upon receipt of confirmation. Otherwise, commitment distribution fails, non-cooperating NPCs are removed from the pool of available NPCs, and the system returns to team formation.

5.5 Team Action Monitoring

Once commitments are distributed, the team executes the social plan. NPCs perform tasks while periodically reporting results to ARAG. ARAG coordinates team actions by monitoring and potentially reconfiguring the plan or dissolving the team to create a new plan. In summary, ARAG develops and proceeds with the social plan as follows:

1. If a social plan is underway, its status (in progress/success/failure) is determined based on reports from teammates.
2. Optional tasks are generated and filtered (see Sect. 4.1). As a standard solution, see [31], option generation is carried out periodically during plan execution to enable adaptation to the changing environment.
3. The best task is selected.
4. If the best task differs from the current one, a new social plan is created. Otherwise, the current plan is kept going and adjusted.
5. The entire process is repeated cyclically while maintaining task prioritizing to adjust to environmental changes.

Algorithm 2: Allocate

Input: *plan* - a plan skeleton with NPCs not assigned to tasks
Input: *team* - the team that should execute the plan
Input: *globalContext* - a copy of a relevant subset of the belief base that is used as
       "working memory" during allocation
Data: *minScore* - the minimal required allocation score set by the user
Output: social plan

$socialPlan \leftarrow plan$ with empty allocation slots
$unallocatedTasks \leftarrow$ all tasks from plan
`/* tasks ready for allocation are determined, as described in Section 5.3          */`
$tasksReadyToAllocate \leftarrow$ ready tasks from unallocated tasks
`// proceed until all tasks are allocated`
while *size of unallocatedTasks* > 0 **do**
    if *tasksReadyToAllocate is empty* **then**
        `// the plan is malformed`
        error
    end

    $bestAgent \leftarrow null$
    $bestTask \leftarrow null$
    $highestScore \leftarrow 0$
    `/* go through the possible allocations and select the best one, based on`
       `opportunity and ability scores          */`
    for $task \in tasksReadyToAllocate$ **do**
        for $agent \in team$ **do**
            $abilityScore \leftarrow$ score based on $agent$'s skills needed to perform $task$
            $opportunityScore \leftarrow$ environment-dependent score based on $agent, task$ and
            $globalContext$
            $totalScore \leftarrow$ t-norm on $abilityScore$ and $opportunityScore$
            if $totalScore >= highestScore$ **then**
                $bestAgent \leftarrow agent$
                $bestTask \leftarrow task$
                $highestScore \leftarrow totalScore$
            end
        end
    end

    `/* if the best score is too low, the allocation phase fails          */`
    if $highestScore < minScore$ **then**
        fail
    end

    allocate $bestAgent$ to $bestTask$ in $socialPlan$
    apply effects of $bestTask$ to $globalContext$
    remove $bestTask$ from $unallocatedTasks$
    remove $bestTask$ from $tasksToAllocate$
    refresh $tasksReadyToAllocate$
end

return $socialPlan$

Algorithm 3: DistributeCommitments

Input: *socialPlan* - a plan with NPCs assigned to tasks
Data: *potentialTeammates* - the set of all NPCs considered for teamwork
Output: success or failure

```
/* attempt to form commitments in the same order that task allocation took place    */
foreach task, allocatedAgent ∈ allocations do
    request allocatedAgent to do task
    response ← response from allocatedAgent
    if response is confirmation then
        │ create commitment
    end
    else
        │ /* if the agent rejects the task or does not respond, it is removed from the
        │    considered set of teammates                                              */
        │ remove allocatedAgent from potentialTeammates
        │ return failure
    end
end

broadcast commitments
return success
```

Algorithm 4: ARAG Update

Data: *currentTask*
Data: *currentSocialPlan*
Data: *commitments* - commitments related to the plan
Data: *potentialTeammates*

```
options ← empty set
if currentSocialPlan ≠ null then
    │ /* determine the plan's status and add new task options based on report monitoring
    │    */
    │ planStatus, newOptions ← Monitor (currentSocialPlan, commitments)
    │ add newOptions to options
    │ if planStatus is success then
    │     broadcast success to all teammates
    │     clean up commitments related currentSocialPlan
    │     currentSocialPlan ← null
    │ end
    │
    │ /* the currently executed task is always added as an option                    */
    │ add currentTask to options
end

add tasks produced by the Opportunity Analyzer to options
bestOption ← option from options chosen by the task selector
if bestOption ≠ currentTask then
    │ /* the current task is replaced                                                */
    │ clean up commitments
    │ currentTask ← bestOption
    │ currentSocialPlan ← ARA(currentTask, potentialTeammates)
end
else if planStatus is failure then
    │ clean up commitments
    │ /* remove tasks that are already finished from the plan and reconfigure         */
    │ remove successful tasks from currentSocialPlan
    │ currentSocialPlan ← ARA(currentTask, potentialTeammates, currentSocialPlan)
end
```

---

6   Discussion of Design Choices

Virtual gaming environments are combined with autonomous agents in an interdisciplinary way to solve NPC collaboration during gameplay. Considering the complexity of turn-based and real-time video games, the effectiveness of specific elements is crucial. This includes:

1. Communication. Only basic speech acts like bilateral communication and announcement are in use. Clearly, they lead to the two distinct kinds of beliefs: individual and shared ones. When contrasted to the whole capacity of collective beliefs, this simplification may be lifted in the future. Similarly, the assumption that ARAG has direct access to NPCs' beliefs will be relaxed, since ultimately beliefs should be accessed via communication.
2. Filtering. During reconfiguration, IRMA-style [4] filtering system is used to narrow down the stream of potential options. Contrary to traditional solutions, ARAG combines not just two, but three streams of optional tasks, including also a monitoring-related one. The user who is in charge of the filter content needs to be cautious about the granularity of these processes.
3. Selecting the winner. Although ARAG makes no explicit assumptions about the selection algorithm, Utility AI [17,26] is one of suitable techniques to select the winning task from among admissible ones. This method permits to aggregate a wide range of decision-related factors.
4. Group topology. The chosen star topology with ARAG as the central node, introduces centralized agent management features and reduces the degree of autonomy enjoyed by individual NPCs. Thanks to this, the multi-phase group commitment setting technique is simplified to a single round.

As our main focus is the impact of a game's adversarial features on teamwork, a systematic oversight of the progress of social plans is necessary. Therefore, in ARAG, we have committed to rigorous reporting on task statuses by the agents. In particular, a lack of a report may warrant an alert and trigger reconfiguration.

7   Proof of Concept

As a proof of concept, we developed Treasure Hunt, a stealth video game [14] using the Unity engine [28]. The game features a player-controlled character and a team of NPCs led by an ARAG-controlled coordinator. These NPCs work together to collect treasures scattered across the map, taking into account their unique abilities and limited fields of vision. Meanwhile, the player tries hard to prevent them from acquiring the treasures.
The player and the NPCs can perform the following actions:

- **Movement**: the player and NPCs move freely across the map, limited only by physical obstacles.
- **Picking up treasures.**
- **Picking up keys**: special keys may be collected to unlock doors.

- **Pressure plates**: some doors require one or more NPCs to stand on designated pressure plates to open them. Once an NPC leaves the plate, the door locks again.
- **Attack**: by hitting an NPC while staying out of its line of sight, the player stuns it. While stunned, the NPC can neither communicate nor act.
- **Reviving NPCs**: an NPC revives a stunned teammate by touching it.

The NPCs take on two different roles: *locksmiths* and *robbers*, each of which has a unique set of abilities. Since only *locksmiths* can acquire keys and *robbers* can gather treasures, a well-formed squad needs both.

The behavior of NPC teams is shown in five scenarios (see the appendix):

- Scenario 1: the player intentionally avoids the NPCs.
- Scenario 2: the player attempts to enter an NPC's field of vision, triggering a pursuit. Meanwhile, another teammate completes the original NPC's task.
- Scenario 3: an NPC is stunned by the player, prompting another NPC to pause its task, revive the ally, and resume the plan without reconfiguration.
- Scenario 4: the player stuns enough NPCs to render the current plan infeasible, leading the team to carry out an alternative plan.
- Scenario 5: following a successful attack by the player, a new team is created to accomplish the task.

Our results show that ARAG greatly improves the gaming experience. Without teamwork, the behavior of NPCs would lead to a less satisfying gameplay. Importantly, the collaboration with other NPCs is crucial for collecting treasures: in some cases NPCs could end up doing nothing when left to their own devices. Table 1 contrasts the behaviors of individual NPCs with those of ARAG-coordinated teams. Moreover, the execution of ARAG does not noticeably affect the game's performance.

Table 1. Comparison of individual and team action facilitated by ARAG.

Individual action	Team action
Only treasures that are not secured in rooms can be gathered by NPCs.	NPCs cooperate to open doors and get access to guarded treasures.
If an NPC is stunned, its task will not be pursued by other NPCs.	ARAG monitors the task's status and reallocates the task to another NPC.
NPCs select tasks without taking others into account.	ARAG assigns tasks to the most appropriate NPCs.
Multiple NPCs might try to perform the same task.	ARAG makes sure that task allocations are unique.

Currently, the evaluation remains qualitative, necessitating further development to establish quantitative metrics and benchmarks for comparing competing solutions. Furthermore, our approach should be applied to diverse adversarial video game types in order to demonstrate its generalizability.

8 Related Work

Teamwork is an active area of research in multiagent systems for three decades already. Building on foundations laid by Wooldridge and Jennings [32], researchers have proposed various approaches to enable effective teamwork of intelligent agents. Dunin-Kęplicz and Verbrugge [7] describe a formal approach to cooperation with collective motivational attitudes as central notions. The role of these notions is highlighted in their Reconfiguration Algorithm. As a process, reconfiguration exploits the concept of *minimal repair*, which is rooted in the maintenance planning literature [19], and further explored in MAS [13].

Among Tambe's contributions, a notable one is the STEAM framework [27]. It employs agents equipped with an explicit model of teamwork, enabling effective communication, monitoring and replanning. Also, the MOISE framework [10] introduces a teamwork model based on roles, groups and missions.

Despite efforts to integrate MAS approaches with game engines [3,16,21], teamwork in video games is largely unexplored. Still, there have been many successful attempts to achieve agent coordination in a centralized fashion. In a typical solution, a single agent assigns tasks to subordinate agents that are not equipped with individual beliefs. Siemonsmeier describes multi-agent planning in a popular tactical game, Gears Tactics [25]. Some aspects of teamwork, such as action allocation, have been studied in the context of real-time strategy games, however, also in a centralized fashion [24]. Despite their effectiveness, these centralized approaches are not suitable for simulating believable behaviors in environments characterized by imperfect information, as they disregard the aspect of limited senses and changing beliefs of individual agents.

Agis et al. [1] incorporated communication and coordination mechanisms into Behavior Trees to simulate a rudimentary kind of teamwork. This approach can handle simple scenarios that do not require planning or efficient task allocation.

Multi-agent systems inspired video games designers in solving problems not solely related to NPC behavior. For example, Lora used MAS related methods to design games by conceptualizing them as a system of interacting agents and defining relevant rules in predicate logic [5].

Convincing simulation of group behaviors is neglected in video game literature. In fact, most of the research focused on action planning, while team formation, intragroup communication, and belief management are overlooked [2]. This is remarkable given the attention for Park et al. [20], who used a Large Language Model to simulate believable NPC behaviors.

9 Conclusions and Future Work

Our interdisciplinary approach to integrating teamwork with adversarial video games greatly simplifies the implementation of NPC collaboration. As an innovative application of MAS-related ideas it demonstrates a fresh attempt to the often-neglected area of NPCs' collaboration. Importantly, video game criteria are different from those of MAS as they aim to provide a convincing appearance of intelligent, human-like behavior rather than to find the best solution.

In this work, we focused on collaboration within a single star group topology. We plan to extend our approach to encompass less centralized group topologies and to consider multiple competing teams. Importantly, video game research is also relevant to robotics, where human-robot and robot-robot interactions face similar challenges related to embodiment and limited senses.

ARAG has been implemented and tested in a prototype stealth game, proving that our approach results in convincing behaviors of NPC groups. Currently, the game is further developed to showcase more advanced teamwork scenarios. While the advantages of incorporating teamwork into video games are mostly qualitative and depend on the player's perception of NPC behaviors as well as their subjective enjoyment of playing the game, we are now developing methods to assess ARAG's quality in a more objective manner. Importantly, in [6], we identified key challenges and outlined a research roadmap to empower teamwork capabilities in adversarial video games.

Acknowledgements. The authors thank Andrzej Szałas for his insightful comments, which greatly contributed to the improvement of this work.

Appendix

A Example Teamwork Scenarios

Treasure Hunt is a straightforward stealth video game with a group of NPCs under the direction of a Coordinator agent, playing against a player-controlled character. The goal of NPCs is to collect treasures placed on the map. In order to do so, they need to work together, taking into account their disparate abilities and a limited field of vision (shown in blue in the screenshots). The player's objective is to stop the NPCs from getting the treasures. The scenarios presented demonstrate ARAG's function in coordinating teamwork and its ability to react to the player's hostile actions. To illustrate how cooperation develops in the new situation, the player typically purposefully refrains from interfering after taking initial hostile actions.

A.1 Scenario 1: No Adversarial Actions by the Player

A group of NPCs tries to find a treasure hidden behind a locked door. To open the door, the team must gather two keys. To illustrate ARAG's uninterrupted functionality, the player intentionally avoids the NPCs. Two locksmiths retrieve the required keys, the door opens, and a robber NPC collects the treasure hidden behind the door and leaves the room. This concludes the plan (Fig. 4).

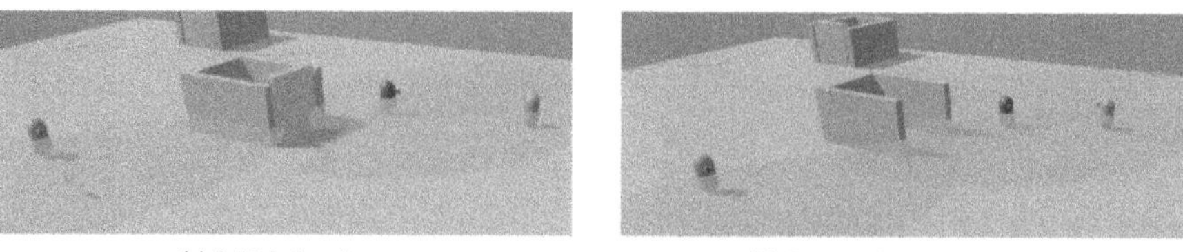

(a) Initial situation.

(b) *Locksmiths* pick up the keys.

(c) *Robber* gets the treasure.

(d) *Robber* NPC leaves the room.

Fig. 4. Scenario 1.

(a) Initial situation.

(b) NPC starts chasing the player.

(c) Another NPC picks up the key.

Fig. 5. Scenario 2.

A.2   Scenario 2: NPC Chases the Player During Plan Execution

In a similar setup (with two keys required to open the door), the player tries to distract an NPC. Upon retrieving the keys, the NPC recognizes the player and begins to chase it. The player dodges, forcing the NPC to become preoccupied with the chase and neglect its task. After some time without task status updates from the NPC, the Coordinator reassigns the task to another teammate (Fig. 5).

A.3   Scenario 3: NPC Is Stunned by the Player During Plan Execution

This example shows how the team would act with non-significant interruptions. When an NPC approaches a key, the player attacks and stuns it, making it temporarily immobile. As seen in the previous scenario, this could lead to plan reconfiguration if the stunned NPC did not respond for too long. However, another NPC notices the stunned teammate, pauses the ongoing task for a while, and revives the ally. After that, the original plan is resumed without reconfiguration (Fig. 6).

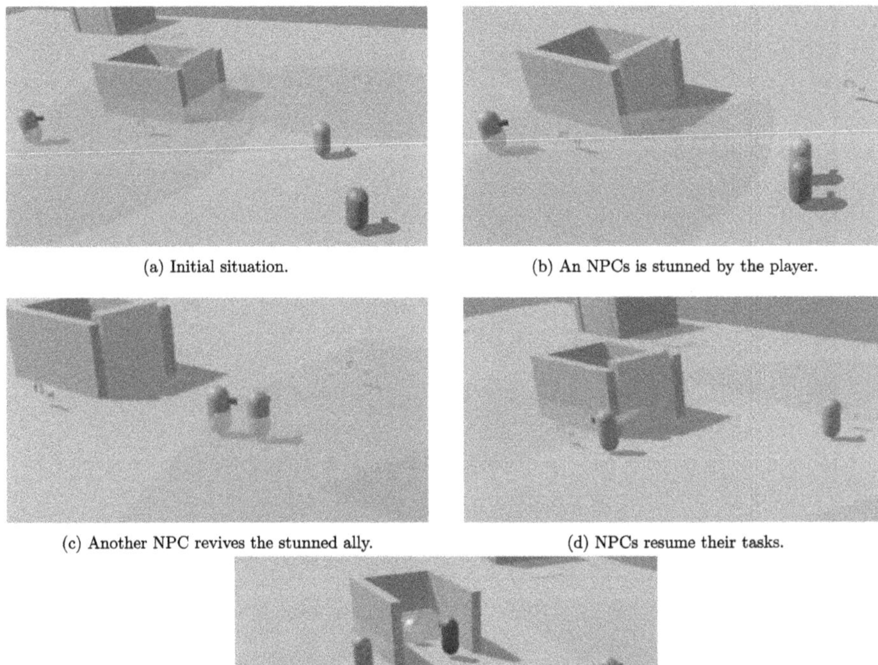

(a) Initial situation.

(b) An NPCs is stunned by the player.

(c) Another NPC revives the stunned ally.

(d) NPCs resume their tasks.

(e) *Robber* picks up the treasure.

Fig. 6. Scenario 3.

A.4   Scenario 4: Plan Becomes Infeasible During Execution

NPCs can select from multiple treasures. They start with the most valuable one, locked behind a door guarded by two pressure plates. Because two NPCs are needed to open the door (by standing simultaneously on the pressure plates), the plan requires three teammates. One of the NPCs is stunned by the player before it reaches its designated pressure plate and becomes unresponsive. After a period without status reports, the Coordinator attempts to reallocate the tasks. However, only two responsive NPCs remain, which makes this social plan unfeasible. Therefore, another treasure is chosen, leading to a new social plan. Once the plan is completed, the Coordinator resumes the original plan. This time the team is successful, as in the meantime the stunned NPC has regained the ability to respond (Fig. 7).

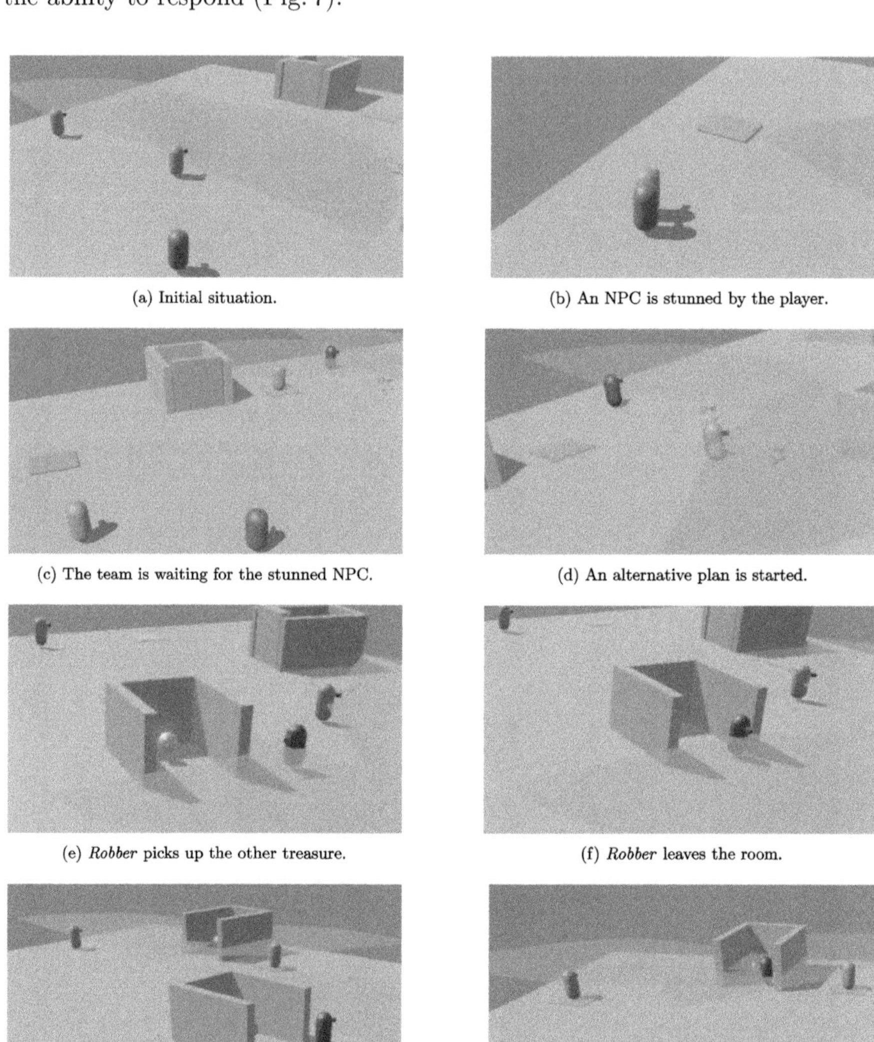

(a) Initial situation.

(b) An NPC is stunned by the player.

(c) The team is waiting for the stunned NPC.

(d) An alternative plan is started.

(e) *Robber* picks up the other treasure.

(f) *Robber* leaves the room.

(g) The team goes back to the initial plan.

(h) *Robber* gets the treasure.

Fig. 7. Scenario 4.

A.5   Scenario 5: Plan Reconfiguration Using Another Team

The goal is to retrieve a treasure hidden behind a door that can be opened by collecting two keys. However, one of those keys is locked behind another door, unlocked by pressing two pressure plates. The plan requires three teammates, while there are four NPCs on the map. The player interrupts the first attempt by attacking one of the team members. The Coordinator replaces the non-responsive NPC with the fourth one. During its task, the new teammate takes the time to revive the stunned ally. The new team successfully obtains the treasure (Fig. 8).

(a) Initial situation.

(b) An NPC is stunned by the player.

(c) The team is waiting for the stunned NPC.

(d) Another NPC approaches to pick up the key, notices and revives the stunned ally.

(e) The NPC goes back to its task after reviving the ally.

(f) The NPC picks up the second key.

(g) *Robber* starts moving towards the treasure.

(h) *Robber* picks up the treasure.

Fig. 8. Scenario 5.

References

1. Agis, R.A., Gottifredi, S., García, A.J.: An event-driven behavior trees extension to facilitate non-player multi-agent coordination in video games. Exp. Syst. Appl. **155**, 113457 (2020)
2. Barambones, J., Cano-Benito, J., Sánchez-Rivero, I., Imbert, R., Richoux, F.: Multi-agent systems on virtual games: a systematic mapping study. IEEE Trans. Games (2022)
3. Brännström, A., Nieves, J.C.: A framework for developing interactive intelligent systems in unity. In: Engineering Multi-Agent Systems, EMAS 2022 (2022)
4. Bratman, M.E., Israel, D.J., Pollack, M.E.: Plans and resource-bounded practical reasoning. Comput. Intell. **4**(3), 349–355 (1988)
5. Lora, C.M.: Game Development Based on Multi-agent Systems. Ph.D. thesis, Universitat Jaume I (2022)
6. Dunin-Kęplicz, B., Tyl, R.: Empowering adversarial video games with teamwork. In: Proceedings of the 19th KES International Conference on Agents and Multi-Agent Systems, KES-AMSTA 2025. Smart Innovation, Systems and Technologies, vol. 464. Springer, Heidelberg (forthcoming)
7. Dunin-Kęplicz, B., Verbrugge, R.: Teamwork in Multi-Agent Systems. A Formal Approach. Wiley (2010)
8. Grant, J., Kraus, S., Perlis, D.: Formal approaches to teamwork (2005)
9. Gregory, J.: Game Engine Architecture, 1st edn. Taylor & Francis Ltd. (2009)
10. Hannoun, M., Boissier, O., Sichman, J.S., Sayettat, C.: MOISE: an organizational model for multi-agent systems. In: Monard, M.C., Sichman, J.S. (eds.) IBERAMI-A/SBIA -2000. LNCS (LNAI), vol. 1952, pp. 156–165. Springer, Heidelberg (2000). https://doi.org/10.1007/3-540-44399-1_17
11. Van der Hoek, W., Wooldridge, M.: Multi-agent systems. Found. Artif. Intell. **3**, 887–928 (2008)
12. Knuth, D.E.: The Art of Computer Programming, Volume 4A: Combinatorial Algorithms, Part 1, Algorithm R. Pearson Education India (2011)
13. Komenda, A., Novák, P., Pěchouček, M.: Decentralized multi-agent plan repair in dynamic environments. arXiv preprint arXiv:1202.2773 (2012)
14. Konzack, L.: Video game genres. In: Encyclopedia of Information Science and Technology, 3rd edn., pp. 3070–3076. IGI Global (2015)
15. van Linder, B., van der Hoek, W., Meyer, J.C.: Formalizing abilities and opportunities of agents. Fund. Inform. **34**(1–2), 53–101 (1998)
16. Mariani, S., Omicini, A., et al.: Game engines to model MAS: a research roadmap. In: WOA, pp. 106–111 (2016)
17. Mark, D.: Behavioral mathematics for game AI. Course Technology Cengage Learning (2009)
18. Mirsky, R., et al.: A survey of Ad Hoc teamwork research. In: Baumeister, D., Rothe, J. (eds.) Multi-Agent Systems. EUMAS 2022. LNCS, vol. 13442. Springer, Cham (2022). https://doi.org/10.1007/978-3-031-20614-6_16
19. Nakagawa, T., Kowada, M.: Analysis of a system with minimal repair and its application to replacement policy. Eur. J. Oper. Res. **12**(2), 176–182 (1983)
20. Park, J.S., O'Brien, J., Cai, C.J., Morris, M.R., Liang, P., Bernstein, M.S.: Generative agents: interactive simulacra of human behavior. In: Proceedings of the 36th Annual ACM Symposium on User Interface Software and Technology, pp. 1–22 (2023)

21. Poli, N.: Game Engines and MAS: BDI & artifacts in Unity. Ph.D. thesis, Alma Mater Studiorum Universita di Bologna Bologna, Italy (2018)
22. Politowski, C., Petrillo, F., Montandon, J.E., Valente, M.T., Guéhéneuc, Y.G.: Are game engines software frameworks? A three-perspective study. J. Syst. Softw. **171**, 110846 (2021)
23. Pynadath, D.V., Tambe, M.: Multiagent teamwork: analyzing the optimality and complexity of key theories and models. In: Proceedings of the AAMAS'2002. ACM (2002)
24. Rogers, K.D., Skabar, A.A.: A micromanagement task allocation system for real-time strategy games. IEEE Trans. Comput. Intell. AI Games **6**(1), 67–77 (2014)
25. Siemonsmeier, M.: Gearing the tactics genre: simultaneous AI actions in gears tactics. gameaipro.com (2021)
26. Świechowski, M., Lewiński, D., Tyl, R.: Combining utility AI and MCTS towards creating intelligent agents in video games, with the use case of tactical troops: Anthracite shift. In: 2021 IEEE Symposium Series on Computational Intelligence (SSCI), pp. 1–8. IEEE (2021)
27. Tambe, M.: Towards flexible teamwork. J. Artif. Intell. Res. **7**, 83–124 (1997)
28. Unity Technologies: Unity (2023). game development platform. https://unity.com/,
29. Warpefelt, H.: The non-player character: exploring the believability of NPC presentation and behavior. Ph.D. thesis, Department of Computer and Systems Sciences, Stockholm University (2016)
30. Wooldridge, M.: Reasoning About Rational Agents. MIT Press (2003)
31. Wooldridge, M.: An Introduction to Multiagent Systems. Wiley (2009)
32. Wooldridge, M., Jennings, N.: The cooperative problem solving process. J. Logic Computat. (1999)

Towards Engineering LLM-Enhanced Multi-agent Systems: A Critical Examination of Roles

Tansu Zafer Asici[1]($\boxtimes$)(iD), Önder Gürcan[2](iD), and Geylani Kardas[1](iD)

[1] Ege University, International Computer Institute, 35100 Izmir, Türkiye
`91200000857@ogrenci.ege.edu.tr`, `geylani.kardas@ege.edu.tr`
[2] NORCE Research AS, Center for Modeling Social Systems, Kristiansand, Norway
`ongu@norceresearch.no`

Abstract. This paper proposes a structured approach to integrating Large Language Models (LLMs) into Multi-Agent Systems (MAS) by revisiting and extending the fundamental Agent-Oriented Software Engineering (AOSE) concept of "roles." Traditional AOSE methodologies provide well-defined processes for modeling agents, roles, goals, and interactions, yet contemporary LLM-based MAS frameworks typically lack such systematic engineering foundations. We highlight how ad hoc development practices in LLM-enhanced MAS—often driven by prompt engineering or role-playing strategies—can lead to inconsistencies and reduced maintainability. Through a critical examination of role definition, specification, and implementation, we identify several gaps in terms of software engineering. To bridge these gaps, we propose a hybrid role-based architecture where we treat *roles as first-class entities at run-time* encapsulating both traditional AOSE design principles and LLM-driven functionalities. By laying this groundwork, we aim to foster more robust, scalable, and transparent engineering of LLM-enhanced MAS.

Keywords: Multi-Agent Systems · Large Language Models · Agent-Oriented Software Engineering · Role Abstraction · Action Execution

1 Introduction

Large Language Models (LLMs), with their advanced natural language processing capabilities, have opened new avenues for enhancing the capabilities of Multi-Agent Systems (MAS). Examples of these include improved resource coordination and decentralized collaboration [45,85], enhanced memory and context handling with hierarchical memory models [85], advanced problem-solving [31] and simulation capabilities [26], scalability and flexibility through frameworks for rapid prototyping [15] and scalable deployment [17]. The rapid advancement of LLMs has also sparked growing interest from research and industry leveraging agent-based solutions, accelerating the development of practical MAS applications and dedicated innovative tools. LLM-enabled MAS applications span multiple domains, including education [44], 6G communications [43], healthcare [4], financial analysis [78], agriculture [49], crime detection [70] and social simulations [32,33]. Dedicated tools and frameworks aiming to leverage the benefits of LLMs to create more efficient, autonomous, and scalable MAS, facilitating their application across various domains, are being proposed at an increasing pace [16,45,52,84].

However, the existing tools and frameworks often lack a dedicated engineering methodology, resulting in LLM-enabled MAS applications being frequently developed in an ad hoc manner, which can lead to inconsistencies and inefficiencies in their implementation and deployment. This challenge is further compounded by a significant gap in integrating LLMs within MAS, particularly in leveraging the extensive body of knowledge from Agent-Oriented Software Engineering (AOSE). AOSE provides a rich set of principles, methodologies, and tools specifically designed to address the complexities of developing agent-based systems [8,37,76]. The under-utilization of established AOSE methodologies [11,25,58,61,80] and frameworks for integrating LLMs into MAS hinders the optimization of design and implementation, ultimately affecting system quality, reliability, and maintainability. Because, by providing structured processes and clear guidelines, these methodologies help development teams systematically plan, implement, and test multi-agent software, reducing the likelihood of errors and costly rework.

Software engineering methodologies are built upon conceptual elements that serve as high-level representations (or "blueprints") of concepts within a system. Since they do not strictly dictate the underlying details, these elements can be implemented in many ways depending on the chosen technology, programming language, system constraints, or performance needs. The AOSE literature outlines key conceptual elements such as agents, roles, goals, actions, interactions, organizational structures, communication protocols, and mental states (e.g., beliefs, desires, intentions). However, adapting them to real-world LLM-enabled MAS applications remains *underexplored*.

Based on this observation, in this paper, as a first step towards engineering LLM-enhanced MAS, we study the role concept and its realization, as it is the standard building block for specifying agents in AOSE methodologies [1]. The contributions of this study are as follows:

- We survey and categorize current LLM-powered MAS tools and frameworks (e.g., AutoGPT, CAMEL, MetaGPT, LangChain), analyzing their development workflows and methodological limitations.
- We identify gaps between traditional AOSE methodologies and contemporary LLM-enhanced MAS implementations.
- We provide a comprehensive, structured analysis of the role concept in MAS, covering its definition, specification, and implementation from both AOSE and LLM-enhanced perspectives.

– We propose a hybrid architecture that treats roles as first-class run-time entities, encapsulating both AOSE principles and LLM functionalities.

The organization of this paper is as follows: Sect. 2 provides a brief background about engineering MAS. Section 3 describes how LLM-enabled MAS are engineered in practice and provides an evaluation in terms of AOSE. Section 4 undertakes a comparative analysis of the role concept in both AOSE and LLM contexts—across the dimensions of definition, specification, and implementation. In Sect. 5, we propose a hybrid role-based architecture that encapsulates both traditional AOSE design principles and LLM-driven functionalities. Section 6 concludes the paper by summarizing the findings, and outlines potential future work.

2   Engineering Multi-agent Systems

MAS methodologies provide structured frameworks for the analysis and design of agent-based systems, enabling agents to perform specific tasks effectively. For example, GAIA [80] offers systematic modeling for complex systems by explicitly defining agent roles, responsibilities, and interaction protocols. Roles represent specific functionalities and responsibilities assigned to agents, whereas protocols regulate interactions among agents. The MaSE [55] methodology supports the design process by analyzing systems as sets of roles and tasks. These tasks and roles are linked to agent goals and subsequently combined to define agent classes in the design phase. O-MaSE [18,20] extends MaSE by introducing meta-models and modular components, emphasizing agent-environment interactions. This facilitates modeling of systems involving environmental processes and rules. Tropos [11] views agents as social actors structured around concepts such as goals, plans, capabilities, and beliefs. In Tropos, roles represent abstract behaviors of actors within specific contexts, while positions indicate the set of roles an actor may assume. Prometheus [58] simplifies agent design by adopting a goal- and plan-oriented approach, linking goals explicitly to functionalities. Functionalities are defined in terms of actions, messages, and data handled by agents, thereby streamlining system development. ASEME [72] takes a platform-independent, abstract, and modular approach, modeling actor behaviors and control flows by integrating actors, roles, goals, and use scenarios. In the final step, code compatible with agent development platforms such as JADE is automatically generated. The AGRE [25] model defines agents in terms of roles, groups and environments within an organizational context. This allows agents to adopt flexible and adaptive behaviors across multiple roles, facilitating the design of dynamic and modular systems (see [67] for a detailed example).

Although existing AOSE methodologies provide various tools for the structured definition of roles, responsibilities, tasks, and interactions, they lack the flexibility and creativity offered by LLMs. This constitutes a significant challenge for traditional methodologies in adapting to today's rapidly evolving application domains.

3   Practical Engineering of LLM-Enabled MAS

This section describes the design principles and configuration approaches used by current LLM-powered MAS development tools to support practical engineering, highlighting features that enhance their overall usability.

3.1   Existing Tools and Frameworks

Current tools for developing LLM-enabled MAS can be grouped into three categories based on their primary functionality:

- Autonomous Task-Oriented Frameworks: Tools like AutoGPT[1], BabyAGI[2], SuperAGI[3], and XAgent[4] use iterative task loops and autonomous planning-execution mechanisms to achieve goals with minimal human intervention.
- Role-based Collaborative Frameworks: CAMEL [53], ChatDev [63], and MetaGPT [40] configure multiple agents with specialized roles, using structured interactions to collaboratively perform complex tasks, particularly in software development contexts.
- General Multi-Agent Orchestration Frameworks: AgentVerse [17], AutoGen [81], CrewAI[5], AWS MAO[6], OpenAI Swarm[7], and LangChain[8] facilitate flexible configuration and management of agent interactions, emphasizing modularity, scalability, and integration.

3.2   Common Development Workflows and Practices

Developers in practice leverage these tools to rapidly prototype and implement LLM-enabled MAS for a variety of tasks. A common workflow begins with defining the roles or objectives of each agent, often via careful prompt engineering or scripting using the framework's API. For example, using a library like AutoGen or LangChain, a developer can instantiate agents with distinct personas (e.g., a "Planner" agent and an "Executor" agent) and then script an interaction loop between them. Typically one agent may be tasked to break down a problem and another to solve sub-problems, or one may critique and improve the other's outputs. Similarly, with role-based systems such as Chat-Dev or MetaGPT, the developer provides an initial high-level task (for instance, a software feature request), and the system spawns multiple agent instances

---

[1] AutoGPT, https://agpt.co/, accessed June 26, 2025.
[2] BabyAGI, https://babyagi.org/, accessed June 26, 2025.
[3] SuperAGI, https://superagi.com/, accessed June 26, 2025.
[4] XAgent, https://github.com/OpenBMB/XAgent/, accessed June 26, 2025.
[5] CrewAI, https://www.crewai.com/, accessed June 26, 2025.
[6] AWS Multi-Agent Orchestrator, https://awslabs.github.io/multi-agent-orchestrator/, accessed June 26, 2025.
[7] OpenAI Swarm, https://github.com/openai/swarm, accessed June 26, 2025.
[8] LangChain, https://python.langchain.com/, accessed June 26, 2025.

(developer, tester, manager, etc.) that message each other to gradually refine and implement the solution. In these multi-agent conversations, each agent's prompt template encodes its persona and scope of work, which guides the agent's behavior throughout the dialogue. Developers often iterate on these prompts to steer the agents toward productive interactions (e.g. ensuring the "tester" agent knows how to systematically find faults in the "developer" agent's code output).

Another prevalent development pattern is the use of autonomous task loops, epitomized by AutoGPT and BabyAGI. In this pattern, once a user supplies an initial goal, the agent system itself iteratively generates sub-tasks, executes them, evaluates results, and adjusts the plan or creates new tasks as needed. Developers employ such patterns to offload not just single-step queries to LLMs, but entire project workflows. For instance, a user might ask AutoGPT to "research and write a report on market trends", upon which the system will autonomously break the job into smaller tasks (e.g. data gathering, analysis, drafting) and cycle through them until completion. In practice, frameworks like SuperAGI or AWS's MAO provide higher-level interfaces for running these autonomous agents, allowing developers to configure resources (for example, a vector database for long-term memory) and to monitor the agent's progress through a dashboard.

Building LLM-enabled MAS today is an iterative and experimental process. Developers rely heavily on observing agent behaviors through logs or real-time monitors and then refining the system. If the MAS fails to converge to a good solution, one might adjust the prompts, add a new agent (for example, an agent whose sole role is to critique solutions or to summarize the discussion so far), or tweak the interaction protocol (for instance, enforcing that agents communicate in a structured format or brief bullet points to reduce ambiguity). In summary, current best practices involve defining clear agent roles, endowing agents with the necessary tools or external knowledge sources, simulating their interactions in a controlled environment, and iteratively improving their prompts and logic. Over time, repeated patterns (such as a planner-executor pair, or a questioner-responder-reviewer trio) are becoming templates that developers can reuse across projects, gradually forming an evolving playbook for how to effectively combine multiple LLM agents for different classes of problems.

3.3   Methodologies and Guidelines in Current Tools

Given the relative infancy of LLM-enabled MAS, most of the existing tools do not prescribe a rigorous software engineering methodology for design or implementation, nor do they explicitly reference classical AOSE frameworks (e.g., Gaia, Tropos) from the MAS literature. Development is often guided by example use cases and the built-in templates provided by each tool, rather than by a formal process model. For instance, AutoGPT and BabyAGI emerged as experimental prototypes shared via open-source repositories; users typically follow the provided README or community-written guides to adapt them to new tasks, engaging in a lot of trial-and-error. The emphasis is on achieving functional goals (e.g., *"let the agent autonomously handle my email workflow"*) and tweaking the agent's prompts or code as needed when issues arise, rather than on adherence to a standardized development lifecycle. In essence, the methodology is *ad hoc* - developers iteratively refine the system until it performs the desired behavior, which is feasible given the high-level nature of LLM prompts but lacks the guarantees of traditional engineering approaches.

Some frameworks do offer informal guidelines aligned with their design philosophies. For example, MetaGPT incorporates the concept of Standardized Operating Procedures (SOPs) from human teamwork as part of its prompting strategy. This provides a semi-structured template for how agents should collaborate on a complex task (e.g., a defined sequence of phases such as requirement analysis → design → implementation → testing in a software project). A developer using MetaGPT is encouraged to follow this template when setting up agent roles and conversation order, which is a form of methodology albeit specific to the software-development domain. Similarly, ChatDev's enforced structure of a virtual software team implicitly serves as a development guideline: it suggests that to solve a problem (say, build a new software feature), one should instantiate a team of agents with complementary roles and have them communicate in a logical order reflecting a typical software engineering process. These tool-specific conventions (often inspired by real-world workflows) provide starting points for developers, but they are not generalizable frameworks one could apply to any MAS project in a systematic way. Notably, we find little to no evidence that these new platforms build on established AOSE methodologies – for instance, their documentation and papers do not mention using Gaia's role models or Tropos's goal diagrams to design agent societies. The emphasis is more on empirical effectiveness (does a given configuration of agents solve the task?) rather than a priori design correctness. In practice, the lack of formal methodology means that much of the development knowledge is tacit, residing in the experience of the developers or shared through blog posts and forums rather than encoded in the frameworks themselves.

3.4   Incorporation of Software Engineering Principles

Current LLM-enabled MAS frameworks implicitly support software engineering principles like modularity and reusability by dividing complex problems into specialized agents with clearly defined roles. Tools such as LangChain emphasize role specialization, which simplifies the development, testing, and potential reuse of agent components across projects. Role specialization aligns well with the principle of single responsibility, enhancing overall system maintainability.

However, significant challenges persist. The behavior of agents, defined largely through prompts, lacks transparency and formal analyzability, complicating maintainability—minor prompt changes can unpredictably influence entire systems. Frameworks like AutoGen offer visual debugging to mitigate this, but robust, systematic methods remain scarce. Additionally, runtime-based traceability provided by logging agent interactions doesn't easily map back to original requirements, limiting systematic verifiability and role clarity.

Scalability also poses issues. While selective message routing and orchestrators, such as those employed by OpenAI Swarm and AWS MAO, improve manageability of agent interactions by efficiently handling multiple agent roles, empirical evidence of their effectiveness in large-scale scenarios remains limited.

Overall, while current frameworks demonstrate foundational support for modular, reusable agent roles, the absence of formal methodologies, traceability mechanisms, and comprehensive scalability strategies highlights critical areas needing development to fully integrate classical software engineering principles into practical MAS engineering.

4   A Critical Examination of Roles

AOSE has long provided solid analytical and design foundations for MAS. AOSE methodologies encompass fundamental concepts such as agents, roles, goals, actions, interactions, organizational structures, and communication protocols. Among these concepts, the *role* is a key concept as it is used to define responsibilities and capabilities of agents. In many AOSE methodologies, a common method is handling agent roles and then aggregate them to form complete agents [1]. Consequently, as a first step towards bringing AOSE methodologies and the practical LLM-enabled MAS development together, we start by critically examining the role concept which is a fundamental conceptual element in AOSE.

In software engineering, conceptual elements are typically characterized by three facets: their definition, specification, and implementation. Accordingly, we will examine, in order, the role concept's definition (Sect. 4.1), specification (Sect. 4.2), and implementation (Sect. 4.3).

4.1   Role Definition

In AOSE, a role is an abstract definition that encapsulates a set of *responsibilities*, *behaviors*, and *interaction protocols* expected of an agent within a MAS. By decoupling the expected behaviors from the agent's concrete implementation, the role concept promotes modularity, reusability, and flexibility, allowing agents to adopt or change roles dynamically as system requirements evolve. Roles specify what actions an agent should perform, how it should interact with other agents, and what obligations or constraints it must observe in a given organizational, social, or physical context (also called environment). Environments define the context, resources, norms, and possible interactions available to agents [79]. They shape and constrain how roles are interpreted and executed, enabling situated reasoning and behavior adaptation.

Different methodologies approach the concept of role in various ways. GAIA [80] emphasizes that roles encompass responsibilities, protocols, and permissions to perform specific functions. MaSE [55] structures roles through use case scenarios and sequence diagrams during system specification. O-MaSE [18,20] extends MaSE to include environmental interactions, deepening the modeling of roles. Tropos [11] defines a role as an abstract representation of the behavior of a social actor in a specific context, while Cabri et al. [13] highlight the interactional aspects of this approach. Prometheus considers a role as an element that reflects system functionality and defines the actions performed by agents. ASEME [74] presents dynamic role models derived from system use case scenarios, modeling the influence of roles on agent-internal behavior through control flow. Finally, AGRE [25] defines a role as a functional position within a group, emphasizing that multiple agents can share the same role as an abstraction.

In AOSE, roles are typically an *analysis* and/or *design-time* concept rather than a *run-time* concept. In some cases (e.g. GAIA), the role concept is only used during the analysis phase and does not exist in the design. Over the years, one of the significant problems faced by the MAS community was the transition of the concept of a role from an abstract design to a concrete implementation within an agent framework, mainly because roles often did not exist at run-time, making effective mapping challenging [9].

In the context of an LLM, a *role* can be defined as a predetermined behavioral profile or identity assigned to the model (such as "an experienced medical advisor" or "a technical support expert"). This role guides the model's responses, language style, information prioritization, and context awareness to effectively perform specific tasks or interactions. Here, the role concept is a *design-time* concept, interpreted and executed by the LLM at *run-time*. However, an LLM role does not inherently encapsulate interaction protocols—structured sequences of messages and actions that govern multi-agent communication [56]. Instead, it primarily defines the responsibilities and behaviors needed to produce appropriate, task-specific responses. While LLMs do not natively support interaction protocols, such protocols can be implemented and managed externally using recently proposed dedicated interoperability protocols [24]. For example, Model Context Protocol (MCP)[9] servers can be used to coordinate and mediate communication between LLM-based agents, ensuring adherence to protocol logic, turn-taking, and state management[10] [68]. Moreover, even though an LLM role can interact with environments mediated by tools and frameworks, the relationship between roles and environments can not explicitly be defined or integrated within the LLM itself [54,56]. This poses problems in multi-agent settings[11].

At *design-time*, the developer defines what role the model will assume and how it should behave, while at *run-time*, the LLM actively applies and adapts these guidelines dynamically during user interactions. However, at *run-time*, the LLM processes these guidelines as instructions or contextual cues rather than maintaining explicit "roles" and "actions" in the agent-oriented sense (with goals, behaviors, or organizational structures). Essentially, the concept of roles and actions is supplied and interpreted by users and developers through prompts and conversation structure, rather than by the LLM's own inherent representation. While LLMs can appear to perform roles and actions (e.g., adding two numbers), this "execution" is still just a text-based transformation (generating a

---

[9] MCP, https://modelcontextprotocol.io/, accessed on June 26, 2025.

[10] See, as an example, Coral Server of the Coral Protocol, https://github.com/Coral-Protocol/coral-server, accessed on June 26, 2025.

[11] Cognition, https://cognition.ai/blog/dont-build-multi-agents, accessed on June 26, 2025.

numeric answer) rather than an explicit representation of action, roles, or goals as understood in AOSE. It is effectively a pattern matching or textual reasoning process, not an agent-based execution driven by internally modeled objectives.

4.2   Role Specification

The specification of a role provides a detailed, often formal, description of the actions it can perform and how it can interact with other roles [35,47]. The behavior is often described in terms of permissions, responsibilities, activities, and interactions [5]. This detailed breakdown is used to guide the implementation of the role. In the following, we give an ordered list of methods for specifying roles, arranged by increasing levels of formality and precision—from the most informal, conceptual descriptions to the most rigorous, mathematically precise and verifiable specifications:

1. Natural Language Description: The use of natural language in role definition offers both accessibility and flexibility. In this approach, users define a role by explicitly and comprehensively describing its tasks, responsibilities, interaction patterns, and objectives using natural language expressions.
2. Graphical Modeling Languages (e.g., UML[12], SysML[13], AUML[14]): These provide visual diagrams to depict roles, their relationships, and interactions. They strike a balance between clarity and formality, making them well suited for conceptual modeling and communication among stakeholders [6,30,71].
3. Business Process Modeling Languages (e.g., BPMN[15]): Designed for illustrating business workflows, BPMN specifies roles within processes clearly. It is more structured than free-form graphics yet still primarily serves as a communication tool rather than a formal specification [57].
4. Architectural Description Languages (ADLs) (e.g., ACME [27], AADL [3]): ADLs focus on system architecture, detailing how roles (often as components or connectors) integrate into and interact within an overall system. They add structure by specifying interfaces and inter-component relationships [23,60].
5. Programming Code: Implementing role specifications in programming languages makes them executable. While this approach is concrete and precise in terms of behavior, it often intertwines specification with implementation details rather than remaining purely abstract [66].
6. Domain-Specific Languages (DSLs): DSLs are custom-tailored to particular domains. They capture role details and constraints that are specific to the domain context, offering both precision and relevance while potentially varying in formal rigor [21].
7. Behavioral Modeling Languages (e.g., Statecharts [36], Petri nets [62]): These languages emphasize the dynamic aspects of roles—modeling state transitions, interactions over time, and concurrency. They provide a formal way to describe how roles behave under various conditions [14,73].

---

[12] OMG UML, https://www.omg.org/spec/UML, accessed on June 26, 2025.
[13] OMG SysML, https://www.omgsysml.org/, accessed on June 26, 2025.
[14] AUML, https://auml.org/auml/, accessed on June 26, 2025.
[15] BPMN, https://www.omg.org/bpmn/, accessed on June 26, 2025.

8. Ontology and Semantic Web Languages (e.g., OWL[16], RDF[17]): By defining roles within a network of semantically related concepts, these languages offer a formal framework that supports logical inference and interoperability. They are especially useful when roles need to be integrated into larger knowledge representation systems [34, 41].

9. Logic Programming Languages (e.g., Prolog [29]): Using a declarative, rule-based approach, logic programming languages allow you to specify roles in terms of logical constraints and relationships. This method supports formal reasoning and can automatically infer properties of roles [39].

10. Formal Specification Languages (e.g., Z [75], Alloy [42], TLA$^+$ [50], VDM [46], B [2]): These are the most mathematically rigorous methods available. They provide precise, unambiguous specifications that can be used for formal proofs and verification, ensuring that role properties and interactions meet strict correctness criteria [28, 59, 64].

These various methods for role specification comprehensively outline the theoretical framework and expectations of a role within a system. These methods not only determine which actions a role will perform and how it will interact with other roles but also provide crucial insights into how these abstract concepts can be transformed into concrete actions during the implementation process.

In the context of LLMs and LLM-enabled agents, role specification relies solely on natural language descriptions. These textual inputs are interpreted and refined through a detailed prompt engineering process, enabling LLMs to capture the user's intent. This process ensures that the generated responses align with the desired expertise or narrative style, thereby improving overall performance. In essence, natural language serves as a vital bridge between human intent and model behavior—the clarity and scope of the language used in defining a role directly shape the quality and relevance of the model's outputs. However, to achieve less error-prone role specifications, it is preferable to use the more precise methods described above. These specifications can then be *translated* into natural language descriptions when interacting with LLMs.

Besides, role specialization and reusability are partially feasible within LLM-based systems, particularly when supported by structured prompt engineering and modular design frameworks. By defining roles through detailed persona descriptions—encompassing aspects such as background, expertise, tone, and communication style—LLMs can consistently emulate specific behaviors across various contexts. This approach not only enhances the model's ability to maintain a coherent persona but also facilitates the reuse of these role definitions across different tasks and applications. However, challenges remain in ensuring that specialized roles do not lead to overfitting or reduced generalization capabilities. Techniques such as Role Prompting Guided Domain Adaptation (REGA) [77] address this by preserving the general capabilities of LLMs while allowing for effective domain-specific adaptations. REGA employs strategies like

---

[16] OWL, https://www.w3.org/TR/owl-ref/, accessed on June 26, 2025.

[17] RDF,https://www.w3.org/TR/rdf11-concepts/, accessed on June 26, 2025.

self-distillation and role integration to mitigate issues like catastrophic forgetting and inter-domain confusion. Having said that, while frameworks and methodologies are emerging to bring more structure to LLM role definitions, LLMs still lack the formal structure of object-oriented programming (OOP), making it challenging to ensure consistency and reusability across different contexts, and they do not yet match the rigor and predictability offered by OOP paradigms.

4.3 Role Implementation

A role defines a set of actions that an agent can perform to achieve its objectives within a MAS. These actions are guided by the structural arrangements associated with the role, which may include interacting with the environment, gathering information, making decisions, and communicating with other agents. By adopting roles, agents can dynamically respond to changing conditions and collaborate effectively on complex tasks. The specific actions associated with a role can be implemented in the following ways.

Fig. 1. Actions Directly Called within Code.

Actions Directly Called Within Code. Roles are implemented using programming languages and are invoked directly by agents within their code. As shown in Fig. 1, an action is first added to the relevant role. Then, Agent requests to perform the role. For an Agent to perform its Role, it has to execute various actions. After execution, actions produce outcomes, which are returned to the agent by the role. This method is more common in AOSE methodologies such as GAIA [83], Prometheus [58], MaSE [55] and is based on the implementation of role definitions directly as methods or plans in the agent code.

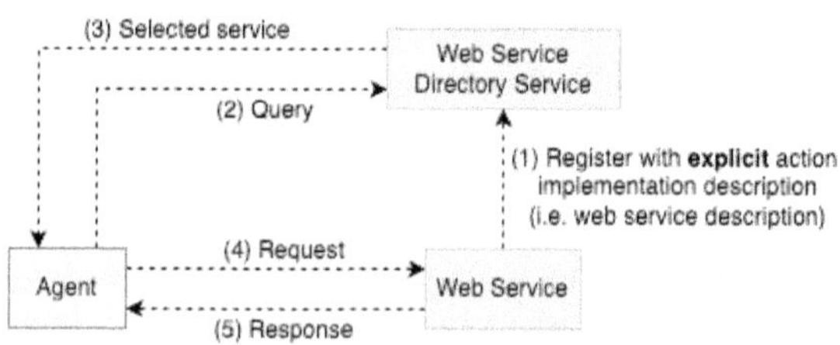

Fig. 2. Actions Called as Semantic Web Services.

Actions Called as Semantic Web Services. Agents dynamically discover and invoke actions via services, aligning with modern microservices architectures. In Fig. 2, firstly the action as *Web Service* registers its capabilities to Directory Service. Then, at any time, Agent sends a request to find the appropriate service. Once selected, *Web Service* is invoked, performs the required operations, and returns the output information in (5) [12].

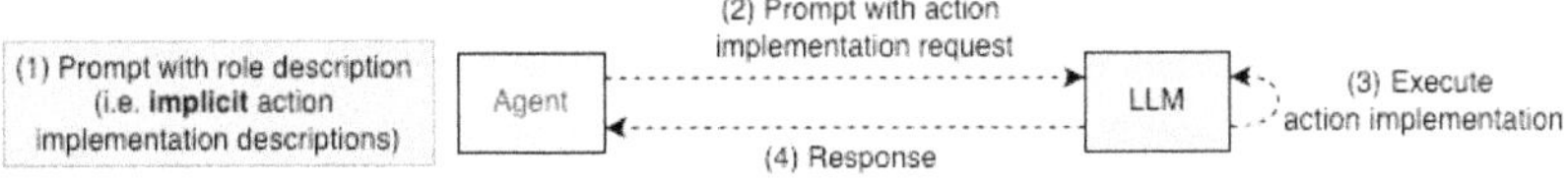

Fig. 3. Actions Triggered for LLM to Perform Its Role.

Actions Triggered for LLM to Perform Its Role. An LLM autonomously performs tasks by assuming a specific role, enabling artificial intelligence to exhibit autonomous behavior. In the first step of Fig. 3, Agent initiates a two-stage prompt process before forwarding it to LLM. In (2), Role supplies its description, and in (3), it sends a prompt containing the action request. In (4), LLM executes the required action-whether generating a response, handling a query, or performing another designated task and returns the output or action outcome back to Agent [17,53,63].

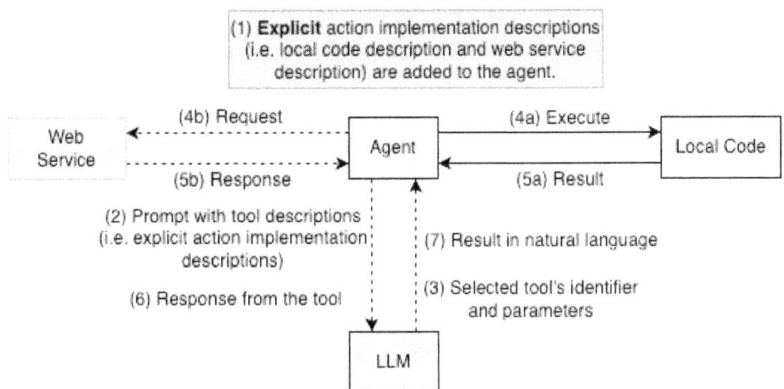

Fig. 4. Actions Triggered by LLM-controlled Tools.

Actions Triggered by LLM-Controlled Tools. Agents use natural language queries or commands to trigger actions through LLMs, leveraging advancements in AI and natural language processing. As shown in Fig. 4, in (1), a specific action definition is explicitly added to the Agent. Then, in (2), the Agent sends a prompt to the LLM, including descriptions of the defined tools or actions. In (3), the LLM selects the most suitable tool from the available options. The chosen action is then either executed by the Agent within *Local Code* in (4a) or performed by sending a request to the *Web Service* in (4b). In (5a), the result from the *Local Code* is returned to the Agent. In (5b), the response from the *Web Service* is returned to the Agent. In (6), the Agent forwards these results to the LLM. Finally, in (7), the LLM translates these results into natural language and returns them to the Agent.

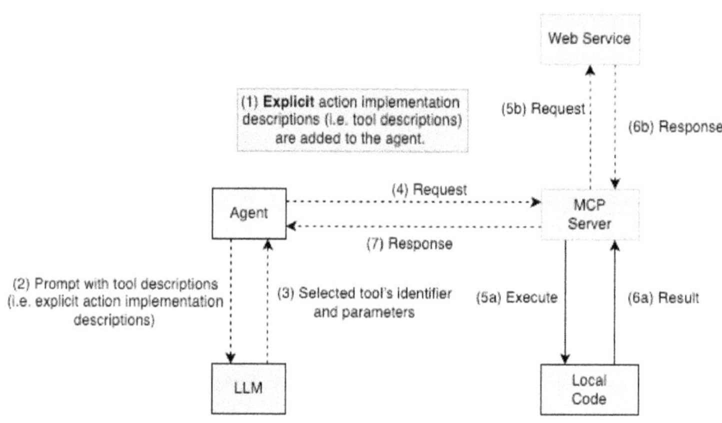

Fig. 5. Actions Triggered by LLM-controlled MCP.

Actions Triggered by LLM-Controlled MCP. MCP is a robust and open protocol specifically designed to facilitate seamless integration of data sources and external tools into LLM-enhanced MAS. MCP operates on a client-server model, systematically managing resources (e.g., documents, databases), tools (e.g., API calls, file operations), and standardized prompt templates required by LLMs. As shown in Fig. 5, MCP Server provides these resources and tools, while LLM acting as MCP Client establishes connections, enabling Agent to efficiently discover and utilize available resources.

In LLM-supported MAS, the selection of role implementation methods must be carefully evaluated based on various criteria, including system performance, security, flexibility, and maintenance ease. Directly invoked actions within code provide developers with full control, enabling efficient debugging, performance optimization, and security. While this method ensures minimal latency and high computational efficiency, its static nature limits flexibility, leading to issues such as code redundancy, maintenance complexity, and scalability challenges. On the other hand, actions invoked as semantic web services enhance dynamic adaptability and reusability through runtime updates and service extensions. While centralized maintenance facilitates cross-platform integration, dependency on external service providers introduces risks such as API changes, service outages, security vulnerabilities, and network latency [48]. Actions triggered by LLM-controlled tools simplify complex operations via natural language interactions, providing a user-friendly environment and supporting rapid prototyping [69]. However, this approach comes with the risks of unpredictable LLM behavior [22], potential errors [82], and high resource consumption [19]. Additionally, actions triggered by an LLM assuming a role offer high adaptability, creativity, and continuous learning capabilities. The ability to assign roles using natural language further enhances accessibility. However, this method also presents challenges such as a lack of transparency [38], security and privacy risks [65], and significant computational demands. Finally, the LLM-controlled Model Context Protocol (MCP) provides a standardized layer for resource and tool discovery, thereby offering flexibility, but it also raises protocol complexity and initial deployment costs. Consequently, architectural design must consider the performance, security, scalability, and maintainability dimensions to determine the most appropriate implementation method for each role.

In this section, we have shown that roles are not necessarily explicitly represented an implementation of a concept. In AOSE, roles are often used as abstract concepts during *design-time* and typically lack explicit representation at *run-time*. However, this absence hinders the clear mapping between agents' behaviors and their corresponding roles, thereby limiting the system's dynamic adaptability. As highlighted in frameworks such as ROPE [7] and JaCaMo [10], this limitation underscores the need for explicit run-time role modeling. Lhaksmana et al. [51] further stress the critical advantages of defining roles explicitly at run-time, particularly in self-organizing MAS. We thus argue that, in LLM-supported MAS, roles should be treated as *first-class entities at run-time* to effectively manage diverse application domains and support adaptability. Such an approach enhances agents' ability to adapt dynamically, increases run-time flexibility, and promotes overall system sustainability. This shift toward explicit run-time role representation is embodied in the hybrid role-based architecture presented in Sect. 5.

5   Proposed Role-Based Architecture

Based on the aforementioned observations, this section lays the foundation for an initial architecture for LLM-enhanced MAS engineering. Our goal is to establish a comprehensive framework that integrates traditional AOSE concepts (e.g., role, role implementation) with LLM-based dynamic capabilities. Due to the requirements of hybrid usage and encapsulation, we propose maintaining role definitions explicitly within agents. By encapsulation, we mean bundling data and the actions that operate on that data in a role into a single unit. This way, we can protect the role's internal state from unintended interference or misuse. Moreover, encapsulation promotes modularity and maintainability, making it easier to modify and debug the role while ensuring data integrity.

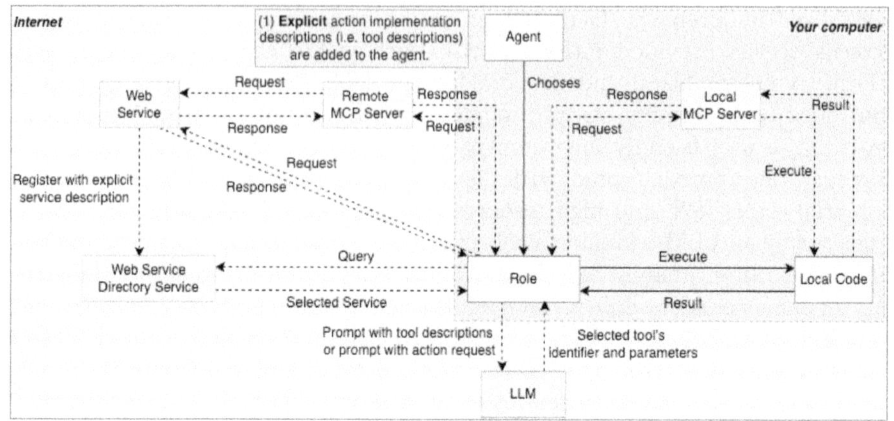

Fig. 6. Proposed Role-based Architecture.

Role definitions can encompass one or multiple role implementation approaches outlined in Sect. 4.3 (Fig. 6). This means that a role may involve actions that are executed locally, actions accessed via web services, tasks performed by locally implemented LLM tools, or operations carried out directly by LLMs.

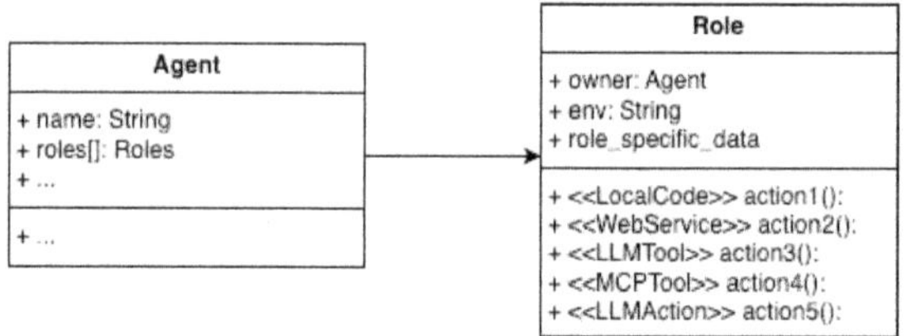

Fig. 7. Proposed Role Concept in UML Class Diagram.

Consequently, we design the LLM-enabled role concept using the UML graphical modeling language since it is more precise compared to natural language. Figure 7 shows a simple UML class model of an agent with roles. Each Role belongs to one Agent (its owner), has a string indicating the environment where the role is played, and may include various role specific data. A Role can have five types of "actions" with different stereotypes—indicating, for example, Local-Code, WebService, LLMTool, MCPTool, or LLMAction—that can be invoked when an agent is acting in that particular role.

When an agent intends to determine or guide its actions within a specific role using outputs generated by an LLM, it employs a dynamically generated prompt. This prompt is constructed by selecting one of the two prompt templates depicted in Fig. 8. Figure 8(a) illustrates a scenario in which the

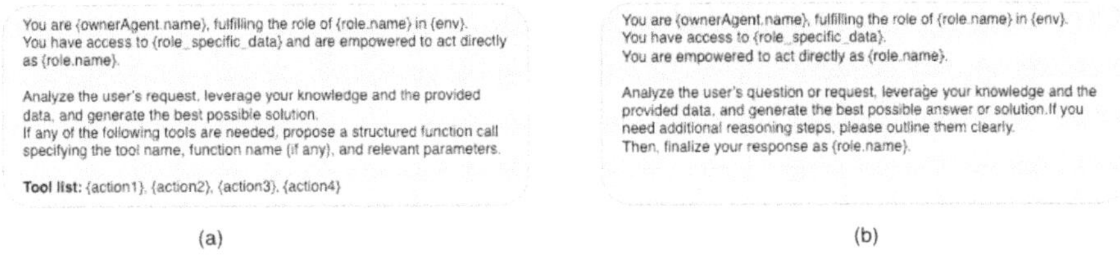

Fig. 8. (a) A prompt template for a role configured to use tools when necessary. (b) A prompt template for a role that generates a response directly through the LLM.

agent performs an action by utilizing external tools based on recommendations provided by the LLM, whereas Fig. 8(b) represents a scenario in which the agent directly utilizes the textual output from the LLM as its response. Placeholders in these prompts-such as `ownerAgent.name`, `role.name`, `env`, and `role_specific_data`—are dynamically replaced at runtime with concrete values derived from the respective role instance and its owning agent. Consequently, the LLM obtains explicit contextual information about the agent's identity, the role being enacted, the operational environment, and the available capabilities. Thus, the agent interprets the output generated by the LLM and either executes appropriate actions through designated tools or directly incorporates the LLM's response into its communication processes.

6   Conclusion

In this study, we shed light on the fact that existing LLM-based tools and frameworks do not sufficiently leverage AOSE's extensive body of knowledge. While LLM-based frameworks and tools have made impressive strides in enabling powerful and flexible agent behavior, they often do so through ad hoc design approaches that compromise maintainability, reusability, and scalability.

To address this issue, we conducted a focused study on the concept of roles, a foundational element in AOSE, and examined how it is defined, specified, and implemented in both traditional AOSE and LLM-based systems. Our analysis revealed key differences and limitations in current LLM-enabled role modeling, particularly the absence of formal structure and runtime support.

However, adapting the concept of "role" in LLM-assisted MAS development and transforming it into concrete actions brings both new opportunities and challenges. Hybrid solutions that combine the solid principles of traditional AOSE methodologies with the innovative dynamism of LLMs can be effective in overcoming these challenges. Based on this observation, we proposed a hybrid role-based architecture that encapsulates both traditional AOSE design principles and LLM-driven functionalities. This initial architecture is able to express roles that have various actions types while encapsulating them.

By bridging the conceptual foundations of AOSE with the dynamic potential of LLMs, our work lays the groundwork for a more principled engineering methodology for LLM-enhanced MAS. Future work will focus on refining this architecture and validating its effectiveness through practical case studies involving real-world MAS applications.

References

1. Abdalla, R., Mishra, A.: Agent-oriented software engineering methodologies: analysis and future directions. Complexity **2021**(1), 1629419 (2021)
2. Abrial, J.R., Hoare, A., Chapron, P.: The B-Book (1996)
3. Aerospace, S.: SAE architecture analysis and design language (AADL) annex volume 1: Annex a: Graphical AADL notation. Annex C: AADL Meta-Model and Interchange Formats, Annex D: Language Compliance and Application Program Interface Annex E: Error Model Annex, AS5506/1 (2011)
4. ALMutairi, M., AlKulaib, L., Aktas, M., Alsalamah, S., Lu, C.T.: Synthetic Arabic medical dialogues using advanced multi-agent LLM techniques. In: Proceedings of The Second Arabic Natural Language Processing Conference, pp. 11–26 (2024)
5. Bakar, M., Ghoul, S.: A methodology for AUML role modeling, pp. 74–81 (2011). https://doi.org/10.1109/ISIICT.2011.6149600
6. Bauer, B., Odell, J.: UML 2.0 and agents: how to build agent-based systems with the new UML standard. Eng. Appl. Artif. Intell. **18**(2), 141–157 (2005)
7. Becht, M., Gurzki, T., Klarmann, J., Muscholl, M.: Rope: role oriented programming environment for multiagent systems. In: Proceedings Fourth IFCIS International Conference on Cooperative Information Systems. CoopIS 99 (Cat. No. PR00384), pp. 325–333. IEEE (1999)
8. Bergenti, F., Gleizes, M.P., Zambonelli, F.: Methodologies and Software Engineering for Agent Systems: The Agent-oriented Software Engineering Handbook, vol. 11. Springer Science & Business Media (2006). https://doi.org/10.1007/b116049
9. Beydoun, G., et al.: FAML: a generic metamodel for mas development. IEEE Trans. Softw. Eng. **35**(6), 841–863 (2009)
10. Boissier, O., Bordini, R.H., Hübner, J.F., Ricci, A., Santi, A.: Multi-agent oriented programming with JACAMO. Sci. Comput. Program. **78**(6), 747–761 (2013)
11. Bresciani, P., Perini, A., Giorgini, P., Giunchiglia, F., Mylopoulos, J.: TROPOS: an agent-oriented software development methodology. Auton. Agent. Multi-Agent Syst. **8**, 203–236 (2004)
12. Cabral, L., Domingue, J., Motta, E., Payne, T., Hakimpour, F.: Approaches to semantic web services: an overview and comparisons. In: Bussler, C.J., Davies, J., Fensel, D., Studer, R. (eds.) ESWS 2004. LNCS, vol. 3053, pp. 225–239. Springer, Heidelberg (2004). https://doi.org/10.1007/978-3-540-25956-5_16
13. Cabri, G., Leonardi, L., Puviani, M.: Service-oriented agent methodologies. In: 16th IEEE International Workshops on Enabling Technologies: Infrastructure for Collaborative Enterprises (WETICE 2007), pp. 24–29. IEEE (2007)
14. Celaya, J.R., Desrochers, A.A., Graves, R.J.: Modeling and analysis of multi-agent systems using petri nets. In: 2007 IEEE International Conference on Systems, Man and Cybernetics, pp. 1439–1444. IEEE (2007)
15. Chandrasekaran, M.: Enhancing efficiency and flexibility of rapid prototyping for scalable multimodal intelligent agents. In: 2024 Artificial Intelligence for Business (AIxB), pp. 66–71. IEEE (2024)

16. Chen, G., et al.: AutoaGents: a framework for automatic agent generation, pp. 22–30 (2024)
17. Chen, W., et al.: AgentVerse: facilitating multi-agent collaboration and exploring emergent behaviors (2024)
18. Dam, K.H., Winikoff, M.: Comparing agent-oriented methodologies. In: Giorgini, P., Henderson-Sellers, B., Winikoff, M. (eds.) AOIS -2003. LNCS (LNAI), vol. 3030, pp. 78–93. Springer, Heidelberg (2004). https://doi.org/10.1007/978-3-540-25943-5_6
19. Dang, Y., He, Y., Xu, M., Ye, K.: Resource management for GPT-based model deployed on clouds: challenges, solutions, and future directions. LNCS (including subseries Lecture Notes in Artificial Intelligence and Lecture Notes in Bioinformatics), vol. 15252, pp. 95–105 (2025). https://doi.org/10.1007/978-981-96-1528-5_7
20. DeLoach, S.A., Valenzuela, J.L.: An agent-environment interaction model. In: Padgham, L., Zambonelli, F. (eds.) AOSE 2006. LNCS, vol. 4405, pp. 1–18. Springer, Heidelberg (2007). https://doi.org/10.1007/978-3-540-70945-9_1
21. Demirkol, S., Challenger, M., Getir, S., Kosar, T., Kardas, G., Mernik, M.: Sea_l: a domain-specific language for semantic web enabled multi-agent systems. In: 2012 Federated Conference on Computer Science and Information Systems (FedCSIS), pp. 1373–1380. IEEE (2012)
22. Deng, Y., Zhang, W., Pan, S.J., Bing, L.: Multilingual jailbreak challenges in large language models (2024)
23. Dissaux, P., et al.: The smart project: multi-agent scheduling simulation of real-time architectures. In: Embedded Real-Time Software System (2014)
24. Ehtesham, A., Singh, A., Gupta, G.K., Kumar, S.: A survey of agent interoperability protocols: model context protocol (MCP), agent communication protocol (ACP), agent-to-agent protocol (A2A), and agent network protocol (ANP). arXiv preprint arXiv:2505.02279 (2025)
25. Ferber, J., Michel, F., Baez, J.: AGRE: integrating environments with organizations. In: Weyns, D., Van Dyke Parunak, H., Michel, F. (eds.) E4MAS 2004. LNCS (LNAI), vol. 3374, pp. 48–56. Springer, Heidelberg (2005). https://doi.org/10.1007/978-3-540-32259-7_2
26. Gao, C., et al.: Large language models empowered agent-based modeling and simulation: a survey and perspectives. Humanit. Soc. Sci. Commun. **11**(1) (2024). https://doi.org/10.1057/s41599-024-03611-3
27. Garlan, D., Monroe, R., Wile, D.: ACME: An Architecture Description Interchange Language, White Paper. Pittsburgh PA, submitted for publication, Computer Science Department, Carnegie Mellon University (1997)
28. Ghafarollahi, A., Buehler, M.J.: Automating alloy design and discovery with physics-aware multimodal multiagent AI. Proc. Natl. Acad. Sci. **122**(4), e2414074122 (2025). https://doi.org/10.1073/pnas.2414074122
29. Giannesini, F., Kanoui, H., Pasero, R., Van Caneghem, M.: Prolog. Addison-Wesley Longman Publishing Co., Inc (1986)
30. Guedes, G.T.A., Vicari, R.M.: Applying AUML and UML 2 in the multi-agent systems project. In: Heuser, C.A., Pernul, G. (eds.) ER 2009. LNCS, vol. 5833, pp. 106–115. Springer, Heidelberg (2009). https://doi.org/10.1007/978-3-642-04947-7_14
31. Guo, T., et al.: Large language model based multi-agents: a survey of progress and challenges, pp. 8048–8057 (2024)

32. Gurcan, O.: LLM-augmented agent-based modelling for social simulations: challenges and opportunities. In: HHAI 2024: Hybrid Human AI Systems for the Social Good, Frontiers in Artificial Intelligence and Applications, vol. 386, pp. 134–144. IOS Press (2024). https://doi.org/10.3233/FAIA240190
33. Gurcan, O., Falck, V., Rousseau, M.G., Lima, L.L.: Towards an LLM-powered social digital twinning platform. In: Proceedings of The 23rd International Conference on Practical applications of Agents and Multi-Agent Systems (PAAMS 2025) (2025)
34. Haarslev, V., Möller, R.: RACER: an owl reasoning agent for the semantic web. In: Proceedings of the International Workshop on Applications, Products and Services of Web-based Support Systems, in conjunction with the, pp. 91–95 (2003)
35. Hameurlain, N., Sibertin-Blanc, C.: Specification of role-based interactions components in multi-agent systems. LNCS (including subseries Lecture Notes in Artificial Intelligence and Lecture Notes in Bioinformatics) **3390**, 180–197 (2005). https://doi.org/10.1007/978-3-540-31846-0_11
36. Harel, D.: StateCharts: a visual formalism for complex systems. Sci. Comput. Program. **8**(3), 231–274 (1987)
37. Henderson-Sellers, B., Giorgini, P.: Agent-oriented methodologies. IGI Global (2005)
38. Hepenstal, S., Zhang, L., Wong, B.L.W.: The impact of system transparency on analytical reasoning (2023). https://doi.org/10.1145/3544549.3585786
39. Hjelmblom, M.: Deontic action-logic multi-agent systems in Prolog. Högskolan i Gävle (2008)
40. Hong, S., et al.: MetaGPT: meta programming for a multi-agent collaborative framework. In: The Twelfth International Conference on Learning Representations (2023)
41. Hui, K., Chalmers, S., Gray, P.M.D., Preece, A.D.: Experience in using RDF in agent-mediated knowledge architectures. In: van Elst, L., Dignum, V., Abecker, A. (eds.) AMKM 2003. LNCS (LNAI), vol. 2926, pp. 177–192. Springer, Heidelberg (2004). https://doi.org/10.1007/978-3-540-24612-1_12
42. Jackson, D.: Alloy: a lightweight object modelling notation. ACM Trans. Softw. Eng. Methodol. (TOSEM) **11**(2), 256–290 (2002)
43. Jiang, F., et al.: Large language model enhanced multi-agent systems for 6G communications. IEEE Wirel. Commun. **31**(6), 48–55 (2024). https://doi.org/10.1109/MWC.016.2300600
44. Jiang, Y.H., Liu, T.Y., Zhuang, X., Hu, H., Li, R., Jia, R.: Enhancing educational practices with multi-agent systems: a review. In: Enhancing Educational Practices: Strategies for Assessing and Improving Learning Outcomes, pp. 47–65 (2024)
45. Jin, A., Ye, Y., Lee, B., Qiao, Y.: DecoAgent: large language model empowered decentralized autonomous collaboration agents based on smart contracts. IEEE Access **12**, 155234–155245 (2024). https://doi.org/10.1109/ACCESS.2024.3481641
46. Jones, C.B.: Systematic Software Development Using VDM, vol. 2. Prentice Hall Englewood Cliffs (1990)
47. Koning, J.L., Hernández, I.R.: Limitations in AUML'S roles specification. IFIP Adv. Inf. Commun. Technol. **163**, 79–82 (2005). https://doi.org/10.1007/0-387-23152-8_10
48. Kumar, D., et al.: Security challenges in an increasingly tangled web, pp. 677–684 (2017). https://doi.org/10.1145/3038912.3052686
49. Kuska, M.T., Wahabzada, M., Paulus, S.: AI for crop production – where can large language models (LLMS) provide substantial value? Comput. Electron. Agric. **221**, 108924 (2024). https://doi.org/10.1016/j.compag.2024.108924

50. Lamport, L.: Specifying Systems, vol. 388. Addison-Wesley Boston (2002)
51. Lhaksmana, K.M., Murakami, Y., Ishida, T.: Role-based modeling for designing agent behavior in self-organizing multi-agent systems. Int. J. Software Eng. Knowl. Eng. **28**(01), 79–96 (2018)
52. Li, C., et al.: ModelScope-agent: building your customizable agent system with open-source large language models, pp. 566–578 (2023)
53. Li, G., Hammoud, H., Itani, H., Khizbullin, D., Ghanem, B.: Camel: communicative agents for "mind" exploration of large language model society. Adv. Neural. Inf. Process. Syst. **36**, 51991–52008 (2023)
54. Li, X.: A review of prominent paradigms for LLM-based agents: Tool use (including rag), planning, and feedback learning, vol. Part F206484-1, p. 9760–9779 (2025)
55. Loach, S.A.D., Wood, M.: Developing multiagent systems with agentTool. In: Castelfranchi, C., Lespérance, Y. (eds.) ATAL 2000. LNCS (LNAI), vol. 1986, pp. 46–60. Springer, Heidelberg (2001). https://doi.org/10.1007/3-540-44631-1_4
56. Malfa, E.L., et al.: Large language models miss the multi-agent mark (2025)
57. Onggo, B.S., Karpat, O.: Agent-based conceptual model representation using BPMN. In: Proceedings of the Winter Simulation Conference (WSC), 2011, pp. 671–682. IEEE (2011)
58. Padgham, L., Winikoff, M.: Prometheus: a practical agent-oriented methodology. In: Agent-Oriented Methodologies, pp. 107–135. IGI Global (2005)
59. Paiva, P.Y.A., Saotome, O., Brandauer, C.: Specification and verification of a multi-agent coordination protocol with TLA+. In: 2018 VIII Brazilian Symposium on Computing Systems Engineering (SBESC), pp. 207–212. IEEE (2018)
60. Park, S., Sugumaran, V.: Designing multi-agent systems: a framework and application. Expert Syst. Appl. **28**(2), 259–271 (2005)
61. Pavón, J., Gómez-Sanz, J.J., Fuentes, R.: The ingenias methodology and tools. In: Agent-oriented methodologies, pp. 236–276. IGI Global (2005)
62. Petri, C.: Kommunikation mit automaten: Phd thesis/institut f ur instrumentelle mathematik.-bonn, 1962 (1962)
63. Qian, C., et al.: ChatDev: communicative agents for software development. In: Proceedings of the 62nd Annual Meeting of the Association for Computational Linguistics (Volume 1: Long Papers), pp. 15174–15186 (2024)
64. Ramzan, M., Ali, A., Akram, S., Qayyum, Z.U.: Formal specification of multi-agent environment using VDM-SL. In: 2011 6th Int. Conference on Computer Sciences and Convergence Information Technology (ICCIT), pp. 150–154. IEEE (2011)
65. Rathod, V., Nabavirazavi, S., Zad, S., Iyengar, S.S.: Privacy and security challenges in large language models, pp. 746–752 (2025). https://doi.org/10.1109/CCWC62904.2025.10903912
66. Ross, R., Collier, R., O'Hare, G.M.P.: AF-APL – bridging principles and practice in agent oriented languages. In: Bordini, R.H., Dastani, M., Dix, J., El Fallah Seghrouchni, A. (eds.) ProMAS 2004. LNCS (LNAI), vol. 3346, pp. 66–88. Springer, Heidelberg (2005). https://doi.org/10.1007/978-3-540-32260-3_4
67. Roussille, H., Gürcan, Ö., Michel, F.: AGR4BS: a generic multi-agent organizational model for blockchain systems. Big Data Cognit. Comput. **6**(1) (2022). https://doi.org/10.3390/bdcc6010001
68. Sarkar, A., Sarkar, S.: Survey of LLM agent communication with MCP: a software design pattern centric review. arXiv preprint arXiv:2506.05364 (2025)
69. Sathe, G., Choudhary, V., Bhagat, D.: Comprehensive review on large language models (LLMS). **2**, 3097–3102 (2024)

70. Sathya, J., Fernandez, F.M.H.: An optimizing crime detection in social media platforms using multiagent ontology-based approach, pp. 956–966 (2023). https://doi.org/10.1109/ICOSEC58147.2023.10276325

71. Sha, Z., Le, Q., Panchal, J.H.: Using SYSML for conceptual representation of agent-based models. In: Int. Design Engineering Technical Conferences and Computers and Information in Engineering Conference, vol. 54792, pp. 39–50 (2011)

72. Spanoudakis, N., Moraitis, P.: Using ASEME methodology for model-driven agent systems development. In: International Workshop on Agent-Oriented Software Engineering, pp. 106–127. Springer (2010). https://doi.org/10.1007/978-3-642-22636-6_7

73. Spanoudakis, N.I.: Engineering multi-agent systems with StateCharts: theory and practice. SN Comput. Sci. **2**(4), 317 (2021)

74. Spanoudakis, N.I., Moraitis, P.: The ASEME methodology. Int. J. Agent-Oriented Softw. Eng. **7**(2), 79–107 (2022)

75. Spivey, J.: The Z Notation. Prentice-Hall (1992)

76. Sturm, A., Shehory, O.: Agent-oriented software engineering: revisiting the state of the art. In: Agent-Oriented Software Engineering: Reflections on Architectures, Methodologies, Languages, and Frameworks, pp. 13–26 (2014)

77. Wang, R., et al.: Role prompting guided domain adaptation with general capability preserve for large language models. In: Duh, K., Gomez, H., Bethard, S. (eds.) Findings of the Association for Computational Linguistics: NAACL 2024, pp. 2243–2255. Association for Computational Linguistics, Mexico City, Mexico (2024). https://doi.org/10.18653/v1/2024.findings-naacl.145

78. Wawer, M., Chudziak, J.A., Niewiadomska-Szynkiewicz, E.: Large language models and the Elliott wave principle: a multi-agent deep learning approach to big data analysis in financial markets. Appl. Sci. (Switzerland) **14**(24) (2024). https://doi.org/10.3390/app142411897

79. Weyns, D., Omicini, A., Odell, J.: Environment as a first class abstraction in multiagent systems. Auton. Agent. Multi-Agent Syst. **14**, 5–30 (2007)

80. Wooldridge, M., Jennings, N.R., Kinny, D.: The GAIA methodology for agent-oriented analysis and design. Auton. Agent. Multi-Agent Syst. **3**, 285–312 (2000)

81. Wu, Q., et al.: AutoGen: Enabling next-gen LLM applications via multi-agent conversations. In: First Conference on Language Modeling (2024)

82. Ye, J., et al.: ToolsWord: unveiling safety issues of large language models in tool learning across three stages, vol. 1, p. 2181–2211 (2024). https://doi.org/10.18653/v1/2024.acl-long.119

83. Zambonelli, F., Jennings, N.R., Wooldridge, M.: Developing multiagent systems: the GAIA methodology. ACM Trans. Softw. Eng. Methodol. (TOSEM) **12**(3), 317–370 (2003)

84. Zhang, C., et al.: PROAGENT: building proactive cooperative agents with large language models, vol. 38, p. 17591–17599 (2024). https://doi.org/10.1609/aaai.v38i16.29710

85. Zou, H., Li, R., Sun, T., Wang, F., Li, T., Liu, K.: Cooperative scheduling and hierarchical memory model for multi-agent systems. In: 2024 IEEE International Symposium on Product Compliance Engineering-Asia (ISPCE-ASIA), pp. 1–6. IEEE (2024)

Towards Explainable BDI Agents for End Users

Marcel Mauri[(✉)] and Mirjam Minor

Department of Computer Science, Goethe University Frankfurt, Frankfurt, Germany
`{mauri,minor}@cs.uni-frankfurt.de`

Abstract. Explainable agency (XAg) aims at providing users with insights about the reasoning and decisions taken by an agent. Most of the newer XAg approaches are particularly useful as explanations for developers and researchers. In contrast, the novel XAg framework presented in this paper aims to address the explanation needs of end users, including both domain experts and lay users. It is a challenging task since this kind of users is not familiar with the methodological and technical aspects of agency. We propose a representation for end user questions and potential explanatory answers in both a verbal and a formal description as well as a mapping structure of questions to multiple possible explanations. We develop a pattern-based approach to extract explanatory content from an execution log and to validate potential answers to a user question which is based on the TriQPAN decision patterns from the literature [14]. We organize the novel concepts in a four-layered architecture with layers for end user questions, validation logic, TriQPAN patterns, and answer text generation. A running sample from a Jadex-BDI project on autonomous mobility on demand provides a demonstration scenario to illustrate some data structures and pseudocode. Further, it highlights the plausibility of our novel XAg framework.

Keywords: BDI Agent · XAI · XAg · BDI-ABM Framework · TriQPAN · Traffic Simulation · Jadex · Agent Development Framework

1 Introduction

Agent-oriented Programming (AOP) [15] has a rich research tradition of implementing intelligent behavior in complex environments. The decisions of cognitive agents are transparent and well explainable by established notions of agenthood in AI, such as beliefs, desires, intentions, plans or norms. The state of an agent can be 'read' directly from its data structures. Thus, Bordini et al. [2] consider BDI-based approaches [12] per se as *Explainable AI (XAI)* and argue that the intelligibility of agent behavior by end users and other stakeholders is their key-contribution. However, with the advent of larger amounts of data and more complex decision processes involved in modern agent approaches, this transparency claim does not fully hold any more.

Recently, the field of *explainable agency* (XAg) has evolved [1,5,8,14,20,21]. XAg describes the ability of agents "to explain their decisions and the reasoning that produces their choices" [5]. Today, the main target groups of XAg

S. Rodriguez et al. (Eds.): EMAS 2025, LNAI 16407, pp. 221–237, 2026.
https://doi.org/10.1007/978-3-032-18011-7_13

approaches are researchers and developers who have a sound scientific and technological understanding. Ribera and Laprediza [13] categorize explainees of AI systems in three main groups, namely developers and AI researchers, domain experts, and lay users. The end user perspective (domain experts and lay users) has not yet been addressed in depth in XAg. There is especially a lack of methods to communicate generated explanations to lay users. Mualla et al. [8] have published some preliminary work on enriching visual simulations of BDI agent behaviour by summarized beliefs and alerts. Yan et al. [21] recognize that explanations of agent-based systems can be used by different kinds of users but do not yet achieve domain level explanations for end users in their prototypical framework. There is a research gap on developing XAg methods for end users, including their evaluation in real application scenarios. It is a challenging research topic to bridge the gap between the explanations demands from an end user perspective and the agent decisions that have been developed from an agent design and problem-solving perspective.

In this paper, we introduce a novel framework for XAg that takes the end user perspective into consideration. It builds on TriQPAN design patterns [14] for recording agent decisions in an execution trace. The TriQPAN design patterns are particularly useful for expert users (MAS developers) as explanations. In our model, we integrate them with additional layers for the end user perspective. This includes a mapping between the user's information needs and potential answers, a validation layer for (multiple) potential answers, and a verbalization layer with different degrees of granularity for communicating the explanations to the end users. The novel framework is demonstrated by means of a running sample in a Jadex-BDI environment. A fully functional implementation in Java is currently under development. The sample explanation scenario is taken from an Autonomous Mobility on Demand (AMoD) project called *ATRIAS* where a fleet of autonomous e-trikes is simulated [7]. The demonstration serves as a proof-of concept for the novel representation forms and validation mechanisms.

The main contributions of this paper are threefold:

- To develop an *XAg framework targeting end users*. It integrates an existing design pattern approach for expert users with the aim to also let lay users get insights about the reasoning of an agent.
- To integrate TriQPAN with Jadex agents in a *preliminary implementation concept*.
- To demonstrate a further *application scenario for TriQPAN with typical decisions of a fleet of autonomous e-trikes*.

The remainder of this paper is structured as follows: Sect. 2 presents the related work. Necessary background is covered in Sect. 3. The concept design of our explanation model is introduced in Sect. 4. In Sect. 5, we present a first feasibility check of our framework. Using an example, we first show the necessary representation forms to capture all information for future explanations. Then we show how that information can be extracted and validated for generating explanations. Further typical end user questions will be explained by the means of a table with several examples.

Section 6 draws a conclusion and discusses future work.

2 Related Work

Langley et al. [5] describe elements of explainable agency (XAg) in a position paper. The elements comprise representation forms for content that supports explanation, an episodic memory of target agents, as well as methods to access and extract content from episodic memory. Our approach has been inspired by this work in the sense that it uses execution traces from a simulation as episodic memory. Events and decision patterns will provide a structured form of representation in this episodic memory, allowing relevant content to be retrieved and extracted for explanation.

Anjomshoae et al.'s [1] literature review discusses application scenarios, main drivers, social science and psychological background, platforms and architectures, explanatory granularity, presentation and evaluation of XAg. The authors state that most of the studied works either lack evaluations or conduct a user study for relatively simple scenarios. The findings provide a further incentive for our intended work on developing methods for the end user perspective in XAg, including their evaluation.

Mualla [8] provides visual explanation also for end users of a parcel delivery service. However, the explanations are still at an atomic level which makes it rather difficult to grasp the relation to the user's demand for information.

There is a body of XAg work on BDI agents where the agents inform human observers about their internal reasoning such as intentions [4,9], recent actions [3], or decision processes [14,19,20]. Some of the work considers building blocks for explanations with a formal setting. Dennis & Oren's framework [3] uses predicate dictionaries to provide natural language substitutes in semi-formal explanations for domain experts with technical expertise. Winikoff et al. [20] generate explanations of the behavior of BDI agents from goal trees. A goal tree is a tree of nodes, where leaves are actions, and inner nodes are goals that can be decomposed using AND, SEQ or OR. The children of an OR decomposition are options that are selected at run time based on valuings, that means which outcome the agent prefers most in the current situation. The valuings approach has been evaluated in a sandbox scenario with end users to assess the believability, acceptability, and comprehensibility of explanations [19]. Rodriguez et al. [14] describe design patterns for developing explainable-by-design agents. The aim is to explain the agent's reasoning and decision processes based on patterns that have a well-defined structure called TriQPAN. Since our approach uses TriQPAN patterns as a formal setting they are described in more detail below. As an extension to the design approach discussed in the literature [14], our work has a scope on the explanatory demands of end users in an application scenario with real world data.

The issue of creating explanatory narratives for end users of BDI agents has been discussed in the literature [21] by means of a domestic robot running example. It is part of a multi layered framework for different user perspectives. Two perspectives namely the implementation view and the BDI design view are formalized and prototypically implemented. The third layer, the domain view, has not yet been formalized and implemented.

3   Background

3.1   ATRIAS System

ATRIAS [7] for *Autonomous trikes as a service* is a framework that connects BDI agents, implemented with *Jadex* [10] with the traffic simulation platform *MATSim* [18]. It was built upon the BDI-ABM interface [16]. Every Jadex vehicle agent is assigned to an agent in MATSim where the Jadex agents act as the decision making component (brain) where the MATSim counterpart is limited to the execution of actions and perception in the simulation environment (body). This allows complex reasoning capabilities to be combined with a feature-rich simulation platform. The intended scope of ATRIAS is all types of AMoD scenarios including ride-hailing, last-mile delivery or waste disposal logistics. The main focus is on the name giving autonomous trikes which process incoming trip requests on demand. Within ATRIAS, the area of operation is divided into several sub-areas, each with its own *area agent*. Incoming customer requests are sent by the area agents to the *vehicle agents* located closest to the customer in their area. These vehicle agents are designed to work in a decentralized manner for easier scalability and are completely self managed. Following the initial allocation of a customer request, an evaluation is conducted in order to calculate a utility score. The purpose of this is to determine how well an agent is suited to execute this request. If it will be below a certain threshold vehicle agents will use the *contract-net-protocol* (CNP) [17] to try to find a better suited agent for that customer request. When their batteries are low they will also drive to charging stations on their own.

The decision logic of the vehicle agents is designed following the BDI paradigm. Several goals have been specified to handle incoming customer requests. Beliefs about incoming customer requests are stored inside the `DecisionTaskList`. The goal `ManageJobs` processes the `DecisionTasks` depending on their current status and decides about the next action to be executed (evaluate it, negotiate with other agents to find a more suitable vehicle for execution, commit to it, etc.). When the status of a `DecisionTask` is set to 'commit' it will cause the creation of a `customerTrip` which will be stored alongside all other scheduled trips inside the `TripList`. The goal `BatteryLoaded` watches the current battery level and can create a `chargingTrip`. The trips inside the `TripList` then will be executed by the goal `TripService` which sends the corresponding drive operations to MATSim.

ATRIAS has been designed as a framework to simulate AMoD scenarios and to test and evaluate agent behavior. The plan is to port the ATRIAS agents to control a fleet of autonomous trikes that will be operating on the campus of Goethe University Frankfurt. When the development of the ATRIAS framework started, XAg was not part of the project. Therefore, a possible future integration of XAg methods was not considered when designing the agent architecture. This makes it an interesting test case to show how an XAg model designed for end users can be adapted to such a non-optimized architecture. The current code of ATRIAS is available via GitHub[1].

3.2   TriQPAN Patterns

TriQPAN [14] (Trigger, Query, Process, Action and Notify) are XAg design patterns that can be used to explain the behavior of agents to expert users like agent developers. In this paper we want to use TriQPAN as a part of an explainability model to extend the scope of applicability to end users. TriQPAN processes are designed to work with an underlying event store, a log database in which all related events are stored. It has recently been implemented directly into the Sarl programming language [14] in which the capturing of these logs is directly integrated. The use of the pattern itself is not limited to a specific agent language or architecture. To apply the pattern, it is necessary to adapt it to the respective agent architectures specific processes. Therefore these patterns have to be modeled manually.

Every TriQPAN process starts with a **Trigger**. A **Trigger** might comprise perceptions, an update of a belief or the activation of a goal or plan. During the **Query** step the agent retrieves all information needed to execute an action. The **Action** step contains all initiated processes. These can relate to both belief updates and movements of the agent within the environment. The final step **Notify** will list all the changes made during the **Action** step and inform the used components which can trigger other TriQPAN patterns. After a TriQPAN process is completed, all the information it contains is captured within an XAgentProcess and stored together with the other logs generated at runtime at the event store.

Explanation approaches like those using TriQPAN patterns are well suited to explain how an agent's decision was made. This makes them a good tool for agent developers. Since they know the agent architectures and their reasoning mechanisms well, they can directly ask for agent internals such as goals/plans to get the information they need. They are also able to understand answers containing technical vocabulary and extract the information they need from them.

To make them better usable also for end users (lay users), there are some research gaps that have to be closed. First, end users of agents do not possess knowledge about the internals of an agent. A question asked by an end user does not necessarily stand in a direct relation to an agent component/decision or can contain situation specific aspects. Another problem is that the generated outputs can contain too many technical, agent-specific vocabulary or would not directly relate to the question. Therefore, a transformation of the facts given by the patterns into an answer in everyday language is required.

---

[1] https://github.com/M4rc3l-M/ATRIAS.

4   XAg Model for End User Alignment

The novel XAg model addresses the information demands of end users. The explanations shall be understandable without technical background knowledge. It aims to fill the gap between the direct explanation of the decisions of the agents and the more general questions raised by end users. In a preliminary survey of potential end users of the ATRIAS system [11], users were confronted with a mobile application to interact with our ATRIAS framework. A brief evaluation of the user experience with the app revealed, among other things, a few questions they would like to ask the system. The questions which have been formulated are "Why is my trike late?", "What are alternative transport modes?" or "What are the CO2 savings when using the ATRIAS trikes instead of driving by car?".

Our current design is limited to user queries that pertain directly to the vehicle responsible for this specific customer. The system is intended to support direct communication between customers and their respective vehicles. Due to the decentralized nature of ATRIAS, individual vehicles are not able to respond to queries which require information stored only in the belief base of other vehicles. Addressing such questions would require extensive communication between agents, which is not currently planned.

Answering such questions requires mapping the user's query to appropriate patterns that allow explaining the rationale behind an agent's decision relevant to the question, validating their truth within the event store, and verbalising a textual explanation for the patterns in everyday language. Some of the questions require additional knowledge beyond the agent decisions, including the vehicle's consumption of electrical power, which might be recorded in the agents' belief base or even be retrieved from external sources. We have developed a model for the end user questions that are explainable by means of the agents' decision. The model builds on the XAg framework TriQPAN to extract the information on the agents' decision behavior from an event store.

Figure 1 depicts the architecture of the novel model for XAg with an end user alignment. It comprises four main vertical layers (from the left to the right): End user questions, validation logics, TriQPAN patterns, and answer text generation. First, the end user can select a question from a list of possible questions. The questions are formulated as texts using the vocabulary of potential end users and are free from technical terms (that are only understood by agent experts). In the second step the selected question will be processed by the validation logic. This component will retrieve a list of possible answers fitting to the user question. These possible answers are based on the functionality of the agent. A possible answer to the initial user question can depend on multiple different decisions the agent has made in the past. These decision points are captured by the TriQPAN patterns designed for the agent and stored alongside changes made to beliefs inside the event store. The patterns in the event store can be reused to answer different user questions. This is because they can refer to the same patterns.

During this step, a full list of possible answers will be calculated. These can be independently validated. Every possible candidate answer will have a test criterion which will be validated by the use of TriQPAN patterns. Every agent

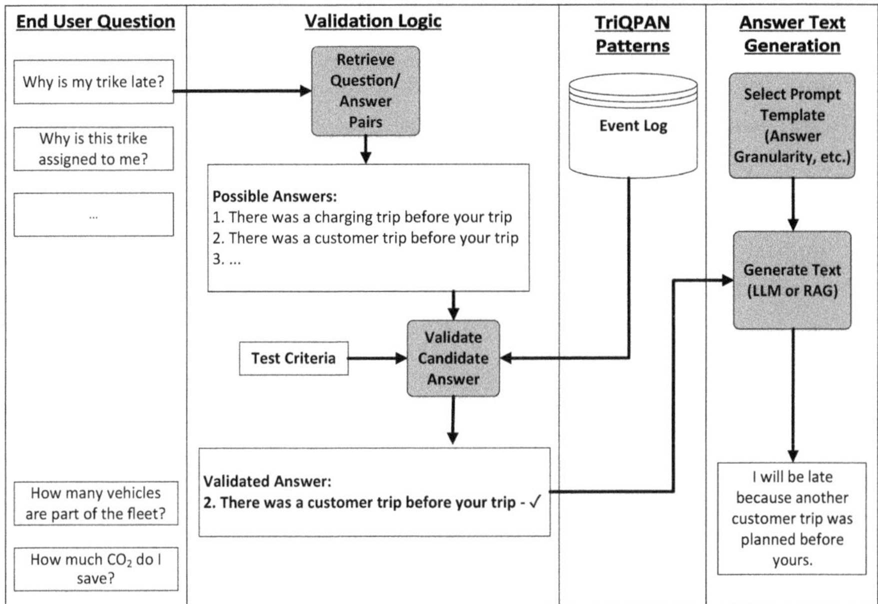

Fig. 1. Four-layered architecture of the novel XAg model.

will store all events and already occurred patterns inside an event store. The validation algorithm will then access the event store to validate the corresponding possible answers by means of pre-defined test criteria. The validation logic then returns a list of identified technical answers to the user's question, along with the corresponding events. In the final step an answer for the end user will be generated. Therefore we will use an *LLM or RAG system* [6] to create an easy to understand answer which will contain all the information given by the validation logic. As customers may have different requirements for the level of detail of the answers, there is also the option to select a prompt template to specify the intended granularity of the answer.

5 XAg Model Feasibility Check

In the following we will carry out a feasibility check by discussing the data structures and pseudo code for a running sample within our ATRIAS framework. It will serve as a preliminary proof of concept of the model presented above.

We will use a typical sample question from end users of our ATRIAS framework: "Why is my trike late?". Based on this question we will explain the measures necessary to log the information required. Then we will explain how we can extract the necessary information out of our logs to generate an answer. Finally, we will look at some of the other questions that end users may ask and the ways in which logs can be reused to generate answers for them.

In addition to the theoretical analysis of the running sample, we have implemented it within our ATRIAS framework. While the overall approach is still under development, the current implementation is functional and demonstrates the practical viability of the concept. The corresponding code is available in our GitHub repository under a dedicated branch[2] associated with this work.

5.1   Information Recording

The question "Why is my trike late?" does not directly relate to an internal goal or plan which could give a direct answer to that question. To answer that question it has first to be connected to internal components from which the necessary information can be extracted. The knowledge base of the XAg system comprises data structures for events and TriQPAN patterns that are assigned to the possible answers.

For the running sample in our ATRIAS scenario, a delay in the arrival of a vehicle can have various causes (possible answers). In the current state of our system, external factors like traffic jams are not yet considered. Thus, a delay is always caused by internal events or decisions made by the agent. In this scenario, the delay results from another trip that has been committed before the recent `customerTrip` but was not completed on time.

We have modeled two possible answers that can be validated independently from each other:

1. There is a `chargingTrip` before your trip, that does not finish in time.
2. There is a `customerTrip` before your trip, that does not finish in time.

A couple of events and TriQPAN patterns are assigned to each of the potential answers. In the following example, we will focus on the events and patterns for the case where another `customerTrip` has caused the delay (possible answer 2). This includes recording the previous `customerTrip` the agent is willing to serve, the agent's decision to commit to the current `customerTrip`, and the estimated time the previous trip will be completed by the agent. The two commit decisions for the previous and the recent customer can be recorded as two instances of the same pattern called `customerTripCreation`.

First, we define the trigger event for `customerTripCreation` named `DecisionTaskCommit`. The event will be logged every time the status of a `DecisionTask` is set to 'commit'. It records the state before and after the change. These and other events relating to changes made to beliefs can be easily integrated into a Jadex agent. Therefore, every write access to a belief will be coupled with the execution of a log operation. The creation of the log has to be coupled to the method that creates new trips. Changes to the `TripList` will be captured by `TripList_BeliefUpdated` events (Fig. 2). Every line in Fig. 2 represents a trip which contains the `TripID`, the `StartTime` and the currently expected `EndTime`. The latter is particularly important for subsequent validation. Its value can still

---

change during future updates of the `TripList`. For better understanding the content of the `TripList` in Fig. 2 has been simplified to focus on the most important elements. Logs containing all the details of a real simulation are available in the GitHub repository.

```
TripList_BeliefUpdated = {
      Old value = [[Trip1, StartTime, Endtime, ...]]
      New value = [[Trip1, StartTime, Endtime, ...],
                   [Trip2, StartTime, Endtime, ...]]
  }
```

Fig. 2. Log of the changes made to the `TripList` (simplified).

```
XAgProcess = {
    name = { customerTripCreation }
    Trigger = { DecisionTaskCommit }
    Queries = { DecisionTaskList }
    Criterion = { A DecisionTask which status equals commit
                  will cause the creation of a customerTrip }
    Actions = { Set DecisionTask.status = committed,
                Create new CustomerTrip = (TripID, StartTime,
                EndTime, ...),
    Notification = {DecisionTaskCommitted,
                    TripList_BeliefUpdated}
    }
}
```

Fig. 3. Sample TriQPAN pattern to be recorded in the event store (simplified).

Figure 3 depicts the pattern for a `customerTripCreation`. The value of the `DecisionTaskList` is recorded within the `Queries` part of the pattern since the agent has used it to take the decision. The `Criterion` part describes the conditions under which the `Actions` take place. It is specified in our example as follows. When a `DecisionTask` within the `DecisionTaskList` has the status 'commit' it will cause the action to create a `customerTrip` and set the status of the `DecisionTask` to 'committed'. The changes made during the execution will cause several notifications which can also be used for other explanations. The pattern shown in Fig. 3 has been simplified again, and the real patterns recorded during a simulation are provided on the GitHub repository.

The XAg model does not currently leverage the full range of functionalities offered by the TriQPAN pattern. Given that our research on the XAg model is still in its early stages, we have deliberately chosen a method for recording agent decisions that is both versatile and well-suited for potential future extensions.

For an integration into an Jadex agent, the first step is to identify the decision points within the agent architecture. The decision logics is complex and each decision comprises several steps that we call decision points. For instance a 'commit' decision to serve a `customerTrip` is part of a sequence of decisions subsumed under the goal `EvaluateDecisonTask` which processes every step in the life-cycle of a customer request. This includes the decision whether a CNP should be started or a request should be delegated as a result of the outcome of a CNP. Not all of these micro decisions are of interest with respect to the user demands. Thus, some of them are explicitly annotated as decision points.

Decision points are derived from state changes of beliefs, goals or plans. When the decision points are identified you can place a logging event at every possible outcome of the decision point. Figure 4 shows a snippet of one of these outcomes in the source code of a vehicle agent. The decision point shown represents the case where the vehicle agent decides to commit to a customer request and creates a `customerTrip`.

```
case COMMIT: {
    // decision point: customerTripCreation
    // creation of a new customer trip
    Trip newTrip = new Trip(currentDecisionTask,
        currentDecisionTask.getJobID(), "CustomerTrip",
        currentDecisionTask.getVATimeFromJob(),
        currentDecisionTask.getStartPositionFromJob(),
        currentDecisionTask.getEndPositionFromJob(), "NotStarted");
    trikeAgent.tripList.add(newTrip);
    // excecution of the logger
    eventTracker.addEvent(event, trikeAgent.tripList,"trike_events/Trike"
        + trikeAgent.agentID + ".json");
```

Fig. 4. A log functionality integrated into a decision point in a Jadex agent.

Every vehicle agent uses an eventTracker to log all the information about the events that took place into a .json file. After a simulation run there will be a .json file for each agent which contains a detailed log history for that agent in the format described above.

While this procedure has been evaluated exclusively with Jadex-based agents, the underlying concept is expected to be applicable to a broad range of agent development frameworks that support reasoning agents, as long as their decision points can be clearly identified.

5.2   Information Extraction and Validation

By storing all relevant information about an agent's past actions and decisions in the event store, it becomes possible to extract meaningful insights from this data. Given sufficient detail within the logs and an appropriate analysis method, the complete decision-making process of the agent can be reconstructed.

In response to the user query, "Why is my trike late?", we consider two potential causes for the delay, each of which must be independently validated. For the purpose of this example, we focus on the cause that: "There is a `customerTrip` before your trip, that does not finish in time". The validation logic within the XAg model can employ various methods to confirm or refute this explanation. In this particular case, validation is more complex, as it requires a specific algorithmic approach to apply the specified test criterion.

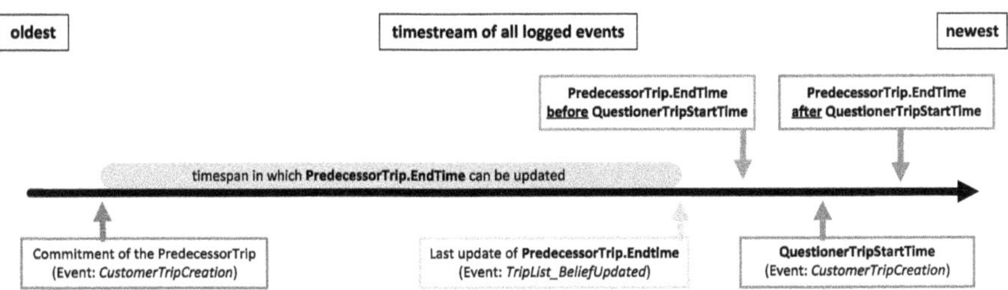

Fig. 5. important events for the validation visualized as a timestream.

We assume that the `TripID` that the customer's question refers to is known and that the entries inside the event store are sorted chronologically. A sample timestream of the events which can be a part of the validation is illustrated in Fig. 5. Below on the left side there is the `customerTripCreation` event of the `predecessorTrip`. This is followed by a timespan during which the `EndTime` of that trip can be updated with the final `TripList_BeliefUpdated` at its end. The second `customerTripCreation` event shows the commitment of the questioners trip. The two alternative time points (before or after) of the `EndTime` for the `predecessorTrip` are shown on the upper right corner.

The code depicted in Fig. 6 shows the pseudocode of the validation algorithm. It searches the event store from the newest to the oldest entry. It will first search for the trip of the questioner, an event with the name `customerTripCreation` where the `TripID` equals the questionerTripID (line 3–9). With its time stamp (`EventTime`) we can narrow down the scope of the further search. From that `EventTime` we search for the `PredecessorTrip` (the next oldest `customerTripCreation`) to get its `TripID` and `EventTime` (line 10–17). For a validation of the potential answer we need the `EndTime` of the `PredecessorTrip`. The `EndTime` of a trip is stored inside the `TripList`, which is logged by `TripList_BeliefUpdated` events (Fig. 2). Should the `EndTime` of that trip have been changed during the runtime of the agent, every change will be stored within a `TripList_BeliefUpdated` event. To get the most recent one we look up the last `TripList_BeliefUpdated` event where the `PredecessorTrip` was mentioned (line 18–20). If the `EndTime` of the `PredecessorTrip` will be later than the `StartTime` of our `QuestionerTrip` we expect a delay and the `CauseOfDelay` is set to true (validation criterion, line 21–23).

```
1    INPUT: QuestionerTripID
2    CauseOfDelay = false
3    EventTimeOfQuestionerTripCreation = init;
4    # search for of the trip of the customer
5    FROM (EventTime: newest TO older){
6        IF ((name == customerTripCreation) &&
7            (TripID == QuestionerTripID)){
8            EventTimeOfQuestionerTripCreation = EventTime
9            BREAK
10       }
11   }
12   # search for the predecessor trip
13   FROM (EventTime: EventTimeOfQuestionerTripCreation TO older){
14       IF (name == customerTripCreation){
15           PredecessorTripID = TripID
16           EventTimeOfPredecessorTripCreation = EventTime
17           BREAK
18       }
19   }
20   # search for the most recent endtime of the predecessor trip
21   FROM (EventTime: newest TO EventTimeOfPredecessorTripCreation){
22       IF ((name == TripList_BeliefUpdated) &&
23           (contains PredecessorTripID)){
24           # validation criterion
25           IF (PredecessorTrip.EndTime > QuestionerTripStartTime){
26               CauseOfDelay = true
27           }
28           BREAK
29       }
30   }
31   RETURN: CauseOfDelay
```

Fig. 6. Pseudocode with test criterion to validate if another `customerTrip` caused a delay.

To fully address the user query, "Why is my trike late?", it is also necessary to validate the second potential cause: that "There is a `chargingTrip` before your trip, that does not finish in time." The algorithm required for this validation would closely resemble the one presented in the current example. Once both potential causes have been evaluated, a list of all positively validated causes can be used for the answer verbalization.

For other types of user questions, the validation procedure may differ and can be significantly simpler. For example, if a query merely requests a value stored within an agent's belief base, no validation algorithm is required, as the information can be retrieved directly.

The current implementation of the XAg model supports the user query "Why is my trike late?" by validating both potential causes of the delays. This validation process can be performed using the provided event stores or with event data generated from custom simulations within the ATRIAS framework. The output consists of a list indicating the validation results for each potential cause.

5.3   Answer Verbalization

The short answer to the running sample discussed above would be: "There is a `customerTrip` before your trip." It hides details like the `EndTime` of the previous `customerTrip`, the commit time of the previous customer, belief updates and so on.

It is still ongoing work to formulate different prompts for degrees of granularity that fit to the particular end user's demand for information. Promising solution ideas are to design a dialogue with the user to request further details and to integrate a dialogue management component into a RAG or plain LLM system. It is a further open issue how to deal with multiple causes that have been positively validated for the same question. A naive solution would be to let the LLM generate a couple of sentences for a conjunction of different causes.

The answer verbalization component is the only part of the XAg model that has not yet been implemented within the ATRIAS framework. Although it has not been evaluated in practice, we are confident in its feasibility. The list of validated answers produced by the validation logic largely consists of content already expressed in near-natural language. Minor linguistic adaptations—particularly when limited to a predefined set of user questions—can be efficiently handled by LLM or RAG-based systems.

5.4   Pattern Reuse

Figure 7 gives an overview of some other questions of possible end users of ATRIAS that can be answered by our model. The question "Why is this trike assigned to me?" refers to the concept of "assignment", which is unknown to the agent. Responsibility can be inferred from various decisions made by the agent. For this special case there would be three possible answers. The agent is assigned to the trip because it "was delegated from the taxi control center and got a high utility score", it "was delegated from the taxi control center, got a low utility score, but was still committed after a negotiation" and that it "was delegated by another trike after a negotiation". In order to be able to validate the circumstances under which the trike committed the trip, the underlying reasoning processes have to be modeled by TriQPAN patterns. These will be "commitNew-CustomerRequest", "CommitDespiteCNP", "CommitAsCNPparticipant".

The validation algorithm shown in Fig. 6 was quite complex and had to be designed specifically for this single question. In contrast, many other possible answers can be validated by a simple approach that can be reused for different questions. For a validation of the above questions, it is sufficient to search for the listed patterns or logs within our event store. If such a pattern or log exists and relates to the `TripID` the possible answer can be validated.

Some other user questions just refer to a simple belief inside the agent and do not even require a reasoning process to refer to. "When will I reach my

User Question	Possible Answer	Pattern & LOGs	Validation Algorithm and Test Criterion
Why is my trike late?	There is a `customerTrip` before your trip, that does not finish in time.	`customerTripCreation, DecisionTaskCommit, TripList_BeliefUpdated`	See Figure 6, (criterion in line 21-23)
	There is a `chargingTrip` before your trip, that does not finish in time.	`chargingTripCreation, estimateBatteryAfterTIP_ BeliefUpdated, TripList_BeliefUpdated`	Similarly to example shown in Figure 6
Why is this trike assigned to me?	The trip was delegated from the taxi control center and got a high utility score	`commitNewCustomerRequest`	Check IF (Pattern & LOGs) exist and contain ID
	The trip was delegated from the taxi control center, got a low utility score, but was still committed after a negotiation	`CommitDespiteCNP`	Check IF (Pattern & LOGs) exist and contain ID
	The trip was delegated by another trike after a negotiation	`CommitAsCNPparticipant`	Check IF (Pattern & LOGs) exist and contain ID
When will I reach my destination?		`TripList_BeliefUpdated`	Take the most recent (Pattern & LOGs) which contain ID
What is your position at the moment?		**`AgentPosition_BeliefUpdated`**	Take most recent (Pattern & LOGs)
When will you arrive?		`TripList_BeliefUpdated`	Take most recent (Pattern & LOGs) which contain ID

Fig. 7. Overview of end user questions and the requirements to our model to answer them.

destination?", "What is your position at the moment?", "When will you arrive?" just require a mapping to the corresponding belief which stores that information.

As the number of possible end user questions we consider increases, it becomes apparent that the events we need to log and the validation algorithms we need begin to repeat themselves (e.g. `TripList_BeliefUpdated`).

With a increasing amount of user questions, we expect this to become even clearer.

6   Future Work and Conclusion

In this paper we have presented an XAg model for end user alignment. It was built upon an existing solution which was aimed at experts and expanded it to this new area of application. Further we carried out a feasibility check by discussing the data structures and pseudo code for a running sample within our ATRIAS framework and provided a simple implementation to simulate the execution of the model on an agent's event store.

We regard the work presented in this paper as an initial step toward enabling system-generated responses to end user questions. We have demonstrated that the core components of our approach namely, systematic logging of agent behavior, as well as the extraction and validation of relevant information are functional. These preliminary results suggest that further investigations could be promising.

Our future work will focus on expanding the range of user queries supported by the XAg model and implementing the currently missing verbalization component. This will allow us to evaluate how easily new question types can be incorporated without requiring modifications to the underlying logic mechanisms. In addition, it will enable a deeper analysis of the complexity involved in implementing new validation algorithms for novel questions. Based on this analysis, alternative approaches, such as the use of counterfactuals, could make validations easier in some cases.

Given the detailed TriQPAN event logs available in the system, the use of LLM or RAG systems to support further tasks within the XAg model could also be a viable direction.

RAG systems may also be beneficial in handling user queries at the input stage. While the current plan involves selecting questions from a predefined catalog, an ideal scenario would allow users to pose unrestricted natural language questions. In cases where fully open-ended interpretation proves unreliable, RAG methods could at least serve to map user-provided questions to predefined entries in the catalog, thereby improving usability and flexibility.

User studies represent an additional future research direction. We are planning an empirical study involving a larger user base than in our preliminary investigation. The goals could be to classify the types of questions users are likely to pose to our agents in particular situations, or to evaluate the LLM-based interaction with the XAg model. A larger, curated set of user-generated questions could reveal user interests and information needs not previously considered.

Once the XAg framework is fully implemented and populated with real user questions, we will be able to systematically evaluate the usefulness and relevance of the system's explanations. A preliminary version of a smartphone application, which enables real-time interaction with a live ATRIAS simulation, is already functional and could serve as a platform for conducting realistic user studies with test participants.

Acknowledgements. The authors would like to thank:
Mahkamjon Raupov for his help with implementing the XAg model. Sebastian Rodriguez, who showed us examples of how TriQPAN patterns can be adapted to ATRIAS. Mariam Rahimi who conducted a preliminary survey on the interests of potential customers of our ATRIAS framework as part of her master's thesis.

References

1. Anjomshoae, S., Najjar, A., Calvaresi, D., Främling, K.: Explainable agents and robots: results from a systematic literature review. In: 18th International Conference on Autonomous Agents and Multiagent Systems, AAMAS 2019, Montreal, Canada, 13–17 May 2019, pp. 1078–1088. International Foundation for Autonomous Agents and Multiagent Systems (2019)
2. Bordini, R.H., El Fallah Seghrouchni, A., Hindriks, K., Logan, B., Ricci, A.: Agent programming in the cognitive era. Auton. Agents Multi-Agent Syst. **34**, 1–31 (2020)
3. Dennis, L.A., Oren, N.: Explaining BDI agent behaviour through dialogue. Auton. Agents Multi Agent Syst. **36**(1), 29 (2022). https://doi.org/10.1007/s10458-022-09556-8
4. Koeman, V.J., Dennis, L.A., Webster, M., Fisher, M., Hindriks, K.: The "Why did you do that?" button: answering why-questions for end users of robotic systems. In: Dennis, L.A., Bordini, R.H., Lespérance, Y. (eds.) EMAS 2019. LNCS (LNAI), vol. 12058, pp. 152–172. Springer, Cham (2020). https://doi.org/10.1007/978-3-030-51417-4_8
5. Langley, P., Meadows, B., Sridharan, M., Choi, D.: Explainable agency for intelligent autonomous systems. In: Proceedings of the AAAI Conference on Artificial Intelligence, vol. 31, pp. 4762–4763 (2017). Issue: 2
6. Lewis, P., et al.: Retrieval-augmented generation for knowledge-intensive NLP tasks. Adv. Neural. Inf. Process. Syst. **33**, 9459–9474 (2020)
7. Mauri, M., Erduran, Ö., Minor, M.: Jadex BDI agents integrated with MATSim for autonomous mobility on demand. In: 12th International Workshop on Engineering Multi-agent Systems, EMAS 2024, Auckland, New Zealand, 6–7 May 2024, Revised Selected Papers. LNCS, vol. 15152, pp. 125–143. Springer, Heidelberg (2024)
8. Calvaresi, D., Najjar, A., Winikoff, M., Främling, K. (eds.): EXTRAAMAS 2020. LNCS (LNAI), vol. 12175. Springer, Cham (2020). https://doi.org/10.1007/978-3-030-51924-7
9. Persiani, M., Hellström, T.: The mirror agent model: a Bayesian architecture for interpretable agent behavior. In: 4th International Workshop on EXplainable and TRAnsparent AI and Multi-Agent Systems, EXTRAAMAS 2022, Online via Auckland, NZ, 9–10 May 2022 (2022)

10. Pokahr, A., Braubach, L., Jander, K.: The Jadex project: programming model. In: Ganzha, M., Jain, L. (eds.) Multiagent Systems and Applications: Volume 1:Practice and Experience, pp. 21–53. Springer, Heidelberg (2013). https://doi.org/10.1007/978-3-642-33323-1_2
11. Rahimi, M.: Explainable agency for users in mobility on demand. Master's thesis, Goethe Universität Frankfurt, Frankfurt am Main, Germany, March 2024
12. Rao, A.S., Georgeff, M.P.: BDI agents: from theory to practice. In: ICMAS, vol. 95, pp. 312–319 (1995)
13. Ribera, M., Lapedriza, A.: Can we do better explanations? A proposal of user-centered explainable AI. In: IUI Workshops, vol. 2327, p. 38 (2019)
14. Rodriguez, S., Thangarajah, J., Davey, A.: Design patterns for Explainable Agents (XAg). In: Proceedings of the 23rd International Conference on Autonomous Agents and Multiagent Systems, pp. 1621–1629 (2024)
15. Shoham, Y.: Agent-oriented programming. Artif. Intell. **60**(1), 51–92 (1993)
16. Singh, D., Padgham, L., Logan, B.: Integrating BDI agents with agent-based simulation platforms. Auton. Agent. Multi-Agent Syst. **30**(6), 1050–1071 (2016). https://doi.org/10.1007/s10458-016-9332-x
17. Smith: The contract net protocol: high-level communication and control in a distributed problem solver. IEEE Trans. Comput. **C-29**(12), 1104–1113 (1980)
18. Horni, A., Nagel, K., Axhausen, K.: The Multi-Agent Transport Simulation MATSim. Ubiquity Press, August 2016
19. Winikoff, M., Sidorenko, G.: Evaluating a mechanism for explaining BDI agent behaviour. In: Calvaresi, D., et al. (eds.) Explainable and Transparent AI and Multi-Agent Systems, pp. 18–37. Springer, Cham (2023). https://doi.org/10.1007/978-3-031-40878-6_2
20. Winikoff, M., Sidorenko, G., Dignum, V., Dignum, F.: Why bad coffee? Explaining BDI agent behaviour with valuings. Artif. Intell. **300**, 103554 (2021)
21. Yan, E., Burattini, S., Hübner, J.F., Ricci, A.: A multi-level explainability framework for engineering and understanding BDI agents. Auton. Agent. Multi-Agent Syst. **39**(1), 9 (2025). https://doi.org/10.1007/s10458-025-09689-6

Engineering the Next Generation of Multi-agent Systems: A Community Roadmap from EMAS 2025

Sebastian Rodriguez[1]([✉]) , Akhila Bairy[2] , Matteo Baldoni[3] ,
Patrick Benjamin[4] , Constantin Blessing[5] , Nicolas Brandstetter[6] ,
Amit K. Chopra[7] , Thomas Clemen[8] , Louise A. Dennis[9] ,
Ahmad Esmaeili[10] , Lu Feng[11] , Angelo Ferrando[12] , Zahra Ghorrati[13] ,
Victor Guillet[14] , Önder Gürcan[15] , Soham Hans[16] , James Herber[17] ,
Viviana Mascardi[18] , Marcel Mauri[19] , Jörg P. Müller[20] ,
John Thangarajah[1] , Rafał Tyl[21] , and Yi Yang[22]

[1] RMIT University, Melbourne, Australia
{sebastian.rodriguez,john.thangarajah}@rmit.edu.au
[2] Karlsruhe Institute of Technology, Karlsruhe, Germany
akhila.bairy@kit.edu
[3] University of Torino, Turin, Italy
matteo.baldoni@unito.it
[4] University of Oxford, Oxford, UK
patrick.benjamin@cs.ox.ac.uk
[5] Esslingen University, Esslingen am Neckar, Germany
constantin.blessing@hs-esslingen.de
[6] Universidad de Chile, Santiago, Chile
nicolasbrandstetter@ug.uchile.cl
[7] Lancaster University, Lancaster, UK
amit.chopra@lancaster.ac.uk
[8] Hamburg University of Applied Sciences, Hamburg, Germany
thomas.clemen@haw-hamburg.de
[9] University of Manchester, Manchester, UK
louise.dennis@manchester.ac.uk
[10] Wichita State University, Wichita, USA
ahmad.esmaeili@wichita.edu
[11] University of Virginia, Charlottesville, USA
lu.feng@virginia.edu
[12] University of Modena and Reggio Emilia, Modena, Italy
angelo.ferrando@unimore.it
[13] Purdue University, West Lafayette, USA
zghorrat@purdue.edu
[14] ONERA (French Aerospace Research Labs), Palaiseau, France
victor.guillet@onera.fr
[15] NORCE Research AS, Bergen, Norway
ongu@norceresearch.no
[16] USC Institute for Creative Technologies, Los Angeles, USA

J. Herber—Independent Researcher

sohamhan@usc.edu
[17] London, UK
jimherber@gmail.com
[18] University of Genova, Genoa, Italy
viviana.mascardi@unige.it
[19] Goethe University Frankfurt, Frankfurt, Germany
mauri@cs.uni-frankfurt.de
[20] Technische Universität Clausthal, Clausthal-Zellerfeld, Germany
jmue@tu-clausthal.de
[21] Grail, Gentle Viking, Warsaw, Poland
rafftyl@wp.pl
[22] KU Leuven, Leuven, Belgium
yi.yang@kuleuven.be

Abstract. This paper presents the outcomes of an open-floor session held at the 13th International Workshop on Engineering Multi-Agent Systems (EMAS 2025), aimed at co-developing a research roadmap for the EMAS community. Participants collaboratively identified and prioritised challenges in engineering large-scale, adaptive multiagent systems, particularly considering the need to engineer systems that can seamlessly integrate *learning* and *reasoning*. Through structured group discussions, four key challenges emerged: explainability in heterogeneous environments, environment modeling, handling dynamic contexts, and communication standardisation. For each of the challenges, participants proposed and ranked potential solutions based on impact and effort. The resulting roadmap highlights concrete research directions toward engineering intelligent, explainable, and interoperable multiagent systems that effectively integrate reasoning and learning in dynamic environments.

1   Introduction

The design, development and deployment of multi-agent systems (MAS) have evolved significantly over the past two decades, driven by advances in artificial intelligence, distributed computing, and autonomous decision-making. As MAS technologies are increasingly embedded in dynamic and uncertain environments, the need to engineer systems that can seamlessly integrate *learning* and *reasoning* has become a central challenge. This integration raises fundamental questions about adaptability, explainability, coordination, and assurance—key concerns for the EMAS community.

In recent years, the rise of large language models (LLMs) [34] and agentic AI systems [1] has further transformed the landscape of intelligent systems engineering. LLM-based agents – or "AI agents", or "Agentic AI agents" – increasingly demonstrate the ability to make decisions, exchange information, and coordinate tasks. Google defines LLM-based agents as *software systems that use AI to pursue goals and complete tasks on behalf of users. They show reasoning, planning,*

and memory and have a level of autonomy to make decisions, learn, and adapt.
Their capabilities are made possible in large part by the multimodal capacity of
generative AI and AI foundation models[1].

Whether LLM-based agents show planning and reasoning capabilities is still open to discussion, with strong claims from some LLMs developers and vendors mitigated by skepticism by some scientists [8,28,44].

Whatever the individual point of view, the EMAS community is discussing about the relationships between agentic AI systems and more traditional approaches in many venues[2]. There is general agreement in recognizing that LLM-based agents may play a role in addressing tasks that are properly coped with by neither traditional symbolic agents nor data-driven learning architectures, and that a synthesis is needed [22,29,52].

This shift opens unprecedented opportunities for building open, adaptive, and human-aligned MAS—but it also introduces new challenges related to controllability, accountability, transparency, and safety. These developments call for a renewed examination of the principles, methods, and tools that underpin the engineering of multi-agent systems.

The 13th International Workshop on Engineering Multi-Agent Systems (EMAS 2025) provided an ideal forum to reflect on these emerging challenges and to chart a shared vision for the next decade of MAS research. In addition to the traditional paper presentations and discussions, the workshop featured an open-floor, hands-on session aimed at collaboratively developing a research roadmap for the EMAS community. This initiative sought to capture the collective insight of researchers and practitioners and to identify priorities that can guide future work in the field.

The roadmap session adopted a participatory and exploratory format. Participants worked together to articulate key challenges, opportunities, and research questions that arise when engineering MAS capable of combining symbolic reasoning, data-driven learning, and emergent capabilities of LLM-powered agents. To ground the discussion, a search and rescue scenario was used as a concrete example, providing a shared context that illustrated the complex interaction between autonomous agents, humans, and uncertain environments. Through structured dialogue and synthesis, participants proposed conceptual frameworks and technical pathways toward addressing these challenges.

This paper summarizes the outcomes of that collaborative exercise. It consolidates the insights generated during the session into a coherent research roadmap that reflects the current consensus and diversity of perspectives within the EMAS community. The roadmap identifies short-, medium-, and long-term priorities for

---

[1] Google definition of AI agent, https://cloud.google.com/discover/what-are-ai-agents, accessed on February 9, 2026.

[2] For example, the *Agents vs. LLMs* panel at the 26th Workshop From Objects to Agents in July 2025, https://sites.google.com/view/woa2025; the *Agent Toolkits 2025 Community Session* at the 22nd European Conference on Multi-Agent Systems in early September 2025, https://interactions.ics.unisg.ch/agent-toolkits-2025/ [14]; the *Rethinking Multi-Agent Systems in the Era of LLMs* Workshop in Oxford in mid September 2025, https://sites.google.com/view/rethinking-mas/home.

advancing the top four challenges identified by participants in the engineering of intelligent, adaptive, and trustworthy multi-agent systems.

Beyond documenting the outcomes, this paper also reflects on the process of collective roadmap creation as a community-building and knowledge-integration activity. By fostering open dialogue across methodological traditions and application domains, the workshop demonstrated how participatory approaches can support the co-evolution of the EMAS research agenda and practice that we hope will influence future editions of EMAS.

The remainder of the paper is structured as follows. Section 2 situates this work in the broader landscape of research roadmap initiatives in agent-oriented software engineering and related fields. Section 3 describes the design and facilitation of the workshop, including participant composition and methodological approach. Section 4 presents the main findings derived from the session discussions. Section 5 introduces the resulting research roadmap, outlining the envisioned directions and milestones. Section 6 offers a discussion of cross-cutting insights and reflections, and Sect. 7 concludes with next steps for sustaining the roadmap as a living artifact of the EMAS community.

2   Background and Related Work

This section summarises the trajectory of previous MAS roadmap and frameworks and defines the key conceptual framing surrounding the challenge.

2.1   Foundational Challenges in MAS

The EMAS community has been active in defining shared views and identifying key challenges to overcome when engineering multi-agent systems. A significant prior endeavor was reported following the 6th International Workshop on Engineering Multi-Agent Systems (EMAS 2018) [31]. That initiative centered on identifying the challenges in three areas: Cognitive Agent Architectures, Agent programming and Machine Learning &MAS. Many of these core challenges are still present today as this work shows.

A crucial implication derived from the persistence of these foundational concerns is that the mere introduction of systems with more powerful capabilities, such as those enabled by Large Language Models (LLMs), does not inherently resolve the underlying engineering deficits. Instead, integrating advanced learning and reasoning must be accomplished on top of robust, verifiable engineering frameworks. Without this foundational rigor, new cognitive capabilities risk inheriting and potentially amplifying existing systemic problems, particularly in areas like complexity, unpredictability, and maintenance overhead.

As noted by Dix et al. [21] over a decade ago, several open challenges persist in the EMAS field. While foundational research remains vital, there is an urgent need to strengthen the engineering dimension, particularly in developing and maintaining large-scale multi-agent systems with clear standards of quality and practice. Technological barriers further limit deployment, underscoring the need for novel engineering techniques and the sharing of empirical lessons from real-world applications using authentic agent technologies rather than general-purpose programming languages [21].

Research of the EMAS community has been tackling these foundational challenges for almost 30 years [51].

2.2   Challenges in Related Areas

The engineering challenges are mirrored and amplified across other key MAS research communities. Challenges that the EMAS community should seek to embrace and provided appropriate methodological support.

The Coordination, Organization, Institutions, Norms, and Ethics in Agent Systems (COINE) community focuses on the scientific and technological aspects of social coordination, organizational theory, normative MAS, and ethics. The close interests of the EMAS and COINE communities were evident in this year's joint panel and discussions[3].

The challenge is the governance of open systems, where agents, their interactions, or the system's purpose may dynamically change over time. Although extensive work has been done in this area on topics such as norms [2,19] still a number of open challenges remain [17].

Furthermore, ensuring the system is *designed responsibly* is crucial to trusting its behaviour. Developing a Responsible AI requires more than some "add-on" features [20], that poses its own set of challenges [5]. The role of the EMAS community to provide the appropriate frameworks is critical in this domain.

The scalability imperative was recognized as a major requirement for MAS applications. Roadmaps, such as the E4MAS community's work [49], focused heavily on techniques for developing Large-Scale Multi-Agent Systems (LSMAS). This research established that achieving efficiency at scale relies on decentralized loci of control, moving beyond monolithic architectures. A crucial architectural realization was that the agent environment—the structure defining how agents perceive, act, and interact—is the primary mechanism for solving scaling issues and managing coordination complexity. That concern is still present in the community today (see Sect. 4).

3   Workshop Design and Methodology

The roadmap session took place during the EMAS workshop, co-located with AAMAS in Detroit, USA. Participants included EMAS authors and general attendees from the broader AAMAS community. They represented a wide range of backgrounds across agent-oriented software engineering, artificial intelligence, distributed systems, and human–agent interaction, united by a shared interest in advancing the engineering principles and methodologies underpinning multi-agent systems. The diversity of perspectives provided a rich foundation for identifying both enduring and emerging research priorities within the field.

---

[3] https://emas.in.tu-clausthal.de/2025/programme.

3.1 Overview

The hands-on roadmap session was designed as an interactive, collaborative exercise. This format emphasises structured, time-boxed activities that move from problem identification to collective prioritisation and solution design. The workshop spanned an entire afternoon and combined individual reflection with group discussion to maximise participation and synthesis.

Participants were introduced to the session goals and briefly reviewed framing materials that summarised current challenges in engineering multi-agent systems, with a particular emphasis on integrating reasoning and learning. In small groups, participants shared their initial thoughts, identified key challenges, and highlighted promising research directions. This ensured a shared understanding of the context and stimulated creative thinking.

In order to co-create a research roadmap for Engineering Multi-Agent Systems, participants then engaged in a sequence of structured collaborative activities. Participants engaged in a silent brainstorming phase to identify key opportunities and problems related to engineering multi-agent systems. Each idea was captured on sticky notes, ensuring that all voices and perspectives were represented. Groups then moved to voting and prioritisation, using dot stickers or stars to highlight the most pressing and impactful challenges. These prioritised items were subsequently reframed into standardized research challenges, enabling a common structure for later analysis.

Once the core challenges had been articulated, participants proposed potential solutions and research pathways, again using sticky notes to encourage breadth and diversity of ideas. After group discussion and voting, the most promising solutions were retained and mapped within an impact–effort matrix. This visual exercise helped distinguish initiatives that could yield immediate results from those requiring more substantial long-term investment.

The session concluded with a plenary sharing and discussion, where each group presented their roadmap and reflected on common patterns, differences, and cross-cutting themes. This final exchange fostered convergence around shared priorities and revealed complementary approaches across the participating groups.

Throughout the workshop, participants used post-it notes, stickers, and handwritten notes to capture challenges, ideas, and proposed solutions. These physical artefacts were collected by the session chairs at the end of the workshop. The materials were later digitised, clustered, and analysed to identify recurrent themes, underlying challenges, and relationships among proposed research directions. The synthesis process informed the thematic structure and roadmap presented in this paper.

3.2 Methodological Reflection and Limitations

The open-floor, participatory workshop format proved effective in stimulating discussion and capturing diverse perspectives from the EMAS community. By framing challenges as research questions and ranking potential solutions by impact and effort, participants were encouraged to move beyond abstract debate toward actionable priorities. This interactive structure fostered inclusivity and creativity, enabling a collective articulation of the field's research roadmap.

However, some limitations must be acknowledged. The outcomes reflect the views of a self-selected group of workshop participants, who—while representative of active researchers in engineering multi-agent systems—may not encompass the full diversity of perspectives within the broader AI and systems engineering communities. Time constraints restricted deeper exploration of interdependencies among challenges and cross-cutting themes such as ethics, scalability, or sustainability.

Future iterations of this roadmap process could benefit from complementary methods to validate and refine the identified priorities.

Then participants were provided with a case study description to ground the discussions. The domain of *Coordinated Drone Swarm & AI-Supported Command for Disaster* was chosen for this purpose. Appendix A contains the guiding material and case study text.

4   Key Challenges and Opportunities

4.1   Opportunities and Advancements

The first phase of the workshop focused on identifying positive aspects and opportunities within the EMAS research community, particularly regarding the integration of learning and reasoning in the design and implementation of autonomous multi-agent systems. Participants highlighted a number of well-estab-lished strengths that position EMAS as a mature yet continuously evolving research domain.

Established Engineering Foundations. Participants emphasized that the EMAS community has developed a solid foundation of engineering principles and abstractions that continue to enable the systematic design of complex autonomous systems [16,43,51]. Core multi-agent concepts—such as centralized and decentralised architectures, coordination mechanisms, and communication protocols—provide proven building blocks for scalable agent-based solutions. Simple yet effective interaction models remain relevant due to their robustness and modest computational requirements.

The community has also achieved significant progress in human–autonomy teaming, multi-level and hierarchical architectures, and normative systems. These efforts have yielded frameworks capable of managing goals, actions, and roles at varying levels of abstraction, exemplified by holonic and hierarchical multi-agent systems [15,35,39]. Extensive work on multi-agent planning and coordination has produced models that support autonomy while maintaining coherence at the system level [48]. Participants also highlighted EMAS's enduring strength in formal methods and safety verification, providing tools for rigorous design assurance even in dynamic and uncertain domains [3,18].

Furthermore, the development of dedicated programming languages and development environments for multi-agent systems continues to distinguish EMAS from broader AI research communities [6,7,26,37]. These languages encapsulate decades of accumulated knowledge about agent-oriented abstractions, decision processes, and interaction patterns—assets that can inform emerging paradigms in agentic AI.

Integration with Learning and Data-Driven Approaches. While traditionally grounded in symbolic and model-based reasoning, the EMAS community has increasingly explored data-driven and hybrid approaches. Participants observed that deductive models remain essential where data availability is limited, such as in time-critical or safety-sensitive environments (e.g., disaster response). At the same time, data-driven decision-making mechanisms have matured to support adaptive command-and-control capabilities and to bridge the gap between autonomous systems and human operators.

Participants noted the opportunity to leverage lightweight cognitive architectures, such as BDI-based agents, in contexts where deploying large language models or deep neural architectures is impractical. The ability to convert raw data into human-readable formats also emerged as a strength, highlighting the community's commitment to interpretability and human-centered design.

Applied Domains and Case Studies. With regards to the provided scenario, participants highlighted the community's ongoing engagement with applied multi-agent domains, such as swarm robotics and collective coordination, and was identified as another area of advancement. Significant progress in swarm MAS algorithms and robotic testbeds has provided both empirical validation and reusable experimental infrastructure. These advances offer a concrete foundation for testing hybrid reasoning and learning approaches in realistic, high-stakes environments such as search and rescue—the scenario anchoring this workshop.

Community Culture and Emerging Opportunities. Beyond technical contributions, participants recognized several cultural and strategic strengths of the EMAS community. There is a shared understanding that meaningful progress requires interdisciplinary collaboration, integrating insights from AI, cognitive science, robotics, human–computer interaction, and software engineering. The community also demonstrates a consistent openness to emerging technologies and paradigms, rapidly engaging with new trends such as generative AI and LLM-based agents to explore their potential for agent programming and coordination.

Looking ahead, participants identified promising opportunities to create shared testbeds and evaluation infrastructures that could foster collaboration and cumulative progress across institutions. Integrating sensing systems and infrastructure into these testbeds, and experimenting with generative AI for agent programming, were noted as particularly fruitful directions for collective exploration.

4.2   Open Challenges

The community identified a wide range of challenges that were grouped into major thematic areas, each reflecting ongoing technical, methodological, and social barriers in the engineering of multi-agent systems.

The most prominent themes were modeling the environment (8 votes), explainability (7 votes), and communication support (6 votes). These highlight the need for more accurate and adaptable representations of complex, changing environments; mechanisms to make agent behaviors interpretable and transparent to humans; and robust communication frameworks that ensure coordination and understanding among heterogeneous agents and between agents and humans.

Other significant areas included dynamic environments (5 votes), emphasising the need for agents capable of adapting to rapidly changing conditions; acceptance of agents (5 votes), pointing to the social and psychological challenges of integrating autonomous systems into human-centered contexts; and natural language to formal representation (3 votes), addressing the gap between intuitive human inputs and formal computational models.

Additional concerns, though receiving fewer votes, remain critical for system robustness and long-term adoption: human–agent autonomy balance, testing and verification (including real-time validation), standards, interoperability, and data fusion. These touch on the reliability, safety, and governance of multi-agent systems—essential factors for scaling and deploying them beyond controlled environments.

Several specialised topics—such as stakeholder engagement, safety and risk management, sensor conflict integration, model representation, scalability, programming abstractions, and hardware restrictions—were also recognized. Although not perceived as the most urgent, they underline the interdisciplinary and practical dimensions of agent-based system design.

Finally, the discussion acknowledged the potential for collaboration with other AAMAS research domains, particularly in areas like multi-agent based simulation to complement real-world testing, multi-agent simultaneous localization and mapping (SLAM) in robotics, and commercialization support. These intersections suggest pathways for advancing both foundational research and applied innovation in multi-agent systems engineering.

5   Roadmap: Solutions for the Top Four Challenges

Following the collective identification of key research challenges, participants were divided into groups to address the four most urgent issues for the EMAS community: Explainability, Modeling the Environment, Dynamic Environments, and Interoperable Communication Platforms. Each challenge was reframed as a research question to sharpen its focus and align it with the community's vision. For each question, participants proposed candidate solutions, then voted on the most promising ones based on two dimensions:

Impact the potential transformative effect on the field if achieved.
Effort the estimated complexity and resources required.

This created a four-quadrant prioritisation (High Impact/Low Effort; High Impact/High Effort; Low Impact/Low Effort; Low Impact/High Effort) that helped identify "quick wins" as well as longer-term strategic objectives. The roadmap below integrates these insights into coherent research pathways for each of the four key challenges.

5.1 Explainability

Research Question: How can we create explainable systems in heterogeneous environments?

Participants agreed that explainability must support heterogeneous ecosystems that include symbolic agents, learning-based components, and human collaborators. They envisioned explainability mechanisms that are not just post-hoc, but integrated into communication and reasoning processes.

Most promising solutions (in order of community votes):

Text-Based Communication that Can be Summarized: Encourage agents to exchange information in structured language formats that can later be summarized for different stakeholders. This approach offers immediate benefits for transparency and debugging.

Formalize Reasoning for Any Action: Develop frameworks that allow agents to produce explicit justifications for their actions—using logical or causal reasoning traces—to enable rigorous inspection of decision processes.

Transparency and Trust Mechanisms: Embed explainability and transparency into design by providing traceability of decisions and provenance of data, forming a basis for measurable trust.

Stakeholder-Tailored Explanations: Generate explanations adapted to the audience—whether human operators, other agents, or machines—using context-aware templates or modality switches.

Multimodal Explanations: Combine text, visualization, and symbolic traces for richer human–agent interaction, particularly in control and mission settings.

Ranked Solutions:

Solution	Votes	Impact	Effort
Text-based communication that can be summarized	5	High	Low
Formalize reasoning for any action	4	High	High
Transparency and trust mechanisms	3	High	High
Stakeholder-tailored explanations	2	High	Low
Multimodal explanations	3	High	High

Roadmap Direction: Short-term work should prototype text-based, summarisable communication within existing MAS frameworks. Mid-term research will integrate formal reasoning traces with stakeholder-aware explanation generation. Long-term, the community should pursue explainability-by-design standards, enabling explainable behavior to be an intrinsic feature of agent architectures rather than an add-on.

Relevant Work: [20,24,25,32,38,40,41,53]

5.2   Modeling the Environment

Research Question: How might we model the environment?

Participants discussed what should be modeled, how consistent centralised or distributed representations should be, and how evolving models can be validated. The consensus was that environment modeling is both foundational and multi-layered, requiring trade-offs between abstraction, accuracy, and computational cost.

Most promising solutions (in order of community votes):

Define What and How to Model, and at Which Level of Abstraction: Propose partitioned spatial and conceptual scaffolds with variable granularity, linked by annotation ontologies for attaching new data, local strategies, and situational knowledge.

Maintain Consistency in Centralized or Consolidated Models: Construct multi-level MAS structures where agents operate at different abstraction levels with specific roles and authorities, ensuring coherence across layers.

Validation of Evolving Models: Employ simulation-based validation, run-time monitoring, and agile experimentation loops to continuously evaluate environmental representations.

Integrate Agents into the Model Itself: *(digital twin paradigm)* Treat agents as both participants and components of the model, enabling co-evolution between the MAS and its digital twin.

Ranked Solutions:

Solution	Votes	Impact	Effort
Define what and how to model, and level of abstraction	7	High	High
Maintain consistency in centralized or consolidated models	7	High	Low
Validation of evolving models	6	High	Medium
Integrate agents into the model itself	3	High	Low

Roadmap Direction: Early stages should define hybrid modeling templates and corresponding ontologies. Mid-term actions include developing simulation-based validation pipelines and model-fusion methods. Long-term efforts should produce standardised hybrid environment representations and open testbeds for benchmarking. This efforts are closely related to Digital Twins required in multiple domains.

Relevant Work: [23,36,49,50]

5.3 Dynamic Environments

Research Question: How might we handle dynamic environments?

This group explored strategies to manage rapid change, uncertainty, and adaptation under resource and time constraints. The core idea was to embed adaptivity within the environment itself, moving from passive to active environments.

Most promising solutions (in order of community votes):

Create an "Active Environment": Develop environments capable of morphing in response to their own internal processes (e.g., earthquakes, floods). The approach requires a library of pre-built models and situations that can dynamically match sensor input and reconfigure accordingly.

Integrate Geotagged Data from Multiple Scouts: Use dynamic, layered maps that evolve over time based on spatially distributed sensor input, enabling situational awareness and faster adaptation.

Combine Accountability, Human Annotation, and Task Reporting: Encourage hybrid systems where agents and humans cooperatively maintain environmental awareness through periodic status reports and manual updates.

Ranked Solutions:

Solution	Votes	Impact	Effort
Create an "active environment"	9	High	High
Use geotagged sensor data from multiple scouts	8	High	Medium
Combine accountability, human annotations, and task reporting	7	Medium	Medium

Roadmap Direction: The short-term goal is to prototype layered environment maps integrating real-time sensor data. Mid-term research should focus on constructing and testing active environment frameworks that dynamically fuse situational models. Long-term efforts should aim for self-adaptive digital twins capable of autonomously reshaping mission models and task allocations.

Relevant Work: [33, 47]

5.4 Interoperable Communication Platforms

Research Question: How might we standardize interoperable communication platforms?

Interoperability was recognized as a critical enabler for collaboration between heterogeneous agents, LLM-powered modules, and human users. Participants highlighted the need for standardization across multiple communication layers.

Most promising solutions (in order of community votes):

Standardized Communication Protocols: Develop and publish standardized protocol languages and wire encodings to ensure compatibility across platforms and domains, along with extensions for message forwarding and adaptation.

Select and Consolidate a Shared Protocol Standard: Reach community consensus on one or a few widely adopted standards, complemented by reference implementations and middleware adapters.

Identify Communication Layers and Semantics: Establish a clear separation of communication layers—(1) Network, (2) Communication, (3) Interaction, (4) Organization, and (5) Coordination—and define their associated semantics.

Ranked Solutions:

Solution	Votes	Impact	Effort
Standardize communication protocols	11	High	Medium
Select and consolidate a shared protocol standard	7	High	High
Identify communication layers and semantics	6	High	High

Roadmap Direction: Initial steps involve defining canonical message schemas and minimal interoperable protocols. Medium-term actions will establish translation adapters between MAS frameworks. Long-term, EMAS can lead a community-wide standardization initiative defining interoperable stacks for communication, coordination, and organization layers.

Relevant Work: [4, 9–13, 27, 30, 42, 45, 46]

5.5   Cross-Cutting Takeaways

The workshop's participatory roadmap development demonstrated that high-impact, low-effort opportunities—such as text-based explainability and ontology-driven environment models—can deliver early wins for EMAS, while ambitious long-term objectives—such as active environments and protocol standardization across communication layers—offer transformative potential.

By structuring research pathways around clear research questions, measurable milestones, and community-shared evaluation artifacts, EMAS is well-positioned to bridge reasoning and learning paradigms, support agentic AI systems, and maintain leadership in the design and engineering of next-generation multi-agent systems.

6   Discussion

The outcomes of this workshop reveal a vibrant and forward-looking EMAS community that is actively redefining the boundaries of multi-agent systems engineering in the era of agentic AI and large language models. The discussions and roadmap activities underscored both the maturity of EMAS as an engineering discipline and the need for renewed integration with recent advances in machine learning, natural language interaction, and human–autonomy teaming.

6.1   Converging Foundations and Emerging Directions

Participants agreed that the EMAS community has built a strong foundation in formal methods, coordination mechanisms, normative reasoning, and architectural design. These provide stable and reusable engineering abstractions—distinct from the more ad hoc nature of current LLM-based agent systems. However, the emergence of LLMs opens an opportunity to revisit long-standing MAS principles through a new lens. The roadmap discussions reflected a shared understanding that the next phase of EMAS research will involve reconciling symbolic, model-driven reasoning with data-driven adaptivity, enabling agents that can both learn and reason in dynamic, human-centered contexts.

6.2   Key Research Priorities

Across the four prioritized challenges—Explainability, Modeling the Environment, Dynamic Environments, and Interoperability—participants consistently emphasized the importance of trust, transparency, and adaptability. These themes are deeply interconnected: explainable reasoning depends on meaningful models of the environment; adaptability in dynamic situations relies on communication and coordination standards; and interoperability serves as the foundation for integrating diverse agent architectures, learning systems, and human interfaces.

The high-impact, low-effort solutions identified—such as ontology-based modeling—represent practical starting points that can yield early community benefits. Conversely, high-impact, high-effort directions, including the development of active environments and standardized communication layers, point to longer-term collective goals requiring shared infrastructures and collaboration across institutions.

6.3   The Role of EMAS in the LLM and Agentic AI Era

One of the most notable outcomes of the workshop is the recognition that EMAS research provides essential engineering principles for the growing landscape of agentic AI systems powered by LLMs. While LLMs offer powerful capabilities, they lack the explicit organizational, normative, and verification structures that EMAS research has refined over decades. The community therefore has a pivotal role in bringing rigor, safety, and accountability to the emerging generation of generative and autonomous agents.

Several groups highlighted that future EMAS research could focus on LLM-augmented agent architectures, where learning-based modules are embedded within well-defined multi-agent frameworks. Such systems would combine adaptive intelligence with verifiable coordination, providing a clear pathway toward explainable, trustworthy, and human-aligned multi-agent ecosystems.

6.4   Toward a Collaborative Research Agenda

The participatory approach used in this workshop, i.e. combining structured brainstorming, collective prioritization, and impact–effort mapping, proved effective in aligning diverse perspectives from across the EMAS and AAMAS community. The resulting roadmap offers both short-term research actions (e.g., communication templates for explainability, hybrid simulation environments) and strategic long-term goals (e.g., standardization efforts, community-wide testbeds).

Beyond the specific challenges discussed, the workshop reinforced the identity of EMAS as a collaborative, engineering-oriented community—one capable of addressing the complexity of modern autonomous systems through rigorous design, interdisciplinary integration, and open research infrastructure.

7   Conclusion and Next Steps

This paper has presented the outcomes of the EMAS 2025 Roadmapping Workshop, which brought together researchers and practitioners from across the AAMAS community to collaboratively identify key challenges and promising directions for the engineering of multiagent systems in the era of LLMs and agentic AI. Through a structured and participatory process inspired by the Lightning Decision Jam methodology, participants jointly explored, categorized, and prioritized issues ranging from explainability and environmental modeling to communication support and system adaptability.

The resulting roadmap highlights a collective vision for the future of multiagent systems engineering—one that emphasizes integrating data-driven and symbolic reasoning, enhancing human–agent collaboration through explainable and trustworthy interfaces, and developing robust methodologies for deployment in dynamic and uncertain environments. The identified challenges and corresponding research directions not only reflect long-standing concerns within the EMAS community but also illustrate its evolving engagement with emerging paradigms in AI.

Beyond the immediate outcomes, the workshop demonstrates the value of community-driven approaches for defining shared research agendas. The roadmap is intended as a living document that can inform future EMAS editions and inspire collaborative efforts across disciplines such as robotics, simulation, and human–AI interaction. Continuing this dialogue will be essential to ensure that the engineering of multiagent systems remains rigorous, transparent, and responsive to the rapidly changing landscape of agentic AI.

We hope that the outcomes of this workshop will serve as the foundation for a living roadmap, to be refined and extended through subsequent EMAS editions and related community initiatives. Continued dialogue among researchers, practitioners, and stakeholders will be essential to ensure that the roadmap remains dynamic, inclusive, and responsive to the rapid evolution of agent and AI technologies.

A   Case Study Notes

Coordinated Drone Swarm and AI-Supported Command for Disaster

A powerful earthquake has devastated a densely populated urban area. Many streets are blocked by rubble or fire, and communications infrastructure is degraded. Emergency services must act fast to locate survivors, assess structural damage, and coordinate rescue.

To support this, the response team deploys:

- **Robot swarms** to search for survivors, map hazards, and relay information. Semi-autonomous robots with perception (e.g., thermal cameras), capable of local decision-making, path planning, and ad-hoc communication with swarm peers.
- An **AI-enhanced Command & Control (C2) system** to help human operators analyse data, prioritize responses, and coordinate ground units and air assets in real time. A centralized or distributed system that:
  - Aggregates drone and responder data,
  - Identifies high-priority zones,
  - Recommends mission plans to human operators,
  - Monitors team status and suggests role reassignments.
- **First Responders** to assist survivors and contain hazards. Ground units (e.g., firefighter bots or human-agent teams) that receive guidance from the C2 system and may themselves be semi-autonomous.

Consider the following points:

- How to engineer the coordination logic for a robot swarm under uncertainty.
- How to design interaction protocols between drones, the C2 AI system, and human operators and first responders.
- How to integrate machine learning for perception and data summarization, and symbolic reasoning for mission planning and role allocation.
- How to ensure trust, transparency, ethics and accountability in a human-AI team operating in a high-stakes environment.
- How to define the engineering process to develop and deploy the system.

Engineering Questions:

- What kind of agent architecture suits the drones, the C2 system, and human interfaces.
- How to handle distributed task allocation and resilience to partial observability.
- How can LLMs or data-driven models assist in reporting or coordination, without compromising latency or reliability.
- How can we validate decisions and ensure safety in the face of ambiguous data.

Main Components to consider

1. System Architecture.
   - Define a modular architecture showing how drone agents, the AI C2 system, and first responder agents interact.
   - Consider modules for Perception; Planning (deliberative agent logic); Communication; Human-AI Interface; Coordination & Data Fusion.
2. Key Specifications for Each Module.
   - Specify whether each module is a single agent or multi-agent subsystem.
   - Clarify which modules will use (non-exhaustive list):
     - ML / Data-driven approaches.
     - BDI (Belief-Desire/Intentions) or Goal oriented; Automated Planning.
     - Rule-based logic for constraints and fallback behaviour.
   - Identify ethics and accountability constraints:.
     - Explainable decision.
     - Human oversight on actions and fail-safes.
3. Interaction Support.
   - Define communication protocols and technologies (e.g., FIPA ACL, BSPL, MQTT, ROS2).
   - Use or design a shared ontology for status, location, health, mission type, etc.
   - Consider bandwidth constraints and dynamic network topologies (ad hoc mesh).
4. Engineering Process.
   - Outline how the system will be:
     - Tested (e.g., unit testing, BDD) and validated (e.g., in simulation, emulated disaster zones).
     - Monitored during operation for faults and accountability.
     - Development and Deployment, including formal methods, agent programming languages, edge-agent deployment etc.
   - Discuss deployment constraints:
     - Energy and hardware limits on drones.
     - Offline fallback behaviour for disconnected agents.
     - Real-time guarantees and failover protocols.

References

1. Acharya, D.B., Kuppan, K., Divya, B.: Agentic AI: autonomous intelligence for complex goals–a comprehensive survey. IEEE Access **13**, 18912–18936 (2025). https://doi.org/10.1109/ACCESS.2025.3532853
2. Alechina, N., Dastani, M., Logan, B.: Programming norm-aware agents. In: Proceedings of the 11th International Conference on Autonomous Agents and Multiagent Systems - Volume 2, pp. 1057–1064. AAMAS 2012, International Foundation for Autonomous Agents and Multiagent Systems, Richland, SC (2012)

3. Bakar, N.A., Selamat, A.: Agent systems verification: systematic literature review and mapping. Appl. Intell. **48**(5), 1251–1274 (2018). https://doi.org/10.1007/s10489-017-1112-z

4. Baldoni, M., Christie, S.H., Singh, M.P., Chopra, A.K.: Orpheus: engineering multiagent systems via communicating agents. In: Proceedings of the 39th AAAI Conference on Artificial Intelligence (AAAI), pp. 23135–23143. AAAI, Philadelphia (2025). https://doi.org/10.1609/aaai.v39i22.34478

5. Barredo Arrieta, A., et al.: Explainable Artificial Intelligence (XAI): concepts, taxonomies, opportunities and challenges toward responsible AI. Inf. Fus. **58**, 82–115 (2020). https://doi.org/10.1016/j.inffus.2019.12.012

6. Bordini, R.H., El Fallah Seghrouchni, A., Hindriks, K., Logan, B., Ricci, A.: Agent programming in the cognitive era. Auton. Agent. Multi-Agent Syst. **34**(2), 1–31 (2020). https://doi.org/10.1007/s10458-020-09453-y

7. Bordini, R.H., Hübner, J.F., Wooldridge, M.: Programming Multi-agent Systems in AgentSpeak using Jason, 1st edn. Wiley-Blackwell, Chichester (2007)

8. Botti, V.: Agentic AI and multiagentic: are we reinventing the wheel? CoRR abs/2506.01463 (2025)

9. Chopra, A.K., Baldoni, M., Christie, S.H., Singh, M.P.: AZORUS: commitments over protocols for BDI agents. In: Proceedings of the 24th International Conference on Autonomous Agents and Multiagent Systems, AAMAS 2025, Detroit, MI, USA, 19-23 May 2025, pp. 490–499. International Foundation for Autonomous Agents and Multiagent Systems (2025). https://doi.org/10.5555/3709347.3743564

10. Chopra, A.K., Christie , S.H., Singh, M.P.: Tools for implementing multiagent systems based on protocols. In: Agent Toolkits. Springer (2025). https://doi.org/10.1007/978-3-032-01082-7_8, in press

11. Chopra, A.K., Christie V, S.H.: Communication Meaning: Foundations and Directions for Systems Research. In: Proceedings of the 2023 International Conference on Autonomous Agents and Multiagent Systems, pp. 1786–1791. AAMAS 2023, International Foundation for Autonomous Agents and Multiagent Systems, Richland, SC (2023)

12. Christie, S.H., Singh, M.P., Chopra, A.K.: KIKO: programming agents to enact interaction models. In: Proceedings of the 2023 International Conference on Autonomous Agents and Multiagent Systems, pp. 1154–1163. AAMAS 2023, International Foundation for Autonomous Agents and Multiagent Systems, Richland, SC (2023)

13. Christie, S.H., Singh, M.P., Chopra, A.K.: Argus: programming with communication protocols in a belief-desire-intention architecture. Artif. Intell. **348**, 104398:1–104398:35 (2025). https://doi.org/10.1016/j.artint.2025.104398

14. Ciortea, A., et al.: Engineering multi-agent systems and generative AI: report from the agent toolkits 2025 community session. In: Proceedings of the 22nd European Conference on Multi-Agent Systems (EUMAS 2025) (2025), in press

15. Correa e Silva Fernandes, K.C.: Systémes Multi-Agents Hybrides: Une Approche Pour La Conception de Systémes Complexes. Ph.D. thesis, Université Joseph Fourier- Grenoble 1 (2001)

16. Cossentino, M., Hilaire, V., Molesini, A., Seidita, V. (eds.): Handbook on Agent-Oriented Design Processes. Springer-Verlag, Berlin Heidelberg (2014). https://doi.org/10.1007/978-3-642-39975-6

17. Criado, N., Argente, E., Botti, V.: Open issues for normative multi-agent systems. AI Commun. **24**(3), 233–264 (2011). https://doi.org/10.3233/AIC-2011-0502

18. Dennis, L.A., Fisher, M.: Verifiable Autonomous Systems: Using Rational Agents to Provide Assurance about Decisions Made by Machines. Cambridge University Press, Cambridge, United Kingdom; New York, NY, USA (2023)
19. Dignum, F.: Autonomous agents with norms. Artif. Intell. Law **7**(1), 69–79 (1999). https://doi.org/10.1023/A:1008315530323
20. Dignum, V.: Responsible artificial intelligence: how to develop and use AI in a responsible way (2019)
21. Dix, J., Hindriks, K.V., Logan, B., Wobcke, W.: Engineering multi-agent systems (Dagstuhl Seminar 12342). Dagstuhl Rep. **2**(8), 74–98 (2012). https://doi.org/10.4230/DagRep.2.8.74
22. Ferrando, A., Briola, D., Collier, R., Mascardi, V.: Agency and generation: friends or enemies? In: Proceedings of the 22nd European Conference on Multi-Agent Systems (EUMAS 2025) (2025), in press
23. Galland, S., Balbo, F., Gaud, N., Rodriguez, S., Picard, G., Boissier, O.: A multi-dimensional environment implementation for enhancing agent interaction. In: Bordini, R., Elkind, E. (eds.) 14th International Conference on Autonomous Agents and Multiagent Systems (AAMAS15), pp. 1801–1802. ACM In-Cooperation, Istanbul, Turkey (May 2015)
24. Gatti, A., Mascardi, V., Ferrando, A.: ChatBDI: think BDI, talk LLM. In: Proceedings of the 24th International Conference on Autonomous Agents and Multiagent Systems, pp. 2541–2543. AAMAS 2025, International Foundation for Autonomous Agents and Multiagent Systems, Richland, SC (2025)
25. Gatti, A., Mascardi, V., Ferrando, A.: Let me talk to you! Natural language interaction between humans and BDI agents via ChatBDI. In: European Conference on Artificial Intelligence, ECAI 2025. Bologna (2025)
26. Hindriks, K.V., Dix, J.: GOAL: A multi-agent programming language applied to an exploration game. In: Agent-Oriented Software Engineering, pp. 235–258. Springer, Berlin, Heidelberg (2014). https://doi.org/10.1007/978-3-642-54432-3_12
27. Huget, M.P.: Agent communication. In: Agent-Oriented Software Engineering, pp. 101–133. Springer, Berlin, Heidelberg (2014). https://doi.org/10.1007/978-3-642-54432-3_6
28. Kambhampati, S.: Can Large Language Models reason and plan? Ann. New York Acad. Sci. **1534**(1), 15–18 (2024). https://doi.org/10.1111/nyas.15125
29. Kambhampati, S., et al.: Position: LLMs can't plan, but can help planning in LLM-modulo frameworks. In: ICML. OpenReview.net (2024)
30. Lewis, J., Matson, E.T., Wei, S., Min, B.C.: Implementing HARMS-based indistinguishability in ubiquitous robot organizations. Robot. Auton. Syst. **61**(11), 1186–1192 (2013). https://doi.org/10.1016/j.robot.2013.04.001
31. Mascardi, V., et al.: Engineering multi-agent systems: state of affairs and the road ahead. SIGSOFT Softw. Eng. Notes **44**(1), 18–28 (2020). https://doi.org/10.1145/3310013.3322175
32. Mauri, M., Minor, M.: Towards explainable BDI agents for end users. In: Rodriguez, S., Feng, L., Müller, J.P. (eds.) Engineering Multi-Agent Systems. Springer Nature Switzerland, Cham (2025). https://doi.org/10.1007/978-3-031-71152-7
33. Moradi, H., et al.: Improving evacuation policies through agent-based modeling and stakeholder engagement in hazard-prone areas. Int. J. Disaster Risk Reduc. **119**, 105280 (2025). https://doi.org/10.1016/j.ijdrr.2025.105280
34. Naveed, H., et al.: A comprehensive overview of large language models. ACM Trans. Intell. Syst. Technol. **16**(5), 1–72 (2025)

35. Odell, J., Nodine, M., Levy, R.: A metamodel for agents, roles, and groups. In: Odell, J., Giorgini, P., Müller, J.P. (eds.) AOSE 2004. LNCS, vol. 3382, pp. 78–92. Springer, Heidelberg (2005). https://doi.org/10.1007/978-3-540-30578-1_6
36. Ricci, A., Piunti, M., Viroli, M.: Environment programming in multi-agent systems: an artifact-based perspective. Auton. Agent. Multi-Agent Syst. **23**(2), 158–192 (2011). https://doi.org/10.1007/s10458-010-9140-7
37. Rodriguez, S., Gaud, N., Galland, S.: SARL: a general-purpose agent-oriented programming language. In: The 2014 IEEE/WIC/ACM International Conference on Intelligent Agent Technology, vol. 3, pp. 103–110. IEEE Computer Society Press, Warsaw, Poland (2014). https://doi.org/10.1109/WI-IAT.2014.156
38. Rodriguez, S., Hilaire, V.: A methodological approach for the analysis and design of human-swarm interactions based upon feedback loops. Expert Syst. Appl. **217**, 119482 (2023). https://doi.org/10.1016/j.eswa.2022.119482
39. Rodriguez, S., Hilaire, V., Gaud, N., Galland, S., Koukam, A.: Holonic multi-agent systems. In: Di Marzo Serugendo, G., Gleizes, M.P., Karageorgos, A. (eds.) Self-Organizing Software: From Natural to Artificial Adaptation, pp. 238–263. Self-Organising Software From Natural to Artificial Adaptation - Natural Computing Series, Springer, 1 edn. (2011). https://doi.org/10.1007/978-3-642-17348-6_11
40. Rodriguez, S., Thangarajah, J.: Explainable Agents (XAg) by design. In: Proceedings of the 2024 International Conference on Autonomous Agents and Multiagent Systems (Blue Sky), pp. 2712–2716. AAMAS 2024, Auckland, New Zeland (2024)
41. Rodriguez, S., Thangarajah, J., Davey, A.: Design patterns for explainable agents (XAg). In: Proceedings of the 2024 International Conference on Autonomous Agents and Multiagent Systems, pp. 1621–1629. AAMAS 2024, Auckland, New Zeland (2024)
42. Schleibaum, S., Feng, L., Kraus, S., Müller, J.P.: ADESSE: advice explanations in complex repeated decision-making environments. In: Larson, K. (ed.) Proceedings of the Thirty-Third International Joint Conference on Artificial Intelligence, IJCAI-24, pp. 7904–7912. IJCAI Org. (2024). https://doi.org/10.24963/ijcai.2024/875
43. Shehory, O., Sturm, A. (eds.): Agent-oriented software engineering. Springer, Berlin, Heidelberg (2014). https://doi.org/10.1007/978-3-642-54432-3
44. Shojaee, P., Mirzadeh, I., Alizadeh, K., Horton, M., Bengio, S., Farajtabar, M.: The illusion of thinking: Understanding the strengths and limitations of reasoning models via the lens of problem complexity. CoRR abs/2506.06941 (2025)
45. Singh, M.P.: Information-driven interaction-oriented programming: BSPL, the blindingly simple protocol language. In: The 10th International Conference on Autonomous Agents and Multiagent Systems - Volume 2, pp. 491–498. AAMAS 2011, International Foundation for Autonomous Agents and Multiagent Systems, Richland, SC (2011)
46. Singh, M.P., Christie, S.H., Chopra, A.K.: Langshaw: declarative interaction protocols based on sayso and conflict. In: Proceedings of the 33rd International Joint Conference on Artificial Intelligence (IJCAI), pp. 202–210. IJCAI, Jeju, Korea (2024). https://doi.org/10.24963/ijcai.2024/23
47. Swarup, S., Mortveit, H.S.: Live simulations. In: Proceedings of the 19th International Conference on Autonomous Agents and MultiAgent Systems, pp. 1721–1725. AAMAS 2020, International Foundation for Autonomous Agents and Multiagent Systems, Richland, SC (2020)
48. Torreño, A., Onaindia, E., Komenda, A., Štolba, M.: Cooperative multi-agent planning: a survey. ACM Comput. Surv. **50**(6), 84:1–84:32 (2017). https://doi.org/10.1145/3128584

49. Weyns, D., Michel, F.: Agent environments for multi-agent systems – a research roadmap. In: Weyns, D., Michel, F. (eds.) Agent Environments for Multi-Agent Systems IV. pp. 3–21. Springer International Publishing, Cham (2015). https://doi.org/10.1007/978-3-319-23850-0_1

50. Weyns, D., Omicini, A., Odell, J.: Environment as a first class abstraction in multiagent systems. Auton. Agent. Multi-Agent Syst. **14**(1), 5–30 (2007). https://doi.org/10.1007/s10458-006-0012-0

51. Winikoff, M.: 30 years of engineering multi-agent systems: what and why? In: Proceedings of the 23rd International Conference on Autonomous Agents and Multiagent Systems (2024)

52. Xiong, H., et al.: Converging paradigms: the synergy of symbolic and connectionist AI in LLM-empowered autonomous agents. CoRR abs/2407.08516 (2024)

53. Yan, E., Burattini, S., Hübner, J.F., Ricci, A.: A multi-level explainability framework for engineering and understanding BDI agents. Auton. Agent. Multi-Agent Syst. **39**(1), 9 (2025). https://doi.org/10.1007/s10458-025-09689-6

Author Index

A
Álvarez-Napagao, Sergio   19
Amjad, Ayesha   27
Asici, Tansu Zafer   200

B
Bairy, Akhila   238
Baldoni, Matteo   238
Bary, Tim   80
Benjamin, Patrick   238
Blessing, Constantin   238
Brandstetter, Nicolas   45, 238
Bravo-Marquez, Felipe   45

C
Chen, Wei   141
Chopra, Amit K.   62, 238
Clemen, Thomas   238
Cortés, Ulises   19

D
Dennis, Louise A.   238
Dunin-Kęplicz, Barbara   177

E
Esmaeili, Ahmad   238

F
Feng, Lu   238
Ferrando, Angelo   117, 157, 238

G
Galland, Stéphane   80
Gatti, Andrea   117, 157
Ghorrati, Zahra   238
Gnatyshak, Dmitry   19
Guillet, Victor   238
Guo, Zhen   141
Gürcan, Önder   200, 238

H
Hans, Soham   1, 238
Herber, James   238
Holvoet, Tom   100

K
Kardas, Geylani   200

L
Li, Binze   1
Li, Zhiyuan   141

M
Macq, Benoit   80
Manjah, Dani   80
Mascardi, Viviana   117, 157, 238
Mauri, Marcel   221, 238
Minor, Mirjam   221
Müller, Jörg P.   238

O
Olmedo, Federico   45

P
Padget, Julian   19

R
Rodriguez, Sebastian   238

S
Shen, Yikang   141
Singh, Munindar P.   62
Sthapit, Saurav   27
Syed, Tahir Qasim   27

T
Thangarajah, John   238
Tyl, Rafał   177, 238

U
Ustun, Volkan   1

V
Vermaelen, Jan   100

Y
Yang, Yi   238

GPSR Compliance
The European Union's (EU) General Product Safety Regulation (GPSR) is a set
of rules that requires consumer products to be safe and our obligations to
ensure this.

If you have any concerns about our products, you can contact us on

ProductSafety@springernature.com

In case Publisher is established outside the EU, the EU authorized
representative is:

Springer Nature Customer Service Center GmbH
Europaplatz 3
69115 Heidelberg, Germany